Siqueiros

Biography of a Revolutionary Artist

D. Anthony White

ISBN: 1-4392-1172-8
ISBN-13: 9781439211724

Visit www.booksurge.com to order additional copies..

Siqueiros in Lecumberri, 1961-1964

Table of Contents

List of Photographs, Paintings and Murals

Cover: *El Coronelazo*, 1945, Self-Portrait in Pyroxylin, Museum of Modern Art, Mexico, D.F.

First Page: Siqueiros in Lecumberri, National Penitentiary, Mexico, D.F., 1960-1964, Photograph, Sala Siqueiros.

p. 32 Lieutenant Siqueiros with General Manuel Diéguez and Staff., 1914-1918, Photograph, Sala Siqueiros.

p. 110 *Peasant Mother*, 1929, Oil on Canvas, Museum of Modern Art, Mexico, D.F.

p. 136 *Street Meeting*, 1932, Exterior Cement Fresco, Chouinard School of Arts, Los Angeles, California.

p. 142 *Tropical America*, 1932, Exterior Cement Fresco, Los Angeles, California

p. 148 *Portrait of Present-Day Mexico*, Santa Barbara Art Museum, Santa Barbara, California.

p. 179 *Portrait of George Gershwin in a Concert Hall,* 1936, Oil on canvas, University of Texas, Austin, Photograph, Sala Siqueiros.

p. 286 *Cuauhtémoc Reborn*, 1951, Pyroxylin on masonite, Palace of Fine Arts, Mexico, D.F.

p. 294 *Man the Master and Not the Slave of Technology*, 1952, Acrylic on Aluminum, National Technology Institute, Mexico, D.F.

p. 298 Siqueiros, Angelica and Diego Rivera in Mexico City, 1950s, Photograph, Sala Siqueiros.

p. 307 *For the Complete Social Security of All Mexicans*, 1952-54. Vinylite on plywood, Hospital de la Raza, Mexico, D.F.

p. 319 *Excommunication and Death Sentence of Miguel Hidalgo*, 1953, Pyroxylin on masonite, University of Michoacan, Morelia, Mexico.

p. 330 *The People to the University, The University to the People*, 1952-1956, Bas-relief and mosaic, Rectory, National Autonomous University of Mexico, Mexico, D.F.

p. 338 *The Revolution Against Díaz, Strike at Cananea,* 1957-1967, Acrylic on plywood, Museum of National History, Mexico, D.F.

p. 348 *Apology for the Future Victory of Medicine over Cancer*, 1958, Acrylic on plywood, Medical Center, Mexico, D.F.

p. 353 *The Theater in Mexico*, 1958-1967, Acrylic on plywood, National Association of Actors, Mexico, D.F.

p. 403 *The Revolution Against Díaz, Revolutionaries,* 1957-1967, Acrylic on plywood, Museum of National History, Mexico, D.F.

p. 404 *The Revolution Against Diaz, The Martyrs,* 1957-1967, Acrylic on plywood, Museum of National History, Mexico, D.F.

p. 439 Polyforum Siqueiros and Hotel de Mexico, Mexico, D.F.

p. 442 *The March of Humanity in Latin America and Towards the Cosmos,* 1967-1971, Sculpture-painting on asbestos-cement, Siqueiros Cultural Polyforum, Mexico, D.F.

p. 443 *Christ the Leader,* 1967-1971, Exterior Panel, Acrylic on asbestos-cement, Siqueiros Cultural Polyforum, Mexico, D.F.

p. 445 *Founders of Modern Mexican Art,* 1967-1971, Sculpture-Painting Wall, Siqueiros Cultural Polyforum, Mexico, D.F.

Preface

After the death of Mexican artist David Alfaro Siquieros in 1974, I learned that he was much more than one of Mexico's three great muralists. He had not only participated in a major movement in modern art, the Mexican Mural Movement, but he had also developed new artistic materials, equipment and techniques, along with challenging theories of art, which he pronounced through journals which he published. While best known as a muralist, he painted countless portraits, landscapes and visual allegories. Between outbursts of intensive creative energy, he immersed himself in political struggles, including the Mexican Revolution and the Spanish Civil War.

While there were plenty of sources on his body of work, they did not explore the relationship between his personality, cultural heritage, social environment and political convictions and the form, style and content of his art. Since he participated in a uniquely Mexican movement and his art was closely linked to his political ideology, this was an oversight that only partially explained the nature and purpose of his art.

Given this lacunae and my interest in Mexican history and culture, as well as the appeal of an obviously energetic, creative and dynamic individual, I decided to research and write a biography which would describe his paintings and prints, as well as his murals, his artistic innovations, his ideas on art, his political convictions and activities and his personal life. Since his art expressed his views on contemporary issues and history and he alternated between intense periods of artistic creation and direct political action, I realized that I would have to describe the social and political environment in which he lived and worked.

I also sensed that the real challenge would not be in describing his life and work, but in capturing his personality, the essence of which I could sense through his art, words and deeds, but which I had not experienced directly. In the process of interviewing his associates, I was struck by the constant reference to his abilities as a storyteller. Since many of the stories he told were recorded, I have included some of them, not only to describe his personal life, relationships and views, but also to provide a sense of his personality, including the theatrical manner in which he told them.

The work of an artist is also a major source for a biographer, providing information on the evolution of his style and technique, revealing the different phases of artistic development and influences and reflecting the artist's state of mind during their creation. Although a work of art may be discussed without consideration of the personality of the artist, the art of Siqueiros was a direct reflection of his personality, mirroring not only personal traits or moods, but also expressing his strong feelings on the subject. Art critics frequently noted that, even in his portraits of other people, Siqueiros was painting himself. I have described his paintings, as well as the process of creating them, therefore, not only to explain his artistic development, but also to describe him.

Besides consulting publications on modern art, Mexican muralism and the art of Siqueiros, I conducted research in the archives and library of Siqueiros and interviewed his widow, brother-in-law and fellow artists, and many others who knew him personally, worked with him or have written about his art. Fortunately, many of his letters, speeches, articles and manifestos, along with reviews of exhibits or murals, are available in several anthologies on his work and life.

His own books, especially *No hay más ruta que la nuestra* and *Cómo se pinta un mural*, as well as numerous published articles, are invaluable sources on his theories and practice of art. The major sources for excerpts from his publications, therefore, are either the books themselves or collections of his manifestos, articles, letters and lectures. Since I have usually stated the publication or source in the text, the notes are primarily explanatory, serving to identify persons and organizations or describing related developments.

For the rewarding experience of researching and writing this book, as well as invaluable assistance, I am indebted to a host of special people. First, I wish to thank my friend Alice Wexler, sister historian and biographer, who encouraged me to undertake a study of Siqueiros.

I also want to express my appreciation for the cooperation and assistance of Siqueiros's widow, Angélica Arenal de Siqueiros. Besides making the library of the Sala de Arte Público available to me and directing the archivist to assist me, she consented to several interviews in spite of her busy schedule and declining health. I could never have conducted the research without her assistance and that of Emma Arriaga, the archivist in the Sala de Arte Público.

Shortly after I arrived in Mexico, I was very fortunate to meet Raquel Tibol, noted art critic and historian. In addition to referring me to her own publications on Siqueiros and Mexican Art, as well as other valuable sources, she provided me with insight and suggestions that guided me throughout the researching and writing of this book. I owe her special thanks and wish to express my appreciation for her prolific scholarship and assistance.

I am deeply indebted to Shifra Goldman, whose article on Siqueiros in Los Angeles was my major source for that period of his life and whose recent book on contemporary Mexican art provided an important perspective on more recent developments. Likewise, Laurence Hurlburt's articles on the Siqueiros Experimental Workshop in New York and his "Portrait of the Bourgeoisie" mural provided much of the information for those sections of book. His excellent *Mexican Muralists in the United States* is a comprehensive study of the subject.

In Mexico, I interviewed a number of people close to Siqueiros, including his brother-in-law and fellow artist Luis Arenal, and Roberto Berdecio, a Bolivian artist who shared a room with Siqueiros in Mexico and New York. I also was introduced to Pablo O'Higgins, an American artist who was an important figure in modern Mexican art.

Another North American expatriate, Bill Miller, told me fascinating stories about Siqueiros and Trotsky's assassin and introduced me to other sources.

Thanks to a College Research Grant from the National Endowment for the Humanities, I spent another semester conducting research in Mexico and writing this biography. Since I conducted research in the Hermeoteca Nacional (the National Periodical Library), the National Library of Mexico and the libraries of the University of California at Berkeley, Stanford University, and Sonoma State University, I want to thank all the librarians who assisted me in my research.

Since the publication of *Siqueiros: A Biography,* I have updated and revised the original, adding new information generated during the 1996 centennial of his birth or recent exhibits or publications. The new title, *Siqueiros, Biography of a Revolutionary Artist*, reflects his dedication to social realism and public art, his innovations in plastic materials, equipment and technique, his prolific theoretical and ideological pronouncements about art and artists, his pivotal role in a unique modern art movement, Mexican muralism, and last but not least, his revolutionary ideology and active participation in the struggle against fascism, imperialism and injustice. After fighting in the Mexican Revolution, he was instrumental in its cultural expression while defending its ideals against enemies, native and foreign.

For Siqueiros, the Mexican Mural Movement was the artistic expression of the Mexican Revolution of 1910. It was an important and unique counter current in modern art and no other country or revolution has produced a comparable movement in monumental public art or as many outstanding artists. As a founder and self-appointed ideologue of that movement, Siqueiros emphasized its singularity and contributions to modern art. He was also very proud of his nationality, his participation in the Mexican Revolution and the international recognition of modern Mexican art. Recalling cherished episodes in his own life, he frequently commented, "It could only have happened in Mexico!"

I. A Young Chinaco

On January 6, 1974, Mexican artist David Alfaro Siqueiros died. Immediately, messages of condolences and tribute came from all corners of the globe, as writers, artists and heads of state recognized his creative genius, artistic innovations, indomitable spirit and lifelong struggle against injustice and imperialism.

After proclaiming twenty-four hours of public mourning and tribute, the President of Mexico, members of his cabinet, close friends and relatives took turns standing guard at the side of his flag-draped casket in the entrance hall of the National Institute of Fine Arts. While images of his creation looked down from his murals overhead, several thousand Mexicans of all ages and social classes filed by, stopping to kiss the flag and honor their friend and comrade for the last time.

The next day, military cadets escorted the coffin to the Rotunda of Illustrious Men. As thousands listened or watched on radio and television, the national flag was folded and handed to his widow and the body was lowered into the earth while hushed mourners sung The Internationale.

Who was this man whom so many honored, what did he mean to the workers and peasants who filed by is casket and why was he, an artist, revered as a national hero? These are just some of the questions which I pondered as I read the obituaries and posthumous tributes which he received.

As I read further, I discovered not just the work of a major artist, but that of an energetic and dynamic personality whose myriad activities and achievements left the impression of several lives or careers: Revolutionary soldier; pamphleteer; union organizer; leader of protests against fascism and imperialism; art theorist and author; innovator in plastic materials, techniques and equipment; commander of front-line troops; agent provocateur; political exile and celebrated prisoner; publisher and editor of countless journals, and prolific painter of murals, landscapes and portraits. Interspersed among these activities were numerous romances, public controversies, arrests, deportations, exiles and long prison sentences.

Now, more than thirty years later after his death, his surviving murals in Mexico, Cuba, Chile, Argentina and the United States, and exhibits of his paintings and prints testify to his creative genius, his commitment to public art and his forceful expression of the human condition. Since he alternated between intense artistic activity and direct political action, his life story is a capsule history of modern Mexico. Because he participated in cultural and political activities in Europe, Russia, Latin America and the United States, his biography also provides a unique perspective on many 20th Century events, personalities and issues.

It all began in the waning years of the nineteenth century.

After more than a half century of civil war, foreign invasions and anarchy following independence, Mexico appeared to be prospering under the benign rule of Porfirio Díaz. After seizing power in 1876, Díaz had established a dictatorship by crushing the opposition, outmaneuvering his rivals and amending the Constitution to permit his reelection. Backed by a well-rewarded army, wealthy landowners, the Catholic Church, and the *rurales*, a notorious rural police force, he stayed in power until 1911.

Despite its strong-arm tactics, Díaz's 35-year rule, known as the *Porfiriato,* brought welcomed stability to a war torn Mexico, encouraged foreign investment and fostered economic growth. New industries emerged, mining flourished and Mexico became the second largest oil producer in the world. In order to attract foreign capital, Díaz offered generous concessions to foreign investors. Impressed by Mexico's material progress, foreign leaders hailed him as a "great statesman."

The expansion of the economy was accompanied by cultural advances. More schools were built and Mexico City was enhanced by impressive new buildings and broad avenues lined with statues. But the emphasis was on European, not Mexican forms of expression, and the European philosophy of positivism became the basis of the educational system, as well as a rationale for perpetuating the dictatorship.

Behind this facade of peace and progress, however, there were serious tensions and contradictions, which were about to tear the country apart. The favored treatment of foreign investors was resented and it was said that "Mexico was the mother of foreigners, the stepmother of Mexicans."

While positivism promised "order, progress and liberty," most Mexicans only experienced the order imposed by the dictatorship and enforced by the *rurales*. Meanwhile, the government was controlled by the old cronies of Díaz, many of whom had been in power since the beginning of the *Porfiriato*, and the *científicos*, a closed group of European-oriented intellectuals, monopolized the important cultural posts.

Nevertheless, Díaz had his supporters and Cipriano Alfaro, a young lawyer in Irapuato, believed in and supported the dictatorship. Originally from Michoacan, he was the son of Antonio Alfaro, famous guerrilla fighter against the French troops of Napoleon III and the conservatives, and of Eusebia, Antonio's second wife. Since his father was a cattle breeder, he was seldom home and Cipriano was raised by his mother, a devout woman who instructed him in religion and shielded him from the rougher aspects of rural Mexico.

Although Antonio was a liberal and a fervent anticlerical who had fought against the Catholic Church, his son became a devout Catholic and entered the seminary in Irapauto as a theological student. While a student at the seminary, Cipriano participated in a protest against the government of General González. After this political baptism, he became a regular activist and was arrested several times as a student agitator. He also wrote articles protesting the government's anticlerical policies, organized protests against the government and marched in demonstrations. Though he left the seminary to study law, he never relinquished his strong faith and he participated actively in Catholic lay organizations and political parties throughout his life.

After law school, Cipriano decided to leave Irapuato and move to the northern border state of Chihuahua where he would set up his law practice. Still sparsely populated and only recently pacified, this developing region was full of promise for young and ambitious Mexicans. Because of its wealthy deposits of minerals, vast stands of timber and large expanses of land for cattle grazing, and close to the United States, Chihuahua was attracting immigrants from all over the republic. Like the rest of the nation, however, there were signs of unrest, and during a recent railroad strike, federal troops burned the town of Tomochic to the ground after it put up a fierce resistance. Only one old woman lived to tell the story.

In Chihuahua the young and dapper Cipriano prospered, building up a successful law practice. Soon after his arrival he met and wooed the attractive Teresa Siqueiros, the daughter of Felipe Siqueiros, a very active state politician and amateur poet. The Siqueiroses were an old Chihuahua family, which many generations before had come to Mexico from Portugal or Galicia in northern Spain. Teresa's grandfather Felipe and his two brothers had come to Chihuahua from Sonora to work in the mines. Among the first settlers in the region, they were active in local government and one of the brothers had served briefly as Governor of the state.

Teresa fell in love with the ambitious young lawyer from Irapauto and, at the age of 16, she and Cipriano were married in Mexico City. They returned to Chihuahua where she gave birth to their first child, but a few months later the baby died. Her second child, a daughter named María de la Luz, survived. Then came José, the first son, born in the town of Santa Rosalia–today, Ciudad Camargo, Chihuahua– on December 29, 1896. Three years later, after a difficult delivery, Teresa gave birth to another son, Jesús. She never recovered and nine months later, she died, leaving Cipriano with three young children to raise.

The oldest son, José, was deeply affected by the loss of his mother. Only four at the time, he could not have known her very well, but he always spoke very fondly of her and later adopted her family name as his own, preferring Siqueiros to his patronymic Alfaro. Since he later exchanged his given name of José for David, he became David Alfaro Siqueiros, and when he became a famous artist, he was just Siqueiros.

José remembered his mother as a strong, sensitive and creative person and he was sure that he had inherited these traits from her. In contrast with the conservative lifestyle and politics of his father, the Siqueiros family was noted for its musicians, poets and actors and a romantic and bohemian way of life. Years later he enjoyed telling stories about his maternal grandfather and his mother's extraordinary sisters, outspoken and liberal, and somewhat eccentric. From others he learned of his mother's restless and, at times, agitated nature, her romantic inclinations, and her ability as an actress to captivate and move her audience, traits which he apparently inherited from her.

José's preference for his mother and her family, therefore, does not appear unusual, and in temperament and political views, he was much closer to his liberal relatives from the north than his father. Through the years his fondness for his mother became an idealization, and his repeated treatment of maternity in his art suggests his memory of her as well as an appreciation of motherhood.

José was only four and Jesús not one when their mother died. Faced with the prospect of raising a young family by himself, Don Cipriano decided to move back to Irapauto where his parents, Eusebia and Antonio, could take care of the children. The grandparents took great joy in the children and Antonio assumed the responsibility of rearing them since "women do not know how to educate men, they make them effeminate." While Eusebia treated them firmly but tenderly, Antonio sought to mold them into macho men like himself by treating them roughly and ignoring their complaints or injuries. As his most famous progeny later described it, Eusebita treated them with an open hand while their grandfather used a closed fist. Since Jesús was younger and more delicate, he spent more time at home with Eusebia, while a vigorous and robust José thrived under his grandfather's rough tutelage.

Antonio Alfaro was the direct opposite of his son. Whereas Cipriano was proper, conservative and devout, his father was rowdy, liberal and anticlerical and led a life of carousing and drinking. He was also a legendary guerrilla fighter who had fought with Juárez against the Catholic conservatives and the French. Serving as a colonel under General Escobedo, he fought against the forces of Maximilian in Jalisco and Michoacan and was known as "Siete Filhos" (Seven Blades), either because of his miraculous escapes from enemy ambushes or his volatile temperament. A great storyteller, he regaled his grandchildren with exciting tales of the "*los chinacos*" (stallions), the shock troops of Juárez, and the war to death between the liberals and the conservatives.

For Antonio there was nothing worse than "*un puto en la familia*" (homosexual) and children had to be educated with fists. When José came home from school complaining that another boy had picked on him, the elder Alfaro struck him and told him that he had to learn to defend himself. If someone hit him, he should return the blow three times. If someone threw a rock at him, he had to throw ten rocks back and hit his target. He must not show fear and be courageous, and if he weakened or expressed fright, his grandfather struck him, sometimes drawing blood. By ignoring his suffering and hiding his feelings, Antonio sought to strengthen his grandson's determination and prevent his dependence on the affection of others.

Accustomed to the rough physical life of rural Mexico, Antonio tried to make his grandsons as tough as himself. When he came across them playing in the fields, he would draw his pistol and after shouting at them to take cover, he would begin to run about and discharge his pistols, the chips flying from the rocks behind which the boys had hidden. This was what he called "the school of men," designed to train machos, not "*muchachitos, hijos de la chingada,*" (little boys, sons of the violated woman).

Antonio was an excellent horseman, breeder of cattle and an expert at buying and selling fighting bulls and cocks. He taught José how to round up wild horses, to tame, saddle and shoe them, how to rope and ride young bulls and to participate in all manner of rural fiestas. He also showed him how to find his way in the dark and how to survive alone in the country. When his grandfather went off to enjoy cockfights, bullfights or rural fiestas, José tagged along, watching his idol's caprichos and learning to handle himself when the fiestas turned into brawls or his grandfather had too much to drink.

During the long hot and dry summers in the region, rabies attacked man and beast and Don Antonio was responsible for tracking down and killing rabid dogs. After receiving a description of the animal, he and José would gallop across the dusty plains, shooting at the fleeing dog until they flanked it, whereupon Antonio dispatched it with several furious swipes of his machete. Afterwards he explained to a horrified José that rabid dogs were so hard to kill because they were possessed of the evil spirit.

Antonio also loved to invent and tell fanciful stories and one day he terrified his grandsons with the tale of a newborn baby which he had found crying alone in the desert. When he brought the child home to Eusebia, he explained, it began to speak, saying, "Look daddy, what big teeth I have!" while displaying a mouth full of teeth larger than those of a full-grown dog. Terrified, Eusebia jumped back and the baby fell to the ground, exploded and vanished. When the children expressed disbelief, Antonio told them to check with Eusebia if they thought he was not telling the truth.

Despite his harsh treatment, José idolized his grandfather and Eusebia worried that he would turn into a monster because of Antonio's influence. When Antonio came home after a long absence, he always had an elaborate explanation and his tales of adventure, romance and women enthralled the young Siqueiros, firing his own imagination and reinforcing his image of his grandfather.

Years later, when José, now a soldier in uniform, came to visit his grandfather during the Revolution, the old man was deeply touched. He had always wanted his grandson to be a soldier like himself and was worried about him becoming an artist. He was also glad to see a bottle of mezcal under his grandson's arm and the old man and his teenage grandson got drunk together.

While the children were still young, Eusebia died. After her death, the family moved to Mexico City and, while the grandfather continued to live with them, the children were now under the control and influence of their father. As soon as they arrived in the capital, Cipriano placed his sons in the Catholic Colegio de los Maristas, while Maria was sent to a Catholic school for girls. The boys were now exposed to the hard discipline and dogmatic routine of the Catholic brothers, in contrast with the rigorous physical training and the warm love of their grandparents.

José also discovered that the priests opposed his liberal anticlerical views and their version of Mexican history contradicted what he had learned from his grandfather. When he defended the Mexican liberal Benito Juárez in class as a great man, he was reprimanded and reminded that Juárez was an enemy of his religion. When he shouted *"Viva Madero!"* in class in support of the major opposition leader to the dictator Díaz, he was sent to the chapel for uttering this blasphemy. Surrounded by bloody figures of Christ and ceilings covered with clouds, stars and floating angels, he marveled at the beauty of the place and wondered how it could be considered a place of punishment.

Life was more comfortable now and José Alfaro grew up with the children of wealthy friends of his father. While most boys walked to school, José and Jesús rode in a fancy carriage imported from England and driven by a liveried coachman in yellow boots and top hat and cockade. His godfather was Don Manuel Amor Escandón, one of the wealthiest and most powerful men in the state of Morelos, and another Amor Escandón, Don Alejandro, became José's riding instructor. During vacations José traveled with his father to visit the estates of his wealthy clients in the state of Morelos, not far from the capital.

These trips not only exposed him to the European culture which the Mexican upper class worshipped, but also to the tremendous contrast between the expensive homes in which they lived for only two or three months out of the year and the humble shacks of the peasants. He also saw the workers put in long and hard days in the fields and observed the excessive punishments which they received for stealing grain to feed their families. It was not difficult, he concluded early, to see that "the rich enjoyed a paradise on this earth while the poor were promised a utopian paradise."

Cipriano was more than just a devout Catholic. According to his son, he was either a Spanish mystic or one of those fanatical Franciscans of the Middle Ages. Before she died, he had insisted that his wife, who was not a religious woman, go to church every Sunday for mass and every afternoon for rosaries. After they moved to Mexico City, the children came to dread Sunday, for their father celebrated mass before and after breakfast, and then dragged them to one church after another before finishing the pilgrimage at the Cathedral.

Mingling with the poor, this elegantly dressed man, a member of the porfirian society and distinguished lawyer, would kneel transfixed for hours in front of the altar, his arms spread in the form of a cross. Since he liked to spend the afternoon visiting even more churches, the children began to devise ways of distracting him and to avoid passing by any more churches. Cipriano also had hopes that his oldest son would become a Jesuit and when José was eleven, he took him to a Eucharist Congress in Montreal.

In spite of Cipriano's religiosity and indoctrination, none of his children remained religious. Even while they lived at home, they rebelled and caused their father considerable anguish by refusing to go to mass. María de la Luz was the first to defy her father and José eventually adopted her liberal views. Ironically, it was one of their father's friends who introduced them to *floresmagonismo*, the anarcho-socialist thought of the anti-Díaz Flores Magón brothers, and Jesús Soto, one of José's classmates, had loaned him works by Kropotkin and Gorki.

In addition to his work as a lawyer for many of the large landowners, Cipriano performed different tasks for the Díaz government, serving as an extraordinary ambassador and traveling frequently to Europe on delicate missions for the government. Since he worshipped France, he had the boys sent to the Colegio Franco-Ingles where they learned to read and spell in French before they could read in Spanish. He also insisted on dressing as an elegant Frenchman, buying his clothes in Paris, while reprimanding his oldest son for his sloppy appearance or spilling food on his new clothes.

In spite of their differences, Siqueiros inherited his father's pride and strong sense of honor and was always an elegant dresser in public. During one of his rare visits to his son when he was in prison, Cipriano greeted his son austerely, barely embracing him and remaining somewhat distant, while he explained why he had come. He said that the government officials who had arrested him did not understand his son's political convictions or his integrity and assumed that he would easily compromise his principals in order to be released.

"They do not know that you are a man faithful to your convictions," Cipriano told his son. After they characterized the bureaucrats as stupid oafs, they laughed, breaking the tension. Before he left, José reassured his father that he would not compromise his convictions or tarnish family honor.

Though he seldom visited his son in prison, Cipriano wrote letters to him as well as sending cigarettes, candies and fruit. Invariably the content of his father's letters was political. While conservative, his anti-communism was neither pedestrian nor a blind rejection of its atheism. He was well read, especially in the history of working associations, and he endorsed the "social Christianity" emanating from Belgium. "Always, to the end of his days," Siqueiros recalled, "he wanted to convert me to his side ... as I wanted to do to him to mine."

Based on the stories which Siqueiros told about his childhood, it would appear that he was a spunky and rebellious child who frequently got into trouble. Most of these incidents were minor, however, and were probably no worse than those committed by other lads of his age and social station. When he took money from home and spent it on candy to treat his classmates, he was caught and severely punished by his father, but without revealing that it had been Jesús's idea to take the money.

Despite their closeness, Jesus always remained a mystery to José, as well as to most other people. As a child, Jesús always had things he was not supposed to have and his older brother thought he would become a gangster. Later, when José was in prison, Jesús would visit him every day, entering unobtrusively, like an intruder. Then, speaking in a low voice, he would hand over the package he had proudly smuggled by the guards that day. When the Chilean poet Pablo Neruda was visiting a middle aged Siqueiros in prison, he suddenly noticed this silent and mysterious person who would appear behind him without any warning. It was Jesús.

Neruda also commented on the uncanny ability of Jesús to change his facial expression from one emotion to another and complimented him on his theatrical ability. While Jesús never won great fame or success on the stage, he performed a unique style of theater in which he wrote the script, arranged for the theater and publicity, designed the sets, printed and sold the tickets, ushered people to their seats, and performed the whole play, including the various parts, all by himself. Since these performances were not financially successful, his brother frequently gave him paintings to sell. Jesús always remained a hazy and impenetrable mystery to his brother, like a "boat, tied up at the pier, but without any destination."

Despite his close relationship with Jesús, it was his sister María de la Luz who influenced him, converting him to her liberal ideas. Although she was spared the rough treatment and physical beatings of their father or grandfather, she was equally strong and rebellious in her thinking, and she was the first to oppose their father's political and religious views. When she visited her brother in prison, they passionately discussed their political views.

While Luz openly expressed her views on the church or against the government in front of her father and his wealthy clients, José's first acts of rebellion were less noteworthy and unintentional. After Díaz resigned in 1911 and left the country, Cipriano supported the presidential candidacy of Francisco Leon de la Barra, Díaz's ambassador to the United States and interim President after Díaz' resignation. When he brought home a silk flag sewn by some Catholic ladies to be used in a demonstration by the Knights of Columbus, he asked his son to paint an eagle, a symbol of the Mexican nation, and "Viva de la Barra!" (Long live de la Barra!) on it. But the next day, when his unsuspecting father presented the flag, José felt a sharp blow on the side of his head. A better artist than speller, he had printed the nonsensical statement "Biba de la Varra!" instead of "Viva de la Barra!," since the Spanish "v" is pronounced like a "b."

José Alfaro's conversion to the cause of Francisco Madero was also confused and tardy. Walking one day with another friend, Juanito Olaguibel, they encountered a ragged mob in the streets of the capital. Running to the head of the demonstration, which was shouting, "Down with the New Era", they marched to a building with "The New Era" printed on it. As the mob began to throw stones at the building, Juanito and José danced in the street, then joined in throwing some burning rags and burlap at the building which caught fire and burned to the ground. When he told Luz of his participation in the stoning and burning of "The New Era," she called him "a stupid animal, an idiot." In his ignorance, he had participated in a demonstration against the only newspaper which had endorsed Madero.

One evening in 1911, when the family was living in Mexico City, a jubilant José arrived home late for dinner. Entering the dining room, he saw a room full of guests and an empty seat at the end of an elegantly set dinner table. When he threw his hat in the direction of his chair, it landed perfectly on the empty seat, evoking laughs from Luz and Chucho, but only stern looks from his father.

Seated around the table were some of the richest men of Morelos and Guanajuato, who were meeting with Cipriano to discuss their problems with the Revolution and the recently elected Madero government. When one of these wealthy landowners turned to José and asked, "Are you one of those who say that what is yours is mine and mine is mine?" he could only respond with a grunt, which provoked more questions, insinuations, jokes and sarcastic comments at his expense.

Suddenly José burst out in a loud voice, "I only know that all the *hacendados* (large landowners) are a pack of thieves!," upon which his father told him to leave the table. Rising slowly to his feet, José walked away from the table very deliberately, staring defiantly at each of the wealthy aristocrats around the table. Exiting the dining room, he slammed and locked the door and began to smash everything he could reach in the next room. He continued to break everything in sight, causing a terrible din, and while his father and his guests tried to open the door, he proceeded from room to room, first locking the door and then destroying priceless objects. After jumping from a window to the street, he bombarded the house with pieces of pavement while his father and his guests looked on, horrified.

After this outbreak, José left home and went to live with a school friend, whose mother took care of him like her own son. Although Jesús was sent to tell him that that his father was very sick, he never went back to live with his father. In order to show that he could support himself, he purchased a fancy suit and sombrero and strutted up and down in front of his father's house. His father never appeared but some former playmates were amused and laughed at his charade. Meanwhile, he had obtained a position as a teacher of drawing in a government school for girls. However, he was soon out of work when some students demanded his dismissal because he gave the best grades to the prettiest girls.

In spite of their differences, it was Cipriano who introduced José to art and encouraged his development as an artist. An expert on Mexico's colonial art treasures and Spanish religious art, he explained this cultural heritage to his son during their weekly pilgrimages to different churches in the capital. Before he could read and write, therefore, José was familiar with the works of los Echave, Miguel de Cabrera, Juárez, and Juan Correa, the masters of Mexican colonial art.

The vivid drama and disturbing themes of this religious art fascinated him and he was struck by the intensity, sense of movement and somber use of color in the paintings. His own use of color, the powerful modeling and the sense of movement in his paintings are similar to that of Mexico's baroque masters. His numerous depictions of maternity and cadavers also resemble the madonnas and pietas he saw with his father and, near the end of his life, he painted several portraits of a bloody, tortured Christ.

José's first painting was also religious. When he was eleven, the family house was being painted and a curious José watched the house painters intensely and plied them with constant questions on style and technique. He also imitated the master painter, aping his dress and walk as he moved from room to room, decorating the ceiling with garlands of flowers and figures of animals in the corners. The painters responded to his queries by explaining their techniques in oil, where they bought their paint and which colors or paints lasted and remained brilliant, while others faded. After an apothecary from a local pharmacy gave him an engraving of "The Virgin of the Chair" by Raphael, he proceeded to copy it directly in oil on a piece of cloth.

When Cipriano saw his son's first painting, he proclaimed that it was a masterpiece and engaged Eduardo Solares Gutiérrez as his art instructor. A disciple of the contemporary Mexican and Spanish masters, Solares imposed a rigorous academic discipline on José and introduced him to a naturalism derived from indigenous art. José responded enthusiastically, absorbing his teacher's directions and developing his talent. Before long, he was winning prizes in the art contests sponsored by the Franco-Ingles School where he was now enrolled.

At one of the award ceremonies, for which the school had sent out embossed invitations and rented a theater, José Alfaro appeared dressed like his teacher of drawing, a very elegantly dressed man. Although his classmates laughed when they saw him march up to receive the first prize, an exact but shorter version of their drawing master, he ignored their derision. After making several grand bows from the stage, he accepted the award, an enormous red and gold book, a history of the Catholic saints in French. This behavior earned him the nickname "el payaso" (the clown).

Life was not all study and art, however, and with the same energy and style that he had approached art, José took up baseball. For his "elegant style" at first base for the school team, "*Los Mascarones*," he was known as "*El Principe Papeles*" (Great Performer) and he basked in the glory of making a graceful pickup or a spectacular backhand stab of the ball and hearing someone shout, "*Ora Principe Papeles!*" His play at first base also earned him a spot on the Mexican national team which competed in the first World Junior Baseball Championships in Houston, Texas.

In 1909 a young artist named Diego Rivera had just returned from Europe and there was an exhibition of his work in Mexico City. Hoping to encourage his son's interest in art, Cipriano urged José to collect some of his drawings and paintings and show them to the artist. More interested in playing baseball, José searched hurriedly through the house and found some vaguely familiar sketches which he took to show to Rivera. Although he was surrounded by reporters, Rivera took time to look at the drawings. Not only did he bestow generous praise on the art which José showed him, but the next day Chucho showed José an article in the newspaper in which Rivera was quoted as saying that José Alfaro would have a great future in art.

While José was only mildly impressed, his father was very excited and asked to see the drawings which he had shown Rivera. When he saw the pictures, however, he was aghast. They were not by his son, but by José's cousin Enrique from Chihuahua. As far as José was concerned, the issue was closed and now he could concentrate on baseball. An "official baseball," bats and gloves were more important than pencils, brushes, or paints. He was always passionate about baseball and he played it whenever possible, even in prison. His cousin, he later learned, died an early and violent death as a gunman for Al Capone.

Before José could pursue his interests and what promised to be a career in architecture, however, the Revolution erupted anew, more violent and destructive than before. Not only were his studies interrupted, but he also became an active participant, first as a student agitator and later as a revolutionary soldier. Although it would be severely tested in coming years, the character of this young *chinaco*, grandson of the legendary "*Siete Filhos*," was already defined.

II. Revolutionary Soldier

In 1910 Mexico erupted in the first major revolution of this century. While the fall of the dictator Díaz was anti-climatic and did not signify a major break with the past, ensuing events promised a new Mexico. After a brief lull, the struggle resumed with greater violence than before. For almost two decades, the country was wracked by civil war and military uprisings. When it was over, more than a million Mexicans had been killed.

The Revolution of 1910 was the culmination of a century-long struggle for social justice, democracy and political, economic and cultural independence. While foreigners praised the economic growth of Mexico under Díaz, very few benefits trickled down to the masses and they continued to live in wretched poverty. Land ownership had become more concentrated and the large estates expanded at the expense of small holdings or the communal lands of Indian villages. Peasants who lost their land were absorbed by the large estates or haciendas and became virtual slaves under a system of debt peonage.

When workers were recruited to build railroads or to work in the mines, oil fields and foreign-owned industry, they tried to organize unions and mount strikes against their employers. But the strikes were brutally suppressed and the leaders were hunted down, sent to jail or killed.

The economy was dominated by foreigners and the Porfirian elite imported or imitated European culture. In the years before 1910, economic conditions deteriorated, triggering rural unrest and a series of strikes which were crushed by the army and the police.

In 1910 Porfirio Díaz was eighty years old and had been in power for thirty-four years. Elections were a farce and the democratic guarantees of the 1857 Constitution were a mockery. However,

Díaz encouraged hopes for a change when he declared that Mexico was ready for democracy and announced that he would retire in 1910. Heartened by this news, an opposition began to form.

One leader who took Díaz at his word was Francisco Madero, the well-educated son of a wealthy northern family. After writing a book which warned against the perpetuation of the dictatorship, Madero ran against Díaz in 1910 as the candidate of the Anti-Re-electionist Party. Although Díaz dismissed Madero as a serious contender, he had him arrested just before the election and announced his own reelection. Madero escaped to Texas and issued a manifesto calling for an armed revolt against Díaz.

Following a series of regional revolts, the *maderista* movement gained momentum. In the south, peasants led by Emiliano Zapata took up arms in the name of "land and liberty," while northern troops under Pancho Villa and Pascual Orozco surprised the federal troops in Ciudad Juárez. When this border town fell to the rebels, an agreement was reached calling for the resignation of Díaz, an interim president and elections to choose a successor. After Díaz departed for Europe, Francisco Madero was elected President in 1911.

The armed revolt against Díaz was preceded by signs of a cultural rebirth and the seeds of a renaissance in the fine arts had been sown before 1910. Influenced by new currents of thought from Europe, a group of young intellectuals had formed the *Ateneo de la Juventud* (Athens of Youth). Although their plans were interrupted by the Revolution, the *atenistas* sought to develop a sense of national identity and called for educational and ideological reform. The precursors of a new intelligentsia, they would enrich national culture through their ideas and public service.

In art several artists had turned to Mexican subject matter and at the Academy of San Carlos, the National Academy of the Fine Arts, a new generation of students was protesting the archaic methods of instruction. While they heard rumors of an artistic revolution in Europe, they were not allowed to improvise or to draw from nature. Instead they were required to sketch from photographs or copies of classic statues, after which they had to correct their sketches by comparing them with photographs of the same view. As they realized the natural beauty and rich artistic tradition of Mexico, including its folk art, they also began to question their teachers' obsession with European art and artists.

In the forefront of this new sensitivity was Gerardo Murillo. The recipient of a government scholarship, he had studied art in Europe and was impressed by the murals of Michelangelo and Tintoretto and attracted to the philosophy of anarcho-syndicalism. In Switzerland he discussed politics with a Russian exile called Lenin and worked on an anticlerical newspaper with an Italian socialist named Benito Mussolini. After obtaining a doctorate in philosophy in Italy, he changed his own name to Dr. Atl, meaning "water" in Nahuatl, the language of the Aztecs.

In 1904 he returned to Mexico in time to help a young artist, Diego Rivera, arrange his first exhibit. Hired to teach at San Carlos, Dr. Atl captivated his students with his tales of adventure and romance and his descriptions of the latest political currents, revolutionary advances in European art and the magnificent frescos of Italy. In 1906 he issued a manifesto to young Mexican artists in which he declared that since there was no market for art in a poor country like Mexico, the only choice for artists was public art fostered by the state and linked to the problems of the nation and its people.

Coming only a few weeks after the bloody suppression of a miners' strike in Cananea by the North American mine owner, Dr. Atl's manifesto reflected the growing unrest in the country. Although it was premature, Dr. Atl's appeal expressed two of the basic premises of the mural movement which emerged fifteen years later: Public art sponsored by the state which addressed national problems and reflected the struggles of the Mexican people.

Besides laying the groundwork for a new generation of artists, Dr. Atl constantly searched for new materials and techniques. Frustrated with traditional paints, he invented his own medium, mixing oil paints, pastels and the juice of the maguey, a cactus-like plant. Using these "Atl-Colors," he painted landscapes featuring volcanos which were characterized by their brilliant color. When he was commissioned to design a glass curtain for the new opera house under construction, he designed a beautiful screen depicting the two volcanos overlooking Mexico City. The subject was Mexican, but the screens were executed by Tiffany of New York and were to be incorporated into a European structure of Italian marble designed by an Italian architect.

In 1910 Mexico celebrated the centennial of Mexico's struggle for independence from Spain. The festivities included thousands of gallons of French champagne, concerts of European music performed by European orchestras and an exhibit of Spanish art. When a group of students learned that the government had appropriated 30,000 pesos for an exhibit of Spanish art in a special exhibition hall and not one centavo for an exhibit of Mexican art, they made plans to exhibit their own art. Calling themselves "The Society of Mexican Painters and Sculptors," they appealed through Dr. Atl to the Director of San Carlos for space in which to display their work. The Director not only gave his permission but also contributed 300 pesos of his own money while the Minister of Education managed to find 3000 pesos for a "Show of Works of National Art" in the halls of the Academy of San Carlos.

According to José Clemente Orozco, one of the student entrants, "the exhibition was a great and completely unexpected success." While he displayed some cartoons and charcoal drawings, Saturnino Herrán presented "The Legend of the Volcanos," based on an Indian myth, and Jorge Enciso exhibited a painting of a life-size Indian entitled "Anahuac." A painting of "Village Women with Flowers" by an unknown student, José Alfaro, evoked comments for its violation of current styles.

After the exhibit, the participants celebrated in a "victory" banquet, making elaborate toasts and expressing their gratitude to Dr. Atl. Flushed by their success and encouraged by their mentor, they formed an "Artistic Center" and pressed for walls on which to paint murals. The Minister of Public Instruction gave his approval and they made preparations to paint a mural in the lecture hall of the National Preparatory School. The scaffolding was barely in place, however, when the revolt against Díaz erupted and the project was postponed indefinitely.

In 1911 a new student enrolled in art classes at the Academy of San Carlos. Just fifteen, José Alfaro was full of youthful energy. His flashing eyes and long narrow face topped by a jumble of uncontrollable curls suggested a spirited and mischievous character. Still living at home, he was studying for a career in architecture at the National Preparatory School during the day and attending art classes at night. Despite the recent turmoil, he was a relatively naive and disinterested teenager who was more interested in making a spectacular play in baseball, engaging in boyish pranks or proving his manhood.

At San Carlos, José followed the traditional course of instruction, studying under German Gedovius in oil painting, Emiliano Valadés in charcoal figure drawing, Saturnino Herrán in dressed figure drawing, Francisco de la Torre in landscape painting, and Carlos Lazo in art history. Although he was acquiring valuable skills, the methods of instruction had not changed and he had to copy from reproductions of classic statues. Even when they had the opportunity to draw from nature, using a live model, the models assumed the frozen poses of the same statues.

Frustrated by these conditions and anxious to do more live figure drawing, José and several other students decided to make their own arrangements. After they obtained permission to use a library in the home of a wealthy friend as a studio, they engaged a model. But just as they started to sketch the nude model they had smuggled into the room, there was a knock on the door which they had locked. It was a servant who wanted a book from the library and José offered to find it and hand it to him through the door. His suspicions aroused, the servant forced the door open and burst in on the students and their naked model. Grabbing her clothes, a half naked "Chatita" and the students fled into the street, pursued by accusations of being "pornographic artists" and engaging a prostitute for an orgy in a respectable home.

After the loss of their studio, the students made other arrangements. Employing Indians as models, they became aware of the different proportions and features of their subjects and developed a preference for Indian over European types. Instead of imitating classic statues, their models also posed more naturally and they began to sketch them in motion.

No one was more excited about the possibilities of drawing the human figure in motion than José Alfaro, or "Alfarito," as he was known to his classmates. He was also interested in speed and he competed with his friend Lupito in drawing large charcoal sketches as fast as possible. When they compared their work, each defended his sketch passionately and their drawing contests sometimes ended in fist fights in the street in front of the school. Although José later conceded that Lupito's sketches were superior, he was faster and the competition had helped him develop a freer and more spontaneous style. Lupito, he learned, died a few years later in the Revolution.

Alfarito's new style was also encouraged by his instructor in oil, German Gedovius, whose motto was "freedom and spontaneity." Impressed by the enthusiasm and progress of his protégé, German wrote José a note, telling him, "It is necessary to have more than just good eyes to paint, one also needs good muscles." A robust and athletic Alfarito accepted the cryptic comment as a compliment.

Inspired by the overthrow of Díaz and news of a revolution in European art, the students anticipated improvements in art instruction as well as social and political change. The Revolution had called for the removal of the *científicos* from public office but Rivas Mercado, the Director of the San Carlos, was a *científico*. He was also an architect who refused to consider changes in the curriculum and was resented by the art teachers and their students. Given the heady atmosphere of the Revolution and the hopes for reform, a confrontation was inevitable.

The clash came when students in a class of anatomy protested the dictatorial methods of the instructor and the mimeographed sheets he sold them for textbooks. Their protest spread and the students held meetings and called for the boycott of other classes.

They wrote slogans and pasted posters on the walls of the school calling for the removal of the *científicos* and the election of a new director as well as teachers. When they blocked the entrances to the school, police were stationed in the hallways. After sending letters outlining their protests to all the newspapers, a delegation of students met with Rivas Mercado. When he refused to accept any of their demands, they called for a strike to explain their position and to remove him as the director.

Meanwhile, a group of students were preparing for an exhibit of their art work as members of the Independent Artistic Center. In August they made an appeal to the Director of Public Instruction and the Fine Arts in which they not only expressed their views on the teaching of art, but also on the role of art in a revolutionary society. The removal of the director, they argued, was based on the Pact of Ciudad Juárez which called for the removal of the *científicos* from public office and, since Rivas Mercado was an architect, he was not only unqualified to direct the training of artists, but he had done nothing to improve the academy or to introduce new methods of instruction.

These protests soon extended beyond the halls of San Carlos and encompassed other issues. Although the architecture students refused to support the art students, students from other faculties of the national university endorsed the strike. The strike became a national issue and the negotiations between the students, the director and government officials were covered by the press. *El País*, the paper of the conservative Catholic party, called the strike "anarchistic" and the students "insects" who should be disciplined by their parents.

The strikers bombarded the newspapers with letters and held art exhibits in public parks and meetings in working class neighborhoods to explain their cause. As the strike dragged on, they increased their demands to include loans for students, one free meal per day for all students and a stipend to cover the cost of all drawing and painting materials. They also called for the nationalization of the railroads and subsoil resources, two major goals of the Revolution.

When government officials promised to investigate the conduct of Rivas Mercado and asked the students to return to classes, they refused, declaring that they would remain on strike until a new director was named. Throughout the strike, which lasted more than a year, the director refused to recognize the newly formed Society of Students of Painting and Sculpture, and mounted police broke up their strike meetings, beating and arresting students. In order to protect themselves, the students adopted diversionary tactics and organized themselves in small cells in which everyone could be identified.

Although he had just entered San Carlos as an evening student, José Alfaro immediately joined the Independent Artistic Center. Like the others, he found the rigid discipline and archaic pedagogy stifling and was disappointed by the indifference of the director and the lack of reforms since the Revolution. As soon as the strike was declared, he became an eager participant, spending most of his time attending strike meetings and listening to the older and more radical students. While he had been exposed to liberal ideas through his sister and his friend Jesús Soto, the strike was his first conscious political act. It was also his first brush with the law.

When the besieged director arrived at San Carlos one morning, José was among the striking students who greeted him with threats and insults. As Rivas Mercado stepped out of his car with his wife and daughter, they pelted him with rotten eggs, tomatoes and rocks. Grabbing one of the student leaders, the director dragged him to the nearest police station while his wife and daughter escaped in the car.

After reinforcements arrived, the police broke up the demonstration and arrested a number of students. Although he was not one of the ringleaders, José had cast a few stones and was arrested along with several of the leaders. While he later expressed his regrets that the director's daughter had seen their attack on her father, he was very proud of his participation and boasted of the support they received in prison, including a box of candy he received from an admirer.

Despite the arrests, the strike dragged on. Even though Rivas Mercado finally resigned, the student movement was eclipsed by a national crisis. A political moderate, President Madero was caught between the revolutionaries who wanted immediate and more radical solutions and the guardians of the old order. When he failed to redistribute more land, Zapata took up arms again and Pascal Orozco led a revolt against the government in the north.

Facing revolts on two fronts, Madero turned to the army to defend his government. But several army officers and the American ambassador were plotting to overthrow him and in February 1913, less then two years after he had taken office, they launched their attack. For ten days the capital was subjected to an artillery bombardment which killed more than one thousand people, most of them civilians.

José was still living at home and had just received a bicycle for his sixteenth birthday when his sister Luz told him that the federal troops had revolted against Madero and it was his duty to ride to the rescue of the President. Taking his bicycle, he rode to the center of the city from where he could hear the sound of gunshots. On the way he met a group of military cadets and President Madero on horseback. Though suffering a few casualties, the escort made its way to the Zócalo and Madero entered the Presidential Palace.

Suddenly, without warning, the cadets turned and fired on the crowd, causing panic and immediately drawing blood. Falling to the ground or taking refuge in the doorways and arches around the main square, the crowd suffered more casualties. Like the rest, José ran for shelter, throwing his bicycle on the ground where it was trampled and bent by the panicking crowd. He was scared and wanted to flee, but he refused to abandon his bicycle. Bullets were still flying everywhere and the wounded were piling up in the doorways. Seeing an opportunity to escape, he rescued his bicycle and ran from the square, carrying the twisted frame over his head.

He had barely fled the battle in the Zócalo when he found himself in the path of an artillery battle between the rebelling barracks and the Presidential Palace. Several hours later he was able to escape and return home, still clutching a battered bicycle frame. Although she was not very concerned about the damage to his bicycle, his sister listened intently as he proudly told about his adventures in the column which had escorted the President to the Zócalo. It was his first experience under fire and exposure to bloodshed. A few days later, they learned that Madero and his Vice President had been murdered.

After Madero's death, the revolution broke out with a new fury. When General Huerta assumed the presidency, Venustiano Carranza, Pancho Villa and Emiliano Zapata joined forces against the government. For more than a year a civil war raged, temporarily uniting these revolutionary factions against the "usurper." When Huerta resigned and left the country in 1914, a power struggle erupted between Carranza and the forces of Villa and Zapata and, for the next year and a half, the country was ravaged by another civil war.

In spite of this turmoil, there were improvements at the National Art Academy during Huerta's short-lived presidency. After Rivas Mercado resigned, Alfredo Ramos Martínez was appointed Director of the School of Painting and Sculpture at San Carlos following an election by the students and faculty. An impressionist just back from Europe, Ramos Martínez insisted on working directly from nature and emphasized the need to develop an awareness of the natural beauty of Mexico. Soon after his appointment he rented a house in the nearby village of Santa Anita Ixtapalapa for classes in which the students would paint directly from nature. It was the first of a series of "open air schools" in Mexico.

Although the school at Santa Anita brought the students into contact with nature and was a welcomed escape from the formal atmosphere of San Carlos, it perpetuated Mexico's obsession with Europe. Ramos Martínez named the school "Barbizón" after the French village made famous by the impressionists and gave each of his students the name of a French impressionist: Renoir, Manet, Monet, etc. Nevertheless, the students learned to paint out-of-doors, working directly from nature, and were encouraged to teach themselves and to improvise, unheard of at San Carlos. They were also exposed to the life of the poor Mexicans in the area and were encouraged to use Indian men and women as their models.

José Alfaro was still living at home but the school at Santa Anita became his second home and frequently he arrived home late at night or early in the morning. Disturbed by his son's late arrivals and irregular sleeping and eating habits, his father requested an explanation from Ramos Martinez. The latter assured him that instruction ended at dusk and explained that while some of the students lived on the premises, his son was not one of them. After his violent outburst in front of his father's aristocratic friends, however, José left home for good.

"Barbizón" had a great impact on José. He reveled in the free and open atmosphere and his sketches acquired a greater spontaneity. Working directly from nature, he did some impressionist drawings and paintings and developed a style approaching pointillism. At Santa Anita he acquired an appreciation of the "uniqueness of the Mexican landscape" and of José María Velasco, the master painter of the Valley of Mexico. He also came into contact with Mexican popular art for the first time: The *retablos* or *ex-voto* miracle paintings; the murals painted on lower class *cantinas* or *pulqueíras;* pottery and weaving from all over Mexico; and the toys, music and dances from different regions.

Imbued with the spirit of rebellion and the success of their strike, the students reacted to the conservative tendencies of their teachers and the director by supporting just the opposite. While their mentors continued to extol the virtues of European art, especially the Greco-Roman standards of beauty, the students rejected that art as ugly and proclaimed that nothing was more beautiful than an Indian and no art was more profound than native art. Peer status among them was measured by the amount of Indian blood in one's veins and the supreme insult was to accuse another student of being "more *gachupín* (Spaniard) than Indian." They also agreed to eliminate black and dark colors from their palettes, colors associated with the formal style of the Díaz period. The more likely influence, ironically, was European impressionism.

During the strike and at "Barbizón," José and other students, mostly upper class and city bred youth, had come into contact with the lower classes and their culture. They had taken to the streets and the popular neighborhoods of the capital where they saw the poverty and became aware of the conditions and issues which had sparked the Revolution. Radicalized by this experience, some went off to fight in the Revolution and from their ranks came many of the peasant and labor leaders of the future, as well as a generation of committed writers and artists.

As the opposition to General Huerta mounted, "Barbizón" was a center of anti-Huerta activities and Alfarito was in the thick of things. When several students were arrested for trying to join the *zapatistas*, José and other students marched in a demonstration to prevent their execution. Since mounted police prevented their march to the Zócalo, the central plaza in front of the Presidential Palace, the students besieged the Minister of Government. Surrounded by students shouting "Government of Assassins," the Minister tried to ring for help. But before he could carry out his intention, Alfarito grabbed his hand and prevented him from sounding the bell. Afterwards, he reveled in the flowery comments of his fellow protesters.

"Barbizón" only lasted a few months and most of the artists soon discarded impressionism for their own individual styles. Even before its demise, José Clemente Orozco despaired of "so much open air" and left Santa Anita to work in his own studio. Although his own flirtation with impressionism was short-lived, a mature Siqueiros was convinced that the experience of the strike and Santa Anita was not only important to his own development as an artist but also to that of modern Mexican art. It was the beginning of a "new aesthetic," he later wrote. Although "childlike," we had launched a permanent break with the archaic and academic pedagogy of the official art academy and it was at Santa Anita where we began to rediscover our own country. "All of our movement of modern painting set out from this pedagogical-political rebellion."

When the police closed their school, many students joined the popular armies opposing the government. Alfarito and his two closest friends, Juan Olaguibel and Jesús Soto, however, had other plans. Convinced of their good looks and a future as gigolos, they set out for the gulf port of Veracruz. There they would stow away on a ship to Argentina, where they would become chauffeurs and the lovers of beautiful rich women. After one successful encounter with the opposite sex on their way to Veracruz, they were confident of a bright future as the paid lovers of rich women.

When they arrived in Veracruz, however, they were broke and destitute. While some *veracruzanos* resented the three cocky teenagers from Mexico City, they became friends with Adolfo Ruiz Cortines, a student like themselves from a rich Veracruz family. Living on charity or occasionally earning a few pesos, they slept on the waste paper on the floor of the offices of the newspaper *El Dictamen*. Although he refused to employ José as an illustrator, the editor of the paper did hire him to translate articles from French and to rewrite articles in correct Spanish.

To escape the heat and humidity of the city, they spent the days swimming in and around an old abandoned ship. One afternoon they met the daughters of the admiral of the American navy, lying off Veracruz. For days they met and played in the water and the three girls shared their lunches with the Mexican youth and gave them some money. On their last day together, they parted tearfully, but with a gift of five dollars from their benefactors. The aspiring gigolos then got drunk and ended up in jail where they were beaten and robbed by the police.

In 1914 the United States Navy bombarded and invaded Veracruz, killing scores of Mexicans, most of them civilians. Watching helplessly, the three vagabonds were enraged by the lack of resistance and the needless bombardment and slaughter of innocent people. "The occupation of Veracruz filled us with shame and I still remember it with tremendous pain," José later recalled. To add insult to injury, they were frequently stopped and searched by the American troops. When they saw Mexican women walking with the marines and sailors, they vented their anger on them as traitors to the country.

Dissuaded from their original plans, José and his friends returned to Mexico City and went back to school. Meanwhile, the Revolution had taken another turn and they were caught up in the forces unleashed by the latest developments. In 1914 Huerta surrendered and went into exile in Europe. When the forces of Carranza occupied Mexico City, Dr. Atl was appointed Director of San Carlos as a reward for his recent work as a *carrancista* agent in Europe. During his brief tenure in that office, he inflamed the students with new ideas.

The first time Dr. Atl addressed the students and the faculty, José listened intently as he declared, "The revolution is also made with bricks!" But they did not know whether they were supposed to throw bricks or that the revolution was building, that is, architecture. Before long they realized that he meant to transform the academy into a practical workshop and that they should start their own art schools, not as elitist centers, but as popular workshops.

In other meetings Dr. Atl talked passionately of monumental art, especially the great mural paintings of the past, and new techniques in art. Although he ridiculed art instruction at San Carlos, he emphasized the value of sound technical knowledge and talked vaguely of collective mural projects. Captivated by his message, the students engaged in heated discussions about monumental art forms and the possibilities for mural painting in Mexico.

The spell of Dr. Atl extended beyond the field of art. After the defeat of Huerta, a constitutional convention was held at Aguascalientes. When Carranza refused to accept the convention's decision to establish a government of civilians, a civil war erupted between the forces of Carranza and those of Villa and Zapata. Surrounded by his enemies, Carranza prepared to evacuate the capital and retreat to Veracruz, recently evacuated by the American forces. Appearing before the Casa de Obrero Mundial (House of the International Worker), an anarcho-syndicalist union which he had organized several years earlier, Dr. Atl convinced many members to join the "Red Battalions" which he organized for Carranza.

Atl's call to arms was also heard by some of his students. Although some of their fellow students joined Villa or Zapata and fought against Carranza, José Alfaro and José Clemente Orozco decided to follow Atl and join the *carrancistas*. When Carranza abandoned the capital, therefore, they left with Dr. Atl and a printing press on the last train out of Mexico City. In Orizaba they appropriated an already sacked church, set up the press and converted the church into a printing shop for *La Vanguardia*, Carranza's official press organ.

While Orozco illustrated the paper with biting anticlerical drawings, José Alfaro was dispatched to the front as a reporter. He was at the front only a short time, however, when he abandoned his assignment and enlisted in a unit of adolescents which the more seasoned soldiers dubbed the "Batallón Mamá," taunting them with "*Mamacita, mamacita*, where are you darling mothers?" when they drilled. Their innocence and inexperience, however, were short-lived.

Since their orders were to join the Division of the West and Villa and Zapata controlled the center of the Republic, the Battalón Mamá had to proceed to the Pacific by way of the Isthmus of Tehuantepec to the south. José's unit was assigned as an armed escort for the train taking the troops to Tehuantepec. Full of confidence and eager to see action, they left Veracruz shouting and singing.

The first night, just before daylight, they were awakened by the sound of shots and the train came to an abrupt stop. Peering out the window, José saw some small flashing lights, coming and going. Thinking to prevent panic, he shouted, "Don't worry, they are only fireflies." But those "fireflies" penetrated the carriage, wounding several of the barely awake teenage soldiers. Grabbing their rifles, they fired into the dark while their attackers rode up and down on both sides of the train.

Soon the train began to move again, picking up speed and eventually outdistancing their pursuers. But several young soldiers, including two of José's classmates from San Carlos, were dead and another twelve were seriously wounded. The train proceeded on to Tehuantepec without further incident, but it had been a sobering experience and convinced the survivors that war was not a game.

Their spirits were soon buoyed, however, by their reception in Tehuantepec. As the train pulled into the station, they were greeted by a profusion of tropical colors, flowers, fruits and beautiful women. Unlike the austere and reserved women of other regions of Mexico, the *tehuanas were* anything but reserved and flirted openly with them. Although they could not understand the language, they had no problem in interpreting their alluring gestures or flirtatious smiles and José cherished the memory of their reception, the most pleasant of the civil war. It was a paradise, a nirvana in which sexual love was the center of life, he recalled, and from which no one wanted to leave.

After recuperating in Tehuantepec, the "Mama Battalion" proceeded up the West Coast to join the command of General

Diéguez and the Division of the West. During the slow trip up the coast in an old steamer, some of the students discussed the problems of national culture and the need to resurrect Mexican art forms, so neglected by the prevailing intelligentsia. When the war was over, they vowed, they would use their art to serve their country.

Upon their arrival in Jalisco, José and his companions were incorporated into the Division of the West and soon saw action in the campaign against Pancho Villa in western and northwestern Mexico. José was assigned to the General Staff of General Diéguez, one of the leaders of the 1906 copper mine strike at Cananea, and in less than a year, he rose from private to second lieutenant. This was not unusual as many former students, because of their ability to read and write, received rapid promotions and were assigned to the general staffs of the different armies of the Revolution. Later José was promoted to second captain and served as an officer of the Yaquis, the Indian shock troops recruited from Sonora by Obregón and Diéguez.

Lieutenant Siqueiros with General Manuel Diéguez
and Staff, 1914-1918

The joys, sorrows, excitement, and terror which José experienced during the Revolution, ran the gamut of human emotions and made an indelible impression on him. At the battle of León, he was in the frontal assault on the town with the Yaqui and Juchiteco infantry. When the battle was over, the fields surrounding the city were covered with bodies and the main street was lined with the shoes stripped from the dead. Afterwards came the parade and serenade for the victors and, the choicest prize of all, the warm reception of the local women.

After they took Guadalajara for the second time, José looked anxiously for his schoolboy friend José Guadalupe Zuno. The city was in a state of terror and the streets were filled with the dead and dying. Arriving in the Zócalo, they found themselves in front of one of the most famous restaurants in the city, but which appeared to be closed. When someone opened a door and peeked out, a sergeant sent him scurrying back into the restaurant with a well-placed shot, leaving the door ajar.

Entering the restaurant, they were surprised to see tables heaped with French pastry, the meals still steaming and bottles of wine from all over the world. Tired and hungry, the soldiers sat down and began to eat. Slowly, the waiters appeared, all dressed in black suits with white aprons, and proceeded to serve them. For these troops, most of them from small villages and just back from months of campaigning in the mountains, it was the best meal of their lives.

In Mazatlan, another companion, Tomás Morán, persuaded José and his close friend and fellow officer Octavio Amador to visit a famous whorehouse, "La Cucona." When some rough irregular troops entered the establishment, they suddenly drew and fired their pistols into the furniture, terrorizing the women and their young clients. In the fracas which followed, Lieutenant Alfaro suffered a slight skull fracture and spent the next week recovering in a hospital.

The Mexican Revolution had its share of atrocities and one of the most impressionable experiences for a young soldier were the frequent executions of captured soldiers, regardless of rank, as well as of civilians caught in the wrong place. After the *carrancistas* had retaken Guadalajara, José was eating breakfast in the Hotel Fénix with

Octavio Amador, who was also on the staff of General Diéguez. Just then they saw a fat colonel, dressed in the northern style, descend the stairs. He appeared to be suffering from a bad hangover and to their surprise, he walked over to their table and greeted them warmly, asking, "Have we already put those *carrancistas* to rout?"

Although they were the *carrancistas* who had just forced the *villistas* to evacuate the city, they invited him to join them and offered him a drink. When Octavio explained who they were, he smiled, trying to convince himself that it was a mistake, a bad joke. When he tried to leave, a sergeant and some soldiers blocked his way and demanded that he be turned over to them. Before they could protest, the soldiers took him outside and shot him in the entrance of the hotel, after which they stripped him of his shoes, watch and anything else of value and left the body where it had fallen.

Those were the orders in those days. No one took prisoners. They were executed on the spot, no trial, no excuse, no last testaments, and the bodies remained where they had fallen, a reminder to the enemy.

Following the battle of Hermosillo, José noticed a familiar face among the prisoners lined up to be shot. When the prisoner addressed him as "payaso," he recognized a former classmate, only 17 or 18 years old. Though the prisoner pleaded to him for help, José could not do anything and gestured helplessly. Regaining his pride, the prisoner shouted, "Very well, go with God and screw your mother!" That night, seeing the corpse of his classmate among the others, he reflected sadly what a waste his death had been. After another battle, José spotted the bloated white body of a young gringo he had known, standing out in a sea of brown corpses.

Not all of the victims were combatants. During the occupation of Guadalajara, orders had been issued that no one was to horde food or supplies under the penalty of death. In their search of the city, José and his men discovered a large stock of food in a wealthy home guarded by two beautiful sisters of Spanish origin and their father, a sick man of ninety. When José explained that their father would be shot within minutes unless they would plead his case with

General Diéguez, they refused, full of pride and never thinking that an old and sick man would be punished.

When José explained the situation to his commander, Diéguez sternly replied, "Those who are dying of hunger in the streets are also old men. Carry out the order!" Minutes later the old man was taken to the plaza where others had been executed, still thinking that it was only a threat, and was shot, his body left in the street to remind others that the orders would be enforced.

Many years later, when Fidel Castro was condemned for the trial and execution of prisoners, Siqueiros reminded his critics of the practices of the Mexican Revolution, no prisoners and the immediate execution of any captives. This included mass executions, which he witnessed, as well as the execution of old and infirm men and decrees which condemned to death all officers and leaders, from second lieutenant up, who remained in the Federal Army after the murders of President Madero and Vice President Pino Suárez. Under these circumstances, life was dependent upon the whim or mood of the arresting sergeant or officer.

The commander with the greatest notoriety for cruelty was Pancho Villa. In the areas which he controlled, Villa forced wealthy landowners to contribute money for his troops. When he shot an old man in front of a group of rich men who had refused to contribute, he was asked why he had shot the oldest. Villa explained that while his victim had some money to donate, the others were much richer.

When José was given an assignment to deliver a message to Pancho Villa in person, therefore, he undertook it with great trepidation. Traveling by train, he arrived at Villa's headquarters. After Villa's hardened *"Dorados"* kidded him about his age and warned him about their commander's temper, he was taken to see Villa.

"So you are one of those little kids who are fighting with *"El Cacarizo?"*, Villa commented, in reference to Dieguez' pocked marked faced, and then asked him if he had read the message. When he replied that he could not have read it since it was still sealed, Villa pointed out that he could have read it before it was sealed. Fearing the worst, José was greatly relieved when Villa handed him his reply and he left hurriedly, accompanied by more taunts about his lack of manhood from the *villistas*.

Years later Siqueiros reflected that the cruelty of Villa was probably exaggerated and that many of the atrocities attributed to him were actually committed by his subordinates or other commanders. He also suspected that Villa's enemies probably encouraged this image in order to destroy his popularity or to cover up their own conduct.

José Alfaro's participation in the student strike and the Revolution made a great and lasting impression on him and was instrumental in molding his personal character, as well as in developing a new awareness and commitment. The student strike constituted his political baptism as well as his exposure to the glories and penalties of direct political action. At Santa Anita he had been exposed to popular Mexican culture and began to paint more spontaneously, working directly from nature. His experiences at San Carlos also convinced him that he was not suited to traditional academic institutions or methods.

In the Revolution he learned to be a soldier, rising to the rank of second captain and acquiring martial skills and attitudes which he could draw upon in the future. Hardened by his grandfather's rough tutelage, he was well prepared for the rigors of combat and the experience of the "fiesta of bullets" inured him to discomfort, as well as to the destruction and suffering of war. The Revolution was one of the proudest moments of his life and he relished telling stories about his experiences in that conflict over and over again.

He was also convinced that the experience of the Revolution had been important artistically. It was, he later wrote,

> the beginning of our direct contact with the people of Mexico. It was not only contact with the people ... but with the idiosyncrasies of the Mexican, the geography, the archaeology, the whole of the artistic history of Mexico, with its popular art, the whole culture of our country ... Without that participation, it would not have been possible

to have conceived or inspired much later... the modern Mexican pictorial movement.

The exposure to the suffering of the war and the economic and social conditions of the country also precluded "the intellectual masturbation" or "the individualism so characteristic of modern artists." For us, he wrote, it ended the notion of indifferent and elite artists, "the apolitical, bohemian, parasitic artist, the typical Montparnassian, the intellectual snob of today," and it gave birth to the idea of citizen artists working for a revolutionary state. By exposing city-bred artists to the richness and variety of Mexican folk culture, the war also showed them how to approach the masses through their popular art forms.

Because the Revolution posed a military problem, he was convinced that it was a valuable experience for those who became militant revolutionaries, providing them with practical knowledge as well as a sense of discipline for developing and defending an art movement at the service of the Revolution. As one of the founders of that movement and its most outspoken advocate, he would draw on these lessons many times

The Revolution also prepared him for other struggles and his participation in the student strike and the Revolution established a lifelong pattern of alternating between intense artistic activity and direct political engagement.

While the outbreak of the Revolution had interrupted plans for the first mural project in modern Mexico, it was the Revolution, according to Siqueiros, which gave birth to the Mexican Mural Movement still to come. "Modern Mexican painting," he later wrote, "is first and foremost the expression of the Mexican Revolution in the field of culture." In 1917 that movement was only a dream, however, and Captain Alfaro had one more military assignment to carry out, this time in Europe.

III. Soldier-Artist in Europe

By 1916 the military tide and political fortunes favored Carranza. Adopting tactics from the war in Europe, General Obregón had employed trenches, barbed wire and machine guns to mow down Villa's cavalry. Zapata's peasant troops were confined to the mountains of Morelos, where he led a sporadic resistance until his assassination in 1919. Now Carranza controlled two-thirds of the country, including the capital, and had been recognized by the United States. After a nationalistic and progressive constitution was drafted, Carranza was elected President and peace returned to Mexico, albeit temporarily.

Before his inauguration, Carranza announced plans for a group show of Mexican artists to travel to the United States. Besides providing an unprecedented opportunity for the artists, it would also create a favorable impression of conditions in Mexico. Although these plans were canceled, there was a group show in Mexico City and later that year, one of the exhibitors, José Clemente Orozco, had his first one-man show. His drawings and watercolors featured schoolgirls and prostitutes, as well as caricatures of public figures, including Carranza. After a cold reception, official favor waned and Orozco left for the United States.

One of the visitors to the show, however, came away inspired. Fresh from his military adventures, José Alfaro sensed a similarity of purpose between Orozco's art and his own aspirations. Here was another artist who had experienced the Revolution directly and, in both subject matter and approach, had developed a unique personal style. He was convinced that the show not only demonstrated Orozco's evolution as an artist, but was also an important milestone in the development of a new Mexican art, the beginning of the "Mexicanization of the plastic arts."

However, José was fascinated by more than the style or technique of Orozco's art. He was also struck by the *mestiza* prostitutes in all their finery and he later confessed, instead of leading us to the masses, Orozco's exhibit led us to the bordellos.

Meanwhile, a group a group of writers, artists and intellectuals had been meeting in Guadalajara since 1914 to discuss the purpose of art and to work towards the development of a new direction in Mexican culture. Expressing their admiration for Mexico's pre-Hispanic art, they had proposed the development of a new national art at the service of the Revolution. When José arrived in Guadalajara in 1915 with the Division of the West, he joined in these discussions and some of the cultural activities of this "Bohemian Center." The Center was also a collective studio where members could write or paint. Two of the members were factory workers who painted some of the first pictures with themes from the lives of the working class.

According to one of the participants, José Guadalupe Zuno, the new recruit seemed to be preoccupied with discovering new artistic materials and procedures which corresponded to the latest advances in science. Attacking the use of oils, watercolors, pastels, fresco, and encaustic as archaic, he proposed "painting with a spray gun ... using enamel paints for the exterior of automobiles ... [and] using colored cement" as superior materials for modern art.

After Villa's defeat, José was no longer on active military duty. Between 1916 and 1918 he met with other artists in Guadalajara to discuss the purpose and history of art in what he later referred to as a "Congress of Soldier Artists," probably the inspiration of the peripatetic Dr. Atl. They also published a journal in which they wrote articles attacking the domination of modern art by the rich or the state and declared that they were ready to serve Mexico and the Revolution through their art. Although they envisioned impressionism as the wave of the future, the ideas which they discussed provided the theoretical base of the Mexican Mural Movement and many of them would contribute to the cultural renaissance of the 1920s.

Relieved from his military duties, José returned to Mexico City and enrolled in a book and magazine illustration course at San Carlos. He also resumed his painting and developed a new style to depict scenes from the daily lives of ordinary Mexicans. In *Tamemes* (Indian porters) he painted several somber Indian figures whose forms filled the canvas. *Sugar Skulls* contrasted upper class girls skipping rope with a squatting Indian woman who is selling her skull-shaped wares on the Day of the Dead.

Combining watercolors and pastels, he painted a black Christ with blood dripping from His wounds. The scene is Mexican, the black Christ representing the mexicanization of Christianity, while His guards are Mexican cowboys or revolutionaries. His *El Señor del Veneno* (Christ of the Poison) received a prize and was reproduced on the front of the magazine *La Revista de las Revistas*.

In 1918 Anna Pavlova, the great ballerina, performed her *Ballet Mexicano* in Mexico City and José painted an art nouveau watercolor of her "The Dance of the Rain." Published in *El Universal Ilustrado*, it depicted the dancer prancing lightly in the rain, the latter suggested by falling rain drops and the ripples which they made in puddles on the ground. In drawings which he did of La Argentinita, a performer of Spanish dance, he seemed to be exploring the development of a sense of movement as well the creation of a dynamic or active space.

In 1919, the first year of peace in Europe, he painted a war torn landscape with a burnt-out cathedral and a naked child in a chariot of flowers pulled by a team of butterflies. He also painted portraits of two other artists, Amado de la Cueva and José Luis Figueroa, filling the picture plane with their figures. While impressionistic, they also suggested the more solid and monumental style of his later work.

Besides having some of his work published, José also received favorable reviews or comments on his art. In a review of his work, Raziel Cabildo, one of the ringleaders of the strike at San Carlos, proclaimed that José Alfaro was one of a new generation of artists who distinguishes himself by "his talent, his restlessness and his rebelliousness." His art is "voluptous," characterized by "opulent" colors, a vigorous and bold technique, and a "peculiar manner of interpreting scenes from life and the psychology of personalities." His portraits, Cabildo continued, "are to be admired for the originality of their composition and the suggestions of spirituality."

In what was more of a comment on his personality than his art, Raziel described him as,

> In full youth, impetuous, intelligent, audacious...We
> end with a fervent wish that this young artist, who starts
> his career with such vigor, may escape being one of the
> many victims of our milieu. May total success crown his
> noble efforts and high aspirations!

Despite this high praise, José had not yet developed his personal style and was still influenced by the romanticism of the masters. The forms in his paintings also lacked density and volume, the subject matter was not uniquely Mexican and there was no message or statement. Nevertheless, he was beginning to develop the emotional elements and impetuosity which would characterize much of his later work and his portraits reflected the psychological as well as the physical characteristics of the subject.

Although he was now committed to art, there was time for other activities. He had met and fallen in love with Graciela Amador, the attractive sister of his companion in the Division of the West, Octavio Amador, and they were married in a Catholic ceremony in 1918. For eleven years "Gachita" was his constant and faithful companion, devoted to him and an active participant in all of his political activities. Sharing his convictions and risking her life many times at his side, she was his "faithful comrade."

They were also passionately in love with each other, alternating between mutual expressions of love and affection and her angry outbursts over his wandering eyes. When she told him that she preferred "David" to "José," he adopted the former. She also convinced him to use his mother's maiden name, Siqueiros, instead of his surname of Alfaro. Henceforth, he would be known as David Alfaro Siqueiros or just Siqueiros.

After his return to Mexico City, David assumed that his military duties were over and concentrated on his art. In 1919, however, President Carranza rewarded him for his military service by appointing him as a military attaché to several Mexican embassies in Europe with the rank of first captain. Although his appointment and official duties were military, David viewed the assignment as an opportunity to study directly the latest developments in European art. His new interest in Mexican culture notwithstanding, the real excitement in modern art was still in Europe, especially Paris, and he was anxious to sample it directly.

In route to Europe, David and Gachita stopped in New York, where they looked up Orozco. Despite their enthusiasm, their first encounter with the modern industrialized society was not very encouraging. Besides encountering racial discrimination, they discovered that Orozco was painting doll faces in a toy factory to support himself. When he had arrived at the Texas border, the border guards had ripped up his sketches and paintings of lower class women and prostitutes because of their "immoral" content, though there was not one nude among them. After a dismal experience in California, Orozco had gone east to New York. Although he had painted some excellent studies of the growing metropolis, he had not been discovered and there was no market for his art.

With the help of Orozco and Juan Olaguibel, an old school mate and sculptor, David squandered the funds for his trip to Europe. When he wired to Mexico for more money, he was told to stay there until he found the funds for his passage. Meanwhile, they shared Orozco's miserable little apartment where they concocted a scheme to obtain funds from a rich friend of a Mexican diplomatic representative in New York.

After Siqueiros managed to scrape up the money for their passage, he and Gachita left New York on an old Spanish liner bound for Spain. Throughout the trip, Siqueiros regaled the other passengers with his tales of the Mexican Revolution, emphasizing the uniqueness of the Mexican, especially the male species, when confronted with eminent death. Proud and chauvinistic, as well as conditioned by the senseless slaughter of the Revolution, he claimed that death had no meaning for Mexicans and bragged that in Mexico they killed for the sake of killing. He relished telling these stories and developed a special flair which captivated his audiences while he elaborated on the unique virtues of being Mexican. Unwittingly, these stories, as well as his own conduct, tended to reinforce the negative stereotypes of Mexicans held by many Europeans and North Americans.

When they arrived in Spain, conditions were more chaotic than in Mexico, which had just undergone a revolution and civil war. The country was suffering under a degenerate and ineffectual monarchy, the army was bogged down in an unpopular war in Africa and the government was brutally repressing an increasingly restless proletariat. Inspired by the Russian Revolution, the workers increased their protests and the anarchist-dominated trade unions had called for a general strike in Barcelona. Management retaliated with lockouts and both sides employed *pistoleros* to blow up union halls or assassinate union leaders, factory owners, politicians and government officials.

Since he identified with the cause of the workers and anarchists dominated the labor movement in Barcelona, he joined their ranks soon after his arrival. Disregarding his assignment as military attaché to the Mexican legation, he attended the funeral of a Mexican anarchist who had been killed by the police and delivered an inflammatory speech. Considered undesirable, he was asked to leave the country and, after only a few weeks in Spain, he and Gachita headed north for France. After changing trains at the border, they headed for Paris.

In Paris Siqueiros met Diego Rivera again, beginning a lifetime association which was sometimes close and supportive, sometimes contentious and antagonistic, but seldom dull. For two years the two artists virtually lived together, and "Don Diego," who had lived and painted in Europe during the Revolution, told his compatriot about the latest in European art, while Siqueiros talked about his experiences in the Revolution. In the process, Rivera began to rediscover his homeland.

Meeting every day in Diego's small apartment, they sung *corridos* of the Revolution, talked about the picturesque personages and macabre heroes of their country and proclaimed that there was no other language like Spanish nor any movement as noble as their revolution. They also vied with each other in inventing and telling outlandish stories. While the rotund and frog-eyed Rivera perched on his chair, listening intently, the curly haired, angular faced and erect Siqueiros spinned his tales of the Revolution. From them Diego created his own versions which had little in common with the original. Exchanging roles, David listened and absorbed the words of "Don Diego," frequently interjecting, but gleaning everything that Diego had to say about recent developments in European art.

One of Diego's favorite tales extolled the virtues of cannibalism. He began by explaining that he had observed that a cat which had been fed on the flesh of other cats had greater vigor and strength, as well as a superior coat of fur. He and some other artists, therefore, agreed to eat human flesh which they would obtain daily from the morgue. Gradually they not only acquired a taste for human flesh but also developed a preference for certain parts of the human, especially female, anatomy. Without batting an eye, Diego would then explain that the abandonment of cannibalism by the human race was the beginning of tooth decay, clouded eyes, heart attacks, deafness, and all assorted human afflictions.

Diego's imagination had no bounds and Siqueiros observed that he would have lied about his own death if it were possible. Not only did he claim that he had fought alongside Zapata and Lenin, but he also said that he was the father of General Rommel. Then, on another occasion, he swore that Pancho Villa was really Rommel's father.

When it came to story telling, David had been exposed to a master of the art through his grandfather and had already demonstrated his own flair for the theatrical. But this exposure to another raconteur, a man whom he admired but with whom he also competed, undoubtedly inspired or reinforced his own inclinations. Those close to him were sure that he would have made a great actor; he loved to tell stories about his personal experiences and presented them with such enthusiasm and eloquence that he appeared to be on stage, even in his own dining room. Although he told the same stories many times, his widow explained that they never bored her because he always added a detail or twist which added flavor or provided new insight into the experience.

In the small apartment in Paris, where Diego lived with his first wife, the Russian artist Angelina Beloff, the two artists discussed art and rediscovered Mexico and its grandeur, each one reinforcing the other with their tales and fertile imaginations. Ultimately they reached the conclusion that Mexico was unique and that the real source of a new aesthetic was not in Europe, but in Mexico because of its special character and originality. They even bragged of the different species of animals, introduced from Europe, but transformed in Mexico into distinctive creatures of different sizes and many colors.

When Siqueiros explained a regional expression, "a male cat of three colors" to denote a male homosexual, since there are no male calico cats, Diego immediately concluded that the cats, originally from Spain, had been modified by the climate and geography of Mexico. Therefore, he deduced, Mexico had its own aesthetic, unlike that of any other country.

The two friends also bragged of the variety and beauty of Mexican folk art, displayed abundantly in the markets and railroad stations throughout the country and chastised other artists for wasting their time in Europe and ignoring Mexican folk art. Another favorite theme was the primacy of the Mexican over the Russian Revolution and the unique and superior features of the new Mexican Constitution.

According to his friends, Siqueiros walked the streets of Paris like a commanding officer reviewing his troops, as if he were still in the uniform of the Division of the North. Sporting a sparse mustache, his posture was erect and martial and he puffed out his chest so much that his friends began to call him "*El Palomo*" (male dove). He was well dressed and, during one of their sessions, Diego sketched him in charcoal, dressed elegantly in suit and tie and with a thin mustache. His favorite conversation topic was still the beauty and horror of the Mexican Revolution, proudly proclaiming that in the face of such violence and terror, man lives the fullest and most meaningful existence, stripped down to the essentials of survival.

Siqueiros told his stories of the Revolution over and over again, serving among other things, to fascinate and conquer members of the opposite sex. Not all of his adventures were crowned with success, however. When two dark skinned Mexican beauties arrived in Paris, he and Diego were chagrined when they preferred some blond Parisians. It was further proof of Mexico's surrender to Europe, they agreed, a disgrace which was all the more unbearable for their names, Adelita and Guadalupe. In another incident, he and another Mexican companion discovered that the objects of their affection were female impersonators.

Thanks to Diego's contacts, Siqueiros met many of the artists in Paris. Although he met Picasso, they were only casual acquaintances and the relationship was that of a disciple towards "el maestro," as Diego always addressed him. After he met Fernand Leger, they became good friends. Meeting almost daily in cafes or in Siqueiros's freezing flat, they talked at length about art and the plasticity of mechanics and the dynamics of modern technology. In New York Siqueiros had been intrigued by the movement and modern structures of the city. When he saw Leger's paintings of machinery, gears and mechanical movement, it triggered a sympathetic impulse and rekindled his own interest in the beauty of machinery and enthusiasm for the modern city of steel and concrete.

Although they agreed on the beauty of modern machinery, Siqueiros later proclaimed that monumental public art was superior to easel painting and, therefore, to the art of the Parisian school, of which Leger was a member. This challenge provoked heated exchanges in which Siqueiros defended his point of view by making caustic comments on the limitations of easel painting. After testing his ideas on Leger, he incorporated some of them into a series of articles, which he sent to *El Universal Ilustrado* in Mexico.

Siqueiros also became good friends with the French cubist Georges Braque. In spite of their different aesthetic approaches, they spent many hours together between 1919 and 1921, deliberately avoiding the subject of art and mainly carousing and discussing women. While Braque had been unfaithful before meeting Siqueiros, their dalliances made his wife suspicious and she believed that Siqueiros was corrupting her husband and suspected that he cheated more on her after meeting Siqueiros.

From time to time Diego and David took walks in a botanical garden in Paris, discussing art and its future in Mexico. Since there was no market for art in their country, they concluded that mural painting sponsored by the state was the only course. Recalling Dr. Atl's manifesto, they became convinced of the need for a type of public art and fueled each other's growing ambition to paint murals. In the process, they developed a disdain for small paintings destined for private homes, galleries and museums. While they were inspired by the work of Ingres and his disciples in Paris, they concluded that there was little interest in or market for this type of art.

When they discussed the idea of teams of artists working under a master artist with other artists, they discovered that they were clearly in a minority composed of a few "romantics." The idea of working in teams was anathema to the reigning cult of individualism, which considered that any cooperative arrangement between artists stifled creativity. Undeterred, they continued to pursue the dream of painting murals and agreed that it was imperative for them to visit Italy and Greece in order to study classical and renaissance mural painting.

Since David was obliged to attend the maneuvers of the French army, Diego went to Italy without him. From Rome, Diego sent several postcards covered with elaborate notes he had made on the secrets of composition which he had discovered in the frescos of Giotto. After six months in Italy, he returned to Paris, ladened with bundles of detailed notes and sketches of the great works of Truscan art and ready to exchange cubism and easel painting for mural paintings featuring mankind. He was also ecstatic about Italy, declaring that it was the only country that could compare to Mexico in the beauty of its women, music, language and art.

When David's turn came to go to Italy, he arrived in Rome just before the inauguration of the new Pope and there were no rooms available. After a long and exhausting search, he located a hotel which had been booked for the Mexican delegation to the consecration, scheduled to arrive the next day. Importuning an employee to let him stay in an empty room, he threw himself on the bed and immediately fell asleep in his clothes. The next morning a clerk woke him abruptly and presented him with a note from his father, a member of the Mexican delegation.

Later that morning, they were reunited and before embracing his son, Cipriano presented him with a ticket for the consecration of the Pope. During the ceremony, he watched his ecstatic father, his arms raised in the form of a cross and crying openly throughout the long ceremony, surrounded by the rest of the Mexican delegation, while all around him people were chanting, singing and praying fervidly.

Like Diego, Siqueiros was very impressed by Italian art, but he preferred different masters. Whereas Rivera favored the masterful compositions of Giotto, Siqueiros was more affected by the realistic representation of the human body by Masaccio and the active mechanism which he gave to that form. When he saw the work of Michelangelo, Rafael and da Vinci, he observed how they had perfected the innovations of Masaccio and Uccello. He also developed an appreciation of Italian baroque art and sensed the similarity with the art of colonial Mexico.

Unlike Rivera, he did not make extensive sketches or take elaborate notes. Instead, he made mental notations of the singular features of each work of art and absorbed those images which moved him. In a letter to Diego, he expressed the importance of working directly from nature, especially the forms of one's own culture, as well as the need to integrate the impulses, passions, convictions and loves of the artist. Art should be integral, he wrote, coming from within the artist himself and the problem with many contemporary artists is their failure to paint from real conviction or to integrate their deepest emotions and impulses in their art.

Besides being impressed by the Italian masters, both renaissance and baroque, David was also struck by the heroic and public nature of this art. Although primarily religious, it was monumental, public and figurative and, therefore, accessible and comprehensible to the masses.

While he was in Italy, Siqueiros encountered another artistic impulse, the Italian futurists. Developing out of an Italian literary movement, these artists emphasized modern life, movement, simultaneity and "dynamism," and had issued several manifestos, which they pronounced dramatically. The emphasis of the futurists on movement and the transitory nature of reality struck a sensitive chord in Siqueiros, already stirred by his exposure to the baroque. His later obsession with movement and the development of multiple images can be traced to this exposure to the Italian futurists. He was also intrigued by their concepts of the violent and dynamic quality of the surface of the canvas and the use of powerful "lines of force" to involve the spectator, ideas and techniques which he later incorporated into his own art.

His interest was also piqued by the emphasis of the futurists on modern life, their revolutionary approach and deliberately shocking and theatrical pronouncements. Combined with the example of Dr. Atl and his own personality, this may have inspired or reinforced his tendency to issue dramatic appeals and sweeping manifestos. Like the futurists, he also denounced the extreme individualism of modern artists and sought to create an art form which would inspire the masses in a new society.

Before he left Italy Siqueiros encountered the metaphysical art of De Chirico and Carra. He met Carra in Milan and was impressed by his solid style as well as by the metaphysical qualities of his art. His portrait of W. Kennedy, painted in 1920, reflected these tendencies.

Artistically, Siqueiros's trip to Italy was most auspicious, both inspiring and influencing his art. Added to his childhood exposure to colonial Mexican art and his subsequent development of an appreciation of Mexican indigenous and folk art, the influences which he absorbed in Italy were crucial in his development as an artist. Although he cannot be classified as the orthodox disciple of any school of art, Siqueiros assimilated several ideas and techniques of the futurists and futurism had a greater impact on his own theories and practice of art than any other modern movement or school of art.

But while he was struck by the modernism and movement of the futurists, he was also inspired and influenced by the realism of Masaccio and by the monumentality and public, figurative nature of the work of the Italian renaissance artists. Consequently, his art became a synthesis of these impulses as well as other currents. While he opposed the dominant influence of Europe, especially that of the "school of Paris," on modern art, he was absorbing ideas and approaches from other European artists, past and present, which would become integral to his own work.

In 1920 Siqueiros returned to Paris to resume his "military duties," overflowing with ideas on art which he wanted to discuss with Diego and put into practice. When he arrived in Paris, however, he learned that Carranza, his benefactor, had been overthrown and killed during his flight to Veracruz. This turn of events immediately placed his appointment and stipend as a military attaché in jeopardy. When the Mexican representatives in Paris sent a telegram to Mexico protesting the change of government, they received a curt reply that they no longer had jobs or salaries.

Lacking a means of support, David took a job in an iron works in the village of Argenteuil near Paris where he drew designs for decorative ironwork. Besides supporting himself and Graciela, this work put him into contact with the French working class since they lived in a pension with French workers. As a factory worker, he experienced the problems of the industrial worker and he and Gachita were soon writing articles for the magazine *La Vie Ouvriere* published by Montmousseau, a member of the French Communist Party.

This exposure to the European labor movement advanced his political consciousness, first triggered by his experiences in the Mexican Revolution. Through his childhood friend, Jesús Soto, he had been exposed to the ideas of Kropotkin and Bakunin, and, before his deportation from Spain, he had been involved with the anarchists in Barcelona. In Paris, he had made friends with members of the Marxist CGUT, as well as exiles from Russia. And after 1917, the most exciting political news was coming from revolutionary Russia.

Since he naturally associated that movement with the Mexican Revolution, he was increasingly drawn to Marxism as a revolutionary ideology.

His ideas about art, especially the function of art and artists in a revolutionary society, were also being shaped by these experiences and his concurrent political growth. Art and politics, his *raison d'etre,* were beginning to merge.

On the lighter side, David enjoyed his working class life and compared his French companions favorably with his own countrymen. Besides regaling his fellow workers with tales of the Mexican Revolution, he entertained them with rope tricks that he had learned from his grandfather, using the rope to trap children or lasso adults.

David was also doing some painting, experimenting with cubism but developing a style that he called "structuralist." Following Cezanne's prescription that a mountain was not a pyramid but a cone, he painted nature as having multidimensional geometric forms and not as objects perceived from only one angle. In his search for a realism corresponding to the reality of nature, his landscapes assumed disconcerting shapes which he "constructed" on the canvas. They were landscapes with volume, the mountains thrusting forward or upward in multiple sculpturesque forms.

Although a few of these works were purchased by a Mexican writer living in Paris, he never showed any of them to Rivera and some he personally destroyed, either because he was disappointed in them or for a lack of appreciation. Despite their fate, some of the ideas and techniques which he developed in France would resurface in the panoramic and sculpturesque landscapes which he painted in the 1930s.

Since he was bored with his work and they were running out of money, David and Graciela decided to try their luck in Barcelona. They had no trouble reentering Spain and not long after their arrival, it was announced that David Alfaro Siqueiros had taken over the artistic direction of a new journal, *La vida americana*. In Mexico the appointment was hailed as a "positive triumph for him," a reward for his art studies in Europe under reputable masters, a generous overstatement. Although the names of other Mexican artists in Europe and several important Spanish and Latin American literary figures were listed in the editorial staff, it was a one-man operation.

According to Siqueiros, he obtained the financial backing for the magazine by blackmailing the Mexican consul in Barcelona. The consul was purportedly a wealthy "dandy" who agreed to provide 400 *pesetas* for its printing if it would contain his portrait with a caption describing all that he had done to improve trade between Spain and Mexico. When the consul decided to retract his offer, Siqueiros threatened to publish a statement about the consul's perfidy and write a letter to General Obregón, the President-elect of Mexico. He received the 400 *pesetas*.

In May 1921, the first and last issue of *La vida americana*, "the Avant-garde Review of North, Central and South America," appeared. It featured a manifesto, a pencil drawing by Siqueiros and several illustrations of local murals by the Uruguayan artist Joaquin Torres García. The manifesto, written by Siqueiros with the help of Graciela, addressed "Three Appeals of Contemporary Orientation to the New Generation of American Painters and Sculptors." In these appeals he called on the artists of America to reject the decadent influence of Europe and to develop a new and appropriate form of art. Although he praised the work of the past, he challenged artists to restore painting and sculpture to their original values while at the same time endowing them with new ones. "Do not let us revert to old fashioned, archaic motifs," he exhorted.

> Let us live our own marvelous dynamic age ... Let us love
> modern mechanics, the dispenser of unexpected plastic
> emotions, the contemporary aspects of our daily life, our
> cities in the process of construction, the sober and
> practical engineering of our modern buildings stripped
> of architectural complexities.

Echoing Dr. Atl's challenge to the students at San Carlos, he pleaded for "the creation of a monumental and heroic art, human art, public art," employing the latest in materials made available by modern technology. While attacking impressionism, the sole aim of which is to "paint light," as a puerile theory of art, he credited Cezanne with restoring art to its essentials. "We painters," he wrote,

> must put the constructive spirit before the purely
> decorative spirit ... Let us impose the constructive
> spirit upon the purely decorative; color and line are
> expressive elements of the second rank, the fundamental
> basis of a work art is the magnificent geometrical
> structure of form and the concept of the interplay of
> volume and perspective which combine to create depth ...
> Let us create volumes in space ... Let us build and mould
> on our personal feelings towards nature, with scrupulous
> regard for the truth.

To illustrate his point, Siqueiros reproduced his recent *Portrait of W. Kennedy* in *La vida americana*. Reflecting the influence of Carra and surreal in nature, this pencil drawing demonstrated the precepts of "the constructive spirit," the "magnificent geometrical structure of form," and "the great primary masses" expressed in his manifesto.

In the third and final appeal to American artists, he recommended,

> Let us approach the works of the ancient populations of
> our valleys, the Indian painters and sculptors ... Let us
> adopt their energy of synthesis, without, however, settling
> for the lamentable archaeological reconstructions
> (Indianism, Primitivism, Americanism) which are now so
> fashionable and which are leading us towards ephemeral
> stylizations.

Rejecting the development of "national art," he exhorted, "We must become universal; our racial and local elements will inevitably appear in our work."

Turning to the teaching of art, he characterized the "open-air academies" as more dangerous than the official academies, "where at least we learned to know the classics. Today, the teachers of art are also commercially oriented and their criticism stifles talent and creativity." As for the art critics, "Let us close our ears to the criticism of our poets; they produce beautiful literary articles, completely divorced from the true values we seek in our work."

The Barcelona manifesto was the culmination of Siqueiros's experiences as a student at San Carlos, his participation in the student strike and the open-air school, the lessons of the Revolution, the discussions of the Centro Bohemio, and his exposure to European art, ancient and modern. It was also the joint product of Rivera and Siqueiros, the result of their discussions in Paris, combined with the contributions of Graciela. Although it was critical of contemporary European art, the manifesto incorporated avant-garde currents of thought and tenets of futurism which American artists were instructed to apply to create a "superior" art of the future. While it called for a new direction in art, the manifesto did not mention political or social change.

Though little remains of his art from this period, Siqueiros's brief sojourn in Europe constituted an important formative stage in the development of his ideas about art, full of portents for the future. Coming as it did on the eve of the Mexican Renaissance, the manifesto was the first theoretical formulation of the Mexican Mural Movement, or modern Mexican art, and it ranks with the contributions of Posada, Dr. Atl, Herrán, Goitía and Orozco in the formative steps of that movement. Within a few months of its publication, the mural movement was underway in Mexico and artists were applying some of the precepts laid out by Siqueiros in Barcelona. The manifesto also influenced a kindred literary movement in Mexico, *estridentismo* (stridentism), whose journals were illustrated by many of the young artists.

After he published the manifesto, Siqueiros wrote to Rivera from Barcelona, telling him of the need to return to mural painting. Before Diego left for Mexico to take up mural painting, he wrote back, "The art of the easel belongs to the individual, mural painting to all the people."

While David had lost his salary as a military attaché, he had arranged through some friends in Mexico for a monthly pension of 300 pesos from the University of Mexico in order to pursue his art studies. Fearful that his sum might be cancelled, he wrote to the new president of the university, José Vasconcelos, asking him to extend it since he was working in his studio in Paris for an exhibition in May.

Meanwhile, Vasconcelos had been appointed Minister of Education and was in the process of launching an educational crusade and cultural revival. He wrote back, assuring David that the allowance would be continued, but he advised him that he would find better opportunities in Mexico than in "those tired old countries." Since Vasconcelos had already hired some artists to paint murals, he wrote another letter urging Siqueiros to return to Mexico to help "create a new civilization." In response, David wrote back, endorsing Vasconcelos's plans

> to create a new civilization extracted from the very bowels
> of Mexico ... Yesterday it was the turn of the
> Orient; tomorrow will be our turn ... to know Europe's
> current work is to touch the very wound of its decadence
> and to acquire faith in our future.

When Siqueiros demurred about returning to Mexico, however, Vasconcelos warned that his allowance would be cancelled if he remained in Europe. Faced with this ultimatum and the prospect of a mural renaissance in Mexico without him, David and Graciela decided to return home. Thus concluded his brief but auspicious exposure to European art, a military assignment with rare cultural significance.

Before they left, they consoled Angelina Beloff, Diego's abandoned wife, and assured her that as soon as they arrived in Mexico, they would have Diego send her money to come to Mexico. After a long journey by steamship in third class, they arrived in Veracruz. Although he was happy to be home, David was impatient to get to Mexico City, where other artists were already painting murals.

IV. Renaissance

As soon as they reached Mexico City, David and Gachita set out to find Diego. Since they had heard rumors that he was painting murals and he had not written or sent money to the wife and child he had left behind in Paris, they were anxious to find out what had happened to him. On their way to his home they met a striking women who was in tears. It was the same Guadalupe Marín whom David had met in Jalisco during the Revolution.

Amid curses and sobs, she took them to the apartment she shared with Diego. Inside they saw a virtual museum of Mexican folk art, superb examples of the art he and Diego had discussed so fervently in Paris. The walls were also covered with portraits of Lupe, most of them in the nude. What would they tell Angelina? Although they lost contact with her, she later came to Mexico and shared an apartment with the abandoned wife of another artist, Graciela Amador Siqueiros.

Meanwhile, Mexico had a new leader and a cultural renaissance was already underway. After his election to the presidency in 1921, General Obregón appointed José Vasconcelos Minister of Public Education. A young intellectual from Oaxaca, Vasconcelos had been a founding member of the *Ateneo de la Juventud*, an anti-Díaz group of young intellectuals, and was editor of a *maderista* newspaper. Forced to flee Mexico, he became a confidential agent for Madero in Washington.

After the assassination of Madero, Vasconcelos returned to Mexico and served as Minister of Education in the short-lived presidency of Gutiérrez. When Gutiérrez evacuated the capital in 1915, Vasconcelos joined the exodus, reaching the United States border just ahead of pursuing *carrancistas*. During the revolt against Carranza, he conducted a propaganda campaign for Obregón in the United States and, after Carranza's defeat, he served briefly as the Rector of the National University before becoming Minister of Public Education.

In 1921 Vasconcelos was bursting with ideas and he immediately launched several ambitious projects. Hoping to improve the literacy and reading tastes of the Mexican people, he printed inexpensive copies of European literary classics and had them distributed throughout the country. He initiated a program of building rural schools and sent young teachers on educational missions to the farthest corners of the Republic. Known as *Casas del Pueblo*, the schools became meeting places for the whole community, hosting political rallies and fiestas. Since there were not enough trained teachers, volunteers were recruited, the only qualifications being literacy and enthusiasm. He also began a program of cultural missions in which small armies of "missionaries" visited villages for several months, providing instruction in health care, agriculture, and crafts, as well as in reading and writing.

Despite the merits of the program, it was difficult to sustain the original enthusiasm under impossible conditions. The rural population outgrew the number of schools and teachers, and the city-bred teachers were often resented as unwelcome intruders. Viewed as representatives of a revolutionary and "atheist" government, some of them were lynched or driven out of town by priest-led mobs.

In 1921 Mexico was celebrating the centennial of its independence from Spain. The festivities included a performance of Verdi's *Aida* in the National Stadium for the Army. Like the distribution of European literary classics, it was intended to inspire and elevate the sensibilities of the audience, mostly rough peasant soldiers and their female companions. But neither had anything to do with Mexican culture and *Aida* had also been performed during the 1910 celebration of Mexico's struggle for independence.

Nevertheless, this fixation on European culture was eroding and the same festivities included a festival of folk dance and music in Chapultepec. There was also an exhibit of folk art in Mexico City arranged by Roberto Montenegro, Jorge Enciso and Adolfo Best-Maugard, and in 1922 the government published *Folk Arts of Mexico*, a two-volume study by Dr. Atl. Although the American writer Katherine Anne Porter helped to arrange an American tour for a collection of Mexican arts and crafts, the exhibit was delayed at the border and closed after a successful showing in Los Angeles.

This interest in folk art coincided with a revived interest in Mexico's pre-Hispanic past. Reacting to centuries of foreign dominance and inspired by the Revolution, a new generation of artists and writers sought to develop a truly indigenous culture based on pre-Columbian roots. In 1921 Manuel Gamio was studying the ancient civilizations of the Valley of Mexico and he hired Francisco Goitía and other artists to sketch the ruins as well as living descendants. Supported by the government, these efforts to study and preserve the ancient cultures unearthed a rich cultural resource.

In addition to promoting literacy and the reading of the classics, Vasconcelos encouraged the composition and performance of Mexican music. The result was a new national music composed by Carlos Chávez and Silvestre Revueltas, the best known of a new group of Mexican composers. In literature the publication of the first novels of the Revolution signaled the development of a new consciousness in Mexican writing. Although they were still influenced by Europe, a new generation of writers were focusing on Mexican themes, developing original forms of expression and laying the foundations of an important literary movement.

Vasconcelos was also a patron of the arts, and the philosophical system which he later developed proclaimed that aesthetic activity was superior to and would replace the rationalist phase of human evolution. Now he talked about a "new civilization" and "renaissance" in the arts and in 1921, he hired some young artists to paint murals in public buildings. While he envisioned a classic revival of mural painting, he unleashed a new and revolutionary impulse in modern art.

Although opinions differ as to when the mural renaissance began or who was responsible for launching it, the participants were building upon national traditions, precedents and prophesies. From the past there were the pre-Hispanic frescos of Bonampak and Teotihuacán, the colonial religious art in churches throughout Mexico, and the popular murals of the lower class *cantinas* or *pulquerías*, all forms of public art or mural painting. Many Mexicans were also familiar with the engravings of José Guadalupe Posada, the most prolific and popular engraver in a long tradition of public art which predated the Revolution.

Dr. Atl's manifesto of 1906 had called for a new type of monumental art, building upon classical traditions. Before the Revolution, he and Jorge Enciso had been commissioned to paint a mural in the National Preparatory School. Saturnino Herrán, instructor to many of the younger artists at San Carlos, had painted humble Mexicans in their daily habitat and developed the concept of *mestizaje*, the fusion of the two races and cultures in Mexico. Francisco Goitía had been the first to paint scenes from the Revolution while Orozco's graphic drawings and prints featuring the lower classes had shocked wealthy patrons and critics. According to Siqueiros, the Congress of "soldier-artists" in Guadalajara had proposed a new "national art" to serve the Revolution.

In 1918 Adolfo Best-Maugard designed sets for Anna Pavlova's *Ballet Mexicano* and his one-man show in New York the following year featured Mexican subject matter. Impressed by Best-Maugard's revolutionary theories regarding creative design, Vasconcelos established the Department of Art Education in which the artist was to use his unique method to instruct teachers of art. Among his students were some of Mexico's finest artists and his "Method of Drawing" became the basic text for teaching art in Mexico and other Latin American countries.

In 1920 Carlos Mérida exhibited a series of paintings of peasants in Mexico City and his choice of scenes and colors from his native Guatemala evoked a sympathetic response. A year later Siqueiros issued his manifesto from Barcelona and an exhibit of Mexican folk art opened in Mexico City.

By 1921, therefore, the foundations had been laid, the manifestos had been issued, and a new generation of artists was ready to participate in a national art movement. Inspired by their own revolution and news from revolutionary Russia, they saw themselves as the builders of a new civilization and, for the first time in many years, Mexico was not torn by civil war. Rejecting Europe as tired and discouraged, they were rediscovering their national culture and even those who had not participated in the Revolution were excited by the possibility of contributing to a rebirth of national culture.

At first Vasconcelos proceeded cautiously, assigning the decoration of the old church of San Pedro and San Pablo, now a lecture hall, to Roberto Montenegro. Just back from Europe, Montenegro was rediscovering his own country and began to paint a mural in oils with motifs taken from popular art. Although his *Dance of the Hours* of twelve beautifully draped females was traditional, it was the first in a series of government sponsored mural projects.

While Montenegro worked on his mural, Vasconcelos was rebuilding the Annex of the National Preparatory School and, before the dust had settled, he commissioned Dr. Atl to decorate one of its patios. This energetic teacher and political organizer had just delivered one of his pronouncements on the future of art and he welcomed the opportunity to put his ideas into action. Using "Atl-colors," he covered one of the walls of the patio with a series of panels depicting Mexican seascapes and tropical nights. They satisfied no one but himself and were soon vandalized by unappreciative students.

Atl's commission was followed by another one to Montenegro. Fresh from his experiences in the lecture hall, Montenegro decided to paint in fresco on the wall of the main stairway of the Annex but none of the artists or their assistants knew the formula for fresco painting. After a fruitless search in the libraries, they told Vasconcelos they had to go to Italy to study fresco painting. Explaining that there was no money for a trip, Vasconcelos told them that, if they were really artists, they would know how to prepare fresco.

The solution came from one of Montenegro's Indian assistants. The son of a house painter, Xavier Guerrero explained that the Toltecs had painted in fresco and that it was still used in the decoration of wealthy homes, churches and private clubs. Several artists then traveled to Puebla where they studied colonial churches covered with fresco decoration and obtained the formula for fresco from the local artists and masons. Rushing back to the capital, they prepared the natural pigments and began to paint on wet plaster prepared by their assistants.

Seizing the opportunity extended by Vasconcelos, the artists transformed the school into a bustling workshop of artists, masons and workers. In the amphitheater of the school, Rivera began work on "Creation," using Mexican Indian women and other artists as models and working in pigments mixed with copal resin, a Mexican encaustic. His assistants were Guerrero, Carlos Mérida, Amado de la Cueva and Jean Charlot, a French artist living in Mexico whose grandparents were Mexican.

While he was assisting Rivera, Charlot was commissioned by Vasconcelos to paint a mural in the Preparatory School. Although Rivera was still working in encaustic, Charlot, Fernando Leal, Fermin Revueltas and Ramon Alva de la Canal decided to work in fresco. After experimenting with this medium, they began painting on wet plaster prepared by their assistants, painting themes from the history of Mexico. Leal painted *The Feast of Chalma*, Revueltas, *Homage to the Virgin of Guadalupe* and Alva de la Canal, *The Raising of the Cross in the New World.* Although the others struggled with fresco or switched to encaustic, Charlot completed his *Massacre in the Main Temple* on the second floor of the school, the first modern Mexican mural painted in true fresco. Aided by Guerrero, Montenegro also finished his *Feast of the Holy Cross* in fresco.

While the artists worked individually in terms of subject matter, concepts and designs, they were assisted by teams of artists and masons with whom they shared the tasks of preparing the pigments. They frequently exchanged roles, artists mixing lime for other artists and the masons taking up the brushes and painting on the damp plaster. After assisting Rivera and Montenegro, Guerrero traded the mason's trowel for the paintbrush and began to paint his own murals.

José Clemente Orozco arrived later and painted a fresco panel in the inner patio of the school which reflected Italian Renaissance art. Later he developed his own unique style, eventually covering three levels of the central court of the building with his iconoclastic views of Mexican history, culture and the Revolution. When some society women covered his paintings with curtains during one of their charitable functions in the school, Orozco caricatured them in fresco as bloated aristocrats paying homage to their "Father God."

Since Vasconcelos could not pay the artists from his budget as Minister of Education, he created fictitious titles and hired them as teachers of art. Rivera was hired as the "Director of the Department of Plastic Workshops," Orozco was a teacher of elementary drawing and Jean Charlot was paid eight pesos a day as "Inspector of Drawing in the Public Schools." The salaries were based on an eight-hour day, usually coming to seven to eight pesos a day for master painter and mason alike. Vicente Lombardo Toledano, the Rector of the Preparatory School, paid for materials from the school budget, contributed some of his own salary and took collections from sympathetic teachers to cover expenses. Occasionally he also grabbed a brush and joined in the painting.

One of the last to arrive was Siqueiros. Although he had been enticed back to Mexico by Vasconcelos's ultimatum, he could hardly remain in a "decadent" Europe, especially when mural painting was being resurrected in Mexico. Soon after his arrival in Mexico City, he rushed to the Preparatoria, anxious to see what the artists were doing. But when he saw the halos around the heads of the figures in Rivera's *Creation,* he was disappointed and wondered what had happened to the ideas which he and Diego had discussed in Paris. The mural, he commented, looked like it was painted by a Byzantine artist affected by art nouveau.

Certain that Orozco, hailed as the "Mexican Goya" after his 1916 debut, would not disappoint him, he was shocked when he saw

Orozco's first fresco. It featured a blond virgin and child surrounded by four blond angels. Although some Catholics were offended by his nude version of the Holy Family, it was not Mexican in theme or revolutionary in execution. After criticizing Orozco for painting a bunch of "nude madonnas...a la Boticelli," Siqueiros accused his fellow artists of betrayal.

While Diego dismissed his comments as jealousy, Orozco quietly defended the use of the ancient masters as guides. It was the first of many heated polemics between the artists, and the movement, still in its infancy, was already divided by personal differences and aesthetic preferences.

Spurred by Rivera's challenge and the head start of the other painters, Siqueiros was anxious to work on his own mural. Before he started, however, he wanted to exhibit his paintings from Europe. But when he opened a trunk full of unstretched canvases, he was disappointed in his own work and decided to exhibit only one painting, a small, loosely brushed landscape which he said Picasso had admired because "it looked like a piece of liver."

Since Vasconcelos was anxious to cover as much surface as possible, he readily accepted Siqueiros's offer to paint the entire vault and four walls of a dark and remote stairway in the Colegio Chico (little school) of the Preparatory School. Like the others, Siqueiros was hired as a teacher, at three pesos per day as "Teacher No. 29 of Drawing and Manual Crafts." He was also assistant to the "Director of the Plastic Workshops" and later he acquired the title of "Assistant Smith in the Bronze Foundry of the Department of Fine Arts," a position which paid six pesos a day.

Although he had chosen an uneven and difficult surface on which to paint his first mural, Siqueiros assured Vasconcelos that his composition would be superior to those of the other artists. But why had he chosen to paint on this stairway, far from the bustle and activity of the other artists or the traffic of the students? Was he timid about his first attempt at mural painting or was he trying to avoid the shadows of the other muralists? Or did he just prefer to work alone, undistracted by gawking spectators or troublesome students?

Perhaps he consciously sought to recreate a baroque chapel in this vault, like those he had admired in Mexico and Italy, and to integrate his painting with the architecture. After viewing Michelangelo's frescos in the Sistine Chapel and other Renaissance murals which covered the ceilings or the inside of vaults as well as the vertical walls, he had concluded that mural painting was much more than the enlargement of an easel painting or the painting of flat walls in two dimensions. It involved painting the total architectural space and should be integrated with the architecture.

He was also interested in movement and perhaps he realized that the concave vault offered a more active surface than the flat rectangular surfaces on which his colleagues were painting. When he tried to share his ideas with Rivera and Orzoco, however, they rejoined, "Mural painting is that which is done on walls and nothing more!"

Before he started, David had a wooden barricade erected around the area and padlocked it when he was not working. Choosing the high vault of the stairwell for his first composition, he began to paint. Using encaustic, in which the pigments are mixed with wax before being burned onto the heated surface of the wall with a blowtorch or hot iron, he painted a woman with wings surrounded by symbols representing the elements. Consciously avoiding traditional or European symbols, he symbolized fire with flaming forms, wind with some ethereal propellers, water as two snails, since they were marine animals, and earth as the cores of tropical fruit.

While the subject matter was traditional, the shawl-draped winged woman with a mask-like face suggested a lower class Mexican woman and her arms were extremely muscular, like those of a man. She was not an idealized angel, he explained, but a woman who has wings since how else does a woman float in space. Although he felt that the figure was too "picassoesque" and considered destroying it, it was more likely inspired by Masaccio. He also concluded that his symbols were too vague and later commented, "Our first subjects were mystical [and] had very little social content ... I painted symbols of physical properties while Orozco painted a la Boticelli."

Despite his assurances to Vasconcelos, Siqueiros frequently abandoned his mural to attend political meetings, issue manifestos, make speeches, or write articles on a variety of subjects, including art. When he returned to work on his mural, however, he frequently did not like what he saw and would scrape the paint off and start all over again. At this rate, the completion of the ceiling alone took eight months.

While other artists chided him for the lack of progress, his patron despaired that he would ever finish. Since the barricade closed off the stairway, no one really knew what was going on behind it, including Vasconcelos. While days, weeks and months passed by, there was no sign of progress. The curious speculated, the critics expressed their doubts and Vasconcelos became more impatient. When passersby reported overhearing heated discussions and the voices of young women from behind the fence, the rumors multiplied.

Siqueiros not only became disenchanted with encaustic but also began to question the established rules of composition. While Diego had insisted on the use of "The Golden Section" developed by the old masters, David concluded that the diagonals he had drawn for the geometric structure of the irregular space were useless and decided that mural painting was not just the painting of independent areas only indirectly connected. *The Elements* was not autonomous or complete, he realized, but an integral part of something else and to paint something next to it, which was completely different, was absurd. Not only must paintings conform to the architecture, but they also have to compliment each other, he concluded.

After he finished the ceiling, David debated whether to continue the subject of the elements on the walls or to incorporate it in another theme. Since Saint Christopher was the vehicle for the transfer of Christianity, he decided to paint him as a symbol of contact between the old world and the new. Directly opposite, therefore, he painted an Indian woman holding a child. The two figures represented the western and pre-Hispanic cultures, as well as man and woman, and the child was a *mestizo*, the mixed offspring of the two cultures. In this way he linked the walls and the ceiling thematically. The winged woman overhead was *The Spirit of the Occident Over Mexico*, while the torches, representing fire, suggested an approaching revolution.

Frustrated with encaustic, David declared that it was archaic and switched to fresco, already adopted by most of the other artists. But the first time he told a mason to prepare the plaster, he failed to show up before it dried. Many times his helpers prepared the walls, only to see them wasted when he never showed up. Once, when they prepared the surface in the afternoon so that he could paint at night, when the school was closed, he failed to appear. But another artist, either Guerrero or Orozco, snuck in and painted a head on the body of an unfinished figure before the plaster dried.

The next day David exclaimed, "Wonderful! Either I did it in my sleep or it is a miracle. I think I'll try it again tonight and see if it works." When the "miracle" reoccurred, he was even more ecstatic and the game was repeated, producing a figure painted by several artists.

When he finished his first figure in fresco, however, he did not like the results and had it destroyed. In its place he painted a female figure with a red Phrygian cap representing democracy. But he did not like *The Angel of Liberation* and had it removed. On another wall he experimented with some symbols and forms derived from native plants. Although they were realistic, his colleagues did not recognize them and attacked them as pure abstractions. Returning to human figures, he painted *The Fallen Myths* with images of God and Satan, two floating women representing monarchy and democracy, a muscular man with a halo and a "popular angel," all reminiscent of Italian Renaissance art.

Gradually, Siqueiros began to realize that if his art was to be Mexican, the figures must be ethnologically Mexican, not classical European types. Furthermore, he became convinced that the classics could not stir the masses or show them the way to decision and action. Inspired by his discoveries, he directed his assistants to prepare the walls and working in a state of frenzy, he painted two massive male figures to represent the Revolution. They were undeniably native Mexicans.

Before he finished this section, however, he started another fresco on the wall of the first level, *The Burial of the Worker*. While he was working on this fresco of four workers bearing the coffin of a dead comrade, David learned of the execution of the revolutionary Governor of Yucatan, Felipe Carrillo Puerto. Writing the name of his martyred friend on a piece of paper, he stuffed it into a bottle and sealed it in the wall behind the painted coffin.

According to custom in rural Mexico, he painted the coffin blue but with a crude hammer and a sickle on the lid. The hammer resembles a cross as well as a tool of the working class and the five-pointed red star, which he placed over the head of one of the workers, suggests a new martyr or resurrection. The coffin, made of rough timber, appears to thrust off the surface of the wall, thanks to an exaggerated perspective and its foreshortened shape. The arms of the workers who carry their dead comrade are linked together and they look straight ahead, stoic, fearless and united. They are also Indians, their features copied from the Olmec ceremonial masks and sculptures which he had studied in the anthropological museum.

On a wall next to the burial scene, he painted a forlorn mother or widow, her face of stone staring blankly. On the adjoining wall, he started to paint another woman breaking her chains and a revolutionary soldier holding a child. But while he was still working on this panel, students attacked it and, before he could repair and finish it, he was discharged from the project.

Siqueiros never returned to repair or complete his first mural project and it remains unfinished and badly damaged in the dark stairwell of the Colegio Chico. Nevertheless, it documents his development as a mural artist as well as his tendency to experiment and develop new theories and techniques as he worked. It also reveals an approach and style of art which characterized his later work.

After beginning hesitantly with his "angel" in encaustic, surrounded by vague symbols of the elements, he had moved down the walls of the stairway, switching to fresco and acquiring more confidence as he worked. His figures had taken on bolder shapes and the Renaissance figures were replaced by figures that were clearly Mexican. They were monumental and sculptural, their forms projecting beyond the painted surfaces, while their mask-like Indian features were psychological in their treatment. Although other artists had painted idealized versions of the Indian cultures, his *Burial of a Worker* was the first modern mural to incorporate the Indian into contemporary society, as members of the Mexican working class.

When some of the other artists saw this adaptation, they recognized that he was approaching the ethnographic quality which was missing in their murals and even Rivera admitted that Siqueiros had achieved "the most complete synthesis of our race" since before the conquest. But when Diego later claimed that he had been the first to incorporate the Mexican Indian into his art, Siqueiros pointed out that Rivera was still using other artists or their women as models and had not yet developed the Indian racial type in his art. However, Siqueiros had not only included the Indians as members of the working class but had also made a political statement by painting a hammer and sickle on the coffin. Later he accused himself of having been an "archaic painter of ancient civilizations" while Rivera was "a renaissance mystic" and Orozco "a bourgeois Jacobin" in their first mural paintings.

Isolated in his blocked off stairway, Siqueiros had proceeded independently, developing and testing theories as he worked and trying out new materials and methods. In the process, he realized that practice must precede theory and that theory evolved from the act of painting. He was also convinced that mural painting was not just the painting of two-dimensional walls but the painting of the total architectonic space and that the different surfaces must be integrated plastically as well as thematically. Although he never finished his first attempt at "integral art", that concept continued to haunt him and became central to his theory and practice of mural painting.

As the murals in the Preparatory School took shape, the artists and their work acquired more notoriety. Reporters visited the patios of the school daily and their papers carried stories on the latest controversy or incident. Rivera provided the best copy. Perched on a scaffold, his huge torso, rotund face and bulging eyes were easy to caricature. He also never shunned publicity and the outlandish stories he told made him the center of attention. After he fell off the scaffold one day, he explained that one of the colossal figures he had been painting had pushed him off the platform and that the spot where he fell was now haunted. Repeated in the press, these stories increased his notoriety and he became the target of newspaper articles and cartoons, even theatrical productions.

One day Diego entertained the other artists with a lengthy discourse on the merits of marijuana, in which he proclaimed that the great art of the past was done under the influence of drugs. When some of the artists endorsed the idea of using marijuana to enhance their creative talents, they requested an expert to instruct them in the use of the magical drug prescribed by Rivera. Two days later Diego introduced "Chema," who proceeded to tell them that "Doña Juanita" was Mexico's most important contribution to the world and that the decadence of the colonial period was the result of the Spaniards' prohibition of the drug.

Although Orozco scoffed at the notion, others responded enthusiastically and agreed to launch a movement to change Mexico's laws against the use of marijuana and to adopt the practice of smoking marijuana before painting. When Siqueiros and an assistant took a few puffs before painting one day, however, the lights failed and, when they reached for a cord, they received a shock and fell off the scaffold. Fortunately, they landed on a pile of sand, but it took them several weeks to recover. After that, both Siqueiros and Rivera agreed that, since they were already "*marijuanos*," they had consumed more than enough to stimulate their creativity.

As public interest in the murals increased, so did the attacks on the artists and their patron. Wealthy art patrons, members of the art establishment, critics, conservative politicians, reactionary students, and members of the foreign community heaped abuse on the murals and their artists. They were accused of destroying colonial architecture, resurrecting ancient idolatry, painting idiots, and setting painting back hundreds of years. Meanwhile their patron, Vasconcelos, was besieged from all sides and barely escaped being lynched by a mob of angry students calling for his resignation.

Thus encouraged, the students of the Preparatoria taunted the artists when they worked, threatened them physically and attacked their finished frescos. Using peashooters and occasionally fists or firearms, the students tried to inhibit the work of the artists and inflicted considerable damage on the already completed frescos. Even leftist students were critical and would stand in front of the walls and bait the artists, provoking them to come down from their scaffolds and exchange blows with the students.

To protect them and their art, the artists decided to arm themselves and wore pistols while they worked. Given the volatile political climate, the experience of the Revolution and the political activities of the artists, the possession or use of weapons was not unusual. Many Mexican males carried pistols, and the artists had to protect themselves and their art from their critics who were also armed.

Since Siqueiros was now involved in anti-government activities and was outspoken in his views, he received more than his share of attacks. While he tried to ignore his tormentors, several times he climbed down and bruised his knuckles exchanging blows with some students. When he found himself outnumbered, however, he pulled out his .44 revolver and fired it into the air, summoning the other artists who rushed to his aid and held off the students. In another incident, the sculptor Nacho Asunsolo and his stonecutters routed a group of students by charging and firing their pistols into the air while they shouted "death to all those who oppose beauty!"

One day a stray bullet ricocheted and hit a student in the eye. To prevent further casualties, President Obregón issued orders to protect the murals and stationed Yaqui Indian troops in the school. Accustomed to idealized versions of their culture or European standards of beauty, however, the Indian soldiers protested that the artists made them look "very ugly" when they painted them in their murals.

But it was impossible to protect the murals at all hours and they were seriously damaged by peashooters, stoning, and the scratching and gouging of pencils wielded by students. While the damage was extensive, the work continued and these artists, many of them veterans of the Revolution, were not to be deterred from their mission by some reactionary students. The attacks on them and their art and the publicity only served to stimulate more interest in the murals, as well as strengthen the convictions of the artists. Where else did artists receive so much attention? While their murals were not as accessible to the masses as they had hoped, they had become public figures and their art was a major public issue.

Not all of the controversy was provoked by their confrontations with adversaries. Using the name of a fictitious engineer, Siqueiros and Jean Charlot wrote a series of articles on "The Contemporary Movement of Painting in Mexico," in which they applied the ideas of the Barcelona manifesto to the conditions of post-revolutionary Mexico. By praising their own work and attacking that of their colleagues, they also pitted the artists against each other and stirred up more controversy. Rivera was not without weapons, however, and he chided Siqueiros for his lack of progress and brooding because "giant loudspeakers" had not proclaimed his greatness.

In spite of their differences, in 1922 the muralists met in the home of Diego and Guadalupe to discuss an organization to promote and protect their murals. Diego argued that as muralists they were not aloof intellectuals but simply manual workers, at best technical workers, and they should defend their craft by organizing a union. They wore overalls and worked on scaffolds and their work was done in public, not in a studio, and it was also very physical. Just as there had been guilds of house painters who had opposed Díaz, they needed a union of revolutionary artists to promote and protect their work.

After a long and heated discussion, the artists decided to form "The Syndicate of Revolutionary Painters, Sculptors and Technical Workers." Before departing, they chose an executive committee consisting of Siqueiros as Secretary General, Diego Rivera and Fernando Leal as Secretaries of the Interior and Xavier Guerrero, Treasurer.

At the next meeting, Rivera proposed that they join the Communist International (Cominterm). But no one knew anything about the workers' movement or how to apply to the Cominterm. Nevertheless, they passed a resolution to join the Cominterm and drafted a message announcing their adherence to its program. Before they adjourned, they vowed that their first duty as members of the working class movement was to get drunk in the lower class *pulquerías* with the masses, but only in those decorated with mural paintings.

As Secretary General, Siqueiros was assigned to draft a manifesto. Aided by Graciela, he wrote an appeal addressed to the

> native peoples humiliated for so many centuries, to
> soldiers who have been transformed into butchers by
> their officers, to workers and peasants treated with the
> whip of the rich, and to the intellectuals who do not
> flatter the bourgeoisie.

Next he called for the socialization of art and declared that the art of the Mexican people is "our greatest treasure. Great because it belongs collectively to the people and this is why our fundamental aesthetic goal must be to socialize artistic expression and wipe out bourgeois individualism." We also

> repudiate so-called easel painting and all the art
> of the ultra-intellectual circles because it is aristocratic
> and we glorify the expression of monumental art,
> because it is public property. We proclaim that in
> this time of social change from a decadent society
> to a new one, the creators of beauty should apply
> their greatest energies to works of ideological value
> for the people, so that the final goal of art, which
> is now the expression of individual masturbation,
> should become a figurative, educative art for everyone.

Although the manifesto emphasized native values and serving the masses, it declared that those values should be linked with the international currents of modern art and be aesthetically and technically sound. Finally, it called for replacing egocentrism with disciplined collective work, the development of apprenticeships, and the formation of cooperatives which would guarantee work for everyone. After members of the Syndicate signed the manifesto, a delegation of artists presented themselves to the Minister of Education and a nervous Secretary General stammered out their demands to an amused Vasconcelos.

The manifesto was not just a declaration of their views on art but was linked directly to recent political developments. In 1923 Adolfo de la Huerta, former President and cabinet minister, led a revolt against Obregón's selection of General Calles to succeed him. Opposing the revolt as counter-revolutionary, the Syndicate gave its support to Obregón and Calles. The artists viewed the revolt as a bourgeois reaction to the Revolution which threatened their new aesthetic, and the manifesto predicted that, if the revolt succeeded, there would be a return to "the sugary taste of the bourgeoisie" and the reign of the cute or picturesque in art, music, and literature. Some of the artists also volunteered to join the army to fight against de la Huerta, and when Xavier Guerrero was assigned to purchase weapons, the Syndicate acquired an arsenal of useless antique weapons.

The manifesto's condemnation of pure art was more than just a reaction to the dominant trend in European art. The members of the Syndicate had dedicated themselves to monumental public art with revolutionary and educational objectives. It would not be an elite form of art but a movement directly serving and reflecting the needs and hopes of the working class.

By forming a syndicate which included workers, that is masons and assistants, and insisting on equal pay by the hour or for the surface painted, the artists hoped to destroy the individualism and elitism of artists and to identify with the working class movement. They also pledged themselves to collective art projects in which teams of artists would work together on a project. Since their murals were the joint products of masters and apprentices and subject to criticism by all members of the Syndicate, they also agreed not to sign their work.

The ideal of collective art, however, remained an illusion. The movement was divided from the start by personal, political and aesthetic differences and the artists frequently criticized each other's murals. Although he was a member of the Syndicate, Orozco refused to attend the first meetings because of a personal feud with Rivera. When an old woman, a veteran of the Revolution, suggested that they expel anyone who had a drop of Spanish blood, Orozco declared that she had the same dumb ideas as Rivera. Since Vasconcelos also treated them as individual artists, their only weapon was to withhold their nonessential services.

Although they could agree on the importance of murals or public art, they disagreed on the content of their projects and were soon split into several different factions. The final blow came when Siqueiros and Orozco were discharged from their murals in the Preparatoria and the members of the Syndicate failed to close ranks behind them. When Rivera continued to receive commissions, as well as most of the attention and acclaim, the envy and resentment of his success further divided them.

As the Secretary General, Siqueiros became the spokesperson for the Syndicate and immersed himself in its activities. Anita Brenner, an American writer living in Mexico and one of the chroniclers of the early phases of the mural movement, described him as "the romp and playboy of the Syndicate," bursting with enthusiasm, energy and ideas, none of which he ever questioned. Dressed in blue overalls and covered with paint and ink, he painted, wrote and spoke with eloquence and gusto, thoroughly enjoying himself and mixing play with his work. Occasionally he rested, sprawling on a pile of newspapers and sketches on the floor, a coat rolled up under his head. A few hours later he was attending another strike meeting.

Another American observer, the author Bertram Wolfe, described Siqueiros as "mercurial, high strung, eloquent, bombastic, eager to exhibit himself, trembling with excitement at each of his new enthusiasms" and rushing from one activity to another. He was "aggressively virile,... his cheeks permanently puffed out by a constant stream of his voluble enthusiasms."

Siqueiros also managed to make his wife jealous and more than once Gachita reproached him angrily for his infidelity. A masterful storyteller, charming, and "guilelessly pretty, of baby-fine white skin, with an exaggerated cupid's bow mouth, silky dark hair and deeply fringed, fresh green eyes," he was attractive to the opposite sex. He also had a roving eye, and when Gachita caught him flirting with another woman, she grabbed a knife and threatened to cut out his wandering eyes. Retreating, he protested his innocence and promised to be faithful.

Siqueiros was the mainspring of the Syndicate and, when he left Mexico City in 1925, the Syndicate collapsed, never to be revived. In spite of its short life, the ideas of the Syndicate outlived it, and the manifesto, along with Siqueiros's Barcelona manifesto, provided the ideological basis of the Mexican Mural Movement in its formative years. While some members felt that the Syndicate served only to divide the artists, Siqueiros always maintained that it was a "guild-like organization, which provided an organization and ideological platform, often a very romantic one, to our painting movement." He also insisted that it did not try to enforce a uniformity of style or subject matter, and the only thing the first murals had in common was the artists' insistence on freedom of expression, technical experimentation, and the search for a new art form.

Although he agreed that the manifesto accurately reflected the ideology of the movement, Orozco felt that the Syndicate only provided a rallying point for the socialist doctrines of Rivera, Siqueros and Guerrero. As for their plans for "proletarian art," Orozco pointed out that a worker who has spent 12 hours in a factory does not want to come home to a house decorated with pictures of men working in factories. It was the bourgeoisie, he pointed out, who bought all the "proletarian art" at fancy prices, while the workers preferred cheap calendar art of the upper classes amusing themselves.

"Why," he also asked, "paint for the people? They make their own art" and he protested the portrayal of Indians as members of the proletariat, since most of them were not and were unaware that they had become subjects for Mexican artists. He also objected to the rejection of easel painting and the emphasis on content in art, because it would reduce art to mere illustration or photographic reproduction.

Immersed in his union duties, Siqueiros worked intermittently on his murals in the Preparatory School. But one morning, when he arrived at the school to work on his mural, he found that the doors were locked and all of the students were gathered outside. Summoned by employees of the Ministry of Education, he went around the corner to the office of Vasconcelos. As soon as he entered the office, Vasconcelos declared that he would not tolerate any more disturbances and, as head of the Syndicate, he should do something.

A surprised Siqueiros was then taken to the window, from which he could see Fermín Revueltas sitting on the balcony of the school across the street, brandishing a large pistol. Entering the school early, Fermín had taken it over and locked all the doors and he refused to surrender until he was paid what the government owed him. Since Fermin was "the armed guard" of the Syndicate and David knew that he would shoot it out with the police before surrendering, he persuaded Vasconcelos to pay him. Taking the 250 pesos of back pay, Siqueiros returned to the school and to the applause of the students, turned the money over to Fermín. Adjourning to a nearby cantina, they spent the rest of the day getting drunk on Fermin's back pay.

As Secretary General of the Syndicate, Siqueiros also had to resolve conflicts between artists. When Rivera discharged Amado de la Cueva and Jean Charlot from the team of artists working on his new murals in the Ministry of Education, they appealed to Siqueiros. At the project he found Diego working on the scaffold, his back to him and a pistol strapped to his waist.

When he informed Rivera of the purpose of his visit, Rivera snapped back and refused to discuss the matter. Mustering reinforcements, Siqueiros managed to persuade Diego to stop work and come down. Although they discussed the dismissal of the two artists, Charlot and de la Cueva were not only discharged from the project, but Rivera also had their frescos removed because their contrasting styles destroyed the continuity of his murals in the courtyard of the Ministry. When the syndicate protested the attacks on the murals in the Preparatoria, Rivera disagreed and resigned from the union.

In order to express their views on art as well as politics, the members of the Syndicate decided to publish a weekly paper. Through its pages, they would be able to promote their aesthetic and political views as well as to communicate more effectively with the masses. After agreeing on the name *El Machete*, they discussed the purpose of this tool and agreed that it was used to harvest crops, clear paths, kill snakes and make revolutions. Graciela then composed a poem which graced the fronticepiece under a woodcut of a machete done by her husband. It proclaimed that:

> The machete serves to harvest cane
> To open paths through wild forests
> To kill snakes and mow down weeds
> And to humble the arrogance of the godless rich.

While David provided the general political orientation and contributed articles or illustrations, it was Gachita who edited the articles and composed most of the ballads and poems which were a major feature of the publication. She was the heart of *El Machete* and it would not have survived without her. She was also actively involved in the Syndicate and the Communist Party and shared the work, hardships and dangers of these anti-government activities along with her husband.

There was a long history of this type of publication in Mexico and *El Machete* was preceded by a host of political papers published by different groups or individuals opposing the government. They bore descriptive titles like *The Scorpion, The Shark, The Tickler, The Whip, The Gut Grater, and The Devil's Lantern*. In style and format, *El Machete* also resembled the pamphlets which Posada had illustrated with his engravings before the Revolution.

Like their murals, *El Machete* was "public art," readily accessible and comprehensible to the masses. Its front page, with its bold masthead and red and black print, was very striking and made an effective propaganda organ when posted on walls or handed out in working class neighborhoods. It was illustrated with crude woodcuts by Xavier Guerrero and Siqueiros or devastating ink drawings contributed by Orozco. Although they were primitive and often smudged or uneven, these illustrations competed effectively with the headlines in red and black and the printed text explained the illustrations.

While Graciela edited articles and composed ballads or poems, Guerrero and Siqueiros wrote and illustrated articles and Jorge Pino Sandoval folded, bundled and helped to deliver the paper. Since red ink was more expensive and they had to pay for the printing and the ink, Graciela composed a short rhyme to raise money, "For that heavenly red to stay, pay!" After it was printed, Guerrero and Siqueiros would take copies of the paper, brushes and a pot of glue and paste it on street corners early in the morning before workers got up and went to work.

As the official organ of the Syndicate of Revolutionary Painters, Sculptors and Technical Workers, *El Machete* published articles on the purpose and work of that organization. For its first issue, Siqueiros wrote an article on the importance of the Syndicate and chastised the writers and intellectuals of Mexico and Latin America as servile and ignorant of their own race, land and people. "Painters and sculptors must be craftsmen at the service of the people," he wrote. Members of the syndicate have "united themselves in a communist movement for creating art and carrying out work of social importance." He also attacked the school system for the indifference and hostility of the students towards their art. How, he asked, can Mexican students be so reactionary after the progressive role of the student generation of the Mexican Revolution?

The same issue also featured the first part of a farce, "The Fall of the Rich and the Building of a New Social Order" by David and Graciela Alfaro Siqueiros. In the prologue, called "The Trinity of

Scoundrels," a Mexican politician, a European capitalist, an Anglo-American imperialist, and a reporter react to the protests and arming of the workers, peasants and soldiers. After the defeat of this group, an invisible worker exhorts the masses to kill the false apostles and to adopt communism, which is "practical Christianity."

Another act of this farce appeared in April, entitled "To the Soldiers, Workers and Peasants." It was illustrated by a woodcut by Siqueiros of a worker, a peasant and a soldier bearing the caption, "We three are victims, we three are brothers." Under another woodcut print of a bleeding and kneeling worker, his hands tied behind him, Siqueiros wrote that this is the condition in which the rich industrialists, oil men and landowners want to keep the worker.

On the anniversary of Emiliano Zapata's death, Siqueiros and Orozco dedicated a *corrido* (folk ballad) to him: "The land belongs to the community and its produce to those who work it, the sage advice of Zapata and Montaño." The ballad described the betrayal and assassination of Zapata and ended with a challenge to the survivors, "What have they done since they killed me? What has the Revolution achieved? Have the sacred promises to the poor been forgotten already?" Above the ballad was a woodcut portrait of Zapata by Guerrero surrounded by hammers and sickles.

When an opposition press was attacked and destroyed, David protested the government's inconsistent policy of protecting bourgeois property while ignoring this violation of freedom of the press. "We communists consider freedom of the press more important than freedom of private property," he wrote, and then exhorted students to utilize direct and revolutionary action against the bourgeoisie.

Although Rivera had been expelled from the syndicate several months earlier, Siqueiros, as Secretary General, defended Rivera's "social painting" in *El Machete* and blamed reactionary elements in the Ministry of Public Education for the destruction of the murals in the Preparatoria. We support Rivera, he wrote, as an act of union solidarity and because he is part of our collective work.

El Machete was more than just the mouthpiece of a union of artists and its articles and illustrations covered a wide range of national issues; the nationalization of oil, land reform, labor rights, education and imperialism. But as it moved further to the left and became more strident and anti-government, the muralists were pressured to desist by their official sponsors. When it published an anti-imperialist woodcut by Guerrero, the Ministry of Education withheld Siqueiros's pay and after Orozco drew a caricature mocking President Obregón's alliance with the Catholic Church and Uncle Sam, Guerrero was dismissed from his post in the Ministry of Agriculture.

After the Syndicate folded, *El Machete* became the official organ of the Mexican Communist Party. During its tenure as the paper of the Syndicate it had expressed the aesthetic and political goals of the artists and was probably more effective in communicating with the masses than their murals in the Preparatory School.

For Siqueiros, the experiences of the Syndicate and *El Machete* severed his association with bohemian art and continued the politicizing process initiated by the student strike and his participation in the Revolution. Instead of painting murals for unsympathetic bureaucrats, teachers and students, *El Machete* had taken them into the streets, factories and fields, exposing them to the social problems of the country and giving them a militancy that their murals still lacked. They had also participated actively in union meetings and sat on strike committees, and their exposure to the daily problems of the working class was reflected in their art. Their paper became increasingly militant and identified with the Mexican labor movement. "We came as artists, but in reality we became labor leaders, without ceasing to be artists," Siqueiros later recalled.

After this experience, Orozco returned to the more graphic style of his political cartoons, mocking the bourgeoisie and the clergy, and painting the best murals of this period after a tentative start. In his next project, in the Ministry of Education, Rivera discarded his neo-Byzantine style of the Preparatoria to paint the workers in a victorious struggle against their oppressors, while Siqueiros painted Indians as members of the proletariat and depicted their struggle in *El Machete*.

David not only wrote, drew, printed and distributed *El Machete*, but he also attended workers' meetings and served on strike committees. This intense immersion in the Mexican labor movement further opened his eyes to Marxism. At its second meeting, the Syndicate had adopted a resolution announcing adherence to the Cominterm. Siqueiros, Rivera and Guerrero also joined the Mexican Communist Party and were elected to its Central Committee. When *El Machete* became the official organ of the communist party, David and Graciela continued to contribute articles and illustrations until its suppression by the government in 1929.

From the start the muralists had their share of critics. While some of the criticism focused on the aesthetic qualities of their paintings, the increasing militancy of their murals and public statements provoked an even stronger reaction. Though Rivera received most of the publicity, his murals remained unscathed while those of Orozco and Siqueiros were seriously vandalized. Their work in the Syndicate and *El Machete* also raised a few eyebrows as the articles and illustrations were increasingly anti-government.

Their patron Vasconcelos was also attacked for wasting money on "ugly art" and the earlier enthusiasm of the Obregón government for his educational and cultural programs had waned. Although he gave the artists free rein and continued to support them despite public criticism, Vasconcelos did not appreciate what the artists were trying to do and later expressed regrets about the very movement he had launched. He was also becoming exasperated with Orozco and Siqueiros, who either destroyed their frescos as soon as they painted them or were frequently absent from their projects. Nevertheless, when his decision to hire Rivera to paint a mural in the Ministry of Education stirred up more protests, the Syndicate came to Vasconcelos's defense.

Vasconcelos also entertained presidential ambitions and expected to succeed Obregón. Instead Obregón chose General Plutarco Elías Calles to succeed him in the presidency. When former President and cabinet minister Adolfo de la Huerta led an armed revolt against the government, Obregón assumed command of the military campaign against the *delahuertistas*, while Calles campaigned for the presidency. When the revolt was crushed, Calles's election was guaranteed and Vasconcelos's days were numbered. Since he had opposed Calles, he knew that he would not be reappointed and submitted his resignation to Obregón.

Another casualty of the succession struggle was General Manuel Diéguez, Siqueiros's commander in the Revolution. He had also taken up arms against Obregón and was captured and executed by government troops. Although he had settled down to the life of a gentleman farmer, in 1923 Pancho Villa was ambushed and killed while he was riding through the town of Parral with his bodyguards.

Reflecting this turn of events, Vasconcelos's replacement, Puig Casauranc, was less sympathetic and less tolerant of the artists and he immediately proceeded to terminate many of the mural projects. Members of the Syndicate were warned that if they continued to publish articles critical of the government, their contracts would be cancelled. When the artists met to discuss this threat, they split into three factions. Charlot and some others decided to paint at any cost, including the suspension of *El Machete*. Orozco declared that if politics prevented him from painting murals in Mexico, he would abandon politics and seek opportunities in the United States. Rufino Tamayo, Rodriguez Lozano and Miguel Castellanos also decided to leave Mexico.

The majority, however, led by Siqueiros, insisted that if the government took away their walls, they would "make mobile murals from the pages of *El Machete*." They would not only continue its publication, but they would also improve the quality of its graphics. Refusing to accept the will of the majority, Rivera declared that he would continue to paint murals. Since they had not yet created the new society and he was a mural painter, he declared that he would paint murals attacking the enemy on its own territory. When Diego received new commissions from the government and refused to come to the aid of the other artists, the breach within the Syndicate widened. Siqueiros accused him of opportunism and the next issue of *El Machete* reported that Rivera had been expelled from the Syndicate.

While the movement had been fragmented from the start, the confrontation with the government over *El Machete* further divided the Syndicate and brought about its demise in less than a year after its enthusiastic pronouncement. Meanwhile, the new Minister of Education informed Orozco and Siqueiros that their contracts had been canceled and they were expelled from their half-finished murals in the Preparatory School. Although his discharge from the project was not unexpected, David was surprised to receive a bill from the government saying that he owed money for not completing his murals. In a letter to the Minister of Education, published in *El Machete*, he protested his termination as an attack on freedom of thought and professional rights.

With his dismissal, the mural painting career of David Alfaro Siqueiros was suspended. Although Orozco returned in 1926 to finish his unfinished frescos and painted a series of powerful statements about Mexican history and the Revolution on three levels of one side of the central patio of the Preparatoria, Siqueiros never returned to finish his first experiments in mural painting. They remain unfinished in the dark stairway, showing the scars of vandalism and age.

Even before his discharge Siqueiros had entertained doubts about the efficacy of art in a poor and ideologically underdeveloped country. Following his dismissal, he declared that if art was so little appreciated in Mexico that a painter could not hold a job like a plumber, he personally felt useless in that profession and would not try to survive as some "salon clown." The choice was between painting canvases for the bourgeoisie or joining the proletarian movement and he preferred the latter. Lacking any prospects in the capital, therefore, he accepted an invitation to go to Guadalajara from José Guadalupe Zuno, now Governor of Jalisco.

Leaving behind three unfinished and badly damaged walls, an obscure ceiling, plus many sketches and some paintings, most of them also unfinished, he and Graciela took the train for Guadalajara. Despite this unimpressive inventory, he had developed a strong personal style and explored some important theories of art in his first mural project. The experience of the Syndicate and *El Machete* had helped him to formulate his political views as well as to develop a theoretical basis for modern Mexican art. Although he was highly critical of his own work and discouraged by the slow progress of the mural movement, he would later boast, "there has never been a collective movement equal to that realized by the painters and engravers of Mexico at any time in any part of the world."

In spite of his short-lived tenure, Vasconcelos had provided the impetus and official sponsorship for the first stage of the Mexican cultural renaissance and the mural movement. Unwittingly, he had unleashed a movement which was in conflict with his intentions and personal tastes. Whereas he had thought in terms of a classical revival with artists rendering traditional interpretations of classical themes or subject matter, many of the artists were committed to a collective form of art, revolutionary in technique and content, and executed by teams of artists.

To his credit, Vasconcelos had not only launched a program of mural art subsidized by the government, but he had also left the subject matter and interpretation up to the artists. And as long as he was in the Ministry, he defended the artists against their critics and it was under his auspices that the first modern painted walls of Mexico became a reality.

Orozco later paid tribute to Vasconcelos as the "first among... revolutionary...statesmen." Siqueiros also recognized his role, but added, "We forced him to tolerate us. He hated our murals as soon as he saw them" and they had soon realized that his classical ideas were not capable of inspiring the masses. An ungrateful Rivera painted his former patron as a dwarf riding on a white elephant on the very walls of the Education Ministry.

Perhaps the artists would have been more charitable if they had known what was to follow. His successor, Puig Casauranc, immediately cut the budget for the fine arts and the new head of the Department of Fine Arts accepted his appointment with the statement, "The first thing that I'll do is to whitewash those horrible frescos."

The fate of Siqueiros and his fellow muralists was the result of their radicalization just as the government was moving toward the right. Although Obregón had supported Vasconcelos's cultural and educational efforts and had defended the artists against their critics, their increasing militancy had become an irritating nuisance. The outburst of revolutionary enthusiasm that accompanied his inauguration was waning, and the President had to cope with the real problems of internal stability, presidential succession and tense relations with the United States.

The revolutionary Left found itself increasingly at odds with the government and continued its agitation for revolutionary change. It attacked the domination and corruption of the labor movement, the slow pace of land reform, the growing influence of the United States and the postponement of the nationalization of oil. Further politicized by his recent experiences and despairing of new commissions, Siqueiros abandoned the capital for Guadalajara, where he forsook mural painting for a more precarious occupation.

V. Labor Leader

After Calles succeeded Obregón in the presidency, more than mural contracts were cancelled. In 1925 Calles tried to restrict the leases of the foreign oil companies, but the United States accused him of violating agreements signed by his predecessor and he was forced to postpone one of the major goals of the Revolution. Although Calles redistributed more land than Obregón, it mainly benefited large and medium size property owners and did not address the needs of thousands of landless peasants. Meanwhile, efforts to organize workers into independent unions were blocked by the government controlled Regional Confederation of Mexican Labor (CROM).

When Calles decided to enforce the anti-clerical provisions of the 1917 Constitution, the Catholic clergy declared a strike and a full-scale war broke out between the *cristeros* and the government. For three years central and western Mexico were torn by a civil war. Preoccupied with the *cristeros* and delicate relations with the United States, Calles had little time or resources for revolutionary programs and found himself under attack by an increasingly militant Left for not carrying out the goals of the Revolution.

Although they were warned to desist or forfeit their mural contracts, the more militant members of the artists' syndicate continued their attacks on the government. When the government withdrew its patronage, the mural movement, already weakened by internal divisions, all but disappeared. Only Rivera, Montenegro and Máximo Pacheco received new commissions, while the other artists sought a more lucrative market in United States or found other employment.

Before he left Mexico City for Guadalajara, Siqueiros participated in a number of protests against the "counter-revolutionary" policies of the government and United States imperialism. When he arrived in Guadalajara in 1925, he was ready to participate in a revival of mural painting. José Guadalupe Zuno, an artist, former classmate and comrade from the Revolution, was Governor of Jalisco and had invited Amado de la Cueva, Carlos Orozco Romero, Xavier Guerrero, Siqueiros, and other artists to assist in the decoration of the new state university and capital buildings. Although they organized an "Alliance of Painter-Workers," their efforts to revive the mural movement were preempted.

Meanwhile, Siqueiros and Amado de la Cueva were assigned to decorate the Workers' Assembly Hall at the University, formerly a Jesuit college. Like Siqueiros, Amado had been enticed back from Europe by Vasconcelos and had assisted Rivera on his first mural. Working along side Charlot and Guerrero, he had painted two frescos in the Ministry of Education, but when Rivera complained that their panels clashed with his, they were dismissed from the project and their frescos were removed to make way for his own paintings. Amado then returned to his native Guadalajara and painted three murals in the Government Palace.

From the start Siqueiros insisted that he work as an assistant to Amado, but only for an eight-hour day, since he had joined the union of house painters and masons and had union duties to fulfill. He was also engaged in designing some doors and furniture for a new Governor's mansion and drawing plans for a new market which was never built.

After Amado created some stylized designs of working men, plows, machetes and a soldier guarding the crops for the University meeting hall, the two of them began to paint them in red and black tones on the walls. Over the main entrance Amado painted Zapata flanked by two farmers, while they covered the side walls with products and the workers who produced them, a potterer, miner, weaver, etc.. On the ceiling of the vault they painted clusters of five pointed red stars and the clasping hands of the workers. Although it was more decoration than mural painting, it was unified ideologically and stylistically.

On the first of April the scaffolding was taken down and Amado, known as the "Black Devil" because of his taste for black clothing and daredevil rides on his motorcycle, decided to celebrate. Speeding through town with one of his assistants, he lost control, ran into a car and was killed.

Several months later, Zuno was overthrown as Governor, a casualty of the Cristero Rebellion. Again out of work, David immersed himself in the struggle of the workers and their attempts to organize independent unions. He had already joined a union and had worked with the textile workers and miners in and around Guadalajara. Now he began to organize the miners at "Cinco Minas," "La Mazata," "Piedra Bola," "El Amparo" and other mines. Despite government and company harassment, he managed to organize several independent unions and led them in successful strikes against the American owned companies.

In order to counteract the independent unions, the foreign companies, with the support of the clergy and the government controlled CROM, organized their own syndicates or "white unions," thereby splitting the workers and controlling the "loyal workers." Federal troops were employed to protect these company unions affiliated with the CROM and to break up the meetings and strikes of the independent unions.

Seeing how the "red" and "white" unions fought each other rather than management, Siqueiros became convinced that the workers should organize their own unions and form one large confederation of independent unions. Then they would be able to confront management and combat imperialism and a reactionary government, he argued. Focusing his efforts on the creation of a national confederation, he was instrumental in organizing the National Revolutionary Federation of Miners which elected him president. He also became the Secretary General of the Workers' Confederation of Jalisco and served briefly as the Secretary General of the Communist Party of Mexico.

This exposure to the lives of the workers and their culture had a lasting impact on Siqueiros's political views, as well as on his art.

Since most of his organizing efforts were among the miners, he saw the deplorable conditions under which they lived and worked and the ravages of silicosis. This disease of the lungs incapacitated young men, turning them into weak old men after a few years in the mines and drastically shortening their lives. When the men could no longer work or died in cave-ins, their families often lost their homes and credit. Meanwhile, the government refused to interfere and tried to prevent them from organizing their own unions or mounting strikes against the companies.

As an independent union leader, therefore, he was not only battling the owners of the mines but also the company unions, the representatives of the CROM and the government itself, and he frequently found himself under attack or behind bars in the states of Jalisco, Colima, Chihuahua and the Federal District. Nevertheless, he was full of energy and dashed from mine to meeting hall on an old bicycle, dressed in overalls and an old sweater, its sleeves and pockets full of holes. It didn't matter, he explained, since he was merely a craftsman out of work and had nothing to put in the pockets.

In its October 1926 issue of *El Machete*, the Mexican Communist Party announced the publication of a new periodical, *El Martillo* (The Hammer), and invited comrades to submit articles for publication to David A. Siqueiros in Guadalajara, Secretary General of the Workers' Confederation of Jalisco. The same issue of *El Machete* also featured a poem to a dead worker in Chicago by Graciela Amador. The following year *El Machete* hailed the appearance of another paper, *El 130*, named after that article of the Constitution, founded and edited by David A. Siqueiros.

Although David and Graciela were the editors of these publications, they were union papers and were written and illustrated entirely by the workers. The articles described their problems and conditions and expressed their views on national or international issues, while the illustrations reflected the *retablos* or *exvoto* paintings of their village churches.

Since leaving Mexico City, Siqueiros had assisted in the painting of a mural, organized miners into unions, led several successful strikes, founded and served as the leader of two workers' confederations and established and assumed the direction of two working-class newspapers. Graciela was always at his side and shared all the vicissitudes of his new career, attending clandestine meetings, taking notes, writing articles and editing and publishing the union papers. She traveled with him from mine to mine and meeting hall to meeting hall, often as the only female, and faced the same threats and attacks as her husband. Together they experienced the assaults on the miners' meetings and escaped the bullets of the *cristeros* or goons hired by the company unions. She was, to quote her husband, "the perfect example of the loyal comrade of a revolutionary."

For David, it was an exciting phase of his life, full of adventures and unforgettable characters about whom he often reminisced. One of his favorite characters was Don Macario Huizar, a union deputy from the mine of "La Mazata." A large blue-eyed blond with a grand mustache, Don Macario was a colorful figure who reminded David of his grandfather. When he was accused of having committed a number of crimes by a representative of the Amparo Mining Company, including the wounding of a draughtsman, Macario pleaded guilty. "It was very simple," Macario explained, "I was making love to his wife. If I had not shot him, he would have killed both of us and that would have been an even greater tragedy." Siquieiros learned later that his friend had been killed by *cristeros*.

Throughout 1927 David and Graciela participated in a number of activities, including a celebration of the Tenth Anniversary of the Russian Revolution and protests against U.S. intervention in Nicaragua against Sandino. Because of these activities, as well as his effectiveness as a labor leader, Siqueiros was hounded by the police and detained so that he could not attend meetings or visit the miners where they worked. Government agents also penetrated the Confederation of Miners and removed the Executive Committee led by Siqueiros. When they accused him of misusing union funds, he protested that he had frequently used his own money to pay the expenses of the organizations which he represented. He was not only exonerated and reinstated as Secretary General, but the investigating committee concluded that the unions which he had organized had waged successful strikes and obtained the most satisfactory contracts in the state, if not in all of Mexico.

When "Siete Filhos" died in 1927, David was deeply moved by the loss. Although he idealized his mother and her family, he had spent most of his formative years under the influence of his paternal grandfather. No other person had meant as much to him or had as great an impact on his life, and he always cherished his memories of Antonio.

In 1928 David was chosen to head the Mexican delegation to the Fourth Congress of the International Red Syndicate in Moscow, and he and Graciela sailed for Europe with the rest of the Mexican delegation. In Russia their hosts were impressed by the good manners of the Mexican delegation and were convinced that they were intellectuals, not workers. Through a translator, David explained that these characteristics were derived from Mexico's Indian heritage. Unfortunately, he added, it was the intellectuals who tried to imitate the proletariat and created bad impressions by adopting crude language and bad manners.

Diego Rivera was also in Moscow, having arrived the year before for the Tenth Anniversary of the October Revolution. Whereas David had traveled to Russia as a representative of Mexican workers, Diego had been received as a great artist and honored guest. Since the issue of a new art for the people had not yet been resolved and Rivera was the best known figure in a movement which had addressed the problem, he was greeted warmly by the regime and invited to demonstrate his theories of socialist art.

But Diego had arrived during the leadership struggle between Stalin and Trotsky and the ideological split over "socialism in one country" and "the permanent revolution." In December of 1927, the 15th All Union Congress of the Communist Party condemned any deviation from the Stalinist position and Trotsky and his followers were expelled from the party and banished to the provinces. A year later Trotsky was expelled from the Soviet Union.

Diego not only disagreed with the Stalinist position of "socialism in one country," but he also criticized the false realism and academicism of Soviet art and called for an "October revolution" in the field of culture. Stalin agreed that there should also be a revolution in culture, but he had not proposed any new direction for Soviet art and pointed out that Christian art had continued to use the forms of pagan art for 12 or 13 centuries after the birth of Christ. Disappointed by this response, Diego began to side openly with the Trotskyites in the workers' congress.

When the congress was over, Diego was summoned abruptly to Mexico by the Mexican Communist Party under the pretext that he was needed for its approaching presidential campaign. Although he had been commissioned to paint a series of frescos in the Red Army Club, the project was cancelled and he returned to Mexico with some oil paintings and watercolors he had done of the May Day celebrations in Moscow.

David and Graciela left Russia at the same time and shared a cabin with Diego on the trip back to Mexico. But throughout the voyage they engaged in heated discussions, calling each other names and arguing loudly over their political positions. When it became too unpleasant, they switched cabins and refused to speak to each other. After several days, however, they agreed not to discuss politics for the rest of the trip and they shared the first prize for their outlandish costumes during the rites of the middle passage.

Their arrival in Veracruz was hailed by *El Machete*, which ran several photographs of Diego, David and Graciela together and announced that David and Graciela would deliver a series of talks on the Soviet Union, "Where the workers and peasants govern." A short time later Diego was appointed Director of the National School of Fine Arts from which he had been expelled 25 years earlier. Although his tenure as Director was turbulent and short-lived, he was clearly in the good graces of the government and it was suggested that a special cabinet position be created for him. He was also invited to paint a series of murals in the National Palace, and while he was working on this massive project, the American ambassador hired him to paint a mural in the Cortés Palace in Cuernavaca.

Although he continued to be active in the Communist Party, Diego's support of Trotsky was unacceptable to the Central Committee and he was expelled from the Party. During the session of the Central Committee which reached this decision, Diego accused himself of working for the petit bourgeois government and voted for his own expulsion, declaring that he could not be a member of an "official Stalinist party."

However, Diego defended himself by pointing out that he had been a faithful and active member of the Party and had participated in the establishment of a confederation uniting communist trade unions. Instead of dividing the working class into communist versus non-communist unions, he had worked to unite them and he opposed the Stalinist belief that the capitalist countries would be converted to communism before they attacked the Soviet Union. He insisted that his expulsion from the Party was unjustified and was the result of the insistence of Manuilksy, a Stalinist agent in Mexico, that he Rivera, was a Trotskyite. He had also been expelled, he claimed, because he had painted a portrait of Felipe Carrillo Puerto, martyred communist Governor of Yucatan, in the Ministry of Education.

Although his expulsion was undoubtedly motivated by his alignment with Trotsky, Diego was also receiving commissions from a reactionary government which was persecuting the Party. Moreover, he was always late to meetings and, when he arrived, he tended to dominate the discussions and could not conform to party discipline, the cardinal sin.

While Siqueiros had accused Diego of disloyalty and opportunism and voted for his expulsion, he always suspected that Diego had manipulated the whole affair. He had not only voted for his own expulsion, but the document against him had been written by the American Marxist Bertram Wolfe, who later wrote an adulatory biography of Diego in which he condemned the other Mexican artists who had remained loyal to the party line.

The differences between Rivera and Siqueiros were not just political. While Diego introduced some reforms as director of the art academy, Siqueiros accused him of not taking advantage of the opportunity to introduce the ideas of art instruction and collective art workshops which they had discussed in Paris. The students must learn by doing, he argued, and not by studying art in an academic setting. The government should assign mural contracts to established artists, and the students would learn the art of mural painting by working on a mural project under these master artists.

David also attacked Diego as the "official painter" of an increasingly reactionary government and for painting a mural for the American ambassador when Yankee imperialism was penetrating Mexico and undermining the Revolution. The quality of his art also suffered, he opined, becoming more picturesque and folkloric and creating a superficial nationalism which replaced political content and supported the official demagoguery. By hiring a Marxist painter who paints hammer and sickles in government buildings, the government can hide its repression and appear liberal, he charged.

While Rivera accused other artists of being romantic and idealistic, Siqueiros continued, he painted workers and peasants with weapons in their hands and confident of their victory at the same time that his patron, the government of Calles, was becoming less revolutionary and more repressive. These murals did not compel the government to change its policies and they were located in buildings where the masses would never see them. While his murals in the National Palace and Cuernavaca depicted imperialism, it was that of the Spaniards in the 16th century and made only vague references to the contemporary reality of increasing American intervention in Mexico and the betrayal of the Revolution.

Meanwhile, Siqueiros added, mural painting in Mexico had become the exclusive monopoly of Rivera and other artists have been forced to become teachers of art or return to easel painting. Orozco, he pointed out, had to leave for the United States while other artists paint picturesque scenes of Mexican daily life or abstract studies devoid of content for the new art galleries catering to wealthy tourists and foreign collectors.

In 1928 President Calles arranged the re-election of Obregón and increased the four-year presidential term to six years. Although there was armed opposition to this violation of the principle of "no-re-election," the rebellious generals were captured and executed and Obregón was re-elected. Before he could take office, however, Obregón was assassinated by a religious fanatic. While three "puppet presidents" held office, Calles remained the power behind the throne. Late in 1928 he created the National Revolutionary Party (PNR), the antecedent of the Partido Institucional Revolucionario (PRI), through which he controlled Mexico until 1935, and which has monopolized Mexican politics through 2000.

By 1929 Mexico was exhausted by almost two decades of civil war or uprisings, and most of the revolutionary leaders had been killed. In their stead, new leaders were emerging, men without the same commitments to change and seeking to exploit their new status. Opportunities for graft abounded and the revolutionary generals and union leaders became influence peddlers and opportunistic entrepreneurs. Corruption was more blatant than usual and the street on which government and union officials had homes in Cuernavaca became known as "the street of Ali Baba and the forty thieves."

The stock market crash and depression further aggravated this situation, undermining an already weak economy and worsening the conditions of the working class. Fearful of jeopardizing the economy or provoking United States intervention, the new elite did not encourage reform. Meanwhile, the Left, inspired by the survival of the revolution in Russia and concluding that the economic crisis spelled the end of capitalism, increased its efforts to unite the working class in the final struggle against the bourgeoisie.

After his return from Moscow, Siqueiros returned to Guadalajara and threw himself into this struggle. He joined the Bakers' Union and was elected to its Central Committee. At the Convention of the Workers Confederation of Jalisco, his proposal for a national congress to unify the union movement and to send a delegation to the Syndical Congress in Montevideo, Uruguay later that year were adopted. A short time later he joined the Committee for a National Workers and Peasants Assembly and participated in a convention to discuss a new Workers Code proposed by interim President Emilio Portes Gil.

Elected Secretary of the Convention, Siqueiros responded to statements made by the President and Lombardo Toledano, who represented the labor organizations controlled by the CROM. Defiant and gesturing dramatically, he reminded his audience that the workers and peasants had suffered tremendous losses during the Revolution and that eleven years after the writing of the Constitution, their conditions had not improved. Although he supported Article 123 of the Constitution, Mexico's "Bill of rights for labor," he condemned the proposed labor code as fascist.

After accusing the President of repressing the organization of the workers and peasants in a united syndicalist movement, Siqueiros urged the workers and peasants to oppose this tactic and the leaders who had betrayed them. In conclusion, he proclaimed that the class struggle would continue until the establishment of "socialism and the destruction of capitalism" and the achievement of "new victories for the working class."

In an address to the Ninth Convention of CROM, Siqueiros proposed a pact of solidarity to end the mortal divisions which had hurt the working class and blasted the so-called representatives of the Mexican Revolution as "the new rich of Mexico, the new *latifundistas* (large landowners), the new industrialists, the new landlords."

When a National Assembly for the Unification of Workers and Peasants met in January 1929 and formed the United Syndical Confederation of Mexico (CSUM), it elected Siqueiros Secretary General. Declaring its opposition to the Federal Code of Labor proposed by the President, the CSUM attacked the Pan-American Confederation of Labor as an instrument of Yankee imperialism. It also vowed its support for the efforts to eliminate bossism and bureaucracy within the labor movement and allied itself with the anti-imperialist struggle of Sandino in Nicaragua. As Secretary General, Siqueiros wrote or signed a series of documents and manifestos which protested government support of American companies against the miners and accused local officials of arresting, deporting and killing labor leaders.

Mexico was still torn by political turmoil, and after the assassination of Obregón, there were frequent reports of political intrigues or rebellions by military chiefs. The *cristeros* continued to terrorize parts of the country while the conflict between the "red" and "white" unions approached a state of open warfare and a number of union leaders were arrested or assassinated. Members of CSUM were harassed by state and federal authorities, accused of being in the service of a foreign power and faced death threats, arrest or deportation from Jalisco.

On the first of May 1929 Siqueiros issued a statement to the workers and peasants, proclaiming "a new epoch" for Mexican workers and calling for a day of protest against a government which represses workers and capitulates to imperialism and the national bourgeoisie. Later that month he traveled alone to Montevideo as the representative of CSUM in the Latin American Syndicalist Congress. While most of the discussions focused on defending the Soviet Union against external aggression, David frequently interjected and proposed resolutions for unifying the labor movement in Latin America. When a Latin American Syndicalist Confederation was established, he was elected to its General Council.

From Montevideo he sent telegrams to President Calles condemning the murder of two labor leaders in the state of Durango and the government's surrender to Yankee imperialism. The murder of two comrades, he wrote, was the direct result of the government's surrender to foreign interests and constituted a betrayal of the workers' revolution.

In Montevideo, David also met a beautiful Uruguayan journalist and poet, Blanca Luz Brum. She was from a prominent family and her uncle was President of the country. Faced with a barracks revolt, however, he committed suicide rather than surrender to the military. Talented, restless and high-spirited, Blanca was a good match for David and they became passionate lovers.

Since the Second Latin American Communist Congress was being held in Buenos Aires, he left for Argentina with Blanca right after the

Syndicalist Congress. Entering the country illegally under the name of Suarez, he participated actively in communist party meetings and at one point, called for an armed insurrection to combat the penetration of imperialism. This rhetoric not only startled many of the delegates but also aroused the Argentine authorities, who promptly arrested and deported him.

Traveling with Blanca and her son by a previous marriage, David arrived back in Mexico. In spite of his disagreements with Rivera, they stayed briefly with Diego and Frida Kahlo, Diego's third wife. Many party members, however, were shocked by his desertion of Graciela, his wife and faithful comrade of eleven years. In their eyes, his relationship with Blanca was also a political betrayal, a suspicion which was reinforced by her political views and his continued friendship with Rivera, a Trotskyite who had been expelled from the Party.

In spite of his betrayal, Graciela was not bitter and they remained friends. Two years after he abandoned her for Blanca, David sought reconciliation and asked for forgiveness. By that time, however, she was involved with another man and had developed an appreciation for the peace and quiet of her life since their separation. Nevertheless, she remained fond of him even after their separation and described him as a generous and amiable companion and a courageous and loyal friend.

Although Graciela later expressed her admiration for his artistic genius, she was grateful that she could admire him from a safe distance and declared that she would never wish on anyone the anguish and misery which she had experienced as his spouse. It had been her fate, she continued, to have lived with a genius whose talent had not yet been discovered. Though she had loved him passionately, their life together had been very difficult. Not only was he restless, impatient, egoistic and prone to self-idolatry, but he insisted that she dedicate herself totally to him and his work, while he was not faithful to her.

Despite his behavior, David always expressed his gratitude and appreciation for Graciela's contributions to his political and union activities and her loyal support through all the hardships and real dangers which their life entailed. He recognized her significant contribution to the struggle through her articles, poems and ballads, as well as her work in editing workers' publications and participation in the independent labor movement. Although they were passionate lovers, no children came from their marriage.

Even though he had dedicated himself to organizing workers after the death of Amado de la Cueva, David had continued to sketch and do woodcuts and was involved in a form of "public art" through *El Martillo* and *El 130*. While very little of his work from this period has survived, he participated in a show of Mexican engravers. Salvador Novo wrote a very favorable review of his prints, though denying that he endorsed the artist's politics. These prints reflected his experiences as a labor organizer and his exposure to the lives of the workers and their art forms. Soon he would be able to paint on a full time basis, though not under the most favorable circumstances.

As the 1920s wound down, the government continued its repression against the Left and its attempts to organize independent unions. In 1929 the Communist Party was suppressed and its offices closed. A number of its leaders were arrested and sentenced to prison and *El Machete* was forced to close shop when its offices were broken into and its presses smashed. The government also expelled two Soviet diplomats for interference in Mexican internal affairs and in 1930, Mexico severed relations with the Soviet Union.

The Party was torn by divisions, and the leadership of the Party and its affiliate, the National Peasants' League, was split over tactics. While some members of the Central Committee opposed Calles, others favored joining the newly organized National Revolutionary Party. The vast majority, however, voted to remain independent and continued to work actively in the Party and the League. When the League held its annual convention in Mexico City in 1930, the divisions widened while the government continued its harassment, searching and disarming members before meetings and stationing police in their meeting halls.

Although Siqueiros continued to participate in some of these activities, he was spending more time and energy on his art. Because of his lessened involvement, therefore, he was replaced as Secretary General of CSUM by Valentín Campa, and at its first national convention, he was expelled not only from the Executive Committee, but also from the confederation altogether.

In February of 1930 there was an attempt on the life of the President-elect Ortiz Rubio on the day of his inauguration. While the evidence pointed to a single assassin, a religious fanatic, the attack provided a convenient pretext for rounding up communists, and Siqueiros found himself in Lecumberri, the federal penitentiary.

Prison, however, had its diversions, unique to Mexico. He had just gone to sleep one night when he heard the faint clanging of doors and was suddenly blinded by a bright light. Through half-opened eyes he saw an army officer and several soldiers standing by the door of his cell. Ordered to get up and come with them, he stumbled to his feet, realizing that his escort were not prison guards or police.

As they walked down the dark corridors of the prison, he wanted to shout out to the other prisoners, the guards, anyone. But torn by fear and ashamed of revealing his terror, he lost his voice. As they left the prison and walked through the dark streets of the city, he remembered his experiences in the Revolution, when prisoners were taken for a short walk before they were shot on the pretext they had tried to escape. At every corner he expected them to offer him a last cigarette before standing him against a wall.

After what seemed like an eternity, they stopped in front of an apartment building and the officer told him to climb the flight of stairs inside. At the first landing, he heard a loud clamor and shouts of men and women coming from a room. Peering inside, David saw a room full of half-naked men and women. As he entered, he was doused by a shower of beer and tequila and an old friend, General Jesús Ferreíra, embraced him and welcomed him as the guest of honor. After Ferreíra explained that another veteran of the Division of the West, the Chief of Police, had loaned him for the evening, David discarded his fears and launched himself into a bacchanal of cognac and beautiful women.

With the first rays of morning, however, the party ended and he learned that his escape was only temporary. Accompanied by a few survivors of the evening, he retraced his steps of the previous night and collapsed on his bunk as the cell doors closed behind him. While the circumstances of his arrest were not unusual, Siqueiros mused, his temporary escape to enjoy an orgy at the invitation of a friend of the Chief of Police could occur in only one country–Mexico.

Although he was soon released, a few months later he was back in jail. On the first of May he participated in a demonstration which culminated in a violent confrontation with the police in front of the American Embassy. Arrested along with other demonstrators, he was again taken to Lecumberri, where he was held until December. Besides frequent beatings from the guards, many of which he brought on himself for his open defiance, he froze at night and sometimes received his food in his sweater or bare hands held under the cell door.

He also suffered from his concern for Blanca. He was separated from her and she had no means of support for herself and her son. She did not understand Mexico and had come to fear and hate his countrymen. Seeing the violence around her, she thought that all Mexicans were homicidal and, when she visited David in prison, she expressed her fears and reproached him for abandoning her in such a hostile place.

In her letters to him, fragments of which she later published in a book, *Penitenciara-niño perdido,* the name of the bus which she took every day to the prison, Blanca protested that she and her son were dying of starvation and that none of his friends, former comrades-in-arms or government officials, would lend a hand. She also expressed her concern for his discomfort but exhorted him to remain steadfast and praised him for his revolutionary struggle. In one of her notes she compared his nose to that of the ancient Mayan kings and praised his sensitive and generous capacities. Although they were a source of moral support, her references to their intimacies and his friends were also painful reminders of their separation.

Visiting him regularly, Blanca encouraged him to paint and kept him supplied with pencils, brushes and paints. This not only gave him something to do and bolstered his morale, but also gave her something to sell to support herself. She also brought him books and articles to read, mostly the works of Marx, Engels and Lenin, which he shared and discussed with his fellow prisoners.

Grateful for her loyalty and support, David compared Blanca to his sister Luz and expressed his admiration for her strong and irrepressible personality and ability to write poetic verse. Like Graciela, she shared the ups and downs of his chaotic and sometimes dangerous life. Although she had a mind of her own and they frequently clashed, they were deeply in love and their relationship was an intense one, albeit tempestuous and short-lived.

Another source of concern for Siqueiros was his strained relationship with the Party. Ever since his return from Uruguay, he had problems with the leadership. Like the international movement, the Mexican party was divided between a Stalinist faction and those who sided with Trotsky. Although he remained loyal to the Stalinist orientation of the Central Committee, he was guilty by association with Blanca, who was suspected of being an international police agent, or worse, a Trotskyite. And since she supported Sandino, the anti-imperialist Nicaraguan leader supported by the Mexican government, he was accused of violating party discipline and supporting the enemy through his relationship with her. The Party also feared that he would reveal the whereabouts of comrades or meetings of the Central Committee, of which he was still a member.

Since party obligations took precedence over sentimental attachments, the Party had ordered him to break his relationship with Blanca. He had refused to abandon her, however, explaining that she was all alone in Mexico with her child of three and terrified by Mexico and Mexicans. Although he had agreed to live separately, he located a refuge for her and visited her secretly at night in order to escape the police, as well as the Party.

This harassment continued even in prison, where he was isolated from his comrades and confined to a cell with hardened criminals and denied the privileges of regular prisoners. On the outside, the Party continued its attacks on him, accusing him of violating party discipline and endangering the Party by his criticism of its leadership. Besides his association with Blanca, he had spoken out against the policies of the Party, accusing it of not responding effectively to the radicalization of the masses and of having contributed to the destruction of the CSUM. The case against him was reinforced by the fact that some "*siqueiristas*" had become Trotskyites. After he refused to join an activity in prison, the Central Committee expelled him from the Party, accusing him of endangering it through his lack of discipline and public criticism of the Party.

When Blanca informed him of the calumnies which the leaders were spreading about him, however, he defended the Party. Provoked by his stubborn loyalty, she cursed his allegiance, using the most offensive Mexican expressions she had learned to describe the shortcomings of his character. When other Marxists tried to convert him, he defended the Party and refused to blame it for the erroneous policies of its current leaders. But like Diego, he could not conform to party policy or discipline and he later suggested that the Mexican Communist Party should be called "*El Partido Expulsionista*" (The Expulsionist Party), since it expelled its most prominent and dedicated members and had more ex-members than active ones.

After several years of strenuous political activism and union organizing, David was behind bars and isolated from his woman as well as his comrades. Despite these conditions, his confinement provided an opportunity to return to his art. Working from memory or sketching scenes around him, he did a few engravings and then progressed to "easel paintings," actually "chair paintings," since he did not have an easel.

In 1930, however, neither the future of the Mexican mural movement nor the artistic career of David Alfaro Siqueiros was very promising. After Orozco abandoned Mexico, only Rivera continued to receive mural commissions and he soon left for the United States. Other artists had either left Mexico or had forsaken mural painting and social art to paint canvases for the galleries of Mexico City and New York.

While Siqueiros's artistic achievement was limited to his unfinished murals in the Preparatory School, some scattered oil paintings, and the illustrations he had done for *El Machete*, *El Martillo* and *El 130*, he had renewed his contact with the masses and their popular art forms and heightened his political consciousness and dedication. Confined to his small prison cell, he recreated the images of his recent experiences and surroundings, wondering when he would be able to incorporate them in a mural. The mural movement, meanwhile, was merely exiled until a more sympathetic government and a dedicated band of artists gave it new life.

VI. Prison-Taxco

Despite his status as an artist and veteran of the Revolution, Siqueiros did not receive any favored treatment in prison and at first he was isolated from the other political prisoners and denied their accustomed privileges. When he was allowed to join his comrades, he lived and worked under the same conditions as the other prisoners and shared in their hardships. He also organized study groups among the prisoners to read and discuss Marx, and before they were separated from the other prisoners, the communists read their papers out loud to the other inmates.

The daily tedium and misery of prison life was sometimes forgotten in the camaraderie of the prisoners and the stories which they told about each other. While Siqueiros entertained other prisoners with his tales of the Revolution and other prison terms, he enriched his own repertoire by observing and listening to fellow inmates.

The most celebrated prisoner in Lecumberri was Romero Carrasco, who bragged that he was more popular than the Mexican President. Although he had killed his aunt, uncle and his maid, flocks of female admirers came to visit him. Then there was Willy, an ingenious forger who insisted that he was a skilled artist since he could reproduce anything, especially official documents. Willy always had an elaborate scheme to propose and promised that he could make Siqueiros rich if he would abandon politics and art.

Using materials which Blanca brought him, David adopted the popular art forms of the workers who had illustrated the papers he had edited and began to develop a style and technique that would characterize much of his later work. Since he could not afford fine canvas, he used a rough fabric made from coarse *henequen* fibers or jute, a type of burlap, to develop textural effects. By covering this surface with white paint and a rubber or gum substance, he created a wall-like surface with a rough texture. Then, using a mixture of oil paint and *copal* or resin, he produced volumes with more weight and depth. Placed against a somber background, these denser forms in reds, blues and ochre heightened the sculptural quality of the modeled forms and created a more dramatic and emotional effect.

He also became more basic, minimizing detail and focusing on a single head or solitary figure which filled the two dimensional surface. Combined with the dramatic and sculptural qualities, this gave his prison paintings a monumental character in spite of their relatively small dimensions. Although he later referred disparagingly to them as "easel paintings," they were powerful statements of the human condition. The effect was not beauty, but an emotive force which penetrated and disturbed the viewer.

Drawing upon his experiences as a labor organizer and his prison observations, Siqueiros drew, etched and painted peasant men and women, Indian mothers and their children, miners, prisoners and their families, some folk heroes and several portraits. In a series of poignant paintings of sad mothers, abandoned children and martyred workers set against barren landscapes, he expressed the pathos of the miners and their families. The tone is somber and tragic, but there is also an expression of strength and solidarity in the face of adversity. Although they are destitute, these humble Mexicans are also heroic, sustained by an inner pride and dignity and their mask-like and expressionless faces have a psychological effect which suggests an inner agony and stoicism.

In *By the Prison Gate*, he painted a little girl waiting outside the prison, forlorn and unable to comprehend why her father had been taken away. It not only captured her emotions, but also expressed the plight of the innocent victims of the system, the women and children of the prisoners. In *Prison Visit* three women and a child visit a prisoner in his cell. *The Torment* shows two soldiers looking at a worker strung up by his thumbs in a cell. In several paintings of children begging or playing in the streets or just staring ahead with wide-open eyes, forlorn and terrified, he described the condition of a whole class, the working men and women of Mexico. He signed some of them "*penitenciaría*," a reminder of his whereabouts.

Mixing oil paints with copal gum and working on a large canvas of burlap, he painted a peasant woman tenderly holding her sick child and framed by a desert landscape with several monumental cacti and a horizon with a bright reddish-orange sunset. Although the mother and child are central and dominate the picture plane, they are alone in a barren landscape, framed by three powerfully modeled and sculptural cacti that provide balance and add depth to the composition. *Peasant Mother* is an expression of the love and strength of poor mothers. By changing the title to *The Deported Woman*, however, he gave it a more specific meaning, the desert scenery implying that they are victims of U.S. immigration policy.

Because of these qualities, he was later compared to Goya and Roualt, and one critic wrote that no one could surpass him in the expression of human grief, "not the grief of an individual, but in the grief of a multitude, of a race, a class." An art historian later wrote that while Rivera might paint a man who had suffered and Orozco would paint a man who was suffering, only Siqueiros could paint suffering.

Peasant Mother, 1929, Museum of Modern Art, Mexico, D.F.

However, he was painting more than just grief or misery. He painted peasant men and women praying, working and bathing, drew a lithograph of Zapata, agrarian hero of the Revolution, and painted a portrait of Moisés Saénz, noted Mexican educator and an early patron of his art. In a self-portrait, he painted himself with raised eyebrows, wrinkled forehead, wavy hair and prominent nose, his massive head framed by two walls of stone. Like his other paintings, it is monumental and sculptural and his strong features project outward from a roughly textured surface. There is no sign of despair or surrender and his strongly modeled features dominate the painting, suggesting an inner strength greater than the walls that surround him.

After nine months in the Federal Penitentiary in Mexico City, David was transferred to Taxco, a picturesque mountain village southwest of the capital, noted for its silver mines and a recently discovered haven for American writers and tourists. Although he was restricted to the town limits and could not leave without the permission of the local military commander, he was reunited with Blanca and could paint under better conditions, uninterrupted by prison duties or political activities. Working in an abandoned chapel, within a year he produced more than 100 paintings in oil on burlap or canvas, a series of woodcuts, some impressive lithographs, as well as many drawings and some watercolors.

The subject matter was still the people of rural Mexico, which he could now observe directly, and the dominant theme was their strength and dignity in the face of adversity. He also painted the portraits of friends and several unusual clients whom he met in Taxco. He continued to work in oil and copal resins on burlap, gradually increasing the size of the surfaces. By his own admission, he was still a primitive who executed poorly, but he felt that he was improving in composition and had developed a greater sense of volume and a means of psychological expression.

Siqueiros's brief sojourn in Taxco also brought him into contact with visiting artists and writers with whom he discussed the nature and purpose of art. Through Moises Saénz he met the Russian film director Serge Eisenstein, who was directing an epic film on Mexican history that focused on the Revolution. Since Eisenstein was producing monumental works of art depicting and serving his revolution, and argued that a great artist should be socially conscious and work from a strong ideological conviction, their association reinforced Siqueiros's personal resolve. They were also convinced that revolutionary art would not have been possible without the revolutions in their countries and that experimentation was a necessary component of revolutionary art. Although Eisenstein's film was never produced in its entirety, four segments were later incorporated into a short film, *Sunrise over Mexico.*

While he provided Eisenstein with information on Mexico and its Revolution, David plied the film director with questions on photography and film making and acquired an appreciation and understanding of motion picture cameras and techniques, including the use of montage. Fascinated by the thought of incorporating these techniques into his art, he exhorted other artists to utilize the contributions and lessons of photography and cinematography and later proposed a combination of art and cinematography in which the final product of a mural would be a film of it. This exposure to film making also reinforced his interest in expressing movement and provided him with some of the techniques for achieving it in his art.

Siqueiros also became good friends with the American composer George Gershwin, who had come to Mexico to sample Latin rhythms. In Taxco they discussed the nature of their respective art forms at length, discovering striking comparisons between art and music. After they agreed on the importance of composition in all forms of expression, they discovered that rhythm and movement, as well as the play of contrasts against each other, were essential elements in art and music. While Siqueiros sensed colors and forms in Gershwin's musical compositions, the latter perceived tones and rhythmic patterns in the paintings and drawings of Siqueiros. Their discussions also fueled Siqueiros's fascination with movement in art.

Thanks to William Spratling, an American writer who had helped to revive the silver industry and make Taxco a tourist center, wealthy gringos were flocking to this mountain town. But they were not interested in somber and graphic depictions of poor Mexicans and preferred pretty and picturesque scenes of Mexican villages or peasants.

Although he admired Mexican folk art, David attacked this influence and the promotion of folkloric art. It not only corrupted local artists and encouraged them to imitate Mexican folk art, he charged, but it also reflected an increasing American presence and influence in Mexico and Central America, which coincided with the sabotage of the Revolution under Calles and the persecution of the Mexican Left. He was convinced that these developments were connected and that the destruction of the mural movement could be attributed to Yankee influence and the lucrative tourist market for picturesque or "cute" Mexican art. Therefore, it was not only their duty to oppose overt North American imperialism in Mexico and Central America, but also to denounce the negative impact of tourism on Mexican art and condemn the opportunism of fellow artists.

Refusing to paint pictures to decorate the homes of the foreign bourgeoisie, Siqueiros continued to express the suffering and anguish around him, creating art that was the direct opposite of the cute and picturesque paintings collected by the North American tourists, but for which there was little or no demand. But while he was accusing the United States of undermining mural painting in Mexico, other Mexican artists were receiving commissions to paint murals for American millionaires or prestigious colleges in the United States. Soon he too would join the exodus. Ironically, it was predominantly rich Americans who were promoting or buying Mexican art, including his paintings.

Siqueiros also met the young American poet Hart Crane in Taxco and they became close friends, sharing ideas and discussing the nature and purpose of art. Moved by Siqueiros's poverty, Crane asked him to do a portrait of him and purchased a small watercolor of a Mexican boy. In letters to his friends, Crane compared Siqueiros to Gauguin and commented on the originality and power of his art. Siqueiros is "fundamentally a mural painter" whose smaller paintings have a "tremendous scale" and are uniquely Mexican, he wrote.

After a trip down to the tropics, Siqueiros became very sick with malaria. Since there was no medical care in Taxco, he arrived with

Blanca at the door of Crane's home in Mexico City and had to be carried into the house. While Siqueiros recovered, the house became a refuge for his communist friends who were hiding out from the government. Although he enjoyed the company, Crane complained to friends about rising liquor bills and the noise which prevented him from writing.

Like Siqueiros, Crane was highly critical of the popular trend towards "commercial folklorism" in Mexican art as well as American imperialism. In Crane's poetry Siqueiros discovered new and vivid images of the United States, especially its modern industry and machinery. Frustrated by his confinement and the lack of modern technology in Mexico, these images and the news that Rivera and Orozco were painting murals in the United States rekindled his desire to return to that country.

In 1931 David painted his friend. Avoiding his expressive eyes, he painted Crane with his head bowed, showing only the upper eyelids, a mass of wavy hair and his shoulders hunched. When Crane saw the portrait, he was ecstatic, declaring that the revelation of his character was "astounding!" A few days later, however, a despondent Crane showed his portrait to a friend and attacked Siqueiros as a fraud whose paint was already cracking. Seizing a razor, he slashed the painting and burned the remains in the patio.

Although Siqueiros was soon living in Los Angeles, Hart Crane never saw his native land again. In 1932 he and his sweetheart took a boat for the United States, but in the middle of the Gulf of Mexico, Crane said goodbye to her and left the stateroom, wearing his pajamas. On deck he went directly to the rail and leaped overboard. When he was thrown a lifeline, he refused to save himself and disappeared silently beneath the waves.

While conditions were much improved in Taxco, David had to support himself, Blanca and her son. He produced more than 100 paintings in the space of a year, but there were few interested buyers and those who liked his art could not afford to buy it. Fortunately, William Spratling not only purchased some of his drawings and watercolors, enabling him to buy food, pay the rent or purchase art supplies, but he also arranged for the printing of some lithographs based on his drawings and their sale at the Weyhe Gallery in New York. In the process they became good friends while Spratling acquired a unique collection of 50 paintings and drawings. The American writer also sponsored other Mexican artists, wrote and published books on Mexican culture and arranged Rivera's commission to paint a mural in the Cortez Palace in Cuernavaca, paid for by the American Ambassador, Dwight Morrow.

David had also done some wood block prints and in 1931, Spratling assembled and published 100 copies of *David Alfaro Siqueiros: Trece grabados en madera* (Thirteen Woodcuts). In the introduction Spratling wrote that the artist had achieved a profound and basic force in the use of form and color which few other artists had achieved. Like many of his recent paintings, these woodcuts were very similar to working class *retablos* in subject, as well as in style. Printed on bright orange tissue paper, they portrayed simply, but graphically, the men, women and children of rural Mexico and featured shawl-draped mothers holding their children, women protesting with raised arms while their men struggle, a prisoner with his arms tied behind him and a hammer resting on an anvil.

In Taxco David had some unusual commissions and interesting patrons. One day there was a weak knock at the door. Opening it, Siqueiros saw a little, old peasant lady, about sixty years old. She told him that she had heard that he painted portraits and she wanted one of herself to hang in her house so that her children could see it when they came to visit. Although he was excited about painting her because she was so interesting, he realized that she could not afford to pay very much. They agreed, therefore, that he would paint her for the same fee the local photographer charged for a portrait, three pesos.

Every day she came and sat patiently while he sketched and painted her. Since he found her so interesting, he asked her if she would mind if he painted two portraits of her, whereupon she said that she would pay for two and send one to her *compadre*. When he explained that he wanted a copy for himself, she asked him why he would want a picture of an old woman. Unable to convince her, he decided to paint the portrait and make a copy for himself without telling her. It was one of his most tender paintings and was later purchased by actor Charles Laughton.

After the little old lady paid Siqueiros for her portrait, she had it framed in one of those cheap ugly frames for photographs. When he became famous, she refused to sell it, even when offered a lot of money, and it remained in the same spot on the wall where she had hung it the day she brought it home. It was proof, he said, of how the average Mexican appreciated fine art.

However, not all his patrons understood the difference between photography and painting. When he heard someone pounding on the door and shouting, "*Señor fotógrafo*," early one morning, he opened the door and saw a young boy. The boy explained that his father wanted him to come at once since his sister had died the day before and they wanted him to do her portrait. Without giving Siqueiros the chance to explain that he was not a photographer, the boy dragged him to his home where he found the family waiting expectantly. In front of them was the dead girl, wearing a light green dress and pink bonnet and seated in a multi-colored chair while her older sister held her up.

After he explained that he was not the photographer but would paint her instead, he began to draw her with her sister holding her upright in the chair, using pencil and watercolors. Working from his sketch, he finished an oil painting of the deceased and her sister and presented it to the family. They all agreed that it was a good likeness, but when he offered to give it to them for nothing, the grandfather refused and insisted that if he did not take their money, they would not accept his "photograph." After taking a collection from all the family members, the head of the family gave Siqueiros his fee of ten pesos, fifty centavos.

Early one morning, he heard someone knocking and shouting outside his studio home. This time it was a little old American woman who presented him with a flower for his "beautiful wife." After she declared that she did not want to leave the country before purchasing at least one of his paintings, she looked around and decided to buy two of them, paying him the unheard of sum of two hundred dollars apiece in traveler's checks. After she left with her two purchases, he woke up Blanca and told her of their good fortune.

Since they needed money desperately, they rented a car to drive to Iguala to cash the checks. There, however, they were told that the woman had called and asked them not to honor the checks. Since she had signed the checks, they should have been as good as cash, but they were told to return to Taxco and to work it out with her. But in Taxco they found a note saying that she had to leave for the United States and would settle her account later, whereupon they laughed and breathed a sigh of relief.

Sometime later the same lady appeared at their door, carrying another flower for Blanca but without offering to settle the debt. This time she wanted a larger painting and decided to purchase *Accident in the Mine*, a large, mural-like, oil painting which Siqueiros had recently completed of several miners huddled over the body of a fellow miner, crushed by blocks of stone. Although she offered to pay a thousand dollars for the painting, Chano Urueta, his cousin and agent, insisted that it was worth two thousand.

Refusing to haggle, she told them that she would deposit a check for one thousand dollars with a friend in Mexico City, and if they accepted her offer, they could deliver the painting to him and pick up the check. Excited by the prospect of this generous offer, they rented a car and drove to Mexico City, stopping along the way to buy new boots and clothes. When they went to deliver the painting, however, the lady informed them that she had decided not to purchase it after all.

Disappointed, as well as broke, they drove around the city, trying to think of a way to raise some money. After they ran into Anita Brenner, she agreed to arrange an exhibit of Siqueiros's recent works as soon as possible in Mexico City. While arrangements were being made for David's first one-man show, he returned to Taxco, still no richer for the sales to his fickle patroness.

In spite of his arrest and exile, Siqueiros did not abstain entirely from politics and in 1931, he participated in the formation of the Lucha Internacional Proletaria (International Proletarian Struggle) with other artists and writers. Although it was short-lived, he never abandoned the idea of creating another union or collective of revolutionary artists, even in exile. According to one of the Americans in Taxco, he also organized a union of boys to watch tourists' cars for a fee.

In January of 1932 David openly violated the conditions of his exile by leaving Taxco for an extended stay in Mexico City. The occasion was the opening of the first exhibit dedicated solely to his art, at the Spanish Casino in the capital. It had been arranged by Anita Brenner and was sponsored by Serge Eisenstein, Hart Crane, William Spratling, Salvador Novo, Roberto Montenegro and Eyler Simpson, with the cooperation of the ambassador of the recently established Spanish Republic, Álvarez del Vayo. The show included his most recent work, including sixty oil paintings, a series of woodcuts, lithographs and drawings, many of them on loan from their owners, and it was a great success.

One of the featured paintings was *Accident in the Mine*, which Lombardo Toledano immediately purchased for the National University. When Siqueiros's American patroness showed up at the exhibit and saw the painting, however, she immediately claimed that the painting belonged to her. After Blanca told her that Siqueiros was not a commercial artist who could be bought and he had sold the painting to the National University for 400 pesos, the two women nearly came to blows. Realizing that the American patron was none other than Mrs. Alice Myers, one of the richest women in America and the owner of one of the finest collections in the southwestern states, Miss Brenner separated them.

When tempers had cooled, David agreed to have lunch with Mrs. Myers and Miss Brenner. During lunch his client wanted him to assure her that the colors in his paintings would not fade since he was a communist and would want to seek revenge on the bourgeoisie. Apparently reassured, this eccentric patron of the arts departed, only to resurface in the United States to plague him again, now a personal nemesis.

While *Accident in the Mine* may have provoked the most controversy, visitors to the exhibit were also impressed by the emotional force and artistic qualities of *Peasant Mother*, *The Prison Visit* and *Proletarian Mother*, in which he had painted an Indian mother with three children seated in a cubicle of stone. While two children hover over her, begging for food, her latest child, a baby, lies at her feet, like the Aztec goddess of childbirth. Her desolation and sorrow is conveyed by her mask like face with its eyeless sockets and by the cold stonewalls which surround her, similar to those in his recent self-portrait. Equally moving was *Slave Children*, showing two young boys, crushed under the enormous loads on their backs, a comment on working conditions in the mines of Taxco.

The exhibit also included his portraits of the old woman and the dead child, his self-portrait, an oil painting and a lithograph of the revolutionary hero Emiliano Zapata, a rare painting of children at play, imitating bullfighters, a water color of a woman making tortillas, a study of a peasant praying and oil portraits of Moisés Saénz, Dolores Álvarez Bravo, Luis Eychenne and Hart Crane. There was also a portrait of Blanca Luz Brum, her hair in braids wrapped around her head and signed *"Mi querida Blanca Luz (My dearest Blanca Luz), Taxco, 1931."* The paintings of the anonymous Mexicans at work and play were characterized by dark and somber tones, heavy modeling and emotive power. The portraits not only captured the physical features of the subjects, but also their inner character.

At the opening of the exhibit Anita Brenner noted that this was the first exposition devoted exclusively to the art of David Alfaro Siqueiros. The organizers of the show, she pointed out, had realized that it might be his last, given his rebellious spirit and intellectual and aesthetic integrity in a time when art had become a luxury item, whose worth was dependent upon the capricious fancy of wealthy patrons.

It is impossible, she continued, to write or speak about his art without mentioning politics. The force and beauty of his art are the expression of his incisive ideology, which he expresses with the same convictions using a brush as he does with the spoken or written word and by his personal conduct. One cannot expect that having followed the most difficult path in politics that he would not follow the same route in his art. After she chastised another critic for emphasizing Siqueiros's recent problems with the law and ignoring his prior achievements in art, she declared that he is "one of the three great figures of modern Mexican art," which is "the most significant artistic movement of our time."

Turning to the exhibit itself, she noted that the central theme of the exhibit is one of pain and suffering, that an emotional quality prevails over the purely plastic elements, while the concept is monumental and the oil paintings are virtual murals. His technique gives his paintings a viscous quality as well as a sense of volume and weight, while the simple, solid and enormous figures assume heroic proportions of great precision and power. His portraits, she observed, are physically exact and reveal a psychological dimension.

After noting that he had enlarged his paintings, she declared that the balance he had achieved between ideological unity, emotion and aesthetics in *Accident in the Mine* should be recognized as genius. Like all his work, she concluded, one does not simply enjoy it; it either moves or disturbs, striking the deepest emotions and requiring respect whether one admires or repudiates it.

In his review of the exhibit, Xavier Villaurrutia compared the art of Siqueiros to that of Orozco, concluding that both painted canvases that "emit great dramatic force." He said the exhibit, however, did not surprise him since he felt that the unfinished murals of Siqueiros were the most restless and disturbing of any in the Preparatoria, and were clearly the ferment of the expressive force which is seen here. His art is not a decoration to enjoy but something that enters us, penetrating and touching our innermost sources. It is characterized by this expressive force and his use of color is in perfect harmony with his intentions and makes them endure.

A New York critic, Carlos Zigrosser, also compared Siqueiros to Orozco in terms of emotional intensity, stating that "Power, not beauty, is his prime objective and his works have a tremendous force." Arthur Miller, art critic for the *Los Angeles Times*, was impressed by the same qualities and proclaimed that Siqueiros was one of the great masters of

Mexico and in the use of color and emotive qualities, there was nothing to compare with his work. The Mexican writer José Juan Tablada concluded that Siqueiros's *Military Train* rushing headlong towards an inevitable holocaust with a simple and heroic impulse could only have been painted by a soul possessed of tragedy and inflamed by a deep fervor.

Others were quick to point out that, while European influences were apparent in the paintings of other Mexican artists, the art of Siqueiros was uniquely Mexican and had introduced American values to universal beauty. They also emphasized that his figurative approach and use of human subject matter clearly distinguished his art from that of contemporary Europe. Hart Crane wrote that Siqueiros had brought to modern painting a human content and spiritual axis which had been missing from European art for a long time and noted that Braque and Picasso had contributed little to this essential vision. Never in New York or Paris, he wrote, had he attended a one-man show as powerful.

While some of the critics contended that Siqueiros's paintings were strident and that the militant, political activist dominated the artist, others pointed out that his paintings and prints reflected the perfect mixture of his two personalities, the social and the artistic. His depiction of a mother embracing her sick child in a desolate wasteland in *Peasant Mother*, they argued, expressed his concern for the problems of Mexico but without any anecdotal device or artifice.

Siqueiros's childhood friend, Jesús Soto, was impressed by the exhibit, declaring that he had not only reached the heights of Orozco and Rivera, but

> had surpassed them in the profound expression of
> human pain with the sober hue of a most powerful
> brush, with the somber force of a grimace, of a gesture
> in which truth vibrates. He is above everything, more
> original and more national ...

Sotito added that his paintings are without anecdotes, literary reminders or theatrical effects and their pathetic colors are in perfect harmony with the determined objective. The result was not the expression of the pain of an individual, but the sorrow of a multitude, a race, a class.

After the exhibit, Serge Eisenstein wrote that Siqueiros was

> the greatest proof that a really great painter has,
> above everything, a social consciousness and an
> ideological conviction. The greater the conviction, the
> greater the painter ... Siqueiros is the marvelous syn-
> thesis between the conception of the masses and their
> representation individually perceived ... [he] strikes a
> blow with his brush with the implacable certainty of a
> pneumatic drill on the path leading to the final goal
> which he always has before him.

If there were any doubts about David's views on art or politics, he dispelled most of them in a lengthy discourse at the closing of the exhibit. After clarifying that he considered painting and sculpture as professional crafts for mature people and belittling the work of children or dilettantes as art, he attacked Diego Rivera for not improving the methods of instruction at San Carlos. One does not learn to mix colors by memorizing a recipe but in the practice of painting under a master artist. The national art academy is not only useless to its students, but also to the artists who teach there, who have become "bureaucratic fossils." They should convert the school into a museum and, instead of spending all the money on teaching art, the money should be used to purchase art by Mexican artists who could then afford workshops in which students would work under a master artist. Their paintings and sculpture would be exhibited throughout Mexico and abroad.

While he recognized the value of folk art, he warned, "to make a fetish of popular art and children's art is not only dangerous to the formation of an artist, but also for popular art itself." The most pernicious trend in Mexican painting today, however, is "Mexican Curious," "one of the effects of Yankee imperialist penetration," which increases in direct proportion to the tourist trade. This fetish with popular art affects all Mexican artists and sculptors, leading to the artificial creation or imitation of folk art for export. It is "an alien art dressed up in Mexican clothes."

Instead, he continued, we should look to the work of the Indian masters of America. "They will teach us to understand the great essential masses, the primary forms...that art is not only a problem of the mechanics of composition, it is also a problem of a state of mind." At the same time he warned against the limitations of national art. We must be modern and international and by finding our own artistic values, contribute to a universal art.

Turning to abstract painters, he declared that some of us, in order to escape from "Mexican Curious" art, have fallen into "a type of snob art which is totally alien to our own geographical reality." But the right path was not in Europe, where modern painting and sculpture were "a kind of cerebral masturbation, both characteristic and representative of the decadent bourgeois classes."

Although he rejected recent trends in European art, Siqueiros explained that he did not mean to suggest that they should cut themselves off from those currents. It was their conditions which had given them the unique tradition and opportunity to make a real contribution to universal beauty without any of the "snobbism so characteristic of European culture today." However, they must avoid imitating the values of the masses, since they were the

> final receptacle of the bad taste of the classes which
> exploit and dominate them. The proletariat owes to the
> bourgeoisie not only its economic oppression but
> also its abominable aesthetic taste ... how can they have
> other than bad taste?

Only the peasants still had good taste because they were closer to the ancient cultures and further from the modern bourgeoisie. But, he added, only "an educated minority can adequately evaluate the plastic arts."

Turning to mural painting, he pointed out that good mural painting was more than the painting of separate panels. No matter how meritorious individually, such painted panels were only decorations and not fully integrated murals. Therefore, many of the Renaissance masters could not be considered good muralists and, after Giotto, mural decoration began to decline. The murals we have painted in Mexico, he declared, "will pass into history as a mediocre example of mural decoration" and we must learn from our experiences and produce something superior.

Next he discussed portrait painting, explaining that it presents the sculptor and the painter with a subject of artistic complexity, with all the factors for an integral work of art, as well as requiring an understanding of metaphysical expression. Mexican artists, therefore, should reject false theories and paint portraits.

While much of his criticism focused on the picturesque tendencies of the "*dieguitos*", the disciples of Rivera, he saved some of his venom for "*los contemporáneos.*" This literary and artistic group had sought to combat "excessive Mexicanism" by developing international, as opposed to strictly nationalist forms of expression. In art they were were influenced by Picasso, Braque, Klee, Matisse and de Chirico and they turned away from the original thrust of the Mexican movement to paint abstract easel paintings devoid of social or political statements, or "art for art's sake."

However, Rufino Tamayo, Carlos Mérida, Manuel Rodríguez Lozano, Agustín Lazo, Carlos Orozco Romero, Gabriel Fernández Ledesma and Julio Castellanos were not just rejecting Mexicanism or social art. They insisted that the value of a work of art was determined by its aesthetic qualities and not by its ideological message. They also turned inward, expressing a "tragic sense of life" which focused on man's solitude, the emptiness of existence and the forces of darkness. Drawing their inspiration from the subconscious, their expression was highly personal, internal, subjective and lyrical, and contrasted with the epic, realistic and dramatic expression of the muralists.

Although he recognized their talent, Siqueiros characterized their art as "bourgeois," European and counter-revolutionary. The conflict, therefore, was that of "social art or pure art" and in these times of bitter class war, the artist must serve either the bourgeoisie or the proletariat. While he agreed with his opponents that the ultimate artistic objective was pure art, he argued that type of art had never existed and could only exist in a classless society, one without class struggle or politics, that is, in a completely communist society. Therefore, "I fight for this type of society because in doing so I am fighting for pure art."

As revolutionary artists, he continued, we should not subordinate our tastes to those of the masses, but must give expression to their desires, especially their revolutionary ideology, and create good art. After quoting Eisenstein's statement that "The great revolutionary painter is a synthesis of the ideas of the masses and their representation by an individual," he concluded his discourse, declaring that the "painters and sculptors of today cannot remain indifferent in the struggle to free humanity and art from oppression" and they should work with "the class historically destined to change the old society for the new."

To his surprise, Siqueiros's unexcused absence from Taxco went unnoticed and despite his publicized presence in the capital, he was not apprehended. Encouraged by official indifference, he decided to end his involuntary exile from politics and immersed himself in national issues, becoming more militant and outspoken than before. This did not go unnoticed, however, and not long after the closing of the exhibit at the Casino Español, it was suggested that he either leave the country or return to prison.

Faced with this ultimatum, he decided to head north to California. Ever since his first visit to New York, he had wanted to return so that he could study and apply the technical advances of American industry, unavailable in Mexico. That dream had been rekindled by the verse of Hart Crane and the news that both Rivera and Orozco were painting murals in the United States. He was also frustrated by the relatively small dimensions of his "chair paintings" and yearned to apply his new techniques on larger surfaces or public walls. But there were no opportunities to paint murals in Mexico, especially for a militant leftist, and even though he had not worked on a mural project since 1925, he might have a better chance in "gringo land."

In spite of the hardships of the last few years, his stay in Taxco had been productive as well as profitable, and his reputation as an artist was based on his Taxco paintings and the contacts he had made there. Ironically, it was primarily Americans who had arranged exhibits of his art, purchased his paintings or commissioned portraits by him, and his next three mural commissions were in Los Angeles.

Nevertheless, the experiences of the last few years had also renewed his political consciousness and he yearned to express his opposition to imperialism and depict the current reality of Mexico. But he could only do it from the inside of a prison cell if he stayed in Mexico. Basking in the favorable reviews of his first one-man show, he packed his unsold paintings and sketches and headed for the border with Blanca and her son.

VII. Exile: Los Angeles and Buenos Aires

When Siqueiros arrived in California in 1932, Rivera and Orozco were already painting murals in the United States. While they were the toast of the art community, their murals provoked controversy and censorship. At Pomona College Orozco's nude Prometheus offended the trustees. When he painted portraits of Lenin, Stalin, Gandhi and the Mexican revolutionary Felipe Carrillo Puerto and a "Table of Brotherhood" of the "oppressed races" at the School for Social Research in New York, his fresco panels were removed from public view.

Before he went east, Rivera painted two murals in San Francisco. After a successful one-man show in New York, he was hailed as the new master of fresco painting and Edsel Ford invited him to paint a mural in the Detroit Institute of the Arts. However, his interpretation of the life and history of the city offended local art patrons. When Diego painted a portrait of Lenin in a mural in the new Rockefeller Center in New York City, he was locked out of the building while the artistic community rallied to his defense. After the "battle of Rockefeller Center" subsided, Nelson Rockefeller had the mural destroyed.

Following a trip to Europe, Orozco began work on the mural decoration of the Baker Library at Dartmouth College. His interpretation of American civilization included a panel in which an American army officer, backed by gangsters and capitalists, is poised to stab a Latin American revolutionary in the back.

Thus, even before Siqueiros arrived in California, it appeared that hiring Mexican artists to paint murals invited controversy and protests. In spite of the public outcry, however, most of their work survived and only Rivera's mural in the Rockefeller center was destroyed intentionally. While Siqueiros would live up to this reputation, his murals in Los Angeles were not as fortunate.

When David and Blanca arrived at the California border in 1932, they did not have entry visas for the United States. They were also broke and David was fleeing Mexico in order to avoid going back to prison. Thanks to the good word of film director Joseph von Sternberg, however, they were given visas for six months and entered the country legally.

Shortly after their arrival, they met Luis Arenal, a Mexican artist whose mother ran a boarding house in the Mexican section of Los Angeles. She was Señora Electa Bastard de Arenal, the widow of Leopoldo Arenal, killed during the struggle against Huerta. After his death, she had raised her four children by herself and, in 1923, she brought them to Los Angeles where she supported them for several years as a seamstress. In 1928 she rented a large house where she provided lodging for teachers, writers, and artists who wanted to learn Spanish. In 1932, her sons Luis and Leopoldo and her daughter Angélica were also living with her.

Since David and Blanca needed a place to stay, Luis brought them home and introduced them to his family. When he explained their predicament, Electa invited them to stay as houseguests. David immediately charmed the whole family and Electa's kitchen became his center of operations when he was not painting. Dressed in overalls covered with paint and wearing a wide brimmed felt hat, he regaled members of the family and other guests with his stories of the Revolution. He also discussed his political views and described the problems and conditions of the country they had fled.

In the process he acquired a second family, one whose destiny was to be linked intimately with his own for the rest of their lives. After assisting Siqueiros on his mural projects in Los Angeles, Luis became a permanent fixture in his mural painting teams. Luis and Leopoldo also shared Siqueiros's political views and were accomplices in some of his subsequent political escapades.

Although Angélica sat timidly in the corner, listening to his stories, and did not enter into the conversations around the kitchen table, she was also charmed by David and, like her brothers, she began to share his political views. The attraction was more than political, however, and in spite of Blanca, whom he had recently married, she became enamored of him. David was also falling in love with her and he began to apply all of his personal charm to conquer her.

Soon after his arrival in Los Angeles, von Sternberg introduced Siqueiros to members of the local art community and the film industry in Hollywood. Through their efforts, he was able to bring his paintings and prints across the border and arrange for his first exhibit in the United States. In return for his help, Siqueiros offered to paint Von Sternberg's portrait. Using house paint and commercial brushes, he painted the film director seated at a table, his strongly modeled head and shoulders filling the picture plane and suggesting a dominating presence and personality.

After an exhibit of his lithographs at the Jake Zeitlin Bookshop in Los Angeles, a second exhibit opened in the Stendahl Ambassador Gallery, one of the most important galleries on the West Coast. The show included many of his Taxco paintings, some recent portraits, including one of Blanca, and *Breadline*, a new work depicting the depression.

When two men arrived at the opening and explained that a Mrs. Myers had sent the Mayor of Los Angeles a telegram saying that *The Accident in the Mine* belonged to her, Siqueiros told his version and the Mayor agreed that she should settle her claim with the Mexican authorities since the painting belonged to the National University of Mexico. The incident in Los Angeles, however, was not the last in their stormy relationship.

The reactions to Siqueiros's first comprehensive exhibit in the United States were mixed. More than a thousand people attended during the first few days, including some of Hollywood's finest, and one third of the sixty or so art works were sold. The major criticisms focused on the lack of color or charm and the "distasteful," "ugly" or "primitive subject matter." Others commented that the paintings suggested a sense of tragedy or brooding, but that their dark and somber nature accurately reflected the times. Some were impressed by the fresco-like effect of his oil and copal paintings on burlap and the monumental scale, energy, and sculptural quality of his figures. Even though most of their reviews were negative, it was obvious that the critics had been deeply moved by the exhibit.

The painting of the dead child and her sister, on loan from the family, provoked the strongest reaction. When he overheard an overweight lady comment in a Southern accent that Mexicans must be sadistic to paint portraits of dead children, Siqueiros replied in a loud voice so that everyone could hear him. Imitating her southern drawl, he declared that the custom of painting dead children in Mexico was very primitive, but it had also been the custom in ancient Greece. "Furthermore," he shouted, "as you must know, madam, it is much more savage and brutal to lynch living Negroes."

While some visitors greeted his remarks with applause, many were offended and left abruptly. The next day all the papers took up the story. They agreed that his initial response had been sufficient, but added that he should not have insulted his host country by alluding to the lynching of Negroes in the South. If attendance and notoriety were the criteria, however, the exhibit turned out to be brilliant success, in spite of the generally unsympathetic reviews.

When Siqueiros arrived in Los Angeles, he was destitute and without any promise of work in a city in the throes of a depression. While his exhibits and a few portrait commissions had brought in some money, it was not enough to support the three of them.

However, he had made friends in the local art community, and Millard Sheets, an artist and instructor at the Chouinard Art Academy, befriended David and Blanca, inviting them to his home for meals. He also persuaded Madame Chouinard, the owner of the art school, to permit Siqueiros to offer a class during the summer and he rounded up some other artists and students to study fresco painting with Siqueiros.

Despite the success of his recent shows, Siqueiros had not worked on a mural for eight years and his only fresco project remained unfinished. Moreover, he was a fugitive from Mexico and had made public statements in which he attacked the decadent influence of the bourgeoisie on art and United States imperialism in Mexico. This background was not very auspicious for a teacher of fresco in a reputable private academy of art, especially given the volatile political climate of Southern California in 1932. But the Mexicans were the only contemporary artists who had worked in fresco and the arrangement was just for the use of a studio for an inter-session class in which other instructors would participate.

At the first meeting of the class, Siqueiros promptly announced that "fresco" only meant "wet" or "moist." He also told them that the only way to teach mural painting was to work on a mural and this should be done by a team of artists under the direction of a master painter. Since they did not have any walls to paint, members of the class, many of them established artists, constructed their own fresco panels with wood frames and chicken wire covered with several coats of plaster. Following the directions of Siqueiros, they began to paint in the topcoat of plaster while it was still wet, creating "fresco blocks."

Meanwhile he was looking around the school for a wall on which to paint a mural. But instead of retreating to an obscure corner of the school, he chose an exterior wall facing the street and broken up by three windows and a door. When he announced to "the mural block painters" that they would paint a mural on this wall, they immediately questioned whether it would be possible to paint in traditional fresco, that is on wet plaster, outdoors and exposed to the intense summer sun and winter rains of Southern California.

After making some inquiries, David learned from Richard Neutra, an Austrian architect, that if you place plaster of lime and sand on a surface of cement and sand, the different rates of contraction would destroy the weaker plaster surface. Neutra, therefore, had recommended using white cement instead of plaster as a base for fresco painting.

At the next meeting of the "block painters," David proclaimed, "Traditional fresco is dead!" Although the obituary was premature, Neutra's advice became an obsession and was the beginning of a lifelong search for new methods and materials for mural painting. In the Preparatoria he had become impatient with the tedious process of encaustic and fresco and had concluded that artists must develop new material solutions using the technology of a modern society. Fresco painting might be appropriate for a Renaissance or colonial building, but it was certainly not compatible with a modern building of concrete and steel. It was like playing a revolutionary anthem on a church organ, he argued, "a new society must have new material solutions!"

But since cement dries much faster than plaster, a cement fresco would require a quicker method of application. He had already proposed the use of spray guns to paint murals and now he perceived the utility of the air brushes and spray guns used to paint automobiles, stoves and refrigerators. Surely these tools could be adapted for painting murals on a rapidly drying surface, he reasoned. They would also encourage spontaneity and provide a welcomed escape from the patience and discipline required in true fresco.

But when he announced this discovery, several members of the class protested that an artist must work with his own hands and according to his own senses and rhythm rather than that dictated by an impersonal machine. In response Siqueiros pointed out that using a rock to mark another rock constitutes a type of machine and that brushes and stencils were also mechanical equipment. When he added that artists were using the airbrush to paint posters, the artists replied that they were "commercial, not true artists."

Undaunted, he continued to experiment, testing and then debating the use of new materials or means of application. In the process, he discovered another "absolute truth," that the tools and the materials were determining factors in artistic production. While he had adopted the spray gun in order to speed up the application of paint to a rapidly drying surface, it had created its own aesthetic and offered a completely different and, therefore, revolutionary language. Certainly a pencil drawing was not a pen drawing, he argued, and every sculptor knows that working in wood is different from working in stone. "You cannot paint an oil painting with fresco nor a fresco painting with oil," he declared. "The first thing an artist must do is to listen to his tools and to understand them."

Further testing demonstrated that these new tools increased the reach of the artist, allowing him to extend his range by several lengths and encouraged freedom and spontaneity. They also produced new and unforeseen aesthetic effects or "accidents" which fascinated him. Artistic machines and material not only create their own aesthetic, he deduced, but these accidents are important ingredients of art and should be studied and adapted by the artist.

The new tools, however, posed another problem. The spray guns developed for painting industrial products were designed to use industrial paints. When he suggested the use of commercial paints, however, several artists protested that they could not produce works of art with the same pigment used to paint automobiles or refrigerators. Siqueiros countered by pointing out that oil paints were also the product of the laboratory and no one would suggest that their development had not greatly enhanced the art of painting. The industrial or commercial origin of the paints, therefore, was immaterial.

Sometime later, however, he realized that while the origin of the paints did not prevent their use by artists, the profit making motive behind their development posed a serious deficiency. While they were fast drying and capable of rapid application using spray guns, the new pigments did not last out-of-doors and were not suitable for murals on exterior surfaces. The paint industry, he concluded, was not interested in their longevity and had deliberately developed formulas in which the colors would fade when exposed to ultraviolet rays.

During his search for new materials, Siqueiros became aware of another aspect of mural painting. Like his Mexican colleagues, he had assumed that painting murals was no more than enlarging easel paintings, that is just increasing the size and figures of the painting. Faced with the prospect of painting a mural on a wall that was exposed to the street and could be seen from a variety of angles by moving spectators, however, he began to have doubts. When he visited the Public Library to see a recently completed mural, he was struck by how it expanded as one approached it. On his frequent walks around the city, he also observed how paintings or billboards changed when they were seen from different angles.

From these observations and his limited experience in mural painting, he concluded that traditional perspective was false because it was concerned only with the static spectator. What was needed in mural painting, therefore, was a totally new perspective that took into consideration the "dynamic spectator." Since he lacked a technical solution, he became engrossed in the development of a multiangular perspective for the active spectator. It would become one of his central theories and one of his major contributions to modern mural painting.

After they had completed their research and experimentation with the new materials and equipment, "the mural block painters" began working on their first team project. While they accepted his suggestion that they work as a team on a collective work of art, in reality Siqueiros was the master artist and the other artists were his apprentices. He not only chose the theme of the mural, but he also made the final decisions on materials and the design and did most of the painting.

Although he had submitted some preliminary sketches to Madame Chouinard, each day he started at the top and worked down, painting directly on the wall and disregarding any previous drawings or what he had painted the day before. Working without a master sketch, he made decisions in the process of applying the paint to the wet cement. When he encountered problems, he experimented with different methods, materials and equipment. From these experiments, he derived new theories as well as technical solutions.

Thanks to the new equipment and materials, the mural progressed rapidly. Working on the white cement recommended by Neutra, he used airbrushes and spray guns to sketch as well as to paint the large areas. In lieu of drawings, he painted from photographs of construction sites and labor meetings and employed stencils to paint the shadows of construction workers on the wall. Although he complained of working in a fog of paint created by the mechanical tools and some of his methods had to be discarded, the 19 by 24 foot mural was finished in the prescribed time of 15 days.

Shortly before it was completed, a curious Mme. Chouinard visited the site and asked him what the construction workers he had painted on a scaffold on the side of a building were watching. He explained that they were looking at one of the street artists who performed on street corners in Los Angeles and produced a sketch showing a performer in front of the construction site. Accepting his explanation, she agreed to keep the public away so that he might complete the project on time.

One night, feigning exhaustion, he told his assistants to quit and go home. When they returned the next morning, however, they saw a finished mural. Instead of a street artist, he had painted a labor organizer on a soapbox addressing the construction workers, flanked by a black man and a white woman, each holding a child and listening to the speaker.

Street Meeting, 1932, Cement Fresco, Los Angeles, California

Like his recent show at the Stendahl gallery, the mural attracted a lot of attention and the unveiling, which coincided with a benefit art show for the founding of the New School of Social Research, was one of the artistic events of the year. Addressing an audience of 800, Siqueiros lashed out against capitalism, North American imperialism and the pretentious painting of Europe and the United States. After hailing the technical and mechanical innovations demonstrated by *Street Meeting*, he challenged intellectuals to join in the struggle of the proletariat.

The next day several reviews proclaimed that it was bold, powerful and moving, notable for its brilliant colors, and a break-through in mural painting. Other critics, however, found it "distasteful", "awkward and ugly." *California Arts and Architecture*, respected mouthpiece of the art community, said that "mixed emotions are aroused" by Siqueiros's fresco and warned, "The art of fresco in this country will languish until it is able to free itself from the sorrows of Mexico and the dull red glow of Communism." There were also objections to the subject matter, a workers' meeting, and the presence of a black man in the foreground.

The contents of *Street Meeting*, however, should not have come as any surprise. He was a veteran of the Mexican Revolution who had organized miners' unions and the art which he had exhibited in Mexico and Los Angeles, along with his public statements, should have dispelled any doubts regarding his views on art and politics. In California he was surrounded by the stark reality of the depression, including breadlines and thousands of workers, especially Mexican Americans, out of work. Nearby efforts to organize the farm workers were crushed by the police or goon squads hired by the growers. Throughout the Southwest, thousands of Mexicans and Americans of Mexican descent were being deported as "illegals," while the Los Angeles Police Department's anti-red squad harassed and broke up meetings of "subversives."

Street Meeting had been conceived as a class project and the uproar it provoked probably sealed its fate. According to one account, the anti-red squad descended on the school and demanded that the mural be destroyed and subsequently Madame Chouinard had it painted over. In a similar version, Siqueiros explained that there was a "fascist reaction" to "The Street Meeting" and a wall was erected in front of it, after which it was destroyed.

However, one member of the team recalled that the mural was experimental and had been painted over by Siqueiros himself or other members of the team, while Millard Sheets pointed out that they had worked on such a wet surface that the walls did not absorb the pigments as in true fresco and the colors faded, chipped or ran with the first rain. After several years of exposure, therefore, the mural all but disappeared from natural causes.

Today all that remains are some black and white photographs of *Street Meeting*. From them it appears to have been skillfully designed and executed. Although somewhat theatrical or staged, the gazes of the workers and the man and women in the foreground focused attention on the labor leader, whose bright red shirt in the original centered the composition. While they were out of scale with the features of the wall, the figures of the workers were powerfully modeled and projected forward off the scaffold towards the spectator, casting shadows on the wall. Siqueiros had also integrated the windows and the door into the composition and the workers appeared to be working on the same wall on which they were painted.

Though most of the ideas and much of the painting was his, Siqueiros had followed his own recommendations for training artists by having them work on a project under a master artist, as well as his ideas about a team of artists working together on a collective project. It was also his first experience in painting a mural on the outside of a building and he had explored new ideas and developed techniques that he would pursue on subsequent projects.

The publicity generated by *Street Meeting* attracted more students and the "mural block painters" expanded from the seven to twenty-four. It also brought an offer to paint a much larger and more challenging mural. When F. K. Ferenz, the owner of the Plaza Arts Center, a school of commercial art, offered Siqueiros a contract to paint a mural on the outside of the building and several local companies agreed to supply the sand, cement, paint and spray painting equipment for the project, he accepted and immediately began preparations to paint his second outdoor mural.

Although the proposed site posed greater problems than the exterior wall of the art school, its visibility made it perfect for a work of "public art." It was a large outside wall, sixteen feet high by eighty feet long on the second story of the Plaza Arts Center on Olvera Street, a commercial venture with a Mexican, or preferably, "Spanish" theme. Because it would be seen from surrounding buildings, by traffic approaching the area from several directions, and by pedestrians on the street, it also offered a perfect opportunity to develop a perspective for the "dynamic spectator." On the other hand, he would have to integrate two windows and a door into the mural and find materials that would adhere to the brick surface and last in the sun and the rain.

This project was also conducted as a class and the new members of the team paid a fee to work on the mural. It included a caricaturist, art instructors in the public schools, commercial artists, decorators, scenic designers, and film directors who worked along with Luis Arenal and several assistants. While the sponsor supplied the materials and equipment, volunteers erected the wood scaffolding and strung wires for huge electric lights so they could work at night.

After Siqueiros and his patron agreed on the theme of "Tropical America", *The Los Angeles Times* reported that "its theme is the Mexican tropical jungle," in which an Indian temple would be surrounded by huge trees and green foliage with colorful birds, pumas and natives. The public naturally envisioned an exotic picture of contented natives in a jungle paradise of lush vegetation, flowers, waterfalls and tropical animals and birds.

While Siqueiros was studying the surface, his team of assistants prepared the wall, first roughing the surface with pneumatic drills and then applying a coat of grey cement. After he had conducted a geometric analysis of the area, David made some preliminary drawings. When he felt that the design was satisfactory, he had it enlarged and projected on the wall using an electric projector, a device suggested by Dean Cornwell, a member of the team who had used a projector on the murals he had painted recently in the Los Angeles Public Library. Since this was faster than the painstaking process of tracing sketches directly on the wall, David was ecstatic about the discovery and adopted the projector as a standard piece of equipment thereafter.

His next technical discovery, however, was an accident. In order to rid himself of an inept artist, Siqueiros assigned him to photograph the site from different viewing points. When he saw the prints, however, he realized that the wall would assume different shapes, depending on the location of the camera. This not only proved the value of photography for analyzing the different perspectives from which mural would be seen, but reinforced his search for a new perspective for the moving spectator.

Using airbrushes, spray guns, lineographs and commercial paints, and working night and day, Siqueiros did most of the painting, while his assistants prepared the paints or filled in blocked out areas. Since many of them worked at other jobs during the day, they could only work on the mural at night and the designs could only be projected on the wall after dark. When he was not busy painting, David directed their work and complimented their contributions.

Most nights they worked until midnight, and then huddling around a bonfire on the roof, they shared a bottle of Tequila or whiskey and discussed art. When time permitted, Siqueiros also gave lectures on art in an empty room behind a hardware store in the building. Alternating between English and Spanish, he explained his theories on art and his latest discoveries and techniques.

After a month of steady work, the mural was almost finished and only the central portion had not been painted. One night he told his assistants that he was tired and everyone should clean up and go home. When everyone else had retired, however, he began to paint the central figure, working feverishly in the cold night air.

When the scaffolding came down the next day and the mural was unveiled, passersby were stunned. The bright colors and bold composition of *Tropical America* were inescapable, even in this bustling and congested urban area. At the inauguration, which took place at night in a light rain, Siqueiros stood in the spotlights, his head uncovered, like the conductor of an orchestra. After explaining the mural in his accented English, he declared that the buildings of the future would be covered with dynamic murals created by teams of artists working together towards a common goal. Ignoring the rain, the crowd remained and following his comments, filed across the roof to meet the artist and have a closer view of "Tropical America."

When the message of *Tropical America* began to sink in, however, it provoked angry protests from the community. Instead of the tropical paradise the public had envisioned, he had painted an Indian being crucified on a cross beneath an American eagle, a victim of Yankee imperialism. Behind this central figure rose a Mayan pyramid with broken columns and sculptures representing the destruction of native cultures. To the right, over the door, a Mexican and a Peruvian peasant crouched, their rifles ready to defend their lands against modern imperialists.

The left part of the wall was filled with an octopus-like tree, its undulating arms embracing the ruins of the Indian temple. To heighten the sense of these arms gripping the geometric forms, Siquerios had directed one of his assistants to incise a groove along the edge of the branches, thereby creating a three-dimensional effect. The contrast of the curvilinear forms of the tree and the Indian martyr with the geometric form of the pyramid created a tension characteristic of Mexican baroque painting, while the central pyramid shape created a recessive perspective.

Tropical America, 1932, Cement Fresco, Los Angeles, California

Despite the protests against its anti-American and political overtones, the local art community congratulated Siqueiros on the bold composition, sense of movement, tension, brilliant use of color and sculptural monumentality. Writing in *The Illustrated Daily News,* Don Ryan described how the sculptural forms advanced and retreated and the bold colors commanded the public's attention from great distances. However, he added, federal authorities viewed his art as dangerous propaganda while conservatives addicted to traditional views or art were alarmed by Siqueiros's vision of the future.

Film director Seymour Stern wrote that "Siqueiros is the Eisenstein of painting," not only because of his development of new techniques but also because his art was revolutionary in its content. "Siqueiros," he proclaimed, "is the first true voice of the world revolution in the sphere of the graphic arts which gives a revolutionary message, with a revolutionary form."

This acclaim, however, could not save his second mural painting in Los Angeles or extend his visa. His patron, Mr. Ferenz, yielded to the public outcry by having the central area of the wall painted over with a coat of white paint that did not completely hide the composition. Several years later, one of the tenants of the building refused to renew her lease until it was completely destroyed, at which point the cement fresco was painted over again. Despite recent efforts to preserve or restore "Tropical America," it has suffered from the elements, as well as the overlays of paint and is barely visible today.

Nevertheless, *Tropical America* demonstrated Siqueiros's adaptation of modern materials and tools to mural painting, including commercial paints, Portland cement, the electric projector, still photography, air compressors, spray guns, and airbrushes. Confronted by the challenge of painting an exterior mural in a busy urban area, he had perceived the unique problems posed by mural paintings and begun a search for a multiangular perspective for "the dynamic spectator."

Although it would be years before he would perfect this concept, he had created a dynamic and rhythmic composition through the interplay of the horizontal and rounded forms against the vertical columns and geometric form of the pyramid, and the receding form of the pyramid drew the spectator into the back of the picture plane. In *Tropical America* and *Street Meeting* he had also applied his frequently stated views on teaching art by directing a team of artists working on a mural project.

Besides signifying a breakthrough in Siqueiros's personal style, *TropicalAmerica* also reflected his rejection of picturesque and folkloric art. The martyred Indian, the ruined temple and the revolutionary peasants were not just interesting or cute aesthetic forms. They boldly expressed the current reality and made a statement about the human condition. At a time when content was considered to be irrelevant in art, it was the content which provoked its destruction. Years later, some of these images and ideas, along with Siqueiros's views about art, would resurface in the Chicano movement and the work of its artists.

While he was still working on *Tropical America*, Siqueiros gave a lecture on "The Vehicles of Dialectic Subversive Painting" at the John Reed Club in Hollywood, named after the American reporter who had covered the Mexican and Russian revolutions. In a lengthy discourse, he resumed his attack on contemporary art and the use of archaic methods and expressed the ideas and techniques that he was exploring. After describing the processes involved in *The Street Meeting* and *Tropical America*, he condemned modern artists for using methods which were thousands of years old and pointed out that the "mural block painters" were using modern elements and instruments that were indispensable for modern revolutionary agitation and propaganda.

Even modern artists with a revolutionary ideology have accepted artistic technology as unchangeable and absolute, but anachronistic instruments and materials can only produce an anachronistic aesthetic, he asserted. While the Mexican artistic renaissance had started as a revolutionary movement, it had become opportunistic and counter-revolutionary. We forgot that new social conditions require new methods of expression, "One cannot play psychologically subversive revolutionary music on a church organ."

Therefore, our movement was not modern but archaic, not monumental but picturesque, not proletarian but populist, not subversive but mystical, not international but chauvinistic and folkloric.

Like the voice of the proletariat, the art of agitation and revolutionary propaganda must be dialectic, combative and optimistic.

Paraphrasing Rivera, he declared, "Easel painting is petty private property. Mural painting belongs directly to the masses, to all of humanity." Therefore, the technical revolution is derived from our struggle for the supremacy of monumental murals painted directly on exterior walls facing the street. Collective art, under democratically chosen direction, is preferable to petty individual art and only collective work can provide the proletariat with the support it needs in its daily struggle. Besides, it is the only form of artistic instruction since the apprentices participate in all phases of a project. Collective work is also essential for the multiple reproductions and we have shown the supremacy of multiple productions over singular works of art.

While modern artists are totally ignorant of the physical nature of the materials they use, he continued, our collective has tried to develop a scientific understanding of the psychological as well as the physical qualities of the elements of artistic production. Artists need to know not only the physical properties of the materials they use, but also the objective and subjective elements which form artistic expression, including the psychological effects of color, tone, volume, texture, space and rhythm, and which elements are static or dynamic, reactionary or subversive, active or passive.

Following his introductory remarks, David elaborated on the use of archaic materials and techniques. He described the hand brush as an ancient machine of wood and hair in an age of iron and therefore useless for expressing the revolutionary struggle of an industrial proletariat. Likewise, traditional fresco is useless on a modern building of concrete and was socially dead. Oil paints, watercolors and pastels are also useless for monumental painting or multiple reproductions and are old and inadequate voices for expressing the values of a new age.

Therefore, he declared, the future belongs to the modern fresco developed by the "mural block painters!" The suitable materials and elements for "dialectical-subversive painting" are the electric drill, the cement gun, white waterproof cement, the airbrush or spray gun, the blowtorch, the electric projector and pre-colored cement. Still and moving picture cameras are also indispensable tools for the modern and socially conscious artist and only these modern techniques and materials can express the convictions of the revolutionary proletariat. Today the multicolored poster, employing the airbrush, is also of extreme importance since it can be reproduced and is much more effective psychologically than black and white posters.

However, he warned, technology without revolutionary commitment is worthless and that commitment must endorse the struggle against imperialism, the final stage of capitalism and the first stages of a new society. Since the decrepit bourgeoisie is in rout, without ideas or convictions, only artists of the proletariat can produce emotional art representative of the age. "The other artists, those addicted to the bourgeois ideology, suffer the same degeneration. Their work is the reflection of capitalist decadence." The new art will rise, he predicted, as an art of maximum subversive psychology, of socialist conviction for the transitory stage of the dictatorship of the proletariat. It will be a monumental art of the greatest public service, an art truly free for the first time in history.

Siqueiros concluded his lecture with a declaration that the revolutionary artist can only produce important works of art if he has a solid Marxist-Leninist revolutionary theory, is keenly aware of the living reality of the capitalist society, knows the psychological nature of the plastic elements and has a profound knowledge of his technology. He must also have a collective spirit and be able to work within a team of artists and be militantly active, physically and ideologically, in the struggling proletarian organizations. "Only then can one be a revolutionary painter."

Early one morning, just after he had returned from working on *Tropical America*, the phone rang. It was Dudley Murphy, the film director, who told him that Charles Laughton, Charlie Chaplin, Marlene Dietrich and some other actors were at his house and Laughton wanted to buy one of the paintings Siqueiros had left with him to be sold. When he arrived in the car which Murphy had sent, Laughton offered him $2000 each for several paintings, beginning a life-long relationship in which the actor became a major collector of Siqueiros's art.

Following the tumultuous reception of *Tropical America*, Dudley Murphy invited David to paint a mural in the covered patio of his home in Santa Monica. Although it was not a very promising site for a militant artist dedicated to "public art," it allowed him to work on another mural and to continue his experiments in materials and technique. Besides, there was little likelihood of other commissions after the controversy stirred up by *Tropical America* and there would be no restrictions on the subject matter.

Murphy also invited Siqueiros to live in his home while he worked on the mural. After moving into the guesthouse with Blanca and her son, David began painting a fresco of some female figures grouped around a fountain. When Murphy objected to the absence of any political statement, however, David decided to expand on the theme of *Tropical America* by painting "The Mexican Bourgeoisie, Having Risen to Power in the Revolution, Surrenders to Imperialism," a title that he later simplified to *Portrait of Present-Day Mexico*.

As the original title implied, it was a direct attack on the Calles dominated government and the penetration of Mexico by United States imperialism. Yet it would be seen only by Dudley Murphy and his guests and certainly was not visible to Mexicans or Mexican Americans or the general public in Los Angeles. However, it was the only one of his three murals in California to survive, protected in a private residence.

Working in traditional fresco and assisted by Luis Arenal, Reuben Kadish and Fletcher Martin, Siqueiros painted two columns in front of a stepped pyramid on the cement wall beneath the covered patio. While the pyramid centers the composition, its recessive or three-dimensional form draws the viewer back into the picture plane and its geometric form contrasts with the tropical foliage which he painted around and behind it.

In the center section he painted two shawl-draped women and a half naked child sitting on the steps of the pyramid. The widows and survivor of the two martyred men which he painted on the adjoining wall, these figures resemble the Indian workers in *The Burial of a Worker* and his Taxco paintings, *Proletarian Mother* and *Peasant Mother*. They are solid, sculptural and monumental forms whose mask-like faces stare at an uncertain future. The prone figures of the dead men are greatly foreshortened, their receding bodies creating an exaggerated perspective and a contraction of space.

On the opposite side of the pyramid he painted a seated man with a sombrero representing Calles, the former President and current political boss of Mexico. Calles has shed the red mask of a revolutionary which hangs around his neck and is holding a rifle and guarding the bulging moneybags at his feet. On the adjoining wall he painted a small portrait of J. P. Morgan, since the American ambassador to Mexico in the time of Calles was Dwight Morrow, a partner in the Morgan financial firm which had made substantial investments in Mexico.

On the right side wall, opposite the dead workers and J. P. Morgan, Siqueiros painted a Red Guard or soldier with his rifle ready, much like the armed peasants in *Tropical America*. Its solid figure fills the picture plane and its foreshortened and sculptural modeling projects the figure and his rifle forward, beyond the surface of the fresco.

Portrait of Present-Day Mexico, 1932, Fresco, Santa Barbara Art Museum, Santa Barbara, California.

Although it was not as impressive as *Tropical America*, *Portrait of Present-Day Mexico* revealed Siqueiros's growing mastery of fresco and the further development of his personal style. The figures are powerfully modeled in color, sculptural in effect, while the pyramid provides the geometric structure for the composition and a contrast to the flowing shapes of the human figures and green foliage in the background. By now, his use of color, the interplay of contrasting forms, the sculptural modeling and the exaggerated foreshortening were recognizable traits of a definite personal style, first revealed in *The Burial of a Worker*.

Neither Siqueiros's art nor his comments endeared him to the wealthy and conservative community of Southern California. Although the *Los Angeles Times* had hailed Siqueiros as a "genius" and "the most revolutionary of the Mexicans," members of local art circles declared that archaic Mexican art forms had no place in Los Angeles, in spite of its Spanish and Mexican origins and a large Mexican American community. While expressing admiration for Mexican art, they rejected its depiction of suffering and pagan, primitive and bloody religions as alien to "our national expression."

Still others protested the employment of a Mexican artist, especially an outspoken Marxist, while American artists went hungry. In spite of the liberal artistic community in Hollywood, the Los Angeles establishment was conservative and anti-union, and many Angelinos resented his comments on racism and imperialism or objected to the anti-American and pro-labor messages of his murals.

Thanks to his notoriety, there were demands for his deportation while he was still working in the Plaza Art Center and, after the unveiling of *Tropical America* and his statements at the John Reed Club, the charges mounted to a full crescendo, calling for his immediate expulsion from the country. In a letter to William Spratling in Taxco, Siqueiros explained that the authorities were refusing to extend his visa despite the petitions of thousands of intellectuals on his behalf. While he expressed his regrets about leaving, since he had only been exposed to a small portion of industrial America, he was convinced that he had made an important advance in public art, the painting of outdoor murals.

Since his return to Mexico would have meant a return to prison, especially in view of his recent statements and the subversive message of *Portrait of Present-Day Mexico*, some of his friends took up a collection and arranged passage to South America. Less than a year after their arrival in Los Angeles, therefore, Siqueiros, Blanca and her son sailed from the port of San Pedro, destined for Uruguay and Argentina. While some of the "mural block painters" continued to work together after his departure, the anti-Red squad raided their exhibit of socially oriented murals and shot or bashed in their frescos of black Americans with rifle butts.

Despite the brevity of his visit to the United States, Siqueiros's accomplishments in Los Angeles were impressive and full of portents for the future. His insistence on teamwork and collective projects was more rhetoric than reality, but he had applied his ideas of teaching art by organizing a team of artists and students, and the participants were able to learn by observing him and assisting on the project.

Thanks to the work of the Mexican muralists in Mexico and the United States, mural painting became a respectable art form in the United States, leading directly to government sponsored mural projects all over the country through the Works Progress Administration (WPA). In spite of Siqueiros's warnings, however, *buon fresco* was the medium for most of the WPA muralists.

Nevertheless, he was convinced that he had initiated something totally new, murals painted on the outside of buildings, exposed to the sun and the rain and visible to the general public. In his view, *Street Meeting* and *Tropical America* were revolutionary developments in civic or public art, regardless of their fate. Since he insisted that mural painting was not something applied to a building, but part of the total architectonic space, he had also integrated his murals with the features of the walls on which they were painted.

In Los Angeles Siqueiros had searched for and developed "a new technology for a new age," using cement instead of plaster for fresco, new faster-drying commercial pigments, electric projectors, cameras and photography, airbrushes, spray guns, compressors, lineographs and stencils for the application of paint on modern buildings. Intrigued by the "accidents" produced by these tools, he began another search and it was in Los Angeles that he became aware of "the dynamic spectator" and the need to develop a different perspective for mural painting.

Siqueiros's experiences in California had stimulated new ideas and convinced him that the techniques and materials of modern art were archaic and anachronistic. This awareness, he insisted, had evolved not from abstract theorizing, but from trying to paint a mural on a modern building. The challenge of painting on the outside of modern structures posed new problems which required new solutions and from these experiments evolved the theory. "In my case," he declared, "theory has never preceded practice."

While he later admitted that he lacked professional experience in "these romantic mural experiments," he did not regret painting them even though they had been destroyed. He viewed art as a weapon in the class struggle and the ruling classes had proved this point by attacking his murals. His purpose, he later explained, had always been to create a new muralism against all obstacles and he could rationalize that the publicity generated by his murals focused attention on the causes he supported. Since he had painted his version of contemporary society, North American imperialism and the Calles regime in Mexico in unequivocal terms, no one could have missed his point.

Although both of his "public" murals in Los Angeles would be painted over or destroyed, and the only mural which survived was a fresco in a private residence, his experiences in Los Angeles and the direct contact with the products of modern industry were to give him new energy and new ideas. When time and circumstances permitted, he would incorporate and expand on the theories and techniques that he had developed in California.

Siqueiros's first stop in South America was Montevideo, Uruguay. After her distressing experiences in Mexico and their tumultuous visit to the United States, Blanca welcomed the sight of her native land. But if she hoped for a more restful life, her mate had other ideas and neither his involuntary departure from the United States nor his exile from Mexico had dampened his energy or enthusiasm. He viewed his exile as another opportunity to pronounce his artistic theories, explore new artistic possibilities, and renew his union and political activities. Shortly after their arrival, her uncle, the President of Uruguay, committed suicide rather than surrender to a military coup and the country was now under a military dictatorship. What followed was another short residence in a foreign country, cut short by his deportation and the loss of his comrade and lover.

In Montevideo David gave a talk on the Mexican Renaissance in which he explained how the Indian painters of Mexico had taught the artists how to prepare and paint in fresco and predicted that the Mexican movement had unlimited possibilities. He also gave a lecture on the lessons derived from the Mexican experience and declared that art had degenerated when it was separated from the masses and became cerebral rather than based on emotion or conviction. He spoke about integrating painting, sculpture and architecture, which had been mutilated by their separation, and he called for the painting of sculpture. The art of the ancient civilizations had been ideological, he explained, and the early Christians were revolutionaries who developed a new form of art, an art with a subversive content.

When he spoke at the First of May demonstration of the Confederation of Intellectual Workers of Uruguay, which he had helped to organize, he attacked intellectuals for having become the blind servants of the feudal bourgeoisie of Latin America and collaborators with the foreign imperialists. While "we were the propagandizers of the class culture of the bourgeoisie, a culture of oppression against the working masses ...," he urged them to become "the enthusiastic applicators of a new revolutionary culture which the proletariat is developing." After praising the Soviet Union for launching the final class struggle, he declared that they were using the weapons of the bourgeois class to "make the social revolution" and document the struggles of the working class.

In a letter to the Central Committee of the Communist Party of Uruguay, he explained that although he had been expelled from the Mexican Party for disciplinary reasons, he had continued to work within the movement and asked that he be judged by his actions. After describing his service to the revolution since his expulsion, he explained that he had come to Uruguay to form the "Block of Painters, Montevideo Section," present lectures on agitation painting and collaborate with the Party.

When David went into a paint store in Montevideo to purchase some art materials, the only paint available was a new industrial paint from the United States. Nevertheless, he purchased several large cans of "Duco," the brand name of the commercial pigment, mixed it with oil paint and began to experiment, producing a series of portraits and easel paintings. He had not only discovered Duco, but his chance discovery eventually led to the use of pyroxylin, both of which were to transform his pictorial technique.

When a show of his recent work opened at the Center for the Fine Arts in Montevideo, it included *Proletarian Victim*. Painted in Duco on burlap, it featured a large nude female figure bound to a wooden beam with a coarse rope and her head bowed, a trickle of blood oozing from a bullet wound in the top of her head. It also bore the title of *Contemporary China*, and was probably based on a photograph of an execution during the Japanese invasion of Manchuria in 1932. Sculptural and monumental, it was powerful expression of the oppression and suffering of the working class and indirectly, the persecution of the communist movement.

Following the exhibit, Siqueiros was invited to Buenos Aires to give several lectures to the Society of the Friends of Art. His first two lectures in Argentina, however, provoked such an outcry that the rest were cancelled. While he concentrated on his painting, he also wrote some articles for local papers and gave some informal lectures in which he called for the development of a new aesthetic and a new social order. These talks and discussions contributed to the formation of the Union of Plastic Artists by Argentine artists.

Assuming the role of an art critic, he wrote a two-part review on the 13th Salon of Fine Arts for the periodical *La Crítica*. Although he recognized the talent of several artists, he described the exhibit as further proof of the decomposition of the capitalist regime and, with a few exceptions, characterized most of the sculptures and paintings as merely the "mirror of capitalist decadence." After severely criticizing pieces of sculpture for their lack of color, their treatment as independent objects suspended in space and the absence of any ideological content, he described most of the paintings as "disguised academicism, shamefaced snobbism" and employing anachronistic techniques.

These artists, he continued, paint still lifes, peaceful landscapes and mystical nudes in the midst of the bloodiest campaigns of the desperate capitalist class and the violent attacks of the bourgeois fascists against the proletariat. But, he added, the exhibit of the Fine Arts Salon was no different than that of other colonial countries and most of the displayed works imitated the predominant snobbisms of the imperialistic countries.

For more than a year Siqueiros wrote articles for the Sunday supplement of *La Crítica* in which he expressed his views on contemporary art and described his experiences in the Mexican Revolution. In one article he predicted that "when class oppression by the ruling class comes to an end, [painting will be] ... genuinely pure art, completely free from any decorative, anecdotal, descriptive or imitative intention." In "An Appeal to Argentine Artists" he wrote about taking art out of the museums, galleries and private homes and converting it into a force for public service, producing art on the most visible public walls in working class districts, union halls, sport stadiums and open air theaters.

Besides his comments on art and politics, Siqueiros was also becoming involved in union and political activities. Since the Argentine military and the conservative government repressed labor and the independent trade unions, his public statements and participation in union and political organizations aroused suspicions and he was detained by the police. After promising to refrain from further political activity, he was released from custody.

Temporarily silenced, he accepted a commission to paint a mural for the publisher of *La Crítica* and for several months he was preoccupied with this assignment. Although he had talked about painting the most visible murals on the most strategic walls in the country, his only mural in Argentina was in an obscure and private bar in the town of Don Torcuato, outside Buenos Aires, and the content was neither ideological nor social. But he had no other offers and the site was a tunnel-shaped room in the basement of a private residence in which he could experiment and apply some of his recently derived theories on mural painting.

Working with a five-man team of Argentine and Uruguayan artists, he began a fresco painting over a background of black cement. After analyzing the geometric structure of the space, "the Plastic Box," he had nude females pose in a glass box that could be moved while photographs were taken of them from different angles. Projecting the prints on the wall, David traced the designs on the wall with a spray gun, creating a series of contorted bodies and a sense of motion. Then, using the nitrocellulose pigments which he had discovered accidentally in Montevideo, he painted the images on the wet cement, after which he touched up the whole surface with silicate, another recent discovery.

In order to integrate the total architectonic space with the mural, he had tiles of pre-colored cement laid on the floor while he planned to complement the painted surfaces with colored lighting. He also used movie and still cameras to check the composition and to document the different angles from which a "dynamic spectator" would view the mural. But film and cameras were not just tools to be used by the artist. Envisioning a film of a dynamic mural as a final and superior form of public art, a "pictorial cinematographic art" which could be seen by everyone, he arranged for the filming of *Plastic Exercise* and an exhibit of photographs of the mural.

Although it was private and non-ideological, *Plastic Exercise* was revolutionary in concept and execution, and it demonstrated another advance in his mural technique. In addition to the use of new materials and techniques, it featured an active composition and different perspectives that were triggered by the moving spectator.

In a leaflet that he wrote to explain the mural, Siqueiros described it as a "dynamic, monumental painting for a dynamic spectator," which "barnacled, static spectators, academic cadavers and objectivist snobs will not really enjoy." Since it could not be ideologically revolutionary in a private residence, he explained, "It is only a project of abstract art ... a group art exercise, art practice ... plastic gymnastics." Because of its collective effort, however, it is revolutionary and the use of new techniques will contribute to "an absolutely revolutionary improvement in the plastic and graphic arts."

Meanwhile, he continued, "the decrepit motor of the intellectual bourgeoisie" can only produce "pale expressions in those dark official academies disguised as liberal, modern schools." Those schools, including "popular and archaic Mexican muralists," are out of touch with the modern world and will be worthless in the future. In spite of his obvious debt to the Italian futurists, Siqueiros also condemned them, who "perished in the defense of an abstract theory of movement. Their bier was easel painting ... The enemies of the anachronistic died of anachronism ... now they are fascists."

Although he lived up to the terms of his conditional freedom while he worked on *Plastic Exercise*, his abstinence from political activities was short-lived. Soon after its completion, he attended and spoke at a meeting of the furniture workers' union and was arrested. Although Blanca was with him, she denied that she knew him and abandoned him to his fate. For David this was the unpardonable sin, since he not only took tremendous risks himself but also insisted on the same dedication and sacrifice from his female companion. Though he later wrote to her from New York, their separation was final.

Despite her betrayal and desertion of him, the beautiful and talented Blanca was one of David's truly passionate loves and she had provided emotional support and stuck by him during their difficult times in Mexico and California. She was not only talented, but also restless and emotionally volatile, and her sudden abandonment of him may have been provoked by his own actions. Her experiences with him in Mexico, Los Angeles and Argentina would have taxed the patience and dedication of any woman and must have convinced her of the hectic life she would have if she stayed with him. Given her paranoia about Mexico and subsequent episodes in his life, she probably made a wise choice in Argentina.

Following his arrest, Siqueiros was deported from the country, the second time he had been expelled from Argentina in four years. In the intervening years he had been arrested and served more than a year in confinement in prison and Taxco and had been exiled or deported from Mexico, the United States and Argentina. However, he was leaving Argentina without his female companion of the last five years and, while he had painted four murals in this period, two had already been destroyed and the other two were in private homes, far from the multitudes of the United States or Argentina.

Although he would not have another mural to paint for six years, these years had not been wasted. He had researched new materials and techniques and, in the process of painting murals, had derived new theories which he proclaimed in print and speech. He had also advanced his own pictorial technique and painted more than one hundred canvases, many of them of unusual emotive power. Mural painting was being revived in Mexico and when the opportunity arose, he would be able to apply his discoveries in new mural projects.

The fate of his murals had also served a purpose. He had linked his art to the struggles of the working class and the controversy stirred up by his murals or public statements had enlarged his audience and generated publicity for that struggle. The destruction of the murals increased public awareness of them and revealed the contradictions of the liberal society which he was attacking. He had also stimulated the discussion of the role of art and promoted the organization of artists in the United States, Uruguay and Argentina. The absence of a devoted female companion was only temporary.

VIII. A New Realism

Although his visa had not been renewed in Los Angeles, David obtained permission to reenter the United States after his expulsion from Argentina. Following a brief stopover in Brazil, he arrived in New York early in 1934, destitute and alone. But since his brother was living in New York, he moved in with Jésus, while friends helped him arrange some portrait commissions. Alma Reed, a patroness of the arts who had befriended Orozco, also arranged for a one-man show of his paintings at her Delphic Studios.

Just before the opening, Siqueiros was interviewed by *Art Digest*. Although he talked about teamwork in painting and the use of the still and movie cameras to plan mural compositions, and expressed his hopes to paint "a series of murals, preferably exterior" in New York, those projects never materialized and he left soon after for Mexico.

The show included some of his recent portraits along with canvases he had painted in Taxco, Los Angeles and South America, including *Proletarian Mother* and *Proletarian Victim*. There were also photographs of his Los Angeles murals and *Plastic Exercise*, along with a statement on his experiences and discoveries on these projects signed, "David Alfaro Siqueiros, Member of the International Team of Painters."

After the exhibit, a reviewer for the *New York Sun* wrote that Siqueiros, like Rivera and Orozco, paints propaganda on behalf of the proletariat but has set himself apart from his compatriots by his more intimate treatment of the masses. After describing Siqueiros as an "artist of imagination and power," whose subjects appear to be "hewn from stone," the reviewer praised his easel paintings for their heroic size, powerful appeal and expressiveness.

A few days later, the persistent Mrs. Myers appeared and renewed her charges that he had stolen *Accident in the Mine* from her. Hoping to settle their account, David offered to paint a portrait of her daughter, a beautiful ballerina. When they saw the finished portrait, mother and daughter were ecstatic and showered him with kisses and compliments. A week later, however, an angry Mrs. Myers telephoned and called him a "miserable coward" and "Mexican bandit." Unnerved by her presence when he was painting, he had omitted the "q" from his name when he signed the portrait. Hoping to end an imbroglio that began in Taxco, he corrected his error.

Before he left for Mexico, Siqueiros ignited a heated exchange with Diego Rivera over his art and politics. In 1934 he wrote an article for the leftist weekly *New Masses* entitled "The Counter-Revolutionary Road of Diego Rivera," in which he accused Rivera of degenerating into "archaeologism," chauvinism and academic snobbism. This scathing attack on Rivera exacerbated the conflict between them and sparked a heated debate in Mexico, complete with pyrotechnics and violent exchanges between their supporters.

The polemic which erupted between Rivera and Siqueiros in 1935 had a long history and several dimensions. Diego was the older of the two and an established artist when he introduced Siqueiros to European art and artists in Paris. Although they had worked together in the artists' union, Rivera was the senior statesman and received more attention and publicity than any of the other artists. After Orozco and Siqueiros were discharged from their murals in the Preparatory School, Diego continued to receive mural commissions from the government.

Although both of them had gone to the Soviet Union, Siqueiros went as a labor delegate while Rivera was received as a great artist and was invited to paint a fresco in the Red Army Club. Because of his support of Trotsky and lack of discipline, however, Rivera was expelled from the Mexican Communist Party. Then, while the government was increasing its attacks on the Party, Rivera continued to receive commissions from the government, as well as the American Ambassador, and was appointed Director of the National Academy of Fine Arts.

When he was accused of "painting murals for millionaires," Rivera explained that he had used their money to paint revolutionary murals in workers' centers which did not spare his patrons or the American past. He had painted an unflattering portrait of "Stalin, the executioner," finished two small panels for the New York Trotskyite headquarters, and openly supported Trotsky's newly proclaimed "Fourth International." He had also attacked "academic art" in the Soviet Union and called the Central Committee of the Mexican Communist Party the "international functionaries, petty leaders and intellectual lackeys of Sir Joseph Stalin."

Siqueiros's differences with Rivera, however, were more than just ideological or aesthetic. While he had provoked his share of controversy in Los Angeles and his New York show was a success, his achievements were eclipsed by the notoriety and artistic accomplishments of Rivera and Orozco. They had received critical acclaim in the United States and had completed impressive murals in Mexico and the United States. Meanwhile, his only attempt at mural painting in Mexico remained unfinished and the only other ones which had not been destroyed were in private homes in California and Argentina.

It was in this atmosphere of personal and professional rivalry, as well as the volatile political climate of the 1930s, that Siqueiros launched his attack on Rivera in the *New Masses*. After describing the Mexican muralist movement as the first attempt to develop a collective and revolutionary public art in modern times, he characterized Rivera's art as "snob, folklorist, indigenous, archaeological and chauvinistic." The perfect snob or *montparnasse* in Paris, Rivera had become "the perfect mental tourist... indigenous, folklorist, archaeologist" in Mexico. Besides emphasizing the circumstantial or regional rather than the characteristics of a social class, he idealized the Indian and the peasant and surrendered muralism to his government patron.

Rivera was a "demagogue and an opportunist," wrote Siqueiros, whose idea of the Syndicate was really a means of collaboration with the government. "Proclaiming collective work, he destroyed any possibility of working collectively...[and] took for himself...all official work for the government." In *El Machete* he was a saboteur who never contributed a drawing and only wrote one article in all its years. Since he never had any real union experience and had not participated in the daily struggle of the working class, he could never be anything but a "dilettante" in revolutionary art. His technique "was mystical for the proposition of revolutionary art; inside walls, traditional anachronistic fresco, the painting brush, etc." and his "academic ideas of composition" come from Europe.

Turning to the content of Rivera's murals, Siqueiros wrote that his murals in Mexico were full of generalities, abstract symbols, pseudo-Marxist lessons and academic discourses, instead of instructions for immediate action. Rivera never paints the imperialists, their Mexican allies or their Latin American victims, and Calles never appears as the butcher of working Mexicans. Although he painted the Spanish conquerors for the American ambassador, he ignored this "modern Cortez" who was his friend, and his widow is his "Godmother" in the United States.

After describing Rivera as the preferred painter of the tourists, from whom he earns a fortune, Siqueiros called him "the painter of millionaires." Meanwhile the revolutionary mural painting which they initiated in Mexico had been replaced by Mexican souvenir painting. Rivera painted a female tennis champion in California for the Pacific Coast Stock Exchange Club, but forgot Tom Mooney, the Scottsboro boys and all the problems of the North American working class. In depicting the present, Siqueiros charged, Rivera uses symbols, like the NRA (National Recovery Act), which will increase U.S. profits at the expense of Latin America, while he does not paint portraits of FDR, Calles, Morrow, Machado or their victims, Julio Antonio Mella or the martyred peasant leader José Guadalupe Rodríguez. "Once again Rivera is brave with the dead and cowardly with the living."

The list of charges continued. Siqueiros accused Rivera of being a renegade who attacked the Central Committee in the bourgeois press after his expulsion from the Party. When he became Director of the School of Fine Arts, he established a program of "demagogic mystification." When they were arrested on the First of May in 1930, he had denied that he was in the demonstration.

Despite his criticism of Rivera and Mexican mural painting in general, Siqueiros ended his article in the *New Masses* on a positive note. "The Mexican mural movement is a utopian movement on the way to revolutionary painting," and from its errors "we must learn some useful lessons.... Let us initiate an international team of revolutionary painters!"

Just before he left for Mexico, Siqueiros issued a manifesto entitled "Towards the Transformation of the Plastic Arts," in which he further clarified his differences with Rivera. The Parisian movement and the Mexican Renaissance are disintegrating, he wrote, and artists must develop a new international movement to transform the plastic arts. After he cited the "Mural Block Painters of Los Angeles" and the "Polygraphic Team of Buenos Aires" as useful antecedents, he suggested a course of action. In order to develop an art for the greatest public utility, we have "to eliminate the bourgeois elitism of European art," end superficial folk art called "Mexican Curious" and work collectively against "the egocentrism of modern European art." In the process we shall learn and teach our new art by producing it, using modern tools and materials, painting exterior murals and excluding any form of private art for the privileged elite.

His latest manifesto also called for the establishment of school-workshops to develop public art forms, including colored prints, editions of drawings and colored posters, polychromed sculpture, photogenic paintings, photomontage, documentary photography and cinematography and murals painted on cement and silicate using the airbrush and other mechanical means. They should also develop a theory and practice of the chemistry of plastic materials and a publicity department to display and publish these works of art.

After two years of exile, Siqueiros was going home. In the wake of "the battle of Rockefeller Center," no one was hiring Mexican muralists in the United States and mural painting was being revived in Mexico. Between 1930 and 1933, Fermín Revueltas, Máximo Pacheco, Juan O'Gorman, Rufino Tamayo, Fernando Leal, Alfredo Zalce and Julio Castellanos had painted murals in public buildings around the capital. Rivera and Orozco were also back in Mexico and Diego recreated the destroyed Rockefeller Center mural in Bellas Artes while Orozco portrayed a dehumanized world in his *Catharsis* on the opposite wall. By 1934, Pablo O'Higgins, an American apprentice of Rivera's, Leopoldo Méndez, Angel Bracho, Antonio Pujol, Alfredo Zalce, Pedro Rendón and the American sisters Marion and Grace Greenwood were working on murals in the Abelardo Rodríguez Market. That same year many of these same artists met in Pablo O'Higgins' studio and formed the League of Revolutionary Writers and Artists (LEAR) to unite antifascist intellectuals and to plan a new art movement for the masses.

Although Calles still controlled Mexico, in 1934 the National Revolutionary Party nominated Lázaro Cárdenas for the presidency and adopted a revolutionary "Six Year Plan." These plans to revive the Revolution, however, provoked opposition at home and abroad and throughout Cárdenas's six-year term, Mexico was torn by ideological debates and violent confrontations between the Left and the Right.

As President, Cárdenas redistributed more land than all the previous presidents combined and nationalized the railroads and turned their management over to the unions. When he nationalized the oil industry in 1938, however, the foreign oil companies conducted a campaign of propaganda, boycott and sabotage against Mexico, forcing Cárdenas to sell oil to Germany, Italy and Japan.

The country that Siqueiros returned to in 1934, therefore, was fragmented and volatile. Never an innocent bystander, he welcomed the opportunity to renew his political militancy and although he was not a member of the Communist Party, he participated in many of its activities. When the National League Against Fascism and War was founded, he was elected President and was in the forefront of its efforts. Because of his participation in antigovernment demonstrations or violent clashes with the opposition, he also found himself in the now familiar prison cells of Mexico City.

But life was not all militant politics. Following his return to Mexico City, David became enamored of María Asunsolo, the daughter of a martyred *zapatista* general. They had met in 1930 when he and Blanca were given refuge by her uncle, the sculptor Ignacio Asunsolo. "Mariquita," as David called her, was a cousin of film star Dolores del Río and was considered to be the most beautiful woman in Mexico City. She was the subject of numerous portraits by different artists and her apartment in Mexico City became a gallery of art and a meeting center for Mexican and foreign artists. She also shared Siqueiros's political convictions.

Infected with "*asunsolitis*," David painted several portraits of María which reflected his consuming passion for her. Using a new synthetic paint, he carefully modeled and textured her features, arms and hands, using light and shadow to create a sculpturesque portrait of María as a beautiful young girl in white lace and ribbons in her hair.

In *María Asunsolo Descending a Stairway* he painted her descending stairs and making a grand entrance in a revealing gown. The creases of her skirt suggest movement as she advances down the steps, while the waving curtains on both sides repeat the sense of movement, creating a realistic version of Duchamp's *Nude Descending a Staircase*. This dynamic effect gives life to the figure and shatters the static quality of the two dimensional surface. When they were shown publicly, these rare sensual portraits fueled local gossip.

Although María was married and had a son, she was separated from her husband, thanks to her well-publicized affair with Siqueiros. When her husband won custody of their son, Siqueiros kidnapped the child while he was being taken for a walk in a park, provoking a scandal. While the child ended up being raised by his father in Germany, Siqueiros recorded the experience in a painting in which a man threatens a barefoot woman and grabs the arm of the child she is carrying. After he finished *Abduction*, David presented it to María. Besides expressing his love for her, his painting of María descending the stairs and *Abduction* suggest the more dynamic paintings to come and the impulsive act which the latter commemorates was a harbinger of the future.

Although they never married, David's brief romance with María was one of the most ardent of his life and moved him deeply. Even after his departure from Mexico, he continued to write to her from New York and Europe, addressing her affectionately as *"Generalita del Chilpancingo,"* *"Merita divina,"* *"Mi puma adorable,"* or *"Mariquita de mi Vida."* After expressing his feelings for her, he described his latest experiences in art and war. He was also writing to Blanca Luz Brum in Uruguay and Angélica Arenal in Mexico.

Preoccupied with politics and romance during the day, Siqueiros painted at night in order to support himself. Sharing a room with the Bolivian artist Roberto Berdecio, he usually arrived home late and then dashed off several semi-abstract landscapes which he had promised to a buyer or which he would try to sell the next day. The next morning he would rush off to a meeting or demonstration, often without changing his clothes. However, he was never shabby and women found him charming and attractive.

Although he painted to support himself, he worked like a man possessed, either driven by a need to catch up with and surpass other artists or inspired by his latest discoveries. He also had plans to leave the country and in one final spurt, just before he left for New York, he painted every night for ten days, producing enough paintings to pay for his trip.

Before he left, however, he provoked and participated in one of the most widely discussed artistic events of the decade. In August of 1935 a group of North American educators was meeting in the Palace of Fine Arts in Mexico City and they invited Siqueiros to address them. Since Diego Rivera had spoken the previous night on "The Arts and Their Revolutionary Role in Culture," Siqueiros seized the opportunity to renew his criticisms of Rivera. But while he was summarizing the points he had made in his article in the *New Masses*, Rivera jumped to his feet, denying the accusations and demanding an opportunity to respond to Siqueiros.

When the chairman of the meeting explained that this was a conference, not a debate, Diego drew a pistol and demanded to be heard. After Siqueiros also produced a pistol, the two of them emptied their weapons into the ceiling, producing a rain of plaster and forcing everyone out into the street. No one was injured, but the next day the newspapers were filled with commentary on the incident, probably prearranged, and the discussion on Mexican art.

After this dramatic opening, a debate was arranged between the two adversaries. By mutual agreement, a committee of artists would conduct the debates and Siqueiros's roommate, Roberto Berdecio, would preside. Diego proposed that each of them appoint seconds and he proceeded to choose two Trotskyites, an economist and a labor leader. Siqueiros appointed the Spanish writer Rafael Alberti and his wife, María Teresa León.

At the opening session, María Teresa began to speak in her affected Castilian when Diego's former wife, Guadalupe Marín, stood up in the rear of the auditorium and shouted, "Give your *huevos* back to Alberti," a reference to his sex organs. After the laughter subsided, María Teresa shot back, "Not the eggs, for that is what chickens have, but the balls of Alberti are what interest you, but which for the grace of your *patrona*, the Virgin of Guadalupe, you don't have."

After this spicy start, the debate resumed and for several days, Mexico City was galvanized by a public debate between two artists on the role of art in a revolutionary society and the status and future of the Mexican Mural Movement. The debates were covered by the press and were followed closely, not only by intellectuals and artists, but also by workers who often took sides. Members of the miner's confederation supported Siqueiros and clashed with the pro-Rivera bakers. As the artists made their points, their respective supporters shouted and cheered. At one point, pistols were drawn and shots exchanged in which several workers were injured.

It was a tense situation and more than art was at stake. But, as Siqueiros explained, they had tried to create a "public art" and therefore a dialogue between two public artists should also be public. The American writer Emanuel Eisenberg wrote in the **New Masses** that "Mexico is probably the only country in the world where a controversial meeting between two painters, in much less than a day's notice, could be calculated to attract a thousand people." His analysis, however, failed to consider the volatile climate of Mexico in the 1930s or that the issues were ideological as well as aesthetic. He also underestimated the knack of both artists for creating publicity and the interest generated by the personal clash, *mano a mano*, of two colorful protagonists.

Throughout the debate Siqueiros reiterated and defended the points he had made in the *New Masses* and his recent manifesto: Mexican art was not being produced for tourist export; they should improve on outmoded forms and techniques; they should be more scientific in their methods of composition and perspective and "we should progress from colonial to modern architecture, in which the mural is conceived as an integral part of the design."

He declared that the murals painted in Mexico since 1923 were not accessible to the masses and their techniques and forms were archaic and inappropriate, while the themes were counterrevolutionary, mystical, religious, and demagogic and served the bourgeois government. Rivera was the worst since he painted for the tourists and had not dared to attack Calles. "There is nothing worse in art than overwhelming nationalism," Siqueiros declared, and "the work of Diego Rivera is characteristic of this stagnation despite its great intrinsic value to both the art of Mexico and the world." Although he focused most of his criticism on Diego Rivera, he did not spare other artists, including Orozco.

When it was Diego's turn to speak, he explained that the attack on him had political and personal motives. The official Stalinist party was using Siqueiros to attack him because he, Rivera, was a Bolshevik-Leninist and by attacking his source of income, they could limit his contributions to the Trotskyites. The Party wanted to show that revolutionary artists could not exist outside the official party and to prevent an artist of his international reputation from aiding the more progressive Fourth International.

The Stalinists use Siqueiros because he will do anything in order to be readmitted to the Party, Rivera continued. While they accused him of being an opportunist, he was received in the Soviet Union as a revolutionary artist and was commissioned to paint a mural in the Red Army Club before he was sent home and expelled from the party for being a Trotskyite. He had opposed the suicidal policies of the Central Committee and when he continued to work in the enemy camp, he had to defend himself as much from the Stalinist international bureaucracy as from the bourgeois press.

Although Siqueiros accused him of aiding the imperialist penetration of Mexico, Rivera's enemies in the United States, the KKK and the DAR, protested that Mexican art was invading the United States. If foreigners were interested in Rivera's art, it was because it expressed the beauty and character of Mexico and he had made no concessions to his North American patrons. In Detroit the Catholic women wanted to erase his mural and his mural in New York was destroyed because of its revolutionary content while organized workers and proletarian parties had rallied to his defense.

Rivera then took the offensive. Siqueiros himself admitted that he had painted portraits of bourgeois women, he charged. His friends hailed the mastery of "María Asunsolo Descending the Stairs." "Who then, makes concessions to the bourgeoisie?" Besides, it was stupid and anti-Marxist to condemn the purchase of paintings by capitalists for speculation. It was like accusing an artisan of being counterrevolutionary because rich people purchased his ceramic pots.

Turning to the personal motives, Diego pointed out that he himself sold sixty percent of the art sold in Mexico, Orozco twenty percent and Siqueiros eight percent and all the other artists, the rest. Siqueiros hoped to ally the other artists against him and the attack makes Siqueiros better known, so that he could achieve "talking, that which he could not achieve painting." While he agreed with Siqueiros that an organization was needed to produce multiple copies of revolutionary art for the masses, it was not a new idea or unique to Mexico.

Although Siqueiros claimed that only the revolutionary proletariat could be the judges of what constitutes revolutionary art, where was his work to be found and what were its symbols? He painted an angel, Saint Christopher and some screw-like symbols in a remote corner of the Preparatoria. His work in Guadalajara was in the University and far from the view of the workers and in Buenos Aires, he painted some magical nude women in a private residence. In Los Angeles the sun and rain have erased his work and he painted Christ as an Indian in another mural.

While he agreed with Siqueiros's criticism of his first mural in the theater of the Preparatory School, Rivera explained that the experience had enabled him to correct his errors before his next project. His murals in the Education Ministry, therefore, depicted the people of all races and social classes and thousands of workers, teachers and students passed them daily.

As to the charges that he was cowardly with the living, Diego replied that Siqueiros had painted only one portrait of Calles, in a private home in California. Meanwhile Rivera had painted Calles twice in the National Palace of Mexico, once representing the consolidation of the bourgeois government in Mexico and allied with international finance, and not, like Siqueiros, protected by the border of the United States. He also painted the victims of imperialism and depicted the masses as active and turning their weapons on the capitalist government. Perhaps Siqueiros confused Marx at the top of his mural in the National Palace with Saint Peter or Santa Claus.

Rivera finished his defense by calling Siqueiros's attack a lie and a slander. The facts showed that Rivera was not an opportunist, nor was he afraid of the living or the powerful. The workers of the world would decide and he was not afraid of Calles, Rockefeller, Roosevelt or anyone else, not even a Stalin or a Manuilsky. Neither did he fear self-criticism or criticism as that was the duty of a revolutionary. He was willing to collaborate with his accuser but while "Siqueiros talks, Rivera paints!"

Although there was a touch of personal rivalry throughout the exchanges, Siqueiros insisted that his motivations and objectives were not personal. In defense of his portraits of bourgeois women, he stated that he needed the money in order to live, and because of the penetration of Mexico by foreign imperialists, there was no time or opportunity to paint revolutionary art.

Despite the dramatic opening and the publicity generated by the debates, they sputtered out inconclusively after three days. The

LEAR printed and circulated posters demanding their continuation, but the debates were over. Siqueiros, however, proposed that he and Rivera publish a written analysis of those points on which they concurred. In these "Documents" they agreed that the Mexican Mural Movement had served the demagogic interests of the Mexican government more than those of the workers because of the lack of an ideological preparation. However, it was the first movement in contemporary art to attempt collective art, subjected to discipline and self-criticism and supporting the revolutionary masses in their struggle. They also agreed on the need to develop an "eminently mobile revolutionary art ... capable of reaching ... the poorest areas of the working and peasant masses."

Although the debates ended anti-climactically, they had provided the first collective criticism of modern Mexican art by the artists themselves. Other artists and intellectuals had participated and issues usually reserved for specialized art journals were discussed in public and covered by the newspapers. The subject of art came to be recognized as important in Mexico, ranking with national politics or international affairs and the inauguration of new murals or the openings of galleries were attended by thousands. Nowhere, Siqueiros asserted, did art or artists receive the publicity and attention which they received in Mexico, not even in Paris.

While they had reached agreement on some purely artistic matters, the political differences between Rivera and Siqueiros had not been resolved and would be magnified in coming years. If anyone had any doubts about Rivera's position or was hoping for a truce, he shattered any hopes for reconciliation in a pamphlet which he published in 1935. In "Defense and Attack Against the Stalinists," he defended his art and politics and repeated his charge that the attack on him was political and personal. He also repeated his taunt that Siqueiros talks while Rivera paints.

The abrupt termination of the debates, as well as Siqueiros's departure from Mexico, may have been prompted by his activities on another front. In March the right wing "*Dorados*" (Gold Shirts), led by a former *villista* general, Nicolás Rodríguez, had attacked the offices of the Mexican Communist Party, destroying materials and trashing pictures of Lenin and Stalin. A mixture of former *cristeros* and fascist elements, this reactionary faction had its own calvalry and had attacked teachers and government officials in the countryside. When the Central Committee of the Communist Party learned that they were planning a march on the Zócalo, the central square of Mexico City, on November 20, the anniversary of the 1910 Revolution, members made plans to disrupt the march.

As soon as the two columns of gold-shirted cavalry and infantry began their march to the Zócalo, they found themselves under attack. Although they made it to the square, their way was blocked by automobiles which had been placed in their path and peasants armed with planks which they had taken from the viewing stands set up for the anniversary celebrations. With bugles sounding the attack, the mounted "*Dorados*" turned and charged their adversaries, whirling lariats.

Their adversaries reacted by commandeering automobiles, including taxis, and using them like tanks. Zigzagging around the square, they charged the horsemen and broke up their formations. In the middle of this battle, David Alfaro Siqueiros and Rosendo Gómez Lorenzo suddenly appeared and joined the counter attack, crouching and discharging pistols into the ranks of the "*Dorados*." One of the first casualties was "el general" Nicolás Rodríguez, hit by three bullets, while wounded horses and riders began to litter the pavement. The attack broken, the communists retreated, covered by the two marksmen.

The battle toll included 3 dead and 46 wounded. Siqueiros's participation was captured in a news photo of the "battle" and a reporter called him "*El Capitán Sangre Fría*" (Captain Fearless). The only woman among the defenders of the plaza was Angélica Arenal. Alarmed by the existence of a private counterrevolutionary army, President Cárdenas disbanded the "*Dorados*."

In 1935 the National Assembly of the Producers of Plastic Arts met to select delegates to the American Artists' Congress in New York. After he was chosen, along with Rufino Tamayo and Roberto Berdecio, to represent the Assembly, Siqueiros left for New York.

The LEAR chose Orozco, Antonio Pujol and Luis Arenal to represent the League in New York.

When Siqueiros and Orozco were introduced at the opening of the congress, they received a tremendous ovation. Orozco then read the General Report of the Mexican Delegation, which declared that art had become a luxury item for the rich, kept in their homes and manipulated by the gallery system. In Mexico, however, the League of Revolutionary Writers and Artists was taking steps to raise the cultural level of the masses and to make art, literature, and drama available to the workers.

Next Siqueiros read the paper, "The Mexican Experience in the Plastic Arts," prepared collectively and edited by Emilio Amero and Angélica Arenal, also members of the Mexican delegation. After describing the Mexican mural movement from its origins, the paper repeated the criticisms of opportunism, official reaction and the monopoly of Rivera made earlier by Siqueiros. Fortunately the LEAR has adopted the principle that "revolutionary art is not only a problem of content or theme—but a problem of form." It has also affirmed that revolutionary art must be that which can reach the greatest number of people for the least expense and its members will operate under the principles of collective discipline, self-criticism, and teamwork rather than isolated individualism.

Along with the other delegates, Siqueiros attended a series of receptions and banquets in their honor, never refusing an opportunity to address an audience. When the Communist Party held a banquet for its electoral campaign, he was a guest of honor and sat at the head table with the Party's candidates for the presidency and vice-presidency and Angélica Arenal. When the Latin American community of New York organized a dinner to celebrate the Popular Front victory in the Spanish elections of 1936, he was one of the speakers.

But he was restless and anxious to resume his art and to apply and test some of his theories. He had repeatedly urged the establishment of a workshop to develop new techniques and materials for a modern society, and to produce multi-reproducible art to reach and serve the masses. When the Artists' Congress adjourned, therefore, he invited a group of American and Mexican artists to join him in establishing a laboratory for experimentation in art and a collective workshop to produce art for the people.

A small nucleus of American and Mexican artists responded to his invitation and declared themselves "ready to raise the standard of a truly revolutionary art program." In less than two weeks the experimental workshop opened on West 14th Street. The original members included the Americans Harold Lehman, Sande McCoy, Jackson Pollock, Axel Horn, George Cox, Louis Ferstadt and Clara Mahl, and a Mexican contingent of Luis Arenal, Antonio Pujol, Conrado Vásquez and José Gutiérrez and Siqueiros's roommate, Roberto Berdecio.

The workshop was based on the principles of revolutionary art, collectively conceived, produced and criticized, for a maximum impact on the working classes and linked to the daily struggle of the masses and the population of the country. The members condemned individualists and anarchists, chained to archaic methods, and called for technical teams familiar with the latest technology and conscious of the revolutionary dialectic and the functional reality of contemporary society. Although dedicated to creating art which would serve the masses, they were also confident that it would be transcendent in purely aesthetic terms.

The funds for the operation of the workshop were to be obtained by tuition of five or fifteen dollars per month for the subscribing artists, as well as by donations from wealthy patrons, the most generous of which was George Gershwin. Additional support and commissions came from the Communist Party of the United States, the Farm Labor Party and the *New Masses*.

The first major assignment for the workshop was the design and construction of a float for the May 1, 1936 parade in New York City. Working as a team, the artists designed a massive float described by Siqueiros as "an essay of polychromed monumental sculpture in motion." It featured a figure of Wall Street topped with a swastika holding the emblems of the American political parties. A gigantic hammer decorated with the hammer and sickle moved up and down, crushing a Wall Street ticker tape machine from which flowed a bloody tape.

When he was not working on posters, banners or floats for political campaigns and rallies, Siqueiros was experimenting constantly with new materials and equipment. In Los Angeles he had insisted that tools and materials created their own aesthetic. Now he watched, fascinated by the new shapes and textures which emerged miraculously from his experiments with non-traditional materials.

Spurred on by his energy and enthusiasm, the other artists began to question traditional methods and assumptions and to investigate the use of new substances and equipment. According to Axel Horn, they were going to make the "stick with hairs on its end" obsolete. Using nitrocellulose lacquers and silicones and airbrushes and spray guns, they sprayed it through stencils, over embedded wood, metal, sand and paper. They poured it, dripped it, splattered it haphazardly or hurled it against sheets of plywood, masonite or asbestos panels, developing thin glazes or building it up into thick and heavy gobs. Using a lazy Susan, they poured paint on the spinning surface and integrated the accidental color mixtures into their paintings. Working in a thin haze of paint, the artists, along with the panels, walls, and floors, were spattered with paint.

Astounded by the results, particularly the unique properties of lacquer and the effects achieved through different forms of application, David continued to experiment, observing and analyzing the startling "absorptions" which his experiments created. The tools and medium produced their own effects, he reiterated, and artists should study and apply them in their work. Despite their origin, these accidents constituted important ingredients of art and should be investigated scientifically. Once understood, the artist could utilize them to expand his means of expression, to enhance his plastic language. Working in this manner, first experimenting, then analyzing and applying his perceptions in some experimental works,

Siqueiros developed a theory and technique of "the controlled accident."

In the course of his investigations, Siqueiros produced several striking paintings. Frequently the imagery which he developed in them was suggested by the accidental patterns that the dripping and pouring of paint created on the panels. Using pyroxylin or nitrocellulose, also known as Duco lacquers, a new pigment developed for painting automobiles, he constructed billowing mushroom clouds, bombed out or burning cities and cosmic landscapes.

Siqueiros was ecstatic about the effect and was convinced of the expressive potential of the new materials and technique. Now he could create shapes and textures that were not possible with traditional methods and materials. He could create rather than merely reproduce nature. The new material, pyroxylin, he exulted, makes "biblical fresco, oil, tempura, and water colors obsolete." It offered greater elasticity, transparency and rapid drying features, in addition to producing the most unusual and sensual textures. He was so enthusiastic about the new pigment that the other artists began to call him "*El Duco.*"

Never complacent, he pressed on. In the **Birth of Fascism** he superimposed poured pigment, pyroxylin and lacquer to create a stormy sea representing the current world of capitalism in which the Statue of Liberty is floundering in the wreckage of bourgeois religion, philosophy and morality. Pyroxylin, he declared, meant that he could "create the sea and not merely copy it." In the center of the stormy sea he painted a prostitute on a raft giving birth to a three-headed monster with the faces of Hitler, Mussolini and William Randolph Hearst. In the upper right he painted the sturdy, gleaming rock of socialism, the Soviet Union. Three years later, in the wake of the Hitler-Stalin pact, he repainted *Birth of Fascism*, replacing the portraits of the three "fascists" with an anonymous monster emerging from the womb and painting a swastika in the sea where the Statue of Liberty had floated.

Meanwhile David was writing to María Asunsolo from New York, addressing her affectionately and describing his recent experiences.

After apologizing for not answering her last two letters, he described how he had become disillusioned and depressed in his attempts to harness the spray gun, "this fickle instrument invented by capitalist industry." But he reassured her that he was thinking better politically and was no longer distracted by the purely emotional and sensual aspects of his experiments. On *Birth of Fascism,* he wrote,

> I must tell you that I have finally found the real way
> to use the spray gun ... *Birth of Fascism* is also my
> best work politically, because it is free of the mysticism
> and passivity of my earlier work, is more synthetic
> and more dynamic, and combines the objective with
> the subjective, 'real' realism with mental realism...
> I will serve the revolution using my best voice, my
> best language. You will see! You will see!

For his next project Siqueiros began a study for a photo-mural. By spraying paint over a series of stencils, he created the effect of advancing masses converting an imperialistic war into a struggle against capitalist aggressors. Using the same technique, he superimposed the transparent beams of a lighthouse, representing international communism, over the rest of the painting. The beams not only depicted the positive role of the communist movement but also integrated the different areas of the painting. Although he never finished *Stop the War*, it demonstrated his increasing mastery of the spray gun and a more effective resolution of the problems of composition.

In June David wrote to Blanca Luz Brum, addressing her as "my dearest" and describing his latest discoveries. He bragged that the "Yankee artists" who reviled him for his attacks on Rivera now recognized the validity of his theories and were working with him to open a new stage in propaganda art. "No one can deny that the fundamental problem of revolutionary art is a technical one," he wrote, and "without modern technique, there is no modern art." The ancient materials and techniques are dead, useless voices, comparable to a revolutionary using his hands as an amplifier instead of a microphone.

Next he described the "First of May" float prepared by the workshop as a combination of subjective and objective elements, "a dialectical realism" or "an active realism, objective and subjective at the same time." They were also working on the design and construction of a barge for an anti-Hearst demonstration for the Fourth of July and he expressed his satisfaction that their work had been appreciated by the Communist Party and was politically useful. Our work, he proclaimed, is leading to a "new plastic language... a new and infinitely richer graphic vocabulary for the epoch of the Revolution."

One of Siqueiros's closest friends and the major contributor to the Experimental Workshop was George Gershwin. Meeting frequently in New York, they renewed their discussions on the similarities between art and music. Siqueiros loved to provoke Gershwin by pointing out that painting was superior to music since the former is made by the eyes, "the quintessence of beauty," while music was the product of the ear, "a sad addition to the human body." You might love a woman for her body or her eyes, but never for her ears, he chided, adding that there were innumerable poems written to beautiful eyes, but none to the ears.

When Gershwin asked Siqueiros to paint his portrait, he brought a medium size canvas to Gershwin's Park Avenue apartment. However, Gershwin decided that he wanted a portrait of his whole figure. Then he changed his mind and asked Siqueiros to paint an even larger canvas of him playing a concert in a large theater full of people. Although he told Gershwin that he really wanted a small mural, Siqueiros began to paint him from the rear of the stage, playing the piano in front of a packed Metropolitan Opera House, suggested by splashes of color in the background.

Gershwin was ecstatic when he saw the finished portrait, but he wanted to ask one more favor. Would Siqueiros paint members of his family, his late father, his beloved uncles, his mother, his nephews and his two agents in the audience? he asked. Working in oil, Siqueiros proceeded to paint Gershwin's whole family in miniature, using photographs of Gershwin's dead relatives and arranging sittings for the living.

When the group portrait was finished, they set out to celebrate at the Waldorf Astoria. But in the middle of their celebration, Gershwin suddenly became serious and drew Siqueiros aside and asked him to paint a portrait of himself in the mural. Since Gershwin persisted, Siqueiros inserted his self-portrait in a corner, his elbow resting on the stage, between the footlights and surrounded by the living and dead relatives of the composer, while Gershwin, surrounded by a white halo, plays the piano. Besides its unusual history and many portraits, the painting has a dynamic perspective and monumental quality.

Portrait of George Gershwin in a Concert Hall, 1936,
Oil on Canvas

Back in his workshop, which languished between major assignments, Siqueiros began another painting, applying his latest discoveries and adding still another technique. After preparing a wooden panel with a white primer coat, he added a second coat of reddish brown paint. Then, laying the panel of the floor, he dripped lacquer and paint from a can and a stick on the horizontal surface. As the paint and lacquer interacted, they produced a variety of holes, puddles, waves and textures. With an airbrush he began to paint through stencils to create transparent clouds and other effects. Next he applied pieces of wood cut out with a jigsaw and then painted over them with an airbrush, creating a three dimensional surface or bas-relief.

Collective Suicide depicted the self-destruction of Chichimecas in Northern Mexico to avoid surrendering to the Spaniards. While the subject was not current or revolutionary, it was anti-imperialist and anti-war and marked another advance in his constant search for a new plastic language, revolutionary in form as well as in content. The addition of wood cutouts to *Collective Suicide* was also his first application of another new concept, "sculpture-painting."

Although seemingly pessimistic, *Collective Suicide* implies that the same lack of unity that had led to past disasters would also destroy the collective strategy of the Popular Front for fighting fascism. Ironically, the painting had been commissioned by Gregory Zilboorg, a friend of Gershwin who had fled Russia after serving in Kerensky's Provisional Government and an expert on suicide who contended that mass suicide was the exclusive recourse of "primitive" cultures.

Siqueiros's experimental efforts were not limited to the studio or the workshop. Since Los Angeles he had been interested in painting exterior murals and the use of new industrial paints that would resist sun and rain. But the formulas or special properties of these industrial paints were carefully guarded trade secrets and the efforts of the artists to decipher them or to increase their brilliance and resistance had been thwarted. After several unsuccessful efforts to enlist the cooperation of the paint companies, Siqueiros was convinced that they needed an independent scientific institution to conduct research and provide the artists with accurate information on new paints and materials.

When he was not working on political "sandwiches" (walking billboards), posters or floats, Siqueiros continued to pursue his experiments and investigations with new materials, aided by José Gutiérrez. Then there would be a great spurt of activity as other artists returned to work on floats or posters for a major event or political campaign. Late in June, the workshop began to prepare an allegorical float for a Fourth of July anti-Hearst demonstration. The float would be mounted on a boat which would be sailed by the thousands of New Yorkers celebrating on the beaches at Coney Island.

The float depicted Hearst and Hitler as interchangeable personalities; their heads rotating on a mechanism inside the barge, while bloody hands on the side reflected the suffering of the masses under a regime of fascism. When the day came, however, the police would not let the boat come any closer than 500 yards off shore, where it could not be read by any of the bathers. Rough seas took care of the rest and the artists had to throw the superstructure overboard in order to avoid capsizing.

In 1936 the workshop undertook the preparation of the artwork for the presidential campaign rally of the Communist Party of the United States. While Harold Lehman worked on an enlarged photo-portrait of Earl Browder, the Party's presidential candidate, Siqueiros painted a portrait of James Ford, the Party's black vice-presidential nominee. Using photos of Browder and Ford, they painted their portraits on large masonite panels which were then photographed and projected on even larger panels of masonite and repainted. Applying pyroxylin with an airbrush, they added body and texture to the flat surfaces. When the fifteen-foot high portraits were unveiled at the Party's rally in Madison Square Garden, the audience was struck by the heightened realism of the enlarged painted photographs and the texture of Ford's hair, a mass of heavily encrusted pigment.

Siqueiros and Jackson Pollock with Portraits of Browder and Ford, 1936, New York

Meanwhile, Siqueiros continued to experiment with new materials and techniques and expressed his firm opposition to war and fascism in several small paintings. From a news photograph of a sobbing child taken after a Japanese aerial bombardment in Manchuria, he painted a child in the middle of a bombed city, surrounded by ruins. Its face contorted in pain, the child is screaming through its open mouth. Behind the child's head, he repeated the image, painting a much larger head whose mouth surrounds the smaller head. In the background he painted an oil refinery, its gleaming tanks spared by the aerial attack which has destroyed the city.

Echo of a Scream is devastating, comparable in expressive force to Munch's "The Cry." One can almost feel the anguish and hear the scream as it reverberates across the ruins. It is not only a powerful statement about the human condition, but it also demonstrated Siqueiros's "new realism," in which a contemporary event, recorded by a camera, becomes the basis for his interpretation of that reality. One of several experimental anti-war paintings which he did in New York, it is the first in which he employed photomontage. *Echo of a Scream* is a more direct expression of the suffering and hypocrisy of modern warfare than Picasso's *Guernica.*

Echo of a Scream, 1937, Duco on Wood

In 1936 he also painted two apocalyptic pictures, *The End of the World,* which depicted a burning city with a solitary human figure raising his arms to the sky and *Cosmos and Disaster*, a dark, foreboding image in which he poured paint over pieces of metal, wire and nails attached to a wood and fabric surface. The former probably referred to the German bombing of civilians in Spain, and along with *Echo of a Scream*, *Collective Suicide*, and *Stop the War,* suggests his despair with the spreading conflict in Spain, Africa and Asia. The mood is foreboding and the emphasis is on destruction, chaos and suffering, not victory, resistance or solidarity.

In a more tender but revealing depiction of reality, Siqueiros painted a small girl carrying a baby on her back, set against a chaotic background of smoke and burning ruins, an abstract landscape created by "controlled accidents." Based on a photograph of a poor young Mexican girl with her baby, *Child Mother* is monumental in effect and effectively conveys a sense of human tragedy.

Not all of Siqueiros's art was political or social, however, and he had to accept private commissions and paint portraits of wealthy patrons in order to support the workshop and himself. He had also painted himself in a powerful and dynamic self-portrait at the age of forty.

Throughout his stay in New York David was engaged on another front and was pursuing his objective with his usual flair and passion. Although he still corresponded with María Asunsolo and Blanca Luz Brum, he was actively courting Angélica Arenal. After living in the boarding house run by Angélica's mother in Los Angeles, the Arenals had become his second family. When he left California for South America, they returned to Mexico where their paths crossed frequently.

Luis and Angélica were also members of the Mexican delegation to the Artists' Congress in New York and although she returned to Mexico after the meetings, Luis stayed and became an active participant in the workshop. In June David wrote to Angélica from New York and told her that "You and I must love each other someday" and if it did not come until later, it would be through no fault of his. They had important work which they had to accomplish together, always for the revolution, he wrote.

In anticipation of her return to New York, he described the work they were doing in the workshop and in several subsequent letters, he proudly described their latest projects and achievements. The attraction was mutual and Angélica soon left for New York with her mother and Adriana, her three year old daughter by a previous marriage. David not only conquered Angélica but also captivated Adriana, buying her presents, telling her stories and taking her to the circus, the zoo, on long walks in the parks and to his workshop.

Angélica soon replaced Berdecio as David's roommate and Adriana began to call him "papa." Although they were living together, David was still involved with other women, including María and Blanca, and though she loved him, Angélica decided to go back to Mexico. When it was time to go, however, he begged her to stay and told her how lonely he would be without her. After she left, he continued to write her, telling her of the vacuum in his life and enclosed a photograph of *Child Mother* on which he wrote, "This child is the daughter of our great love." Although he had promised the painting to her, he explained that George Gershwin insisted on buying it. Just before he left New York, he wrote that he hoped that they would meet in Spain to fight against the fascists together.

In 1936 the Popular Front had won a decisive victory in the elections of the Spanish Republic. In July, however, the Spanish generals launched their revolt against the Republic from Morocco. Aided by Mussolini and Hitler, their armies were soon threatening Madrid, while volunteers from all over the world responded to the call to defend the Republic. Siqueiros, whose own art and that of the workshop had contributed to the struggle against fascism and war, could not remain indifferent and early in 1937, he sailed for Spain.

Without his ideas and leadership, the workshop soon disintegrated. It had always been held together by his energy and the strength of his personality, and after completing several ongoing projects, the artists went their separate ways, some abandoning politics altogether, while others carried on the struggle on other fronts. During its short life, however, the participants in the "Siqueiros Experimental Workshop" had lived up to their original objectives. They had worked collectively to produce art for the people, either in the form of posters or large floats for parades and demonstrations, and had exhibited their individual work in an exhibit at the workshop.

More importantly, they had investigated the properties of new pigments, incorporated photography into their art, and developed some revolutionary techniques in the process. Siqueiros had used the opportunity to experiment with new materials and equipment, developing many new techniques and enriching his own plastic language. Although he was proud of the service the workshop had provided for progressive causes, he felt that the most enduring consequence of its brief existence was the development of a new technology for the plastic arts.

Now, he argued, the artist could use a new plastic language to achieve a "new realism" in which nature is created, not merely reproduced. His own work, "revolutionary in form as well as in content," proved his point and it coincided with a wave of neo-realism in art, literature and film. After he mastered the new tools, pigments and techniques, he would combine them in a more effective means of expression. His recent paintings were also impressive in style and technique, as well as in their dramatic force.

Soon after the completion of a paper mache float for the 1937 First of May parade, the workshop dissolved. While Siqueiros was on his way to Spain, the other Mexican artists prepared to return to Mexico. In 1937 Leopoldo Méndez, Luis Arenal, Angel Bracho, and Pablo O'Higgins met in Pablo's studio and decided to establish a graphic arts center in Mexico. Soon other artist members of the LEAR joined and the *Taller de Gráfica Popular* (Popular Graphic Workshop) became a reality.

Like the New York workshop, the Taller was to produce art for the masses and to serve the "democratic forces in the fight against fascism." By producing woodcuts, linoleum block prints and lithographs that could be reproduced in multiple copies and distributed and posted throughout the country, the Taller would serve popular causes and make art accessible to the masses. It was also committed to the investigation of different forms of engraving and painting and was based on the principles of collective work and criticism.

Although Siqueiros was never very active in the Taller, both he and Rivera had recognized the need and called for a cooperative artists' workshop to produce inexpensive art for the masses at the conclusion of their public debates in 1935. *El Machete*, the labor organs of Jalisco, and the New York workshop were similar in orientation and purpose. The Taller, however, has survived and another generation of artists has continued to work in the tradition of Posada, Méndez and many other fine artists. Their work, bold and simple, like ancient codices or *retablos*, was accessible and comprehensible to the people of Mexico.

While some members of the Experimental Workshop continued to create revolutionary art, one member headed in another direction, but greatly affected by the experience. When Siqueiros announced the opening of a workshop in New York, Jackson Pollock had already been exposed to the mural painting of Thomas Hart Benton, Orozco, Rivera and Siqueiros. Although he and his brother were merely assistants who helped to erect scaffolds and painted banners for the floats, Pollock was impressed by the rejection of traditional methods, the use of new pigments, the large scale of the projects and the creation and study of accidental effects.

Although Siqueiros did not view the experiments or techniques as ends in themselves, Pollock adopted the "drip" and the "controlled accident" as final statements, for which he was dubbed "Jack the Dripper," and he used pyroxylin almost exclusively in his later years. While his approach was revolutionary in technique and reflected the technical advances of the workshop, his "action painting" was non-figuratve and devoid of social commentary.

To those who looked for meaning in his art, Pollock pointed out that "It's just like a bed of flowers. You don't have to tear your hair out over what it means." It also commanded the highest prices in New York and Paris and Jackson Pollock was on his way to fame and fortune, as well as personal tragedy. Though Siqueiros recognized Pollock's talent, he lamented that he had been distracted and corrupted by his success in the commercial market.

Just before Siqueiros's departure for Europe, members of the workshop threw a party for him in a loft. But when someone offered a toast to the guest of honor, no one could find Siqueiros or Pollock. Hearing scuffling from another room, they found the two of them under a table, trying to choke each other. Jackson, who had a reputation for being violent and had a drinking problem, was apparently the aggressor and Siqueiros was only saved from strangulation when Sanford Pollock broke his brother's grip by knocking him unconscious.

In another interesting twist, Siqueiros's idea of a new or dialectical realism was in direct conflict with the current Soviet trend of socialist realism and this type of art and free and open investigation was no longer possible in Stalin's Russia. Siqueiros's call for the use of modern technology and stylistic improvements and his insistence on the artist's right to develop his own techniques and interpretations were contrary to the precepts and practice of "socialist realism." When it came to the role of the artist and art in a revolutionary society, Siqueiros was closer to the ideas of the Leon Trotsky than the official art policy of the Soviet Union under Stalin.

IX. El Coronelazo

The forces and issues which erupted in Spain in 1936 resembled those which had sparked the Mexican Revolution in 1910. When King Alfonso resigned in 1931, Spain suddenly became a republic and the new government immediately adopted long overdue measures to improve public education, redistribute land, separate church and state and modernize the armed forces. Although the Left won the 1936 elections, the Right still controlled rural Spain while the hierarchy of the Catholic Church and the military opposed the Republic and blocked its reforms.

A new government had barely been formed in 1936 when there was a rash of bombings and assassinations. When a popular military officer was killed and a Catholic politician was murdered in retaliation, the die was cast. In July military garrisons revolted throughout Spain and in North Africa. With the help of irregular troops, members of the armed forces loyal to the Republic defended Madrid and it appeared that the uprising had been contained. When Italy and Germany airlifted African troops to Andalusia, however, the insurgents gained a foothold in the south while monarchists allied with the army seized towns in the mountains north of Madrid.

While the Civil War had deep roots in Spanish history, it was also part of the greater conflict about to engulf Europe and it immediately assumed an international dimension. From the start the rebel generals received generous contributions of men and equipment from Germany and Italy. After the western democracies abandoned the Republic, volunteers came from all over the world to defend it.

In Mexico the birth of the Spanish Republic had been hailed by the Left as another Mexican Revolution and when the Spanish generals pronounced against the Republic, President Cárdenas promised support. Throughout the conflict, Mexico supplied ammunition and rifles to the Republic and protested the hypocrisy of the non-intervention policy of the western democracies. Mexican volunteers also went to Spain and were incorporated into the Army of the Republic. Mexico also offered homes for children orphaned by the conflict and opened its doors to thousands of refugees after the defeat of the Republic in 1939.

When the war broke out, Siqueiros was still in New York, working on projects for the Party's presidential campaign. After celebrating the victory of the Spanish Left in the 1936 elections, he learned of the generals' revolt and watched as Spain became a battleground between the forces of the Left and the Right. Later that year he decided to go to Spain and offer his new artistic techniques as weapons in the struggle against fascism.

After traveling by boat to Le Havre, he headed south from Paris and arrived in Valencia in January of 1937. At the University of Valencia he gave a talk on "Art as a Tool in the Struggle." Full of enthusiasm, he talked excitedly about the Mexican Mural Movement and his New York workshop and announced plans to organize a collective of Mexican and Spanish artists to produce murals and posters for the Republic. But since most of the young artists were already in the army, these plans would have to wait.

One of the first persons he contacted in Spain was Vittorio Vidali, an Italian Cominterm agent assigned to Mexico in 1927 and a member of the Mexican Party's Central Committee. In Spain he was known as Carlos Contreras, political commissar and commander of the Fifth Regiment, the irregular troops which defended Madrid before the arrival of the International Brigades. He was also the companion of Tina Modotti, who had been deported from Mexico in 1930 as a Soviet agent. After serving with International Red Aid in Berlin, Paris and Moscow, she had also been assigned to Spain.

When Comandante Carlos asked David why he had come to Spain, he replied that he preferred combat to painting and the next day he accepted Carlos's invitation to return with him to Madrid. Surrounded by the enemy and subject to constant bombardment, the capital was a war zone and Siqueiros soon had a taste of combat. Visiting the command post of the Fifth Regiment, he quietly observed action from a distance, but every time someone left for the frontlines, he wanted to know when they would go to the front.

A few days after his arrival in Madrid, he was observing a major operation in the headquarters of Juan Modesto of the Fifth Regiment when the General asked for a volunteer to take a message to a unit which the enemy was trying to encircle. Stepping forward, Siqueiros volunteered, "My commander, I am at your orders!" After studying a map, he took the message, saluted smartly and took off, running towards the front and disappearing among exploding artillery shells. He returned after dark, exhausted and covered with mud, but elated by his participation. That night, the officers opened a bottle of wine and Enrique Lister, the Commander of the 11th Division, toasted "the artist-combatant David Alfaro Siqueiros."

Siqueiros continued to serve as a messenger between the command posts and the front lines. During the battle of Jarama, when the enemy's crack troops, supported by the German Condor Legion's tanks and aircraft, tried to cut Madrid off from the rest of Spain, he had to run across the flat plains under air and artillery bombardment as well as machine gun and small weapons fire. Many messengers were lost and for several days Comandante Carlos could not find his new courier. When he found Siqueiros at the command post, Lister explained that Siqueiros had agreed to stay and they had not called because they did not want to wake him. After the enemy's pincer movement had been broken, the veterans of Jarama talked about the Mexican messenger who had performed so well in his "first battle."

Shortly after the battle of Jarama, Siqueiros enlisted in the Popular Army of the Republic. Since he held the rank of captain in the Mexican Army, he was given the next highest rank, that of major, and was later promoted to lieutenant colonel. In a letter to Angélica he expressed his excitement about enlisting and explained that he could not avoid joining the army. Besides recognizing his rank, he wrote, they were going to assign him to organize attack brigades for the next offensive and there was talk of forming a battalion of Latin American volunteers in which he hoped to play a major role.

After describing a morning of artillery and air bombardment as "splendid," he expressed his satisfaction in knowing that he could be useful in this important struggle. "I am going to work without dismay and I will not leave Spain until after the victory. I want to give the best of the rest of my life to this triumph of our cause," he wrote. He also wrote to María Asúnsolo, but his letters were not answered.

Not long after the battle of Jarama, Siqueiros learned that President Cárdenas had granted political asylum to Leon Trotsky and the Russian exile was now living in Mexico. In wake of the purge trials, the leader of the left opposition to Stalin in Russia was considered an enemy of the Soviet Union and the Communist International by "loyal comrades." Since the Soviet Union was the major ally of the Spanish Republic, many of the Mexicans fighting in Spain felt betrayed by Cárdenas's protection of Trotsky.

This sense of betrayal was reinforced by their personal experiences in Spain. Whereas they had been received warmly and their appearances at rallies had provoked shouts of *"Viva Mexico!"* and *"Viva Cárdenas!"* now they found themselves treated like outcasts or faced open hostility because of their government's policies. When Siqueiros attended the National Congress of the Spanish Communist Party, he was surprised to hear Dolores Ibarruri, the famous *La Pasionaria* (Passion Flower), express gratitude for the aid provided by other nations without mentioning Mexico, which after the Soviet Union, was contributing the most to the defense of the Republic.

Soon they had more reason to resent Cárdenas's policy. Within the Republic, the POUM, an anti-Stalinist, Marxist party, openly opposed the Spanish Communist Party. Although Trotsky had repudiated the POUM, the communists branded it as Trotskyite. In May of 1937 a test of strength between the anarchists and the POUM on one side and the Communist Party and the Catalan State on the other led to a war within the war. For several days Barcelona was torn by intense street fighting, diverting troops and equipment from the front during the fascists' northern offensive and encirclement of Bilbao.

When the struggle was over, the POUM was accused of trying to seize power in Barcelona and sabotage the war effort against Franco. It was not only eliminated as a political force, but many of its leaders disappeared, reportedly at the hands of Soviet agents. After the "May Days," therefore, the Mexicans in Spain were in even more of a quandary. While they were fighting the fascists, their country was harboring Trotsky and the Fourth International, whose agents were undermining the war effort and aiding the enemy.

In Siqueiros's case, the issue had another twist, since it was Diego Rivera and his wife Frida Kahlo who had persuaded Cárdenas to grant asylum to Trotsky. Diego and Frida met Trotsky when he landed in Mexico and he was now living in their home in Coyoacán. They also contributed generously to the Fourth International and Frida had an affair with the Russian exile, apparently to get even with her philandering husband. Trotsky later broke with Rivera and moved into another home which was transformed into a fortress, surrounded by thick walls topped with watch towers and protected by 50 Mexican policemen and Trotsky's personal guards, young Trotskyites from the United States.

When Andre Breton and Trotsky formed an International Federation of Independent Revolutionary Artists, Trotsky drafted a manifesto which Breton and Rivera signed. "Towards an Independent Revolutionary Art" compared art in the USSR under Stalin to that of Nazi Germany and called for an art dedicated to the revolution and a defense of the freedom of art "against usurpers of the revolution."

In spite of the conflict raging around him, David had other things on his mind. Before he left New York, he had written to Angélica about his decision to go to Spain and expressed his hope that they would meet there and work together in the struggle against fascism. When he learned that she had been injured in an automobile accident, he was greatly saddened and wrote her an emotional letter expressing his desperation over her suffering.

Although Angélica's injuries were serious, she recovered and obtained credentials as a reporter for *El Nacional* in Spain. While there were no funds for her passage, General Múgica, the Secretary of Public Works and Transportation, needed a messenger for a delicate mission to the Spanish government and entrusted her with an envelope carrying the codes for the ships carrying grain and arms to Spain. Leaving Adriana with her mother, Angélica went to New York and sailed on a liner with some doctors and nurses going to Spain to serve with the Abraham Lincoln Brigade, the unit of American volunteers fighting for the Republic.

By spring Angélica was in Spain and working as a war correspondent for the Mexican daily. During her first night in Spain she woke up in the middle of an aerial bombardment and when she arrived in Barcelona, the communists, anarchists, socialists and Trotskyites were fighting in the streets. After the "May Days," she proceeded to Valencia, the new capital of the Republic, where she turned the sealed envelope over to the Minister of War. She arrived just in time to participate in the Congress for the Defense of Culture Against Fascism, where she met Tina Modotti and Comandante Carlos.

In Valencia, Angélica arranged to cover the war for the Spanish periodical *El Frente Rojo* (The Red Front). After obtaining credentials as a war correspondent and a safe conduct pass from Comandante Carlos, she proceeded to the front near Cordoba. When she found out that a recently promoted Lieutenant Colonel Siqueiros commanded one of the units in that sector, she went on horseback with the political commissar to see him. In spite of her safe conduct pass, David insisted that she be taken to his command post behind the lines. Furious and hurt, she went instead to another town nearby.

It did not take David very long to find her, however, and they were finally reunited. Every night he galloped up to the door of the house where she was staying and they spent many tender and passionate nights together, temporarily forgetting the war.

During one of the lulls in the fighting, they agreed to meet in Valencia. David arrived before her and went directly to the hotel room and filled it with roses of different colors. When she arrived, he surprised her by proposing that they be married as soon as possible by his commander, Juan Modesto. Before she could reply, he explained that he was like a train headed in a definite direction and that if she wanted to get on and become his wife, they would make a good team. But if she ever got off, he warned, she would never be able to get back on.

Although she loved him, Angélica was developing her own career as a correspondent and writer and was a little hesitant, sensing the demands he would make on her. But David insisted and they were married by his commander, he in a fancy uniform and she in a modest dress. While they were soon separated by the exigencies of war, it was the beginning of a permanent and indestructible partnership. Once on board, Angélica never wavered and as David had warned, he had set his course and would not be diverted from it.

Following their wedding, Siqueiros returned to his command. In November he was commanding the 46th Motorized Brigade at the front in Estremadura when he received orders to go at once to Barcelona. There he was told to go to France to receive further instructions.

Meanwhile, Angélica was covering the war, writing articles for *El Nacional* and *Alta Voz del Frente*, a paper for the troops fighting on the southern front. But when she received a telegram that her mother was very ill, she decided to return to Mexico. After she joined David in Paris, they found out that his special mission was to go to Mexico to obtain some military optical instruments that the Republic needed.

Taking a boat from Le Havre, they arrived in New York and then flew to Mexico, where he met with President Cárdenas. After they had discussed the war and other issues, Cárdenas agreed to provide the needed equipment and gave Siqueiros his own pearl-handled pistol as a gift. The mission was accomplished in less than 3 days and Siqueiros left again for Spain, leaving Angélica behind.

During his stopover in New York, Siqueiros purchased an American army officer uniform and after his return to Spain, he was known as the best-dressed officer on either side. Standing erect in his new uniform with an American style cap with visor, leather strap drawn sharply across his chest, and riding pants tucked into his spit-shined leather boots, he looked like a cavalry officer on parade and stood out among the bedraggled defenders of the Republic. Rumors also circulated that he wore a purple and gold cape into action and when he was queried about his fancy uniform, he explained simply, "What's the sense of being an artist if you cannot design your own uniform?"

Siqueiros arrived back in Spain in December 1937, just in time to participate in the Republican offensive at Teruel, designed to relieve enemy pressure on Madrid. He was anxious to return to action and was assigned to several different units during the battle for Teruel and in the action at Celados, the men under his command seized the main plaza. After fierce hand-to-hand combat in a blizzard, the Republican forces took Teruel, but a few months later it was retaken by reinforced Nationalists.

Since the anarchists hated the Soviet Union and admired Mexico, Mexican officers were often assigned to their units. When Siqueiros was placed in command of a unit composed almost entirely of anarchists, he tried to convince them that military discipline, based on the solidarity of comrades, was necessary even in armies of the people. But they rejected any sense of military discipline and refused to stand at attention, wear insignia, or address officers with the formal "usted." In battle they were unpredictable and would sometimes abandon the front without authorization or would waste precious ammunition by firing their guns into the air.

When one of the anarchist units was relieved at the front, the soldiers refused to leave their heavy machine guns or mortars and left a long stretch of the front without heavy weapons. Reacting immediately, Siqueiros went to the command post of the unit and told the commanding officer to order his men to return their guns to the trenches. But no one moved and several soldiers protested that their weapons would be damaged or lost.

Just then one of their officers approached him with a pistol in his hand. Suddenly he turned around and faced his men, placing the pistol in his mouth and shouting, "If you do not obey the order of the lieutenant colonel, the top of my brains will fly off!" Slowly the men picked up their machine guns and other heavy weapons and loaded them in a truck that was waiting to take them back to the front. To make sure they reached their destination, Siqueiros accompanied the truck back to the front and turned the weapons over to their replacements.

Siqueiros's chauffeur was also an anarchist. One day they were traveling through the countryside in an open car when they were suddenly ambushed and bullets began whistling over their heads. The chauffeur abandoned the car and Siqueiros and disappeared over a hill, never to be seen again. Although the bullets were still flying, Siqueiros remained seated in the back of the car until he realized that his driver was not coming back. Since he did not know how to drive, he finally got out and walked back to headquarters.

In spite of his fancy uniform, Siqueiros won the respect of his troops by fighting with them and exposing himself to the same dangers. During an attack on a blockhouse, he led his men coolly under heavy machine gun fire, carrying a machine gun pistol. He also refused to panic. When he and his men became bogged down in a marsh and watched as the geysers of exploding artillery shells marched towards them, he refused to abandon their position. Only when enemy planes appeared overhead and began to drop bombs on their position did he order retreat. Falling back to the hills, they escaped, but not before they had suffered more than fifty percent casualties. In another battle, he had just given the command to mount horses when bullets started whistling around them. Although everyone else dismounted and sought cover, he remained in the saddle, impervious to the danger.

While he appeared fearless and almost suicidal in his exposure to enemy fire, Siqueiros admitted that he was scared. "Who would not be afraid, who would not tremble in fright?" he asked. But he also seemed to enjoy the thrill of battle and later declared, "For me there is no beauty which can compare with action. Not even art, for which I have dedicated my life."

Siqueiros and Comandante Juan B. Gómez in Spain, 1937

In late 1937 Siqueiros and the Catalan artist José Renau met with Ernest Hemingway in a restaurant in Valencia. Over dinner, they discussed the nature of war and their views of the Spanish conflict. While Siqueiros and Renau listened, Hemingway spoke enthusiastically about the uniquely Spanish character of the war, comparing it to the heroic life and death struggle of the bullfight. He was also fascinated by Spanish regionalism and the individualism of the anarchists, which he viewed as uniquely Spanish.

Fresh from the front, where he commanded a unit of anarchists, Siqueiros took issue with the American writer and said that his views were subjective. While he agreed that the individualism of the anarchists was characteristically Spanish, it was also Mexican and Italian, and therefore it was a question of ideology, not national character. After describing some of his experiences with his unit, he asked Hemingway why only the anarchists resisted discipline and not the communists, socialists and republicans, who were also Spaniards? What we need to defeat the enemy is more effective discipline, organization and solidarity, not more individualism.

After Hemingway returned from fetching another bottle of whiskey, they resumed their discussion and Renau and Siqueiros tried to convince him that the terror and violence of Spain was not due to any peculiar national character, but was the result of fascist aggression and the helplessness of the Loyalists against the machines and tactics of modern warfare.

Siqueiros's experiences in Spain ran the gamut of human emotions and the stories he later told reflected the tragedy and suffering, as well as the tenderness, love and solidarity which he observed. During the struggle for Teruel, David used to pass through a small town everyday. Though they were ordered not to give rides to civilians, when a small boy asked for a ride, he obliged and every day he gave Pepillo a ride and they became close friends. After an aerial bombardment had leveled the town and Pepillo did not appear as usual, Siqueiros went to the neighborhood where he lived, but there was only a pile of rubble. The house, Pepillo and his family had been pulverized by the bombs.

Since many of the soldiers were illiterate peasants who had no idea what the war was about, they often crossed over to the enemy lines. When his men brought him a prisoner one night, it was a young peasant who stumbled into their camp, thinking he had reached the enemy. Realizing his error, he assumed that he would be executed, though no one had said anything about shooting him and Siqueiros had to call headquarters for orders.

The next day orders came. The prisoner was to be shot by members of his own unit after an address by one of their officers. Facing the victim, the captain shouted that since he had wanted to go to the enemy, where Jesus Christ was, they were going to send him quickly to Jesus Christ. Expressionless, the hapless lad muttered, "So be it," just before he was shot by fellow peasants.

When Siqueiros assisted his countryman, Colonel Juan B. Gómez, in the execution of a young Spanish soldier accused of distributing anti-war propaganda among the troops, however, they were reprimanded. Unlike the Mexican Revolution, they were told, summary executions were not permitted in the Army of the Republic.

Although the Mexican volunteers were proud of Mexico's contribution to the struggle, that support presented another problem for them. While their comrades shunned them because of Mexico's protection of Trotsky, the socialists and anarchists emphasized Mexico's contribution to discredit the Soviet Union and when they appeared at public meetings, they were hailed as heroes to the embarrassment of any Russian officials present.

Never one to shun the limelight, Siqueiros was perplexed. How could he avoid the use of Mexico or its volunteers as instruments of anti-Soviet propaganda? Whenever he had the opportunity, therefore, he pointed out that the Soviet Union was supplying the bulk of the military equipment for the Republican forces while the western democracies, especially France, with all of its socialists and Popular Front government, refused to sell munitions or permit the shipment of weapons to the government of Spain.

Meanwhile Trotsky's fortified villa in Coyoacan had become a center of anti-Soviet propaganda, dispensing daily press bulletins and articles attacking Stalin and the Soviet Union. Although the conditions of Trotsky's asylum prohibited his involvement in Mexican politics, he was commenting on almost every political issue in Mexico and was implicated in some of them. Following the purge trials in Russia, Trotsky had also staged a highly publicized counter-trial of Stalin in Mexico to denounce the Soviet leader.

Although many of the Mexican volunteers were serving in different units of the Spanish Army, Siqueiros met with several other Mexican officers and they discussed how Cárdenas was aiding the enemy by his protection of Trotsky. After agreeing that the headquarters of the Fourth International in Mexico should be closed down as soon as possible, Siqueiros, Colonel Juan Gómez, his nephew Antonio Gómez and Ruperto García Arana, all officers in the Republican Army, drew up a detailed plan which they agreed to carry out as soon as the war was over and they returned to Mexico.

Although the war would drag on for another year, Siqueiros's service in Spain was nearly over. In order to avoid the impression of foreign intervention and to persuade Germany and Italy to withdraw their troops, the leaders of the Republic decided to discharge the international brigades and to remove the foreigners from their commands in the Army of the Republic. After receiving his orders, Siqueiros had to proceed back from the southern front by way of Valencia, which was cut off from Barcelona by the Nationalists, and then make his way through the blockade up the coast to France.

Although he had left Spain, Siqueiros had one last mission to perform before he returned to Mexico. In France he was ordered to Italy to obtain an issue of a periodical with an article that provided irrefutable proof of Mussolini's direct military aid to Franco. It was a dangerous mission for someone who had been fighting in the Republican Army and everyone who had been associated with the publication had disappeared.

As soon as he arrived in Rome, he contacted Cárdenas' representative in Italy. When he learned of Siqueiros's mission, however, he refused to cooperate. As he left the embassy, he ran into the Mexican pianist Ordoñez, who introduced him to other Latin

American students studying in Italy. Unaware of his service in Spain and assuming that he was another bohemian artist like themselves, they invited him to the studio of an Italian artist who had painted a portrait of Mussolini and designed the uniforms of the Italian fascists. When some Germans arrived, the gathering turned into a drunken party in which they shouted fascist slogans and sung their hymns.

At the first opportunity, David left the party and returned to his hotel, expecting to be apprehended at any moment. That night, while he was having dinner in a *trattoria*, he saw a copy of the magazine he was looking for on an empty table in the corner. Still apprehensive and expecting to be arrested at any moment, he hid the magazine under his coat, checked out of his hotel and took the train to France.

In Paris, Siqueiros was met by two Spanish officials who congratulated him and explained how important his mission had been. The article not only proved that Mussolini had sent more than 60,000 regular troops to Spain, but that they had suffered more than fifty percent casualties and reinforcements were still being sent to Spain because of pressure from the German high command.

While he was in Paris, Siqueiros looked up his friend, the artist Georges Braque. Though they were old friends, Braque's wife distrusted Siqueiros and warned him not to bother them any more. They met anyways in the home of the Spanish artist Joan Miró and renewed their discussions on art, Pancho Villa and the opposite sex.

Removed from the conflict in Spain, Siqueiros also had more time to think about art and he wrote Angélica that his mind was full of ideas on art, that phantoms haunted him day and night and he was more convinced than ever about his ideas on the development of modern materials and techniques for art. Although he considered his commission and commands in the Republican Army "the most emotional" of his honors, he was also convinced that the experience had been very important in his development as a painter.

Before he left Paris, Siqueiros gave a lecture at the Galerie d'Anjou sponsored by the Maison de la Culture and the Mexican League of Revolutionary Writers and Artists. Relishing this opportunity to speak in this center of avant-garde art, he spoke on the role of art in the contemporary political struggle and contrasted the experience of modern Mexican political painting with "the current of apolitical art of Western Europe."

Thanks to the intervention of Ignacio Bassols, the Mexican ambassador in France, more Mexicans arrived from the refugee camps in southern France. Reunited in Paris, they resumed their discussions on the contradictions of Mexico's aid to the Republic and its protection of Trotsky. By Siqueiros's reckoning, only 59 of the 300 Mexicans who fought in Spain had survived and returned to Mexico. As they recalled the Barcelona uprising and the sacrifice of their countrymen, they were convinced that the sabotage of the Republic by the POUM could not have occurred without the approval of the Trotskyites in Mexico, who were protected by the Mexican police and armed foreigners.

After taking the train to Le Havre, Siqueiros and the other volunteers embarked on a ship for New York. During the crossing, they continued to discuss their plot against Trotsky and the group of conspirators expanded to include David Serrano Andonegui, a Mexican communist who had spent some time in Russia before arriving in Spain, and Néstor Sánchez, a Mexican volunteer who had served with the International Brigades in Spain.

Although there were large demonstrations in New York for the returning American veterans of the Spanish Civil War, immigration authorities refused to let the Mexicans disembark. But after a protest, they were allowed to leave the ship and were welcomed with warm embraces and gifts of badly needed clothing, cigarettes and chocolate from the Mexican community in New York. The reception was short-lived, however, as they were marched off to specially arranged buses, guarded by immigration agents, to take them to the Mexican border. When they arrived in Mexico, they were treated like outcasts. In spite of Cárdenas's support of the Republic, there was no special recognition of their service and many of them were desperate to find work to support themselves and their families.

The Mexico which Siqueiros returned to in 1938 was just as chaotic and politically volatile as when he had left two years earlier. Although Cárdenas enjoyed widespread popularity after his nationalization of the foreign-owned oil companies, he was also caught between the increasingly militant factions of the Left and the Right. He was accused by the Left of selling out to the imperialists; his protection of Trotsky was viewed as a betrayal of an otherwise enlightened foreign policy; and his reforms were belittled as those of a bourgeois idealist. Although Siqueiros admired Cárdenas, he later compared him to Manuel Azaña, the moderate and ineffectual President of the Spanish Republic.

When Trotsky stepped up his attacks on Stalin and the Soviet Union and Cárdenas condemned the Hitler-Stalin non-aggression pact and Russia's invasion of Finland in 1939, the Left, especially the Mexican Communist Party, became more disenchanted. Meanwhile, the communist press increased its attacks on Trotsky, calling him the new pontiff, "Leon XXX" who, like Judas, had accepted 30 pieces of silver. When 20,000 demonstrators marched in Mexico City on May Day with placards calling for the expulsion of the "traitor Trotsky," Trotsky responded that this was how people write who are about to exchange their pens and pencils for machine guns.

While the Left accused Cárdenas of being a "bourgeois idealist," the Right accused Cárdenas of being a "Bolshevik" or "tool of Stalin," even though he had granted asylum to Stalin's enemy and opposed Stalin's foreign policy and Mexico did not have diplomatic relations with Russia until 1942. Conservatives not only opposed Cárdenas's domestic reforms, especially "socialist education," but also his foreign policy.

Faced with an armed revolt by a former cabinet officer, Cardenas took command of the military campaign and revolt was crushed and its leader killed. This situation was compounded by the arrival of thousands of refugees from the Spanish Republic, many of them leftists who continued their internecine quarrels on Mexican soil.

In 1939 Cárdenas' six-year term was coming to a close and after restructuring the National Revolutionary Party, he chose General Manuel Ávila Camacho, his Minister of Defense, to succeed him in the Presidency. General Juan Andrew Almazán, who was linked with the Right and American companies in Mexico also entered the race and Trotsky was accused of secretly supporting his candidacy.

After one of the bloodiest elections in recent history, Ávila Camacho was elected President. Though many of the domestic squabbles persisted, the increasing international crisis eclipsed domestic issues and the twists and turns of global politics reverberated in Mexico. After the Japanese attack on Pearl Harbor, Mexico joined the Allies, including the Soviet Union, thereby realigning the Left for the duration of the war.

After his return from Spain, Siqueiros did not waste any time before injecting himself into this political fracas. When he and the other veterans arrived in Mexico City, they were attacked by reactionary elements and felt betrayed by the government's toleration of fascist and reactionary organizations. To counteract these forces and to carry on the struggle of the Spanish Republic, Siqueiros founded a pro-Loyalist review, *Documental*. Along with other Mexican veterans, he organized the Francisco Xavier Mina Society, named after the Spaniard who had fought for Mexico's independence from Spain, to carry on the anti-Franco struggle in Mexico. In a jointly authored statement, they warned that the fascists had penetrated the cabinet, the National University, the army and the police, just as in Spain, and made an appeal for solidarity against the forces of fascism.

Meanwhile the volatile political situation approached that of a small-scale guerrilla war, with the different factions attacking each other in the streets, as well as in the press. When the Nationalists entered Madrid in March and the Republic surrendered a month later, the Spanish fascists in Mexico held a public demonstration in celebration of Franco's victory at the Casino Español, decorated with large photographs of Mussolini, Franco and Hitler. The Left retaliated, provoking a major confrontation which was broken up by the police. The arrival of thousands of refugees from the Spanish Republic later that spring added fuel to a raging fire.

Siqueiros was in the forefront of many of these activities. During a demonstration against the pro-Franco views of the major Mexico City newspapers, he outlined the capitalistic interests that were behind these papers. Although he pleaded with the crowd to respect freedom of expression and allow the press to combat the press, some demonstrators began to throw rocks at the offices of one of the major Mexico City dailies and clashed with the police. When the papers blamed him for the attack the next day, he was briefly detained by the police but was released without charges being filed.

Unchastened, David continued his political activities but also found time to express his recent experiences in paint and was preparing for a show at the Pierre Matisse Gallery in New York. Working in duco on masonite, he painted a Mexican peasant wearing a black metallic mask. While the mask in *Ethnography* links this modern peasant to a rich but disappearing past, it also disguises his real condition, hidden by the current idealization of ancient cultures. Using a spray gun, he created a dark and ominous cloud of smoke, billowing up over a flat horizon in *The Fire*.

In *Prostrate But Not Defeated*, he painted a powerfully modeled and greatly foreshortened torso of a man lying face down on a heavily textured earth, his muscular back, broad shoulders and head topped with wavy hair projecting forward, down and off the surface of the painting, perhaps a self-portrait. While his fists are clenched in anguish, there is also strength and determination, a tribute to the courage of the Spanish people, and his slightly raised head suggests hope for the future. In *The Sob* he painted a woman, her powerfully modeled arms and clenched fists covering her face but emoting her agony and desperation, a reflection of his own mood in the wake of recent events.

The Sob, 1939, Enamel on Composition Board

In a surrealistic self-portrait, David painted himself in profile with his left eye wide open, looking at the viewer and suggesting a reality which he cannot or does not want to see or paint. He also painted other pictures entitled *Sleep, Crying Child, Tarahumara Child* and some studies of natural objects without any personal statement, conveying a tenderness and calm which was not apparent in his public persona. The sculptural modeling, excessive impastos and wavy or flowing lines, however, were familiar.

After his recent paintings were shown in the Pierre Matisse Gallery in New York, several of them were purchased by the Museum of Modern Art. In his review of the show for the *Daily Worker*, Ray King commented on their originality and wrote that Siqueiros was the only one of *los tres grandes* to develop new ideas.

As a prominent artist and public figure, as well as a proud veteran of the war in Spain, David found himself increasingly under attack by the older Spanish community, predominantly conservative and pro-Franco. While most of these were verbal assaults, which he returned in kind, he also had a small flier, printed which declared, "We are exchanging *españoles* (meaning Spaniards arriving from Spain) for *gachupines* (anti-Mexican Spaniards living in Mexico)."

Poking fun at his frequent references to his rank and role in the Spanish Civil War, a Spanish editor of *Ultimas Noticias,* a Mexico City daily, dubbed him "*El Coronelazo*" (Bigshot Colonel). Recalling that other artists, like Tintoretto, had taken on such sobriquets as their nom de plume, Siqueiros signed several of his paintings, including a self-portrait, "*El Coronelazo*." He also issued a statement in which he cited Freud to suggest that his name caller, because of his excessive use of superlatives. was a homosexual who preferred young boys.

Meanwhile, mural painting had been revived under Cárdenas and a group of artists had painted murals in the Abelardo Rodríguez Market, the Taller de Gráfica Popular and in public buildings and schools in and around Mexico City. Although Rivera was concentrating on easel paintings, he had completed his comprehensive history of Mexico in the National Palace and repainted *Man at the Crossroads* in Bellas Artes, while Orozco had painted *Catharsis* in Bellas Artes and was finishing his masterpieces in Guadalajara.

In contrast, Siqueiros had not worked on a mural since Argentina and his only mural in Mexico was unfinished. While he had resumed painting, he was frustrated by the small surfaces of his recent paintings and was anxious to apply his new ideas and techniques on larger spaces. Moreover, he viewed Mexico as a "second front" where he could apply his new discoveries and carry on the struggle against fascism by painting superior murals.

For years he had also dreamed of directing a team of artists working together on a mural and he had proposed the formation of a collective of Mexican and Spanish artists in Valencia. Since there were many artists among the refugees in Mexico, he decided to organize the "International Team of Graphic Arts." Besides himself, it included his brother-in-law Luis Arenal, Antonio Pujol and the Spaniards José Renau, Miguel Prieto and Antonio Rodríguez Luna. Because he was the oldest and most experienced muralist, they agreed that Siqueiros would be the team leader and would find a site for a collective mural project and make arrangements with the owners and architects of the building.

After some research and negotiation, he obtained permission from the officers of the Mexican Electrical Workers Union and the architect of their new union hall to paint a mural in the stairwell of the building. The site was relatively small and confined, a cubicle formed by three walls and a ceiling and a total surface of only 100 square meters. Like the site of his first mural in the Preparatoria, this narrow stairway, with its walls and ceiling perpendicular to each other, did not appear to be the ideal space in which to paint a mural with an integrated theme. But it would permit him to apply his theories on painting the "total architectonic space," as well as creating a perspective for the "dynamic" or active spectator, and it would be seen daily by members of the working class.

After consulting with the officers of the union, it was agreed that the theme of the project would be imperialism, fascism and war, which after further discussion, was changed to *Monument to Capitalism*, and later, *Portrait of the Bourgeoisie*. It was also agreed that the painters would receive a set wage based on an eight-hour day and the mural would be completed in six months.

After they made a study of the passage of more than 100 subjects as they climbed or descended the stairs, the artists calculated the successive points of view of an "average spectator." These different perspectives were then used to plan the major themes and their progression on the walls. Arenal and Pujol then constructed a scale model of the stairwell on which they traced the outlines of the different perspectives. After preparing the walls for painting, they transferred these compositional lines to the wall with an electric projector.

Now they were ready to start painting. Using a compressor and spray gun and the Dupont paint "Duco," the team of artists began to cover the three walls and the ceiling with their version of capitalism, fascism and war. Seeking to create images which would be familiar to the electrical workers, they worked from contemporary photographs and popular symbols in periodicals or news publications. Since he had worked extensively in photomontage, José Renau directed its application and did much of the painting.

While the project was more orderly than previous ones, there were frequent interruptions, discussions and revisions, and it required fifteen months to complete rather than the six months he had promised. Much of the delay could be attributed to Siqueiros's divided attention. He was frequently absent from the project, disappearing for days and weeks at a time to pursue other anti-fascist activities. When he returned, it was for only a short time during which he criticized portions completed during his absence or helped to complete some unfinished figures.

At times Siqueiros painted directly over the figures painted by the other artists without offering any word of explanation. Just after he had admired the clouds of smoke that he had painted painstakingly over an aircraft carrier, Renau watched Siqueiros paint directly over the billowing forms. Barely restraining himself, he watched Siqueiros model and remodel the clouds with an airbrush, eventually reconstructing them as if from within, like hands working with bread dough. Only after he realized that the result was more effective and was the product of their joint efforts could Renau accept Siqueiros's method. But the other two Spaniards were unable to work under such chaotic conditions, as well as in the fumes created by the spray paints, and they resigned.

While he was working on the project, Siqueiros wrote to José Gutiérrez, still in New York, repeating his view that artistic materials were not inert but living dynamic forces which create their own aesthetic. He declared that the art world is blind to recent chemical discoveries as well as new developments in mechanical tools and urged Gutiérrez to continue his efforts to study and develop new techniques, "because we fight for a new classicism in art."

Despite his frequent absences, the mural began to take shape. As the forms and themes became recognizable, the electrical workers offered their opinions. When Roberto Berdecio joined the team and began to paint a thermo-electrical center on the ceiling, the workers protested, "Haven't you ever seen an electrical tower?" Later, as the political climate shifted toward the Right, union officials insisted that Renau remove the faces of the child victims of the Spanish Civil War that had been painted on the center wall. Renau also removed a portrait of Hitler and painted a yellow parrot over a caricature of Mussolini, thereby eliminating references to the identity of the fascist and capitalist figures.

Thus, whereas the original version portrayed fascism as the final stage of capitalism, the modified version presented a watered down criticism of that economic and social system. Nevertheless, it was still a strong indictment of capitalism and the plaque, which describes Portrait of the Bourgeoisie, predicts the triumph of the revolution and the end of the violence and exploitation with which capitalism sustains itself.

Portrait of the Bourgeoisie is a political poster, a manifesto and a call to battle. As one mounts the stairs in the interior of the Electrical Workers Union, one first sees a figure with the head of a parrot haranguing the mobs and gesturing with his arms, a flower in one hand and a burning torch in the other. The "parrot" or demagogue is activated from underneath by a spring mechanism manipulated by the machinery of capitalism. Behind him there is fighting in the streets while hordes of brown-shirted troops march in precise formation, an effect achieved by spraying paint repeatedly over the same stencil.

Behind the upraised torch the Parliament is in flames, its motto of "Liberty, Equality and Fraternity" partially obscured by a moneybag, while it is dwarfed by the facade of the modern factory building behind it. At the first landing of the stairs, the side wall blends into a scene dominated by the inside of a large machine topped by a metallic eagle, from which hangs the body of a lynched negro, painted directly from a photograph in *Look* magazine. Under the machine, men can be seen working beneath a concrete floor, surrounded by octopus-like tentacles, as a stream of flesh and blood is being sucked up by the machine and converted into a river of gold coins.

Figures in helmets and gas masks representing England, France and the United States stand on one side of the machine, a river of coins at their feet and a Phrygian cap of liberty pierced by a bayonet behind them. Directly opposite stand the militaristic figures of German, Italian and Japanese fascism. In the background troops march off to war in front of a concentration camp, while a mother and child look on in sorrow. Overlapping this central scene and the sidewall of the next flight of stairs is an aircraft carrier, its horizontal lines breaking the angle of the adjoining walls. The clouds of billowing smoke over the carrier suggest the Japanese attack on Pearl Harbor, still a year away.

The final wall is dominated by the figure of a revolutionary soldier, right out of the Spanish Civil War. He is confronting a tank, his rifle pointed at the mechanical monster whose treads are crushing a burning building and the ruins of a classical civilization. The electrical towers and tanks painted on the ceiling culminate in a bright blue sky, glowing sun and the flag of the Electrical Workers' Union representing work, solidarity, peace and justice.

Portrait of the Bourgeoisie, 1939, Pyroxylin on Cement,
Electrical Workers Union, Mexico. D.F.

Although much of the painting on *Portrait of the Bourgeoisie*
had been done by other members of the team and Siqueiros was
a fugitive in hiding before it was finished, the project constituted
another advance in the development of his mural technique. For the
first time he had applied many of the techniques and materials which

he had advocated for years and had been testing in Los Angeles, Buenos Aires and New York. Working as a team, they had painted a continuous pictorial surface, developing an active composition of multiple, overlapping and changing images to be activated by the "dynamic spectator.

Whereas Picasso, in his celebrated *Guernica*, had painted a vague abstract oil on canvas, Siqueiros and his co-artists had painted a specific statement about the same conflict in modern terms, using modern materials, equipment and techniques and expressed in a language which was comprehensible to the masses. The familiar imagery described capitalist exploitation, militarization, the destruction and corruption of democracy, imperialism and war, and the final triumph of revolutionary sacrifice, solidarity and struggle.

But while the message of *Portrait of the Bourgeoisie* is clear and unequivocal, it is not always convincing. The profusion of images, as well as the different styles of painting, either tends to confuse the spectator or restate the obvious. Even then, a plaque was installed to provide an explanation. The number of images and the differing styles also tends to destroy the artistic unity of the mural and makes its comprehension by a moving spectator virtually impossible. One must stop, therefore, at various points along the way or view the mural from the top of the landing in order to fully appreciate its specific or general statements.

In the process of creating a pictorial presentation to be activated by the moving spectator, the team of artists had used photography and photomontage, employed a projector to transfer sketches and compositional lines to the walls and painted a modern industrial pigment on a cement wall using airbrushes, spray guns and stencils. Practicing his slogan of "new instruments, a new aesthetic," they had created a dynamic cinematographic art which could move the masses. Although there were plans to incorporate a piece of painted sculpture as part of the mural, it was never installed, perhaps because of the limited space of the stairway or the sudden disappearance of the master artist.

The most important achievement of this project for Siqueiros, however, was the demonstration of the effectiveness of a collective work of art by a team of artists and students, working under a master artist similar to that of a great symphony orchestra performing under a master conductor. Although the process was not always harmonious or well coordinated, Siqueiros was convinced that it was a collective effort in which all members of the team had contributed to the final creation. While the mural reflects futurist tendencies in its emphasis on machinery, active dynamism, cinematic quality and its depiction of modern warfare, it also owes a debt to early Soviet art and Siqueiros's exposure to Serge Eisenstein and the art of cinematography.

Notwithstanding its imperfections, the composition of *Portrait of the Bourgeoisie* was unique and effective. Incorporating many of the ideas and techniques that Siqueiros had proclaimed for years, it was distinctive for its style, historical analysis and innovative techniques. Rivera and Orozco were still working in fresco, and while their murals were in more prominent locations, *Portrait of the Bourgeoisie* was more accessible to members of the working class. Although the master artist was already answering another call to arms before it was completed, it was also the first mural Siqueiros had finished in Mexico.

X. Agent Provocateur, Fugitive, and Exile

At about 4 AM in the morning of May 24, 1940, twenty men dressed as policemen and led by a man in the uniform of a major in the Mexican Army surprised the police guards outside the fortified home of Leon Trotsky. After disarming and tying up the policemen, they cut the telephone lines and the electrical line to an alarm in police headquarters, and entered the fortress-like walls surrounding the house. Taking up assigned positions in the yard, they opened fire on the bedroom of the Russian exile and shouted "Viva Almazán!"

As soon as she heard the shots, Trotsky's wife Natalya jumped out of bed and pulled her husband down on the floor in a hail of bullets, shielding him with her own body. They crouched under the bed in a corner of the room while the shots continued and the smell of burning gunpowder filled the room. Over the din of the shooting they heard the scream of "Grandpa" and in the flare of an exploding bomb, they saw the silhouette of a man in an army uniform enter the room and fire another round of shots into the bed.

As quickly as it had started, the attack was over. Taking the two cars kept ready for flight, the assailants disappeared into the early morning. When the shooting stopped, Trotsky and Natalya searched for their grandson Seva. Alarmed by a trail of blood leading from his room, they were relieved when the household was assembled in the courtyard and Seva had only a minor cut on his big toe. Despite 300 rounds of machine gun fire and two incendiary bombs, no one had been killed or wounded. But Robert Sheldon Harte, a young American poet and the commander of the garrison, was missing.

When the police arrived, Colonel Salazar, the officer in charge, was amazed that anyone had survived. Moreover, the principle target was calm and unruffled by his narrow escape, even though 73 machine gun bullets had been fired from four different directions into his bedroom. None of the guards seemed to be disturbed and they cooperated cheerfully with the police. Though one of them had been seen holding a pistol during the attack, no one had fired a shot in defense. One of the maids also remembered that Trotsky had held a meeting with his guards the previous night and there were several discrepancies between Natalya's description of the armed attack and her husband's version.

Since Trotsky's cause had declined after his counter-trial of Stalin and an alliance between the United States and the Soviet Union would strengthen Stalin, Salazar wondered if Trotsky had not planned the attack in order to discredit Stalin and generate sympathy and publicity for himself. He still wondered how anyone had escaped and why the guards had not returned the fire. Apparently the attackers were well informed about the layout of the villa and had been recognized at the door and admitted to the compound by someone inside. They also knew about the keys in the cars in which they had made their getaway and there was the unexplained disappearance of Robert Sheldon Harte, only recently arrived from New York.

Trotsky himself was full of explanations and immediately began to suggest possible enemies, whom he called the "gangsters of Stalin." He accused Joseph Stalin, the GPU and all the other agents of Stalin in Mexico, including the Mexican Communist Party and leftist newspapers and periodicals. He recommended that the police question David Alfaro Siqueiros, who had become a GPU agent in Spain, for information regarding this "criminal assault." Ever since his arrival in Mexico these people had accused him of cooperating with the fascists and tried to expel him. Having failed with their pens, they were resorting to machine guns and bullets.

Although Siqueiros could not be found, other arrests were made and when the police located the two stolen cars abandoned nearby, they also found some discarded police uniforms. In the studios of the Taller de Gráfica Popular they discovered more uniforms and makeup and promptly arrested some of the artist members. It was also revealed that two women had weakened the police detachment at the villa by seducing some of the guards and inviting them to a party in their apartment the night of the attack. But the alleged leader of the assault, to whom mounting evidence and testimony pointed, had disappeared along with several other suspects.

Casa Trotsky, Coyoacan, Mexico, D.F.

With Angélica driving one of the cars, the attackers made their escape. After abandoning their uniforms and the stolen cars, they split up and David, Angélica and Adriana headed for Cuernavaca. For several days they stayed in a comfortable home, following the news of the arrests and charges in the papers. As the investigations progressed and Siqueiros's name was mentioned, they decided to leave Cuernavaca and drove back to the capital.

Leaving Adriana with her grandmother, they headed north for Jalisco. In the town of Quemada, they were met by a peasant with two horses. After explaining that he had kidnapped Angélica as his bride and they were fleeing her relatives who had sworn to kill him, they rode for hours. Finally they arrived at a ranchería which they had visited during the fall in anticipation of such a flight. Here they could hide among old friends from the mining unions he had helped to organize.

Although he was among old friends, Siqueiros tried to disguise himself as a peasant, growing a mustache and darkening his skin in the sun and wearing the boots, clothes and sombrero of the region. He took the name of "Macario Sierra" and Angélica was "Eusebita" after his grandmother. Despite his disguise, his old friends recognized him immediately and insisted on celebrating his return with a bottle of mezcal. While Angélica made frequent trips to Mexico City, Siqueiros avoided staying very long in any one place. Every night he slept in a different place, riding into the mountains where he slept in a cave or out in the open.

During the day Siqueiros wrote articles which he sent to newspapers in the capital. Besides justifying the attack on Trotsky, he criticized the government's repression of the working class, including the use of violence against those arrested after the attack. He accused President Cárdenas of repressive policies and aiding the enemies of the Revolution by protecting Trotsky. He also wrote to the police, informing them that he would surrender when and where they would want to meet him, but he never appeared and since the letters were mailed from different parts of the country by friends, they served to confuse his pursuers.

In Mexico City the investigation continued and after the interrogation of most of the participants, a manhunt was launched for Siqueiros. The Communist Party denied any involvement in the attack and did everything possible to disassociate itself from Siqueiros, calling him an irresponsible "pedant with a machinegun" and the leader of uncontrollable elements outside the Party.

A month after the attack, the police discovered the slightly decomposed body of Robert Sheldon Harte buried in a shallow grave and covered with lime in a hut on a small ranch which had been rented by Angélica's brothers, Luis and Leopoldo Arenal. According to police experts, he had been shot in his sleep while resting on a cot which had been purchased by Angélica Arenal de Siqueiros and brought to the ranch by Siqueiros himself. The Arenal brothers were the last to have been seen with Harte alive and had been observed chatting with him in English before he disappeared. The Arenals, however, had fled the country. After identifying Harte's body, Trotsky wept profusely and had a plaque erected in his memory in the garden of the compound.

In August there was a second attack on Trotsky. In an elaborately planned and patiently developed scheme, Ramón Mercader posed as a Belgian businessman and courted an American Trotskyite who worked in the compound. Pretending to be a disinterested businessman and performing small favors, he managed to penetrate the defenses of Trotsky and was invited into the fortress. One hot and muggy afternoon, while Trotsky was reading an article he had written, Mercader took out an alpine pick concealed in the raincoat he was carrying and crashed it down on Trotsky's skull. Though severely wounded, Trotsky fought off his assailant and insisted that his guards who came to his rescue not kill him. The next day the comrade of Lenin and former commander of the Red Army died from massive head injuries.

After the assassin recovered from his wounds, he was tried and sentenced to 20 years in prison. Despite its verbal attacks on Trotsky, the Mexican Communist Party expressed its regrets and blamed the assassination on an "agent provocateur" sponsored by fascist or imperialist elements. When Siqueiros heard the news, he sent a telegram to the press in which he attacked the Party's apology and declared that he would come out of hiding when Trotsky's death had been confirmed. When his surrender came, however, it was not voluntary.

Not long after Trotsky's death, Siqueiros was sleeping in a house in a small village when an old lady knocked on the door and told him that there were federal troops nearby. Since Angélica was in Mexico City, he took off alone without his horse. Stumbling into holes in the dark and hiding in a cave full of snakes, he managed to elude the soldiers.

When he arrived at one of the villages where he and Angélica had hidden previously, he learned that the troops had already been there. Fleeing into the sierra, he tried to sleep in a cave but the mosquitoes were so thick he could not sleep and had to climb higher in order to escape them. Sometime later, he sat down and fell asleep, exhausted.

Suddenly he was wakened by shouts of "Surrender, *hijo de la chingada!*" Looking up, he saw a bunch of soldiers pointing carbines at him. Ordering him to stand, they took his pistol and machine gun, as well as his watch and a few pesos he carried in his boots. After tying his arms behind him, they placed a noose around his neck and marched him off, away from the main road down the mountain. Convinced that they were going to shoot him on the pretext that he had tried to escape, Siqueiros tried to impress his guards with jokes and a stream of nervous chatter.

This charade ended abruptly, however, when some shots rang out and they dove into a ditch and forced his face into the ground. But it was only another group of soldiers who were lost and had stumbled onto them. After the sergeant explained that they were afraid that some miners might try to rescue him and they had been given orders by the President not to harm him, Siqueiros quickly regained his composure and taunted his escort as they resumed the march.

When they came to a road, there was a caravan of automobiles and more soldiers waiting for them. Their commander, Colonel Salazar, apologized for the rough treatment and ordered that his hands be untied, explaining that he was not really a prisoner but a leader and honor to the country. Hearing this, Siqueiros retorted, "In that case, my commander, may I order them to withdraw?"

Ignoring this suggestion, Salazar continued to praise Siqueiros. Although he was a fugitive, he was also a veteran of the Revolution who had served under Diéguez and Obregón and he ordered his men to stand at attention while he and Siqueiros reviewed them. Getting into the cars, they drove back to the village and the prisoner found himself the guest of honor at a banquet, seated between Colonel

Salazar and the commander of the battalion which had captured him. After the banquet, he rode back to the capital in Colonel Salazar's car.

The party was over, however, and Siqueiros found himself in prison awaiting prosecution for his role in the attack on Trotsky. He not only faced charges for the murder of Robert Sheldon Harte, but also for the theft of police uniforms, the impersonation of an army officer, the firing of automatic weapons, the theft of two cars and illegal flight. Nevertheless, he issued a statement from prison complimenting Colonel Salazar and his men for their "cleverness in finding me" and sent a message to the President, insisting on the dismissal of charges against the peasants who had given him shelter. Meanwhile, he reflected that his recent experiences "could only have happened in Mexico."

The next chapter in his life was equally bizarre and could have been possible in only one country. While he was in prison awaiting trial, the Chilean poet Pablo Neruda visited him regularly and at night they would leave with the commander of the prison to have a brandy in an obscure cantina where no one would recognize them. Returning early in the morning, they embraced and Siqueiros returned to his cell.

During these soirees, they schemed to free Siqueiros. Since Neruda was the Chilean Consul in Mexico, he would issue a visa for him to travel to Chile. But when the Chilean ambassador learned of their plans, he not only cancelled the visa, but also suspended Neruda from his consular duties.

When he was interrogated, Siqueiros did not deny his involvement in the attack. Instead, he attacked the laws of Mexico as the products of bourgeois capitalism and since his action had been purely political, he argued that they did not apply to him. He also described how the Trotskyites had sabotaged the anti-fascist struggle in Spain and denounced the financial support that Trotsky had received from reactionary forces, including Yankee imperialists. He insisted that they had not intended to kill Trotsky and that he had every right to attack and destroy the headquarters of Trotsky because his asylum and protection by the police was a violation of Mexican law.

The conditions of Trotsky's asylum in Mexico, he argued, stipulated that he was not to become involved in internal political matters, but his cooperation with counter-revolutionary groups in Mexico and his frequent attacks on Mexican political organizations in the press violated these terms. The attack, therefore, was intended to frighten Trotsky, to demonstrate that he could not be protected in Mexico, to publicize his illegal activities and to point out the hypocrisy of Cárdenas in pretending to be a friend of the Soviet Union while he sheltered one of its enemies.

Meanwhile, Angélica and his brother campaigned for his release, petitioning government officials and using the newspapers to defend his case and publish his statements. The Communist Party, which had condemned the attack and characterized its leader as "irresponsible," now defended him. Fifty Mexican and Spanish intellectuals signed a petition to President Ávila Camacho in which they declared their solidarity with Siquieros and demanded justice for him on the basis of his artistic achievements and contributions to national culture. The Mexican Confederation of Labor called for the release of Siqueiros and others arrested in the struggle against "Trotskyism" and organized a committee to work for their freedom.

Despite the protests of Natalya Trotsky that this "cynical resolution" not only defended the terrorist acts of Siqueiros but also those of the real assassin, Siqueiros was released. Whether influenced by the appeals on his behalf or under orders from higher officials, the judge dismissed the major charges, and after almost five months in the Federal Penitentiary, Siqueiros was released on bail, pending a trial for damaging property and stealing two cars.

According to the subsequent testimony of the participants and official investigations into the armed assault on Trotsky's headquarters, Siqueiros was the ringleader. The plot had been hatched in Spain and the original band was expanded to include other veterans, some Spanish refugees, David's brother Jesús, Angélica and her brothers Luis and Leopoldo, the artist Antonio Pujol and some miners from Jalisco. In the fall David and Angélica had gone to Jalisco to arrange for a hiding place and to recruit accomplices from his old comrades. It was also Siqueiros who arranged the meetings and distributed funds from an unknown but generous source to cover their expenses, including those of the two women assigned to seduce the police agents.

On the night of the attack, Siqueiros had dressed in a custom-fitted uniform of a Mexican army major and disguised himself with a pair of dark glasses and a handlebar mustache with upturned ends. At the home of Trotsky, he had spoken to the policemen outside the walls, after which he entered the stockade with the help of an inside accomplice. Not only did all the evidence point to him, but Siqueiros never denied his role in the assault and declared many times that it had been one of the most honorable acts of his political life.

While there was little mystery about the identity of the participants in the attack, the motives were less clear and there seemed to be as many versions as there were sources and the case was never brought to trial. Trotsky insisted that Siqueiros had become a Stalinist in Spain and was an agent of the Soviet Union or the GPU. While Siqueiros assumed responsibility for the attack, he always insisted that they were not trying to kill Trotsky, but only trying to point out that he could not be protected in Mexico and to create such a scandal that his asylum would be revoked.

Angélica corroborated his version, explaining that he had tried to persuade President Cárdenas that Trotsky was violating the terms of his asylum by his involvement in Mexican politics. He had pointed out that Trotsky was receiving money from American imperialists and was taking advantage of his protection by the Mexican government to attack progressive sectors in Mexico. These activities explained why he had been denied exile in Europe, she wrote. Having failed to convince the President, therefore, Siqueiros and the others had vowed in Spain to arouse public opinion against Trotsky and persuade the government that he could not be protected in Mexico. This would explain the anti-Trotsky demonstrations before the attack, as well as why no one was injured in an attack by twenty well-armed veterans of the Spanish Civil War.

The attack on Trotsky's villa and his subsequent death at the hands of Ramón Mercader proved that the government could not protect him, though another version contends that the first attack was only a subterfuge which Mercader used to win the confidence of Trotsky before killing him. Since Trotsky had a large library and was writing a biography of Stalin, the incendiary bombs were intended to destroy his papers and the manuscript, but this part of the plan had failed when the bombs did not ignite.

Although Trotsky blamed the Mexican Communist Party, Lombardo Toledano and Comandante Carlos for the verbal and physical attacks on him, the Party was divided and Marxist doctrine condemned individual acts of terror as counterproductive. Hernán Laborde and Valentín Campa, members of the Central Committee of the Mexican Communist Party, had refused to cooperate in any scheme of the Third International to eliminate Trotsky. They argued that Trotsky's cause was in decline and that his assassination would work against the interests of the Party, the Soviet Union and the international communist movement. In his memoirs Campa also wrote that Siqueiros, who was not a member of the Party during Trotsky's exile in Mexico, had revealed that Stalin had provided unlimited funds for the liquidation of Trotsky and a Soviet agent, an Argentine named Vittorio Codovilla, known in Spain as Colonel Leonid Eitington, had arranged everything, including the final and fatal attack by Mercader.

Others, including the detective investigating the case, contended that Trotsky, whose cause was suffering, could have arranged the attack in order to provoke a scandal, evoke sympathy for his cause, and discredit Joseph Stalin. Supporters of this thesis insist that Trotsky was either warned or in on the plot and spent the evening resting comfortably in the Hotel Ritz. Hence his miraculous escape and calm demeanor when the police arrived.

According to this conspiracy thesis, Robert Sheldon Harte played the role of a double agent, aiding the attackers, but at the same time, warning Trotsky so that he would escape unharmed, with more public attention and sympathy. An American veteran from Spain whom Siqueiros had tried to recruit claimed that he had seen Harte with Siqueiros before the attack and that Harte was a Trotskyite who had become disillusioned because of his leader's acceptance of money from the fascists. This informant also stated that the money for the purchase of the weapons and uniforms had come from a recent purchase of Siqueiros's paintings by the Museum of Modern Art in New York.

Still another version of the episode describes Harte as an inexperienced and idealistic American who panicked at the surprise attack. In this scenario, Harte decided to leave with the attackers, either because he dreaded being reprimanded by Trotsky or feared for the defeat of Trotskyism. Some sources contended that Harte, who had only been in Mexico for six weeks, was actually a GPU agent and had set up the whole affair by posing as a Trotskyite. No one knew very much about him before he came to Mexico, although one source states that he kept a picture of Stalin in his room in New York and his girl friend was sure that he was a Stalinist.

Much of the evidence does point in this direction, especially since there must have been an inside accomplice and Harte not only left with the attackers without offering any resistance, but actually drove one of the getaway cars and was observed talking with some of the attackers in English during the flight and just before his death. His murder, therefore, could be attributed to his being a Soviet agent who knew too much or a double agent who had betrayed the conspirators by warning Trotsky.

Were it not for this personal tragedy, the attack had the appearance of a comic opera. The false mustaches, the dark glasses, the police uniforms, the seduction of the guards, the shouts of "Viva Almazán!," the firing of 300 rounds and the failed incendiary devices without inflicting any casualties and the escape in Trotsky's own cars were almost comical and did not enhance the military reputations of the alleged conspirators.

The leader's escape from prosecution further suggests the burlesque. Either members of the government did not take the first attack seriously or were in sympathy with the attackers, and after the death of Trotsky, the matter was closed. On the other hand, a trial would have given Siqueiros a public forum, more notoriety and a chance to attack the government as well as the Fourth International. He was also a friend of Cárdenas, a veteran of the Mexican Revolution and an internationally known figure whose imprisonment would disrupt the delicate fabric of Mexico. Justice, Mexican style, prescribed absolution and exile.

While Siqueiros denied that they had tried to kill Trotsky, political violence was not uncommon in Mexico, especially during this period of political polarization and international tension. Many leftists believed in the Moscow trials and the charges that Trotsky had conspired to assassinate Stalin and other Soviet leaders. And for the veterans of the Spanish Civil War, there was also the bitter memory of the "May Days" in Barcelona.

If the assault had been an attempt on Trotsky's life, it had been bungled and provided him with more publicity and a renewed opportunity to attack Stalin, the Soviet Union and his Mexican adversaries. As Laborde and Campa had warned, the assault discredited the revolutionary Left in Mexico, as well as the Soviet Union, and was followed by increased persecution of the Party.

Despite his refusal to identify himself as anyone other than Jacson Mornard or to talk about his attack on Trotsky, most of the mystery surrounding the origins, background, motives and sponsors of Trotsky's assassin has been unraveled. His mother, Claridad Mercader, was born in Cuba and had been involved in communist activities in Barcelona during the Civil War. She was linked romantically with Vitorrio Codavilla or Leonid Eitington, and following Trotsky's assassination, she was honored and given refuge by the Soviet Union. Her son had also joined the movement and was assigned to Mexico, presumably to liquidate Stalin's archenemy.

While several writers contend that Siqueiros knew Mercader in Spain and provided him with a cover in Mexico, the only evidence linking the two is that both were in Barcelona during the war and Mercader had once given a room number as his office in a building in Mexico City where Siqueiros had also rented a room. The latter would appear to be more than just coincidental, however, given that both men made separate attacks on Trotsky within a period of three months and Comandante Carlos had also used the same address when he returned from Spain. There is also the testimony of a motel operator that several men came to visit Ramón the night of the first attack and left, carrying away a large trunk and several suitcases, presumably the uniforms and weapons used in the attack. And it was just after this attack that Mercader made his first direct contact with Trotsky.

Those sources who assert that there was a connection between Mercader and Siqueiros, contend that Siqueiros was already a Soviet operative in the late 1920s and his expulsion from the Party was a subterfuge to protect him from government persecution, or that he had become a GPU agent in Spain. In his recently released memoirs, the former head of Soviet counter-intelligence confirmed that the assassination of Trotsky was a state priority and had been assigned to three separate teams. When the Siqueiros-led team bungled their assignment, therefore, it was Mercader's turn. In this scenario, the cries of "Viva Almazan" and leaving the uniforms in the Taller de Gráfica Popular were diversionary tactics to blame the assassination on a Trotsky supporter, Diego Rivera.

Since some of the early testimony from the first assault mentioned an American "Jewish type" who financed and directed the first attack, the killer of Trotsky may have been that same agent, especially since the "Jew" spoke with a French accent. This implicated Mercader, who claimed to be Belgian even though he had entered Mexico with the passport of a Canadian reported missing in Spain, a fact which linked him to the GPU, since the passports of volunteers were turned over to the political commissars and used as covers for agents when a volunteer was killed. However, recently released information establishes that the "Jew" was Soviet agent Iosif Grigulevich and since Harte had recognized him at the door, he had to be eliminated. However, Néstor Sánchez, a Mexican veteran of Spain who participated in the attack, wrote in his memoirs that the account of the American Jew was a diversionary tactic he had invented during his own interrogation.

Although Mercader probably expected a lighter sentence since Siqueiros and the others involved in the first attack were never prosecuted, he received the maximum penalty and spent the next 20 years in prison. He was a model prisoner who taught other prisoners how to read, arranged painting classes and set up a radio and electronics repair shop to train them for careers. Throughout his imprisonment, his mistress visited him regularly, arriving at the prison gates in her new American car.

He was also honored with frequent visits by members of the Communist Party or by leftist sympathizers. Although there were rumors of attempts to free him, he apparently did not encourage them, perhaps out of fear of what might happen to him if he did escape. He studied Russian and when he was finally released, he went directly to Cuba and then to Russia, where he was made a "Hero of the Soviet Union" and given a lifetime pension. Later he moved to Czechoslovakia but was expelled under Dubcheck, only to return after the Russian invasion of 1968. Refusing to discuss his activities in Mexico, he took his secrets with him to the grave.

Although Diego Rivera had befriended Trotsky and was one of the most generous supporters of the Fourth International, he claimed that he had escaped the roundup when Paulette Goddard warned him that his house was surrounded by police and drove off with him hiding under a blanket in her car. Since Diego's wife Frida had known Mercader in Paris and had a brief love affair with Trotsky, she was also a suspect and was interrogated by the police. Diego even claimed that he had lured Trotsky to Mexico in order to trap him.

While Rivera later made Stalin the central figure of a mural, Siqueiros never painted the Soviet leader and was increasingly critical of the "academic formalism" of the Russian social realists. Artistically at least, he was much closer to the ideas of Trotsky on revolutionary art than the precepts and practice of socialist realism under Stalin. Trotsky had called for "every liberty in art" and proposed "a broad and flexible policy in the field of art." He had also recognized the need for a new technology in art and insisted that art should participate in and serve the revolution and that the artists must be permeated with the content of that struggle.

In the meantime, Mexican justice had not run its course and the leader of the attack on Trotsky still faced the charges of property damage and car theft. Just before he was released on bail, however, Siqueiros was taken to the home of the President, General Ávila Camacho. Arriving at the rear entrance, he was conducted into the house and greeted cordially by the President in his riding boots and military uniform. After expressing concern for his health, Ávila Camacho proposed that Siqueiros accept voluntary exile in order to avoid retaliation by the Trotskyites. The Mexican ambassador to Chile had arranged for him to paint a mural in that country and his Minister of Government, Miguel Alemán, would arrange all the legal documents for his travel to South America.

Despite the offer, David protested that he had been cleared of the charges of homicide and should be released on probation. But Ávila Camacho pleaded with him, declaring that he did not want his death on his hands. Thus, without ever standing trail for leading the armed attack, impersonating a Mexican army officer, stealing two cars or killing Sheldon Harte, Siqueiros was encouraged to violate the terms of his release from prison and to leave the country with the blessing of the President of Mexico.

The day of his departure, Miguel Alemán accompanied David, Angélica and Adriana to the airport and presented them with their papers and tickets to Santiago, Chile. Despite the President's assurances, David was apprehensive that he might be detained in route. Instead of going to Panama from Cuba as arranged, therefore, they flew directly to Bogotá. Still afraid of discovery, they rented a car and drove through the country towards Ecuador, and after crossing the border, drove on to Peru. In Peru they heard rumors that Chile had decided not to let him enter the country, but they proceeded anyway and hired a small plane to fly to Arica, the northernmost city in Chile. When they arrived in Arica, they were exhausted and took a room for the night, hoping for some quiet and time to rest.

Early the next morning, however, they were wakened by a policeman, who informed them that they had entered the country illegally since the arrangements for their visit had been revoked. After the Mexican ambassador explained that Siqueiros had been commissioned to paint a mural in the Mexican school in Chillan and would be confined to that city, they were allowed to continue on to Santiago. After two days in the capital, they took the train to Chillan in the Central Valley, south of Santiago.

When Chillan was devastated by an earthquake in 1939, the Mexican people had raised funds to rebuild the local school and a new building had risen out of the rubble. It had also been proposed that Mexican artists be commissioned to paint murals in the "Mexican School" and Xavier Guerrero was already working on a mural in the school. When Siqueiros arrived, he was invited to paint a mural in the library, named after Pedro Aguirre Cerda, the President of Chile.

The room was long and narrow and the sidewalls were lined with bookshelves or broken up by windows and doors and the two end walls were not very large. Nevertheless, Siqueiros immediately began to make tracings with crayons and rulers. outlining the composition that he would paint on the end walls and the ceiling. In order to create a continuous surface of mural painting, he had masonite panels mounted where the walls and the ceiling came together, thereby creating a vault overhead on which he could paint images uniting the two end walls.

Before he started to paint, however, he tried to recruit some Chilean assistants, but since he had no money to pay them, he had to start work with the help of some Chilean workers. They were enthusiastic but they knew nothing about art or color and he had to redo most of their work. When a fire broke out in the school and damaged one of the finished sections, it had to be rebuilt and re-painted. Meanwhile, needing money to support his family, he interrupted his work on the mural to paint some pictures to sell, though there was not much of a market for art in Chile.

When several young artists arrived from Santiago, their government scholarships were not enough to support them and Siqueiros, who was living in the small quarters of the concierge with Angélica and Adriana, shared his food with them. He also discovered that they were "more academic than his instructors at San Carlos" and one of them had the audacity to sign his name on a portrait he had painted in the mural. However, one of them was a mathematician who helped him to develop an understanding of geometry which he needed to solve the problems of composition.

Although he referred sarcastically to his mural as "*oratoria pictórica*," a label that his critics had adopted for "public art," the theme of the mural was the struggle of the Chilean and Mexican people for liberty and independence, or "*Death to the Invader.*" After tracing the compositional lines on the ceiling and curved walls, which now formed a "rounded box," he proceeded to paint the walls and celotex panels, using pyroxylin paint and air brushes.

On the north wall he painted the struggles of the Mexican people, symbolized by a massive figure with multiple arms and legs representing Cuauhtémoc, the Aztec leader who led the final resistance against the Spaniards. A dead conqueror, his chest pierced by a shaft, lies at the figure's feet, and a cross, which is also a dagger, thrusts downward from the ceiling at the chest of Cuauhtémoc. To the left of this pulsating figure he painted the portraits of Hidalgo, Morelos and Zapata, heroes of the Mexican independence movement and the Revolution of 1910. To the right of Cuauhtémoc he painted Juárez and Cárdenas, Mexican leaders linked by their liberalism and nationalism.

On the opposite wall Siqueiros painted a massive figure with multiple arms and lances astride the armor-clad bodies of fallen Spanish conquerors. This central figure has two heads, that of Galvarino, the Araucanian Indian hero, with bloody stumps for arms, and that of Francisco Bilbao, the Chilean liberal who rejected the Catholic Spanish past and called for a free and united Latin America to confront the United States. Flanking this symbol of Chilean independence are the portraits of other Chilean heroes, from Bernardo O'Higgins, the liberator of Chile, to the Indian hero Lautaro and Recabarren, the founder of the Chilean Communist Party. Overhead, a volcano erupts while the struggles of the Chilean and Mexican people are linked together by the extension of the raised bow of Cuauhtémoc and the lances and flags of the Chilean patriots from the end walls onto the ceiling and by a series of lines and geometric forms which extend across the ceiling.

Death to the Invader, 1941–1942, Pyroxylin on Masonite and Plywood, Mexican School, Chillán, Chile.

Like his mural in the Electrical Workers headquarters in Mexico, *Death to the Invader* is an illusion which is set in motion by an active spectator, taking on different shapes and moving as the viewer moves about the room. It is a tour de force in which the spectator is visually assaulted by large pulsating forms, multiple images, vibrating lines and a variety of textural effects. It has a strident quality, the severed arms and screaming face of Galvarino seeming to shout at the spectator as he lunges forward, stepping over the bodies of the conquerors.

The day of the unveiling, a section of the Mexican wall just beneath the portraits of Hidalgo, Morelos and Zapata was still unfinished. In the morning, while the dignitaries were arriving from

Santiago, Angélica posed while Siqueiros painted Adelita, popular heroine of the Mexican Revolution, her upraised arms and clenched fists framing the other revolutionary heroes. Thanks to the spray gun and fast drying paints, he finished the figure just before the ceremony began.

The unveiling was a major event and the President of Chile, other government officials, members of the diplomatic community, intellectuals and the press participated in a grand fiesta. The reactions, however, were mixed. Although they recognized the power of the mural, several critics found it inappropriate for an elementary school. Others commented that the figures moved with frightening rapidity and the loud shouts of violent men transformed the mural from "the pictorial to the phonetic."

Siqueiros replied that these criticisms only proved the effectiveness of "pictorial oratory" and the negative reaction of the critics was more than offset by the school children who dubbed the library "The Room of the Giants" and pointed proudly to their heroes. To them the massive undulating figures were not monsters but magical figures which moved as they ran about the room.

After Lincoln Kirstein, Director of the Latin American Section of the Museum of Modern Art in New York, visited Chillan, he wrote that the school children understood Siqueiros and that the "spectator, instead of quietly observing, finds himself physically involved in a violent combat." One hears the clash of arms, the crushing of flesh against armor and the screams of the warriors, he wrote. "It is not pleasant, but without question, one is affected forever." Kirstein went on to say that Siqueiros had established the beginnings of a "tremendous plastic and spatial revolution, the most important synthesis of plastic elements since the cubist revolution of 1911," and when compared with Picasso's *Guernica*, the triumph of Siqueiros is obvious. He also compared it to El Greco's *The Burial of Count Orgaz*.

Kirstein also ranked Siqueiros's optical illusions as one of the most extraordinary experiments since da Vinci's camera oscura. After declaring that Siqueiros's latest work was superior to that of Orozco and Rivera, Kirstein predicted that some day special trains would take students to see the optical solutions and innovations in composition which Siqueiros had developed in Chillan. He concluded with a reference to war in which innocent bystanders are killed, but in which this artist is "neither innocent nor standing still."

In letters to his friends, Siqueiros expressed his own satisfaction with the mural. Writing to Pablo Neruda in Mexico, he described the mural and confided that it was his "greatest effort yet in public art." Although he complained to José Renau about his frustrations during the project, he wrote that his Chillan mural was the logical progression of "the most important political painting in Mexico," their *Portrait of the Bourgeoisie*. Now, he wrote, "I am more convinced than ever of the need for teamwork in modern social art."

He also sent pictures of the mural and an article "My Painting in Chile" to the Mexican daily *Hoy*. Hoping to arrange an exhibit of enlarged photographs of the mural at Inés Amor's Mexican Gallery, he sent her some articles he had written in which he expressed his sense of achievement and described his latest mural as an "obvious improvement over my previous murals," as well as "a step forward in my effort of twelve years to develop a new public art, of a greater and new art of the state."

In a pamphlet which he wrote on the mural, *Arte Civil*, he explained that his active composition contrasted with the static art of his Mexican colleagues or that "snob agility" characteristic of modern Parisian art. Nothing, he wrote, proved his point more than the very words of his critics who attacked the power and movement of his figures. "*Oratoria pictórica*," therefore, refers to the "eloquence" with which modern social art can communicate its ideological message. In all the classic periods of the past there was an epoch of public art, and today's private snob art of the decadent bourgeoisie will yield to a new public art representative of a modern industrial society.

In a long letter to Lincoln Kirstein, Siqueiros suggested that the Museum of Modern Art exhibit his work and publish a monograph on the Chillan mural. Reminding Kirstein of his praise for the mural and favorable comparison to Picasso's *Guernica*, he pleaded with him to support what would be the first publication dedicated to his art and asked, "What reasons are there against it? Political reasons? Have I not been the most active anti-fascist in Mexico for the last 20 years?"

Siqueiros also reminded Kirstein that since the museum had held an exhibit of war posters to promote the cause of the democracies, it should commission him to paint a mural on the outside of a building in the heart of New York City. The museum would determine the theme and it would be painted by a team of North American and Latin American artists, using the latest in pigments and tools developed for painting automobiles and billboards, donated by their manufacturers. Together, he assured Kirstein, they would "open a new world of art."

Despite difficult conditions and frequent interruptions, *Death to the Invader* marks the successful application of new materials and techniques and constitutes a logical progression from the cinematographic *Portrait of the Bourgeoisie*. Although constrained by the size and shape of the room, he had modified the architectural space and created concave surfaces on which he painted overlapping forms, thereby integrating architectural elements with the mural. Using pyroxylin paint and working with an airbrush, he had painted these forms as they were projected on the walls and ceiling by an electric projector. In the future, he predicted, muralist and architect would cooperate in creating the ideal space for mural paintings in new buildings.

The effect was overwhelming, the powerfully sculptural figures seeming to leap off the surface and move as the viewer moves about the room. Through the use of multiple images, the fusing of figures and the tracing of geometric lines, he had created a dynamic surface, one which changes and takes on different shapes from different perspectives. The cross doubles as a sword, the flag as a lance, blood becomes a flame, and a scream is transformed into positive action. His portraits of Mexican and Chilean patriots are strong and expressive, suggesting their turmoil and strength and their pairing reflects similar traits or achievements. It was also the first time that a Mexican artist had painted Cuauhtémoc as a triumphant hero, the defender of the patria against foreign invaders.

With the completion of *Death to the Invader* and *Portrait of the Bourgeoisie*, Siqueiros joined Rivera and Orozco as the recognized masters of Mexican muralism, albeit very different in style and interpretation. Whereas Orozco had expressed despair and disillusionment with current ideologies and movements in his latest frescos, Rivera was inexplicably silent about the mounting world conflict. Siqueiros, on the other hand, had just completed two eloquent statements against fascism and imperialism, using new materials and techniques and working with teams of artists from several countries.

After a trip to the south, he returned to Santiago and made plans to tour other South American countries to mobilize artists for the allied war effort. Before leaving, he announced that his trip would end in New York, where he would continue his campaign against fascism by painting an exterior mural with other artists using materials from modern industry and with the financial backing of the Museum of Modern Art.

He also wrote and issued a manifesto, "In War, The Art of War," in which he summoned the artists, writers, musicians and actors of America to contribute their artistic talents to the war effort. After urging them to demand that their governments establish workshops, sponsor artistic, literary and theatrical productions and provide the latest in equipment and materials, he advised them, "You ... must understand that art can be converted into a weapon ... which enters the eyes, the ears...through the most profound and subtle of the human senses." He concluded his latest manifesto with an appeal to the artists and writers to join the struggle for human liberty and the self-determination of all peoples, as well as to develop a truly great "public civilian art for peace."

Early in 1943 Siqueiros left Chile on a tour of several South American nations in what he described as a campaign to organize the artists and writers of the continent against fascism and for the triumph of the democracies. In Lima he gave a talk on the "Experiences of the Mexican Mural Movement for all of Latin America," in which he emphasized the responsibility of the government to sponsor young artists. After Peru, David and Angélíca visited Ecuador, Colombia, and Panama and at each stop, he continued his efforts to mobilize artists against war and fascism and to organize "groups of war artists" who would carry on wartime cultural propaganda within their respective countries. His next stop was Cuba, where he planned to carry on his campaign before traveling to New York and launching a new mural project.

In Havana, however, Siqueiros learned that in spite of his recent efforts on behalf of the democracies, an anti-subversive law prevented him from receiving a visa for the United States and the State Department would not allow an exhibit of his work at the Modern Museum of Art. The denial of a visa not only frustrated his artistic plans, but also aggravated their financial situation since he could not return to Mexico out of fear of arrest and retaliation for the attack on Trotsky. His banishment from the United States would also become permanent, lasting until his death in 1974.

Forced to cancel his plans, David announced that he would paint a mural in the land of José Martí, the "apostle" of Cuban independence. But after he found a suitable location in an old fortress, the project was cancelled, reputedly because of pressure from the American embassy. Therefore, when he was invited to paint a mural in the narrow corridor of a private residence owned by María Luisa Gómez Mena, a wealthy sugar plantation owner, he accepted. Although it was not an ideal site, he announced that he would unite the three walls and the ceiling by constructing a shell out of masonite panels, on which he would paint "a more active composition."

The theme would be "Allegory of Racial Equality and Fraternity Between the White and Black Races in Cuba," and as soon as the space had been reconstructed, Siqueiros began painting the walls and ceiling using an air compressor, spray gun and pyroxylin paint. After working all day, he would return home, unshaven and covered with paint, only to stay up late to draw and prepare for the next day's work. In spite of the intense summer heat, frequent interruptions and the constant commotion in the house, the mural began to take shape.

On one side he painted a seated black woman, symbol of the African race, and on the other her twin for the white or European race. The hand of the black women is draped over the raised knee of her white counterpart while the white woman returns the gesture. Directly overhead he painted a muscular figure, its head and arms aflame. Representing fraternity and equality, this humanized sun pulsated with energy and plunged downward towards the viewer, while its receding body drew one back into the space overhead.

But one morning when he arrived at the house, he was told that a woman had died of a drug overdose in the house the night before. After one newspaper accused Siqueiros, and another reported that Angélica had killed the woman out of jealousy, he was locked out of the house. Despite his pleas, the owner refused to let him or anyone else enter the house and see the mural. When he circulated leaflets in which he asked the public to demand to see the mural, saying that the Señora was the only one who give permission to view it, she closed the house and moved to another one she owned.

Though the mural was dismantled and destroyed, it marked another advance in Siqueiros's mural technique, particularly the resolution of painting the total space, the use of concave surfaces and the development of a perspective for the dynamic spectator. In the confined space, the dramatic distortions, multiple images and sense of movement created by the concave surface were overpowering. In subsequent murals he would apply and master these techniques, as well as recreate the image of the human-sun.

Siqueiros and *The Allegory of Racial Equality and Fraternity in Cuba,* 1943, Havana, Cuba

Notwithstanding the scandal, a committee headed by Nelson Rockefeller, now at the State Department, offered him $2500 to paint a "transportable mural" for the Institute of Cuban-American Cultural Relation in Havana. Desperate for funds to pay their bills at the Hotel Sevilla-Biltmore, he gladly accepted the commission. While the project only called for a flat canvas surface of 40 square meters, he created a concave section above the flat surface on which he painted *Two Mountains of America: Martí and Lincoln*, featuring monumental portraits of the Cuban and American heroes.

While he was still working on this painting, he received another assignment to paint a small portable mural for the entrance of the Hotel Seville-Baltimore, where he was staying. On a small flat surface of masonite he painted *New Day of the Democracies* in pyroxylin, in which a female figure emerges from smoking volcanoes, her raised arms and clenched fists projecting upward and outward. In less than a year he had painted one major mural and two portable ones, each time experimenting and gaining valuable experience. Viewed in retrospect, they were preliminary studies or experiments for future projects.

Meanwhile, he was invited to give a series of lectures on art in Havana. Besides describing the origins of the mural movement in Mexico, he stressed the importance of the return to public art and a new humanism which would constitute a "new realism." Like Mexico, he asserted, Cuba did not have a substantial market for art and Cuban artists, as well as artists throughout Latin America, should seek government support. Mexican artists had taken advantage of the Revolution to win the support of the state and Cuban artists should seize the opportunity of the war to develop an art that is authentically Cuban. Today, he said, artists could and should play a major role in the struggle of the democracies against fascism.

At the school of San Alejandro, he attacked academies that had not produced one great painter and were "producers of pedagogy rather than producers of art." Because of the lack of a market for their art, artists were forced to accept positions as teachers and then their students repeated the cycle, he noted. The only way for students to learn was by doing the work and the Mexican movement had been a major advance in this direction, he concluded.

In another lecture, he elaborated on the history of the evolution of the physical tools of artistic production and the unquestionable relationship between the society, technology and industry and the aesthetic of any historical period. There had never been nor would there ever be an art movement of any transcendence without the application of the most advanced technology of the age.

Turning to the work of Cuban artists, he praised their monumental style and uniquely Cuban styles or themes, but also noted some obvious Parisian tendencies and recommended that they abandon certain styles or techniques. Since Latin Americans had different racial compositions and different cultural traditions than Europe, they should not copy European art. Because of their similar cultures, races, histories and languages, Latin America was like one country with 21 provinces and the great pre-Columbian and Spanish colonial traditions belonged to all of them, even to the people of the United States.

Banned from the United States and apprehensive about returning to Mexico, Siqueiros asked his brother to inquire if he would be prosecuted for jumping bail or if he faced additional charges for the Trotsky attack. Assured by Jésus that he would not face prosecution if he returned to Mexico, David and Angélica prepared to leave, even though none of his murals in Cuba had been unveiled.

Just as they had left Mexico with little fanfare three years ago, he and Angélica returned to their homeland in semi-secrecy and moved into her mother's home. Though apprehensive, they were relieved to be back in Mexico. Their life in exile had not been easy, and even when he had been able to paint, it had not been under ideal conditions.

If Angélica had any doubts about their life together, the experiences of the last few years should have dispelled any notions of a dull and routine existence or a life of luxury and comfort. She and Adriana had shared in all the hardships of exile, proving their mettle as well as their commitment to him and his work. It was a bond that would be tested many times.

XI. Los Tres Grandes

Although his brother Jésus had assured him that he would not be prosecuted for the Trotsky affair, David was still apprehensive that he might be arrested for jumping bail and he kept a low profile after his return to Mexico. When his presence in Mexico was discovered, several newspapers immediately called for his arrest. Since the case was not reopened, rumors were rampant and ranged from the application of the statute of limitations to the mysterious disappearance of the Siqueiros-Trotsky dossier.

When he was questioned about his role, Siqueiros did not deny his responsibility, stressing that he had acted as an independent agent, and declaring, "I consider my part one of the most honorable acts of my life." Although the Trotsky case was apparently closed, he knew that his liberty depended on his abstinence from politics, especially protests against the government during wartime. Besides, Mexico was now allied with the United States and the Soviet Union in the struggle against fascism.

Fresh from his experiences in Chile and Cuba, Siqueiros was anxious to continue his art and he welcomed the opportunity to concentrate on painting. Taking advantage of this period of relative calm and living and working in the privacy of his mother-in-law's home in Mexico City, he produced some small but monumental easel paintings. Working with pyroxylin, he painted several landscapes, literally creating and shaping the forms of nature on flat surfaces. In *The Wounded Centaur* and *The Centaur of the Conquest,* he painted a centaur which represents the Spanish conquerors, half horse and half man. In the latter, he painted a large and muscular centaur rearing up over a volcanic landscape, one arm holding a sword while the other grasps a menacing cross. Although seemingly invincible, the centaur has been mortally wounded by a lance thrown by an unseen enemy.

Soon he was painting a much larger centaur, this time in the hallway of the Arenal home. Although the two-story surface, joined by two narrow walls and crossed diagonally by a stairway, was not an ideal surface for a mural painting, he converted it into a concave shell, much as he had done for the *Allegory of Racial Equality and Fraternity in Cuba*. Aided by Luis Arenal, he created a concave surface by joining the three surfaces with curved, celotex panels, upon which he began to paint *Cuauhtémoc Against the Myth*.

On the left side he recreated a massive centaur rearing up, its hooves multiplied and repeated on the lower stairway, producing a threatening movement. In its multiple hands it holds the beads of a rosary, a cross that is also a dagger and a flaming torch. But the centaur has been wounded and an obsidian-tipped lance, thrown by Cuauhtémoc, like the biblical David, is about to strike a mortal blow to the beast. Although it is an uneven struggle that the native leader cannot win, his act of resistance destroys the myth of the God-like invincibility of the Spanish conquerors.

In the background Siqueiros painted the defeated Aztec leader Moctezuma pleading with his people to surrender, along with a burning temple representing their defeat. While he worked feverishly on the walls, Luis was modeling the severed head of a Spaniard and a copy of pre-Columbian sculpture representing Quetzalcoatl, the plumed-serpent God whose prophesized return had demoralized the Aztecs. After Siqueiros painted them in bright colors matching those on the wall, they placed the head of the Spaniard and Quetzalcoatl beneath the painted stairway and in front of the wall.

Cuauhtémoc Against the Myth, 1944, Pyroxylin on Celotex and Plywood, Tecpan de Tlateloco, Mexico, D.F.

According to Siqueiros, the painted sculpture, combined with the painting of the total architectonic space, including the two sidewalls and the stairway, was "truly integral art." The painting of the sculpture was not an innovation, he explained, since the sculpture of ancient civilizations was painted, and unpainted sculpture lacks form and plain white or dark sculptures merely produce white or black silhouettes. Besides adding another dimension to the two-dimensional surface, the two pieces of sculpture anchored the vertical sidewalls and balanced the concave upper section. They also implied that there were no victors in the struggle, Spanish or Indian.

In June *Cuauhtémoc Against the Myth* was unveiled. Standing in front of his historical allegory, Siqueiros read a personally drafted manifesto and announced the establishment of the Center for Modern Realism in his mother-in-law's home. Mexican mural painting was the first art movement in Latin America to have an international impact, he declared, one which was even more important than the literary modernism of Rubén Darío and was the first artistic impulse in Latin America that was not colonial in nature. It was a new public art form, the equivalent of the Mexican Revolution in the arena of culture. More than just a reflection of the past, it was a product of the Revolution. Otherwise, it would be merely elitist, picturesque or snob art.

Today, he continued, they faced a crisis in Mexican art and had to avoid the picturesque trend and those pseudo-nationalists who were degrading the country by indulging in superficiality and mediocrity. The first period in the Mexican movement was necessarily primitive, purely emotional and instinctive, a romantic period which led to "a second experimental-technical stage and final determination of its doctrine" and "a new realist art, complete realism, a truly modern realism" in its social purpose, as well as in its forms and technique. This new realism would be promoted by artists with a social conscience, faithful to the original program and willing to contribute their talent to the struggle against fascism.

The Center for Modern Realism, he explained, would consist of a theoretical institute and a school to investigate and study everything related to the plastic arts, including history, chemistry, psychology and mechanics, as well as a functional workshop to produce painting, sculpture, sculpture-painting and graphics. It would constitute an alliance and consultative organ for the promotion and defense of Mexican art through the publication of a monthly review entitled *Realismo*, and it would sponsor conferences and expositions on the nature and purpose of modern art.

The reactions to the mural and Siqueiros's manifesto were varied. Orson Welles, who visited the Center for Modern Realism with

Rita Hayworth, declared that no other artist had painted with such boldness within the architectonic space since Michelangelo. The film director and actor described the figures as surging from the surface of the wall. "We feel that they project themselves towards us." Paul Westheim characterized the mural as "Movement impelled with an unbridled passion. A volcano, a Paricutin, surrounded by a sea of flames whose eruption cannot be prevented by anything or anyone." Siqueiros "is a man for whom his vision is reality, the only reality which he is disposed to recognize."

While most critics recognized the sense of power and movement the mural produced, some felt that the multiple forms clashed in the narrow hallway. Others noted that a mural in a private residence was inconsistent with the artist's advocacy of "public art." Opinion was also divided on the contribution of the polychromed sculptures and the painting of the stairway to the total effect of the mural.

To counter the criticism that he had reverted to archaic symbols of Greek mythology, David explained that the centaur was really a man-horse since the Indians had believed that the Spaniard and the horse were one being with two heads which spit out fire. This was part of the myth that was destroyed by the resistance of the Aztecs, led by Cuauhtémoc. "I present recognizable objects," he added, "so that the people may understand what I want to say."

Although David's proposal for a Center for Modern Realism provoked little reaction, his latest manifesto was attacked by several colleagues as presumptuous and its ideas, obscure or contradictory. While he agreed that the lack of a social platform had led to degenerate folklorism or purely sensual qualities and recognized the need for self-criticism, José Chávez-Morado attacked the "Plan Siqueiros" because it had all the "polemical and dominant character of its author" and was issued from above so as not to encourage discussion or self-criticism. Siqueiros's ideas, therefore, were not only divisive but also inconsistent with his proposal for a Center for Modern Realism.

Chávez-Morado also rejected the idea that only monumental art can be "public art," since easel paintings can be transported and exhibited in many places. Throughout our history, Chávez-Morado argued, popular portraits, prints and lithographs have been part of our artistic tradition and Indian pottery, retablos and other forms of folk art should be appreciated as much as the great pyramids and cathedrals which Siqueiros emphasizes.

The intensity with which Siqueiros had worked following his return to Mexico left him exhausted and combined with an old liver ailment, forced him to bed. But he was hard pressed financially, since he and the Arenals had financed his last mural and the Center for Modern Realism, and he was anxious to return to work, especially since it appeared that the charges against him had been dropped. Following a brief rest, therefore, he resumed his frenetic pace, working simultaneously on several fronts or projects.

After *Cuauhtémoc Against the Myth*, Siqueiros longed to incorporate some of his recent studies in another mural project. Not long after the unveiling of *Cuauhtémoc Against the Myth*, he received an invitation to paint a mural in the Institute of Fine Arts, or the Palacio de Bellas Artes, the lavish opera house started by Díaz before the Revolution and in which Rivera and Orozco had already painted murals. It was his first government commission since his eviction from the Preparatory School in 1924, and it meant that he had been recognized as a major artist by the official art establishment and implied an official pardon for past transgressions.

However, the site for his mural in Bellas Artes was hardly ideal. It consisted of a small section of wall divided into three spaces and topped by a cornice on a very narrow balcony which could be viewed only from up close or from another balcony, where two vertical columns obstructed the view. He was also warned not to tamper with the architecture. Despite these conditions, he began to work immediately on panels of celotex covered with cloth, to which he added different types of plant fiber to heighten the surface quality. Using pyroxylin, he began to develop the theme of "Life and Death."

After painting a volcanic landscape dotted with craters, he modeled a female figure based on a photograph of a bare-breasted Angélica. Similar to his *New Day of Democracies* figure in Havana, the highly modeled figure emerges from an erupting crater, her shackled arms thrusting upward and outward as she breaks free of her chains, grasping a torch in one hand and a flower in the other. Her red Phrygian "liberty cap" reflects the color and shape of the flames of the volcano from which she is emerging. These images extend up over the edges of the overhanging cornice, destroying it visually and creating a three dimensional effect. Behind and below one of the raised arms he painted a muscular third arm, its tightly clenched fist thrusting directly at the spectator. This mysterious force appears to have defeated fascism, a grey cadaver with blood-drenched hands which he painted from a photograph of himself stretched out on his back.

New Democracy, 1944–46, Pyroxylin on Canvas, Palace of Fine Arts, Mexico, D.F.

A year later, after the Allied victory, he added two side panels. On one side he painted a prostrate human figure with bound hands and whip lashes across its back, the "Victim of Fascism." For the opposite side he painted "Victims of War," the bodies of an embracing couple, their mutilated bodies stretched out on the ruins of war. In both panels, the rounded shapes of the human figures contrast with the rectangular shapes of the steps on which they are sprawled. They also recede towards the back of the picture plane, offsetting the forward thrust of the central figure of *New Democracy*. Along with the fallen conquerors in *Death to the Invader*, these radically foreshortened cadavers resemble Mantegna's dead Christ and Uccello's dead warrior which Siqueiros had studied closely.

Although *New Democracy* was overshadowed by Rivera's *Man at the Crossroads* and Orozco's *Catharsis* in Bellas Artes, Siqueiros had achieved a remarkable effect in a difficult space. Seen from the opposite balcony, the brilliant color and sculptural forms are striking and the exaggerated torso of the figure of liberty appears to lunge forward beyond the edge of the balcony. This effect, however, is counterbalanced by the receding figure of fascism and the accompanying side panels. Up close, the texture and rounded shapes of the human figures seem to have been molded out of moist earth or cement.

While some critics attacked the poster-like quality of *New Democracy* and the use of such obvious symbols as the torch, the flower, the Phrygian cap and the chains, others recognized it as "realism combined with expressionism," in which the forms of nature are not just copied by the artist, but are given a new meaning and existence. The symbol of liberty and democracy reminded some viewers of Delacroix while others compared his cadavers to those of Mantegna. One critic wrote that while Orozco allowed the viewer to interpret his work, Siqueiros did not give him any choice. Furthermore, he wrote, the approach was too simple, the forms were exaggerated and the message was obvious. Rufino Tamayo suggested that an airplane would have synthesized "liberty" in modern terms more effectively than the Phrygian cap.

Siqueiros rejoined that his super-realism was intended to communicate and to make sure that no one missed his message. He also declared that the art of the future would be baroque, dynamic, morbid, passionate, impetuous, sculptural and with "an obvious theme." With its sinuous forms, bright coloring and sense of movement, *New Democracy* was baroque, dynamic, passionate and sculptural, and its message was inescapable.

During the summer and early fall of 1944 David and Angélica wrote a series of ten articles on the subject of Mexican art and artists which appeared in the magazines *Hoy* and *Mañana* and the daily *El Nacional*. These articles provoked considerable controversy and rekindled the public debates on the origin, purpose, and status of modern Mexican art. In the first article Siqueiros reiterated his views on the origins, nature and importance of modern Mexican painting, "the first sprout of profound reform in the art of the contemporary world," and the "equivalent of the Mexican Revolution, and revolution in general in the arena of culture."

After proclaiming that the Mexican movement was the first artistic expression in Latin America to receive international recognition; the first artistic impulse which was not colonial or a mechanical reflection of fashionable French art; the first demonstration of a new political and public art, a greater art of the state, and the only theoretical and practical rebellion against traditional forms in the modern world, he proclaimed, "ours is the only way!" Given the lack of a private market for art in Latin America and the muted voices of yesterday, those modern currents of Paris, "ours is the only solution!"

His next article was dedicated to Diego Rivera, "the first practical exponent of our art." After admitting his differences with Rivera over technique, he described him as the most important and prolific founder. "Early in our movement," he wrote, "Mexican painting was Diego Rivera and nothing more." He was the first Mexican artist living abroad who recognized the transformation which was occurring in Mexico and he allied himself with the young artists who had fought in the Revolution. Rivera's ideas had also inspired his Barcelona manifesto in 1921, "the first theoretical formulation of our movement," and without his enthusiasm for public and heroic European art, the movement would have stalled.

Mixing praise with criticism, Siqueiros wrote that it was Diego who recognized the value of our pre-Hispanic, colonial and popular forms of art, though it is a shame that he has remained in such a "primitive phase." It was also Diego who pointed out the importance of good craftsmanship and professionalism, who demonstrated how to apply the theories of the Barcelona appeal and who proved that the movement was international and had universal values. He showed the way by challenging the routine teachings of the academics as well as by defying the "false ingenuity" and "dilettantism which the snobs of the modern school of Paris so admire." He was the first to develop "an ideological objective associated with the problems of mankind and society" and he was the first to paint a work of "public art."

Not only was Diego the first practical interpreter of our art, Siqueiros concluded, but he also remained faithful to mural painting and has accepted the program of the Center for Modern Realist Art. It is impossible to measure the contributions of Rivera. His work, along with that of Orozco, is the first expression of "public art after a long period of decadence in the plastic arts."

In his third article Siqueiros paid tribute to "the young Dr. Atl, the political and theoretical precursor of our movement," who provided the first idea, the first enthusiasm for mural painting, the idea of a return to public art, to a new classicism. As an instructor and Director of the National Academy of Art, Dr. Atl encouraged the break with the "pseudo academic training" at San Carlos. He was responsible for the artists' participation in the Revolution, which not only exposed them to the rigors of war, but also made them aware of the conditions of their country and the diversity and richness of national culture. The Revolution also destroyed the notion of indifferent and elite artists and fostered the concept of citizen artists working for a revolutionary state. Dr. Atl was the first to express his appreciation of Mexican popular art and he was responsible for the state's first efforts to foster and preserve this art.

Dissatisfied with traditional methods, Dr. Atl searched continually for a medium corresponding to the age and his restlessness led to the discovery of the "immutable principle" that an artist's tools and materials determine the nature of his art. Dr. Atl was the first to express his dissatisfaction with traditional methods of composition and perspective and it was he who fostered a spirit of monumentality, breaking with the "retrograde art" of the galleries and so-called modern artists." He was also the first to develop a panoramic sense of the landscape, using a new perspective of the earth made possible by the airplane.

Siqueiros's next article was an open letter to "José Clemente Orozco, the Formal Precursor of Our Painting." After comparing art critics to those of the bullring who do nothing but promote their favorite bullfighters, he turned to the subject of modern Mexican art. It would be wrong, he wrote, to conclude that its only source was Mexico's pre-Columbian and colonial culture because many other countries in Central and South America have similar cultural backgrounds, but none of them have produced a similar modern art movement. Had it not been for the Revolution, therefore, Mexican painting would have been as "intellectually colonial and domestically snobbish as it was in pre-revolutionary Mexico and still is in Spain and the rest of Latin America." Modern Mexican painting, therefore, is the cultural expression of the Revolution and without it, Orozco and other artists would have had to emigrate to a more positive environment.

With the exception of Dr. Atl, no one played a greater role in the process of the Revolution than you, Orozco, and your art and theories were the most faithful reflection of that revolutionary, iconoclastic period of our art. You created the best anti-clerical art ever produced in Mexico and were "the artistic precursor of the incipient school of Mexican social art." You supported the collective decision to paint murals and contributed to the development of the revolutionary program of the Barcelona manifesto. "You were as powerful a political cartoonist on the walls as you had been on paper," Siqueiros wrote, and you realized that a truly social art needs social forms that must be large as well as public.

Since you were involved from the first protests against the dictatorship of Díaz, your contributions were more extensive than Rivera's. Noting that his own participation began during the student strike at San Carlos, Siqueiros complimented Orozco for being the first muralist to become dissatisfied with traditional techniques and the first to experiment with new materials.

Turning to contemporary art, he posed the question of how anyone can believe that modern art is free just because artists do not have to reflect the ideology of their masters, when the artist must paint for a small minority of society and satisfy their "chic, epicurean and infantile taste?"

After admonishing Orozco for becoming isolated and losing his ideological support, Siqueiros advised him to ignore interpretations of his art by the critics and to improve, to experiment. While "you have improved both technically and artistically, your social involvement should keep pace with these improvements." You are still young and will recover from your current intellectual crisis and stagnation.

Siqueiros concluded his letter to Orozco with a challenge and a response. We must become truly collective, developing an ideology and a modern technique. Our production must increase, becoming a national and functional expression, but acquiring more universal values. The subject should be more concise, more powerful. Otherwise, the movement will fail and lose its international significance, like other artistic movements, he concluded.

In subsequent articles Siqueiros touched on a number of issues, but the underlying theme was the importance of modern Mexican painting, not only for Mexico, but as an example for other countries. In "There is No Other Way But Ours, the National and International Importance of Modern Mexican Painting," he analyzed the conditions of artistic production in three historical periods: ancient Greece, medieval and renaissance Italy, and contemporary France. After comparing pre-Hispanic America to ancient Greece and colonial Latin America to medieval and renaissance Italy, he pointed out that contemporary Spanish America could not be compared to contemporary France in its economic, social and cultural conditions. Therefore, the decadent aspects of modern French art were greatly accentuated in America.

However, the modern Mexican artistic movement is an exception, a pro-classic movement that searches for a new classicism, a new realism, through "the reconquest of the public forms lost since the end of the Renaissance, in the social and technical conditions of the democratic world." This movement already has twenty years of practical experience and is "without any doubt, the only possible universal route for the near future!"

In an article on the Center for Modern Realism, Siqueiros analyzed the current crisis in art and proposed moving to a superior phase based on the original platform of modern Mexican painting. The destiny of modern Mexican painting, he wrote, is directly linked to the destiny of the Mexican Revolution and if its progress is detained, Mexican painting will face a crisis. If the Revolution disappeared, Mexico would become the mediocre and insignificant intellectual colony which it was during the *porfiriato*. The health and progress of Mexican art, therefore, depends on the progress of the Mexican Revolution.

In other essays Siqueiros discussed the importance of the Taller de Gráfica Popular and the need to modernize its production; the participation of the artists in the campaign against illiteracy; the art of Picasso and descriptions of his own murals in Cuba and Chile. In 1945 these articles were collated and published in a book by the Ministry of Public Education. Entitled *No hay mas ruta que la nuestra* ("Ours Is the Only Way"), it was a manifesto on behalf of modern humanist and realistic public art. It immediately sparked protests, as much for the dogmatic tone of the title as its contents, and Siqueiros was accused of ignoring the contributions of other artists and being as exclusive and sectarian in his views as the Europeans were in theirs.

In the introduction he stated that Western Art had experienced a period of decadence since the Italian Renaissance until the Mexican movement, with the exception of the artists David, Cezanne and Picasso. In Mexico, in spite of its semi-colonial status, the first major reform in art occurred after three and a half centuries of decadence and this "public art...a truly modern functional art...neo-humanist" would replace the old and traditional formalism as well as the new snob academicism of the economically advanced countries.

In the first chapter, "Modern Mexican Painting, the First Sprout of Profound Reform in Contemporary International Art," he repeated his view that the Mexican movement was the first non-colonial artistic impulse in Latin America, was not dependent on French art and had universal significance. We are the first to develop a new political art, the only country where the great social forms of expression have been rediscovered since the Renaissance. But while they were working towards a "new realism, neo-humanist ... a new and greater classicism," the program was being abandoned by its very founders, surrendering to commercialism. But, he added, it was not too late to reverse this process.

Following this introduction came the chapters or articles on Dr. Atl, Orozco, and Rivera which combined expressions of praise and admiration with criticism and admonition. Although *No hay mas ruta que la nuestra* continued to spark controversy and debate in years to come and its implications of exclusivity were resented by younger artists, it remains an important document on the evolution of modern Mexican art by one of its major figures. Like his other manifestos, its tone was polemical and it combined self-criticism with praise. It was intended to remind others of the original goals of the movement, as well as its achievements, and it restated many of his own ideas on art in general and the Mexican movement in particular.

Feeling cramped by the small dimensions of *New Democracy* and anxious to apply some of his ideas, Siqueiros searched for another site, more challenging and more suitable to his aspirations and technique. While he was still working on his mural in Bellas Artes, he discovered an expansive stairway with a large overhead vault in the Old Customs House on the Plaza of Santo Domingo in the heart of Mexico City.

From the start he ran into problems. Since he wanted to modify the structure, he had to wait seven months for permission from the bureaucracy responsible for historic buildings. Then he proceeded, first erecting an elaborate wooden structure over which he had celotex panels covered with canvas mounted, thereby creating more curved and concave surfaces that joined the ceiling and the walls. When the framework and panels were in place, however, there was no pyroxylin paint available, and when it finally arrived, its cost had multiplied several times. Although the government of the Federal District had promised to cover his expenses, he had not received any money and had to use his own funds. Finally, the men assigned to assist him did not appreciate art and he complained that they worked on the mural as if they were paving streets or working on a construction project.

Despite these problems, he made some progress and worked on it throughout 1946 and 1947. After carefully studying the space and the different viewing points, he constructed a model of the structure on which he tried out different ideas. For a theme he chose "Patricians and Patricides," in which the Mexican heroes Hidalgo, Morelos, Juárez, and Zapata would rise to confront the traitors and enemies of the people, the Santa Annas, Iturbides, Huertas and the Catholic clergy. He would paint the latter as horrible monsters with horns, huge ears and metallic claws, representing the negative forces of tyranny, imperialism, feudalism and religion, all of which would be pushed into oblivion by the positive forces of revolution.

Using a projector to transfer sketches to the ceiling, he began to paint the evil forces on the ceiling. As the monsters took shape, their figures hurtling down towards anyone mounting the stairs, a flood of criticism was directed at him. His demons were characterized as unconvincing and primitive or as "comic" rather than terrifying. He was accused of turning the colonial building into a theater of the absurd and a workshop filled with tools, scaffolding and assistants, while his modification of the space clashed with the original stone structure.

Rivera joined the chorus of critics. After reminding Siqueiros of his criticism of other muralists for not integrating mural painting into architectural structures, Diego accused him of sticking cardboard on a stone building and creating homes for rats. "Siqueiros' painting is nothing but stage decoration, a sort of allegorical chariot or triumphal arch built in the street for a patriotic pageant," and he violates his own principles and tries to hide it by accusing others of committing the offense.

Siqueiros returned the favor, declaring that all the rectangular spaces in Rivera's murals were "virtual stadiums for rats, certainly more comfortable and healthier than mine" and that his Anachuali, the replica of a pyramid which Diego had designed and built as a studio and a museum to house his collection of pre-Columbian art, was an anachronism in the twentieth century, a "cave for dinosaurs." In defense of his modifications of the architecture of the Customs House, he pointed out that it had been necessary to modify the colonial buildings in which they were working and that painting the total architectonic space was more than just adding simple decorative elements to unite separate panels.

In response to other critics, Siqueiros explained that his composition was more baroque or post-baroque because of the baroque architecture and "contains all the elements of a new technique of painting ... whose consequences will appear gradually during this second stage of our movement."

All this criticism and debate were academic, however, as the mural was destined to remain unfinished. It had been plagued with problems from the start and while he was painting the demons on the ceiling, moisture began to seep through the colonial structure. He continued to have problems with funding and protested the failure of the Federal District to supply the promised funds for expenses to Carlos Chávez, the Director of the Institute of Fine Arts. This delay, he warned, would seriously affect the international recognition which their work had received and showed that the government of the Federal District did not support cultural and artistic activities.

Frustrated by technical problems and the lack of adequate financing, Siqueiros abandoned the project in 1947. In 1950 he negotiated another contract to finish it and returned to work on it sporadically in the 1950s and again in 1965 for the last time, without ever finishing it. While all that remains are the swirling demons on the ceiling, a portrait of Angélica representing the heroine of the struggle for independence, and some compositional lines, it was an impressive concept and is distinctive for its baroque quality and polyangular perspective.

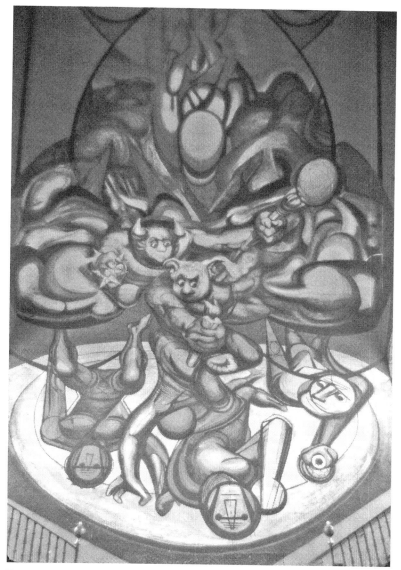

Patricians and Patricides, 1945–1968, Pyroxylin and Acrylic on Masonite, Customs House, Plaza Santo Domingo, Mexico, D.F.

After the publication of *No hay mas ruta que la nuestra*, David and Angélica continued to write articles that provoked controversy. In August of 1945 *Hoy* published "The Function of the Photograph" by

David Alfaro Siqueiros in which he resumed his attack on the literary method of art criticism. In Mexico, he wrote, they were still debating whether photography is one of the fine arts when it offers a new vehicle for preserving images and is able to create an art of its own, a photographic art.

"Photography offers a vehicle, either accessory or direct, which could lead to a more integral, truer and more realistic realism," he wrote. Its function is "to serve, in a documentary sense, as an objective and psychological collaborator which can 'check' the plastic process of both painting and all other art." How can photography be seen as serving science, technology and everything else, but not the plastic arts? he asked. Photographers may "contribute their own particular aesthetic expression ... [and] all the tools used to produce art are machines, even the most primitive." He concluded with a statement that art must be capable of being mass-produced if it is to be public and democratic.

In September the magazine *Así* published an open letter from Siqueiros to Jaime Torres Bodet, the Minister of Public Education, in which he attacked the current program for dehumanizing culture and debasing the platform of the Mexican Revolution. It has become a commercial gallery of art, sponsoring exhibits by mediocre artists and has failed to generate any debate on pedagogy in the plastic arts. Siqueiros pointed out that there was nothing in the aesthetic program of the Ministry which conformed to Torres Bodet's previous activities and philosophy of education and he should discharge all those employees who support "art purism," the partisans of the aesthetic of "the ivory tower," and reconsider all plans for exhibits of abstract art.

Turning to the subject of the Mexican film industry, Siqueiros wrote an article on "National Cinema: True or False." In it he accused the Mexican film industry of having sold out and imitated the styles, themes and techniques of Hollywood. The birth of the film industry, he pointed out, coincided with the birth of the mural movement and was the logical outcome of the Revolution. The first films, therefore, were experimental and primitive, as well as full of social comment, much like the murals. "But then what happened?" he asked. Although foreign influences were instructive at first, speculators came in to exploit the market, building studios and importing foreign technicians, writers and actors. Mexican film corrupted the intellectuals who wrote for it and has falsified Mexico and its people. "It has tuned our horsemen into theatrical tenors or dolled-up cowboys, in a servile transcription of the 'Mexican gunmen' invented by Hollywood."

This disaster can only lead to economic catastrophe, he wrote, since better box office profits would be derived from fewer, but superior films. Moreover, cinema or film should serve the Revolution and eventually the industry should be nationalized as the state's best educational medium, as other countries have already done. Leaving it in private hands would be like converting the Ministry of Public Education into a private capitalistic enterprise.

While they were writing articles for several other publications, David and Angélica were also involved in the direction of two new reviews. Named for the year in which they first appeared, the mastheads of *La 45* and *La 46* proclaimed, "In Defense of the Social Progress of Mexico: Monthly Review Produced by Painters, Engravers, Writers, Draughts men and Photographers." Luis Arenal was the art director and the pages were covered or dominated by large illustrations, what Siqueiros called "cartículos," a blend of the Spanish words for poster and article but also close to "cartuchos," or cartridges. These "cartículos" were plastered on walls throughout Mexico City or were used as posters for political rallies.

Besides defending the Revolution against the conservative opposition, *La 45* and *La 46* took up the defense of the Spanish Republic and developed a foreign policy for an independent Mexico that opposed war, fascism and imperialism and advocated the self-determination of all peoples. Another common theme was the need for a revolutionary press, film industry and theater. Incorporating the work of the best writers and artists in Mexico, and foreigners like Orson Welles, Pablo Neruda and the Cuban poet Nicolás Guillén, the issues were very popular and sold out almost immediately. Although short-lived, these publications brought together diverse writers and artists in a cooperative effort.

For years Siqueiros had expressed his disenchantment with traditional plastic materials and tools and his enthusiasm for the new synthetic materials was well known. After he stumbled upon "Duco," he incorporated it into his paintings and he had organized a workshop in New York to explore new materials and techniques. Declaring that there could be no transcendental art employing technical anachronisms, he had encouraged José Gutiérrez to continue his investigations and he had issued numerous statements calling for a truly modern technology, using the latest industrial technology to produce a modern art for a modern age.

In 1945 his insistence was rewarded when Jaime Torres Bodet announced the establishment of the Institute for the Chemical Investigation of Plastic Materials at the National Polytechnic Institute in Mexico City. Gutiérrez was named director and during the next twenty years he conducted experiments in the use of plastic materials for industry as well as for artists.

In response to the requests of the muralists who needed a rapidly drying paint with bright colors which would last indefinitely, even outdoors, Gutiérrez and a chemist, Manuel Jiménez Rueda, developed "politec" paints from acrylic emulsions. Manufactured in Mexico, the Politec paint resists fading, oxidization and climatic changes and is used today by artists throughout the world. Besides investigating the properties of the different pigments, the institute studied the porosity, adhesive qualities and durability of different surfaces and pigments under various conditions of heat and light.

It also trained hundreds of artists from many countries in the use of the new media and became a mural workshop where the artists in residence learned how to use the new paints by painting on its walls.

In addition to a plethora of articles and mural projects, David was busily painting "studies" for future murals. After posing in front of a camera, he painted his self-portrait, *El Coronelazo*, with his paint-spattered fingernails, knuckles and clenched fist thrusting forward, as if scratching the surface of the painting, and symbolizing his militant posture in art and politics. Meanwhile, his foreshortened arm leads back to his face and torso draped in a red tunic. He also completed a lithograph study for a painting he would later call *Our Current Image*.

Using himself as a model, he had his picture taken with his chest bared and arms and hands outstretched, and then used the photograph to draw his image on a lithograph stone. In a second version, done in pyroxylin on masonite, he exaggerated the foreshortening to create a muscular male figure whose outstretched hands dominate the picture plane. The palms are open, the fingers point down and out, as if to offer or receive an unseen force or gift. The head and the face consist of an undefined and surrealistic grayish block of lava, similar to some of the monsters he had painted in the customs house.

Our Current Image was painted on a seven by five-and-a-half foot surface and its powerfully modeled hands, figure and block-like head fill the plane and project beyond it, directly confronting the viewer and at the same time, drawing him into it. While the figures in both *El Coronelazo* and *Our Current Image* project out and away from the surface of the paintings, that projection is offset by a perspective which draws the viewer back into the picture, towards the face or head, thereby creating a sense of alternating movement.

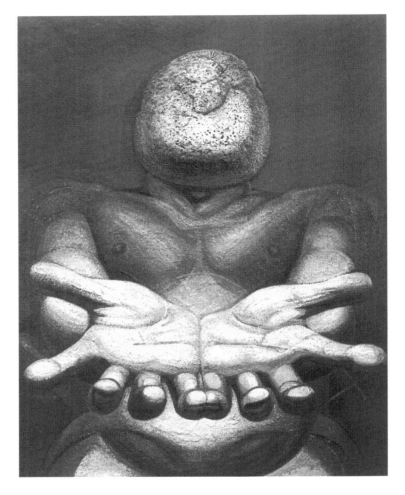

Our Current Image, 1948, Pyroxylin on Masonite,
Museum of Modern Art, Mexico, D.F.

When a photographer accused him of plagiarism because he had copied a photograph, Siqueiros demonstrated that he had conceived the idea before the photographs were taken and pointed out that anyone comparing the two art forms could see that while one was a photographic document, the other was clearly the inspiration and creation of the artist. Unlike Rivera, Siqueiros did not make elaborate sketches and increasingly worked directly from photographs that he had taken of himself, Angélica, his assistants or natural landscapes.

In 1946 David was fifty years old and in the prime of life. If 1945 had been a productive year, 1946 was to be equally fertile and his best years and work were still to come. The *New Democracy* commission and the publication of "Ours Is the Only Way" by the Ministry of Public Education signaled his acceptance by the establishment and more commissions would follow. Along with Rivera and Orozco, he was now recognized as one of *"los tres grandes,"* the three masters of modern Mexican art.

XII. El Maestro

While 1945 was a good year for Siqueiros, it also signified a turning point for Mexico as a modern nation. The war effort had united the country and bolstered the economy. Cut off from foreign suppliers, Mexico had expanded industrial production while lend-lease equipment and technical assistance from the U.S. had improved the transportation system.

Although Cárdenas remained in the government, Ávila Camacho's election to the Presidency signaled a move to the right. Instead of social reform, official policy promoted economic development, industrialization and increased productivity. In the countryside agricultural production took precedence over land reform and the pace of redistribution declined drastically. The labor movement also lost ground and many of its more radical leaders were eased out and replaced by moderates during the war.

While some of these changes were dictated by wartime priorities, they also reflected the emergence of a new industrial and commercial elite in Mexico. When Miguel Alemán Valdés succeeded Ávila Camacho in 1946, he became the first elected civilian President since Madero. He had not fought in the Revolution and his election signaled the emergence of a new political generation, the sons or protégés of the revolutionary generals and government technocrats. The PRM also became the Institutional Revolutionary Party (PRI), a government party that dominated politics at every level.

While Mexico experienced unprecedented economic growth between 1946 and 1952, providing more jobs and expanding the middle class, the benefits were distributed unevenly and were eroded by inflation. The "dance of the millions" was occasioned by excessive corruption, even by Mexican standards, with a corresponding disillusionment with government officials and the Revolution. The government not only controlled the official labor confederation but also intervened in the independent unions, replacing elected leaders with government stooges.

On the other hand, the government was building schools and training more teachers and the increase in government spending and private wealth expanded the market for writers and artists. There were more mural opportunities as artists were hired to decorate the offices of new government agencies, schools and public works projects. But Mexico not only welcomed foreign capital but also imported culture and revolutionary nationalism, the Indian and his heritage were no longer considered appropriate symbols for a modern and progressive nation. Nationalistic art was considered passé and destined to yield to more avant-garde and universal forms of expression.

Although the new wealth spawned more art galleries and a market for easel painting, their patrons tended to prefer abstract expressionism or picturesque folkloric art to social realism. The climate of the Cold War also discouraged social realism or "political art," especially since the patrons were wealthy members of the new oligarchy or private corporations, and Mexican cultural institutions were influenced by North American cultural institutions. A new generation of artists was also emerging which had not participated in the struggles of the past and the younger artists were trying to express themselves in the different reality of the postwar years. Exposed to cultural currents from Europe or the United States, their fame and fortune depended on their discovery abroad or recognition and promotion by a foreign sponsor.

Although he would profit from these developments, Siqueiros was critical of recent trends and spoke out against the counter-revolutionary policies of the government and United States imperialism under Truman. He was also critical of the opportunism of other leftists and labor leaders.

Lacking a new mural project and frustrated after his last two attempts, David concentrated on "mural studies." Using pyroxylin, he developed modeled impastos of thick and bulky forms, which took on a life of their own. The swirling and heavy forms of nature in the landscapes appear to move and their solid forms and rough surfaces can be felt as well as seen. They also seem to be animated and endowed with human characteristics.

In *Pedregal*, a landscape study of a lava-strewn area of Mexico City, the lava seems to be alive and moving. In another painting of the same area he included three human figures which are overshadowed by the natural landscape and a stormy sky endowed with a human energy. In *Intertropical* the forms of nature appear to be locked in combat while the three squashes in a still life seem to interact with each other, like three human figures. While he called these studies "subjectivizations," a critic wrote that Siqueiros "humanizes the most abstract elements of his paintings."

In October of 1947 a show of "70 Recent Works" by David Alfaro Siqueiros opened in Bellas Artes. For the first time many of his most important paintings and prints of the last fifteen years were presented together. In the catalog Siqueiros explained that the paintings and drawings were studies for current or projected mural projects, and they provided visual proof of many of the ideas he had expressed recently and were an effective response to the criticism stirred up by his articles and his most recent mural, **New Democracy**.

The catalog also contained an extensive biography of the artist by Angélica, in which she described his experiences from childhood to the preparations for the exhibit and included many of his statements on art and the origins, nature and significance of modern Mexican painting. She quoted him on the superiority of pyroxylin and vinylite, "constituting a superlative oil ... with greater possibilities of thickness, texture, veladuras, etc." She also repeated his characterization of the Mexican muralists as "pre-primitives of a new Renaissance," which neither they, nor the next generation, would achieve.

The "70 recent works" included *Pedregal*, *Three Squashes* and *Our Current Image*. Besides *El Coronelazo*, there was another self-portrait of Siqueiros in an elegant overcoat and fedora, which Angélica explained, "is a study for the objectification of the subjective elements of the figure." In a tribute to Orozco, which he signed *El Coronelazo*, he had painted his fellow artist seated in a chaotic landscape of swirling forms. For a study of Josefa Ortiz de Domínguez, the heroine of independence, he had painted a portrait of Angélica in which her powerfully modeled figure fills the plane of the picture and stands out against a turbulent background. The treatment is psychological as well as realistic. Her image not only dominates the picture plane, but her intense expression evokes an inner strength and determination.

The exhibit also included a series of mural-like allegories. To commemorate the nationalization of the oil industry in 1938, Siqueiros had painted a large female figure, based on a photograph of Angélica, clutching oil wells to her bosom in *Sunrise of Mexico*. It is monumental in its effect, the highly sculptural and geometric figure filling the picture plane. In a large, mural-like study, *The Devil in the Church*, the viewer looks up from the altar at a monster breaking through the roof of the cathedral to be adored by the humble masses while the rich look on from the balcony. Although he referred to it as "a study in perspective," it was a commentary on religion and society, monumental in its style and force.

In *Cain in the United States* he protested racism by painting a group of white demons lynching a black man. *The Death and Burial of Cain* represented the death of Mussolini, who according to a Mexican saying, "died like a chicken." It featured a yellow plucked fowl draped across a mountainous landscape surrounded by the celebrating masses. In *Image of Mexico* a large, heavily modeled male figure lies face down, his body sprawled across the rough terrain of the country.

The exhibit included more portraits, several other nude studies, some "cataclysmic" or "animated" landscapes and a series of abstract paintings or "plastic exercises" with titles like "Rotation," "Vibration" and "Forward Movement." In all of them Siqueiros demonstrated his use of new materials and techniques and an increasing mastery of the medium. The forms are full and round, the thick and dense material has a life of its own and the forward projection of the figures is counterbalanced by a receding perspective that draws the viewer back into the painting. With the exception of the abstract studies and portraits, the approach is didactic and direct, even brutal, and the effect is frequently overpowering, evoking strong emotions.

The response to the show was generally favorable and there was little doubt that Siqueiros had established himself as a major artist and one of "*los tres grandes*." One review called the exhibit "an aesthetic revelation" and "an aesthetic note of the first order which places Mexico at the vanguard of revolutionary painting." Although the writer cautioned that Siqueiros "is an apocalyptic painter and prophet of communism," he emphasized the sculptural and corporal value of the forms which are "animated by the magic of the artist" and the masculine, firm, precise and vigorous nature of his technique. The portraits, he wrote, lose their pictorial essence and assume "an astounding elasticity." His colors have an intensity and luminosity, which when compared with those of the masters, make the latter appear mental or superficial, while the synthetic resins created thick, dense, bubbling and volcanic forms which appear to move in a constant, pulsating agitation.

Another observer wrote that in *Our Current Image* Siqueiros uses surrealism to make "reality concrete" and abandons traditional perspective. Rather than drawing the spectator into the picture, he is determined that the spectator raise his hands to his face in order to protect itself against figures which thrust themselves towards him. The landscapes are "original," the critic wrote, the result of "invention" rather than pure imitation, while his abstract paintings are much more than a simple play of forms. The paintings reflect "the tormented spirit and the combative will of the artist" and are "violent, thundering, terrifying... disquieting for someone who seeks tranquility in art."

At the close of the exhibit, Siqueiros gave a talk in which he described the Mexican mural movement, "the first manifestation of Latin American art to find an important place in the ranks of world culture." After reviewing his own experiences in this process, he listed the "tricks" of technique which he began to develop in California. Besides using pyroxylin as superlative oil" which can produce textures impossible to achieve with other materials, he had used the camera and its photographic documents, an electric projector and new commercial paints applied with an airbrush or spray gun. Insisting on painting the total architectonic space, he had created more active surfaces, developed polyangular forms and produced a perspective for "the dynamic spectator." This new realism, he declared, is a "poetic combination ... of objective and subjective elements, because my reality is made of recognizable things and of things prone to suggestion."

He also challenged those who condemned "the monopoly of the Big Three," that is Rivera, Orozco and himself, as if they were holy men, to develop a systematic plan of criticism which attacks the archaic and archaeological technique of Rivera, the purist art tendency of Orozco and the mystical, neo-classical, frequently sentimental and spectacular elements in his own paintings, as well as the obvious contradictions and mistakes in his theory and practice. They should also study and criticize Rufino Tamayo, Manuel Rodríguez Lozano and Carlos Mérida, who had deserted the movement and surrendered politically, technically and formally to art purism. However, he did not deny the importance of the "School of Paris" in destroying traditional approaches to art.

Returning to the subject of murals, he called for the criticism of the murals painted in old and modern buildings, including those painted on the exterior, and commented on the historical significance of the Mexican movement. In spite of the negative aspects of that movement, Mexico was achieving its historic destiny of discovering all the positive plastic values and developing a "more integral and accurate realism. We can desire nothing better than post-Baroque art!" he concluded.

Although he had hoped that the exhibit would travel to the Museum of Modern Art in New York, those plans were cancelled, a casualty of the Cold War. Meanwhile, a show of "45 Self-Portraits by Mexican Artists" had opened in Mexico that included several of his personal studies. He also wrote a section for the catalog entitled "The Creed of David Alfaro Siqueiros," which contained few surprises.

After declaring "the modern art movement of Mexico, of which I am one of the founders, is the most important art trend in the world today," Siqueiros recognized that the Parisian school had broken the old routines. He also commented on his fellow artists. Much as I admire the heroic and monumental work of Orozco and bow before the craftsmanship of Diego Rivera, he wrote, I would prefer different methods or interpretations. As for Rufino Tamayo, "I understand his contributions to the use of color, his discoveries of 'local color,' but I would discard the chic Parisian elements which have crept into his work."

When it came to his own creed, he explained that he was faithful to the "Mexican School" and concentrated his efforts on murals and reproductions using the latest technology to produce public forms for the socialist society which will replace capitalism.

Throughout 1948, Siqueiros continued to write articles and give lectures on the subjects of art and art criticism. In "Towards a New Integral Art," he called for a unitary art, like that of the past, in which architecture, painting and sculpture were united or integral. Despite the resurgence of art and architecture in Mexico, he wrote, they have not been integrated and the current independence of the arts from each other is not liberation, but a mutilation, a consequence of the individualism of a liberal society.

The new architecture, he continued, will be monumental and integrally artistic as in the past. It will use the latest in materials, the synthetic paints, artificial lighting and "stuccoes and finishes which absorb paint through an electrical discharge." "The old forms are too static, too mechanical and would not be right for the active spaces of active architecture... We need new voices, voices of an integral art which can only come from new throats."

When Luis Cardoza y Aragón wrote an article on him, David responded with "Art Criticism as a Literary Pretext." After declaring that the artistic conflict in Mexico was between the non-realism of Paris and the new realism of Mexico, he proceeded to illustrate how that struggle was reflected in the art criticism of our country. In Cardoza y Aragón's article on him, Siqueiros explained, there was no analysis, only praise. He says that "the best of my work continues to be easel painting" and asks, "Where is his great mural work?" when

I have always admitted that all our earlier works were conservative and primitive and that we needed to launch a new phase.

When the same critic wrote that Tamayo "does not or never will accept being a voice in the chorus of the Three Giants: Rivera, Orozco and Siqueiros" and he was a worthy successor in the artistic tradition of Mexico because his work was just the opposite of "los tres grandes," Siqueiros responded, what is the merit in not being part of our tendency and being part of the non-realist and formalist tendency of Paris? Since these critics are ignorant of the nature and historical transcendence of the "School of Paris," he asked, how are they going to understand the nature and transcendence of our movement? How can they appreciate our movement if the social issues which gave rise to it are considered distasteful or are ignored and how can they assess its contributions if they are caught up in a movement which is directly opposed, antithetical to ours?

According to Cardoza y Aragón, he wrote, our school is "only an interesting graft of the same tree," the school of Paris. Why, he asked, do they refuse to accept that a semi-colonial country like ours can produce a superior movement and example for the whole world? The "monocle of the art purists" prevents them from seeing the contradictions between their tendency and ours. They, the art purists, seek form for the sake of form, while "we seek form as an illustrative and eloquent means, like the artists of the great periods of the past." In addition, he hoped that these discussions would lead to an appropriate method of criticism for their movement and a new realism.

Sixteen years after his first experience in teaching "fresco" or mural painting, Siqueiros received an offer to apply his theories on teaching art and to work with a group of art students. Through Graciela Amador, his former wife, he was invited to give a series of lectures on mural painting at the School of Painting of the University of Fine Arts in San Miguel de Allende, in the state of Guanajuato. Needing a vacation from his hectic schedule in Mexico City, as well as the offer of three thousand pesos for three lectures, plus food and lodging for himself and Angélica, Siqueiros accepted the offer.

Although other Mexican artists were also invited, in August of 1948 Siqueiros began to offer the first course on mural painting in Mexico. In an ironic twist, most of the students at the school were veterans from the United States and the same government that refused to grant him a visa, paid for these students to study under him in Mexico. Not only was he able to expound on his ideas on art, but he also renewed his acquaintance with North American students and artists, and when time permitted, he played baseball with them.

After his first three lectures, he agreed to offer more on the technique of mural painting. But since he was convinced that the only way to teach mural painting was to work on a mural, they obtained permission from the director of the school to paint a mural and began to look for a wall. After a search around San Miguel, they found an appropriate site, a narrow vaulted dining hall in the eighteenth century Convent of Santa Rosa. Since the town was named after Ignacio Allende, local hero of the war of independence, they agreed that the theme should be the life and work of Allende, or *Monument to Ignacio Allende*.

Although he sensed that the directors of the school were not very enthusiastic about the prospect of a mural in a building that did not belong to them, Siqueiros immersed himself in the project, working in a frenzy of activity and ignoring everything else. He divided the students and some of the teachers from the school into nine teams which were to research and develop some theme or aspect of Allende's life, from his birth to his execution for leading the revolt against Spain. In the process, the whole community became involved, contributing documents or anecdotes on local history and the Allende family.

Since there were no drawings of the building, they took measurements of the interior and constructed a model to develop a structural analysis of the space. Then, following Siqueiros's directions, the students analyzed the different viewpoints of a moving spectator. From this information, they determined the lines of the composition and painted them on the walls using an electric projector.

Photography was also used extensively throughout the project. Instead of sketching horses, photographs were taken of horses in the countryside, from which sketches were drawn for different sections of the mural. When the various sections had been planned and some preliminary sketches had been applied to the wall, photographs were taken of them to study the different forms and shapes they assumed from different points of view. Studies were also made of the impact of color and the relationship of blocks of color to each other by painting large areas and then analyzing the effect.

Because of the height of the room, some sort of scaffolding was needed to reach the higher areas, but which would also permit an unobstructed view of the surface under study. After holding a competition for a solution, the students found an answer. They built four towers mounted on wheels that could be easily dismantled or joined and moved about. One team of students also developed a special lens for the projector which permitted the teams of artists to make adjustments for the different perspectives. Now they were ready to transfer "Monument to Ignacio Allende" onto the walls of the convent.

When the students began to transfer their sketches to the walls and ceiling, however, Siqueiros was disappointed. Instead of creating a unified composition that would totally involve the spectator in developing an understanding of the life of Allende and the struggle for independence, they had painted separate areas without any sense of unity.

One morning, however, David arrived at the convent and found the entrance locked. When he was told that it was time for vacations, he demanded that the convent be opened immediately so they could resume work on the mural. While he waited for a response, the students told him that he was the only real instructor in the school and the other so-called "teachers" were actually students who were paid a small stipend by the school. But they lived constantly under the threat of deportation for working without a permit from the Mexican government.

The students also explained that the Director had not paid the rent for the school buildings with the excuse of spending the money on repairs. But the buildings were in ruins, there was no library in the school and there were no easels or art materials for the students.

Many of them, therefore, merely came to receive their certificates, which they received after paying three thousand pesos and spending eight days in San Miguel. David then realized that the convent had been locked because they did not want him to finish the mural and by keeping him there, they could attract more students.

Incensed by the interruption in his work, Siqueiros met with Campanella, the Director, and threatened to destroy his lucrative operation. When he tried to salvage the project by explaining that the school could still make a profit and at the same time, contribute to the projection of Mexican art and culture in the United States, Campanella was intransigent and told him that he could not understand how a communist could object to cheating the government of the United States.

Frustrated in their efforts to reopen the convent, the students and their teacher organized a strike and sent a delegation to Mexico City to meet with the Minister of Public Education. They also met with Carlos Chávez, the Director of the National Institute of Fine Arts, and suggested that the government take over the school and create a truly continental school of mural painting. There would be no charge for Mexican students, while the fees paid by the foreign students could be used to purchase materials for teaching mural painting. Meanwhile a group of sculptors, painters, engravers and photographers joined the protest and organized a boycott of the school.

In July of 1949 Siqueiros wrote a letter to the students and professors of the school and some public officials. In it he explained that he would have to interrupt his work on the mural until the dispute was resolved by the proper government agencies. He would honor his contract, but he refused to cooperate with a director who knew nothing about the plastic arts, was never at the school and whose only interests were commercial operations of questionable legality. After calling for a boycott of the school, he protested the use of the prestige of modern Mexican painting for opportunistic mercenary interests.

The dispute dragged on and *Monument to Allende* remained locked up in the convent. Campanella refused to budge and accused Siqueiros of painting a naked Virgin of Guadalupe and using photographs instead of having his students sketch from live models. Siqueiros had the support of the local community, however, and even the office of veterans in the United States Embassy supported the boycott and suspended its contract with the institute.

In August the government decided to incorporate the school into the National Institute of Fine Arts, but most of the students had already left. Having exhausted his funds, Siqueiros returned to Mexico City, leaving behind the tracings of another unfinished mural.

The termination of Siqueiros's project in San Miguel de Allende meant that he had not finished his last two mural projects, *Monument to Allende* and *Patricians and Patricides*, and the only murals that he could claim since his return to Mexico were *New Democracy* and *Cuauhtemoc Against the Myth*, neither of which justified his lofty status along side Rivera and Orozco. While the delays, lack of funds, and the misadventure at San Miguel were discouraging, he was determined to finish both projects. He had also advanced his ideas on mural painting as well as his technique and in 1951, he incorporated these ideas and lessons into a book, *Como se pinta un mural* (How to Paint a Mural). Based on his experiences on *Monument to Ignacio Allende*, it described that project and provided a practical manual for muralists.

Como se pinta un mural is a synthesis of many of his previously stated theories on art and mural painting and it contains excerpts from his essays in *No hay mas ruta que la nuestra*. After a preamble in which he wrote that muralism disappeared after the Italian Renaissance and then resurfaced in Mexico in 1922, the first chapter provides an analysis of the Mexican movement as the first attempt at the re-integration of the plastic arts.

While the development of integral art must use the new mechanical and scientific technology already adopted in modern architecture, not all painters, sculptors and artists understand it. After calling for a total integration of the arts according to their function, he summarized the history of modern Mexican art, the only movement, he contended, committed to recovering the lost values of integral art.

As its title implies, *Como se pinta un mural* is also a manual for painting murals and it includes diagrams, preliminary sketches and photographs to illustrate his points and several appendices with formulas and instructions for using fresco, encaustic, pyroxylin, ethyl silicate and vinylite. It also addresses the problems of painting modern murals in old buildings; the organization of a team of artists working under a single director; the use of the camera, photography and electric projector for making realistic studies and analyzing the progress of the painting; the careful analysis of the structure; the utility of a scale model; the study of the different perspectives and the use of appropriate materials and equipment. But, he warned, if you paint in fresco, you produce pre-Christian or medieval art and public art requires an even greater knowledge of plastic materials.

On the subject of composition, *Como se pinta un mural* insisted that "it must conform to the normal transit of a spectator" and use a multiangular approach from the many different points of view. Therefore, most of my murals and those of my colleagues are not yet mural painting.

In terms of unitary art, Siqueiros declared that even the best mural paintings of the past were not truly mural paintings. The Sistine Chapel is a work of genius, but it is a series of murals painted horizontally and from top to bottom and joined by ornamental details. Each panel has its own unitary composition, joined to the whole by simulated architectural elements.

Rivera, "the new Michelangelo," painted his most complete work at Chapingo, he explained, since it is not just a succession of panels but "a harmonious coordination of many panels ... linked together by *trompe l'oeil..*" All true architectonic space is a machine, he wrote, and its parts, the walls, floors, vaults, arches, etc. are wheels of that machine, an active machine in rhythmic movement with a geometric play of infinite intensity. The spectator is the only switch that can activate this machine, the current which gives the necessary movement. When the spectator stops, the machine also stops.

On the subject of perspective, Siqueiros wrote that the traditional solutions were inadequate. Both rectilinear and curvilinear perspectives assume that the spectator is a fixed statue that looks at the mural from one point or moves along an axis and looks with a fixed gaze at a straight or curved horizontal line and a single vanishing point. A real spectator is not a statue but someone who moves along a plane, activating the different geometric forms around him. In the process, a rectangle becomes a truncated pyramid that inclines towards the right from one view and from another, towards the left. Since traditional methods ignore the distortions created when a spectator moves, a new perspective and composition is needed, a new concept of active space within the architecture.

Next he described the process of adding color. Once the different angles or points of view have been determined and the tracings of the composition have been transferred to the wall, masses or flat areas of color should be applied, since color has spatial value and suggests different depths. Because there are no scientific formulas on the spatial qualities of color, Siqueiros wrote, they had to learn from their experience at San Miguel, using only their eyes and their sensibility, and arriving at the principle that "colors have neither value nor belligerency by themselves; their life is a result of their chromatic relationship with the colors which surround them in greater or lesser proximity."

Returning to his experience in San Miguel, he observed that when they divided the room into flat color areas, they exaggerated the anatomy of the structure, increasing the concavity of the space and the relationship of the arches and they had planned to add color to the floor, using colored cement. As in any type of painting, he advised, mural painting should proceed from the general to the particular, but given the great distance from which it will be seen, superfluous elements should be eliminated since they will only weaken the pictorial structure.

In another chapter he described the experience and significance of designing a new type of flexible and mobile scaffolding. Our experience, he also wrote, proved the importance of photography and in the future, cinematography will be more important. "The camera is the indispensable tool of a new realism ... It captures pictures; how then can we, the creators of pictures, ignore or despise it?" Earlier he had also discovered that films could reproduce the path of a spectator in front of a mural and had suggested that the final product of a mural painting would be film of it, a film which millions could see anywhere in the world.

In the final chapter he dealt with style, "the last extreme, the final wrapping, the physiognomy of the work," but which cannot be determined a priori. It must be the result of the social function as well as the modern materials, tools and technique of the mural, including the methods of composition and perspective. He concluded this chapter with his comparison of ancient, medieval and modern art and repeated his conviction that modern Mexican painting was the only exception in a long period of artistic decadence, "the only and possible universal route for the near future."

Though it would be several years before he would have the opportunity to apply the techniques of *Como se pinta un mural* on a project of his own, and work had been suspended on his last two murals, Siqueiros had received an important but unofficial distinction. He was now referred to and addressed as "maestro," a term of respect which means both "master" and "teacher." He had also become one of the most popular portrait painters of the Mexican bourgeoisie, receiving commissions to paint public officials, artists, writers and society women. His stature in Mexico secure, it was time to conquer Europe.

XIII. Triumph at Home and Abroad

While he waited for another mural commission, Siqueiros worked intermittently on *Patricians and Patricides* and completed several portrait commissions. He was also experimenting and turning out more studies. Using pyroxylin, he painted a series of whirling and interlocking forms in a "plastic exercise" he called *Rotation*. With the same materials, he painted two "studies for murals," a portrait of Maclovio Herrera, an old friend from the miners' union, on horseback, and a powerfully executed head of a horse. In another study, he painted the hands of two people gripping each other by the wrist. Set against a turbulent background, the powerfully drawn hands vibrate with the tension between two invisible figures.

In 1950 Siqueiros was invited to paint another mural in Bellas Artes for the balcony directly opposite *New Democracy*. Before starting on the wall, he painted a study of Cuauhtémoc, the Aztec leader, in Spanish armor, standing over a dead centaur and surrounded by the adoring masses. Using his customary tools, he transferred it to three panels totaling 400 square feet. After the panels were installed, he continued to work on it, finishing and signing it early one morning on the day of the unveiling.

In *Cuauhtémoc Reborn* the Indian hero stands over a writhing centaur, its torso pierced by a pointed lance. When patriots objected to this symbol of nationalism in Spanish armor, like a "tinned hero," and pointed out that the horse was treated more passionately than Cuauhtémoc, Siqueiros explained that *Cuauhtémoc Reborn* is both Indian and Spaniard. Native in flesh and European in dress, he represents the birth of the *mestizo*, the mixture of Indian and European which began with the conquest. Cuauhtémoc's victory also suggests the reconquest of Mexico by native forces and implies that the Indians would have defeated the Spaniards if they had possessed their weapons.

Cuauhtémoc Reborn, 1951. Pyroxylin on Masonite.
Palace of Fine Arts, Mexico, D.F.

Defending the meaning of *Cuauhtemoc Reborn*, however, was easier than satisfying stylistic objections. Critics pointed out that although he had emphasized the dynamic qualities of concave surfaces, he had painted the mural on a flat rectangular surface and created a static composition with a stiff and awkward Cuauhtémoc. Siqueiros explained, however, that he had not tried to develop a multiangular perspective for moving spectators because the panels were placed on a wall on a narrow balcony and could only be seen from the opposite balcony.

While he was still working on *Cuauhtémoc Reborn*, Siqueiros was designing another panel of equal size for the adjacent wall. First he did several studies of Cuauhtémoc in pencil and then Cuauhtémoc surrounded by Spaniards in armor and grieving Indian women. For the greyhounds used by the conquerors against the Indians, he took photographs of dogs in different poses and used the prints to draw and paint one of the fierce animals in the mural.

Painting directly on the panels, he depicted the *Torture of Cuauhtémoc*, in which the hero's feet are being burned while faceless conquerors watch, like mechanized robots, their glowing suits of armor reflecting the flames. One of them restrains a fierce looking dog with its fangs bared, while Malinche, Indian mistress of Cortez, stands behind the conquerors. Cuauhtémoc's women and children stand directly opposite, their mutilated figures pleading while cities burn in the background. At the unveiling, Siqueiros explained that it was an allegory of the unequal struggle of the weak nations against the strong ones. "I have stressed the armor, the horses, the dog and the harquebus in order to record how the great industrial nations dominate the weak."

Despite its effective expression of the grief and suffering of the victims, contrasted with the cold indifference of the Spaniards, there is no sense of movement in the *Torture of Cuauhtemoc*. As he admitted, it confirmed his contention that a static flat surface could only produce an inactive or static composition.

The high point of these years for Siqueiros, however, was not another mural commission, publication or technical breakthrough. In 1950 Rufino Tamayo, who had been living and painting in the United States and Europe, received an invitation to the International Biennial of Venice. It was the first time that a Mexican artist had been invited to participate in a major European competition, but after an Italian artist came to Mexico and discovered the work of "*los tres grandes*," the invitation was expanded to include their work.

When the exhibit opened, therefore, the Mexican section included twelve paintings by the late Orozco, seventeen by Rivera, sixteen by Tamayo and fourteen by Siqueiros, including some earlier works like *Peasant Mother*, *The Sob*, and *Echo of a Scream*, along with his more recent *The Devil in the Church*, *Our Current Image*, *Cain in the United States*, *The Centaur of the Conquest*, *Pedregal with Figures*, *Three Squashes*, *El Coronelazo*, *Angélica*, a portrait of Margarita Urueta, *Ethnography* and *Intertropical*.

From the reviews, it appears that the Mexican pavilion was the major surprise of the show. One French commentator described it as "the greatest revelation of the Biennial... a totally original creation... developed outside European influences and which imposes itself with such a violence that it is impossible to resist." Jean Bouret concurred. "The great victors were the Belgians and the Mexicans," he wrote, and "we did not realize that the Mexicans had reached such a point in the sense of grandeur and nobility ... [or] the constructive power..."

Another European critic wrote that the Mexican salon was the most successful and surprising of the Biennial. It reflected a long artistic tradition, comparable to that of China, but it was not art for the sake of art, since it dealt with contemporary issues and was linked with the past and future of its people. Other writers contrasted the work of the European artists with those of Mexico, emphasizing the living force of the Mexican art, "its overflowing virility."

Struck by the power and force of Siqueiros's paintings, especially the exaggerated foreshortening and reverse perspective of *El Coronelazo* and *Our Current Image*, one critic wrote that no one had used "such strong means of optical illusion" and Siqueiros is "a man of excess, as much in his life as in his art," whose art is "an attack and a violation."

Another review declared that his *Three Squashes,* in which the inanimate objects appear to interact with each other, was painted with the "fullness and vigor of a master of the baroque style." After noting that his paintings were too large for a private home, Clay Elliot described Siqueiros's portraits as "heroic" and added that he had achieved an unusual sense of depth and richness through his use of pyroxylin.

The real surprise of Venice, however, was the announcement of the award of the Second International Prize to David Alfaro Siqueiros. Donated by the Museum of Modern Art of Sao Paulo, Brazil, this 500,000-lira prize was decided by a jury of 20 artists from all over the world. Since the first prize for a non-Italian painter had gone to Henri Matisse, in recognition of his long career in art rather than for any recent work, Siqueiros's selection was even more impressive. Considering that the original invitation had not included him and the competition had included Picasso, Braque, Leger, Utrillo, Portinari, and Marin, as well as his Mexican colleagues, it was a major coup for Siqueiros. The other prizes for non-Italian artists went to the German Max Beckman and Constant Permeke from Belgium.

The Venice Biennial was a many-sided triumph for David. Exhibiting with three other Mexican artists who had received more international recognition, he had come away with the honors. Secondly, Mexican art had won acceptance in Europe and his selection over major European artists was a national as well as a personal triumph. Venice had also vindicated his contention that the figurative and realistic art of Mexico was a fresh and important movement in contrast with the stale, purist art of Europe. In view of his frustrated plans to exhibit in the United States, the invitation to compete in the Venice Biennial and his unexpected triumph were doubly gratifying.

When he accepted the Brazilian prize, Siqueiros declared that Venice demonstrated that Mexico's "neo-classic, neo-humanist path" was superior and contrasted with the decadence of Europe. To the Mexican press he confided that he was pleased that Europe had acknowledged their movement, "the first sprout of a new realism," and his award recognized the importance of human and social content in modern art. He then pointed out that in contrast with the idea of art for art's sake and of form for the sake of form, their paintings presented a new humanistic expression with man again at the center, especially when humanity was searching for a new humanism after being lashed by two wars and facing the prospect of another. The experience of Venice proved that Europe was tired of formalism and a "recreational art" which ignores human problems. This indicated a movement back to humanism, a movement which favored the trend in Mexican art.

Commenting on the other Mexican artists, he declared that Tamayo was a member of the Parisian school and the Mexican elements in his art were no more than those which any Parisian artist could acquire on a short visit to Mexico. His art, therefore, was a colonial reflection of that intellectual center. Most of Rivera's paintings were portraits or picturesque paintings of Mexico and cheated those who anticipated that Mexico would be presenting the issue of social art in Venice. Unfortunately, he added, the paintings of Orozco included some semiabstract paintings of his last period which were not representative of his major work.

National acclaim followed international recognition, a development which underscored Mexico's cultural dependence. While commenting that Mexican art had demonstrated its own "vigorous racial originality," a Mexican newspaper proclaimed that after the Biennial, Mexican art was now of the first category and that the triumph of Siqueiros was the most impressive since the prize to Matisse had been based on earlier work. Although some critics protested that the judges were all leftists who favored social art, the award to Matisse, as well as the balanced composition of the jury, belied their charges.

In the wake of Siqueiros's victory in Venice, the first monograph devoted to his work appeared. Written by Antonio Luna Arroyo, "David Alfaro Siqueiros, A Painter for Our Time" included an updated essay written in 1947 by the author, an introductory letter-prologue by Fernando Gamboa and an "Epilogue" by Dr. Atl. After a brief biography, Luna Arroyo provided an analysis of Siqueiros's social thought, his aesthetic theories and his draftsmanship, which he compared with Picasso's. On the Venice triumph, he wrote, "Mexican art has achieved an ecumenical acknowledgment and David Alfaro Siqueiros, his definitive historical consecration." Dr. Atl noted that Siqueiros embodies the spirit of the Revolution and is "an archetype of the revolutionary intellectual," a man of action and artist who is renovating painting.

That same year, the American art critic Paul Westheim wrote an article on Siqueiros in which he compared him to "a volcano which throws flame and lava in perennial eruption." He is "full of vitality, loaded with energy, dominated by a burning passion and intoxicated by his own exaltation," and it "appears that ecstasy is ... a normal state." These qualities are similar to those of Van Gogh, Westheim continued, "Both are obsessed, obsessed with their own mission, obsessed with their ecstasy" which "makes them give their creations the maximum intensity, and" both had similar experiences; Van Gogh as a lay priest among the coal miners and Siqueiros as a union organizer among the miners of Jalisco.

Between his mural and easel projects, David managed to sandwich a number of other activities. Working together, he and Angélica wrote 28 articles between 1949 and 1950 on the "Criticism of Art Criticism" for the editorial page of the Mexican daily *Excelsior*. In 1950 he participated in a series of conferences in Bellas Artes on "Fifty Years of Achievement in the Plastic Arts of Mexico," in which he gave two lectures, one on his own work and the other on the "affirmations and contradictions in the plastic arts of Mexico."

He was also active in the international peace movement, collecting signatures on peace petitions and participating in protests against the use and testing of nuclear arms. When Pablo Neruda arrived in Mexico as a political exile from Chile, Siqueiros and Rivera contributed lithographs for two editions of his epic poem, *Canto General*. Meanwhile he was also drawing and painting, producing more studies of Cuauhtémoc, painting portraits and constructing vibrant landscapes.

In 1951 *Como se pinta un mural* came out, followed by an attractive monograph published by the National Institute of Fine Arts entitled *Siqueiros: Por la via de una pintura neorrealista o realista social moderna en México*. ("For the Way of a Neo-realist Painting or Modern Social Realism in Mexico") With Spanish, English and French text, it contained more than two hundred black and white reproductions of his murals and paintings. It described his art as "an explosion of force" which corresponds in the plastic arts to the triumph of the Revolution and stated that his concept of art was monumental and dynamic. It also included statements by Siqueiros and given his well-publicized opinions, there were few surprises.

On the content of art, he wrote that art without ideology is transformed "into a society juggling game for ladies and gentlemen..." and is determined by the market place, just as "an electric generator corresponds to its current." Since the great movements of the past had been characterized by an integral and accurate realism, the Mexican movement was the most solid at this time. Now, he declared, they needed a national art with a social purpose, linked to national traditions, not "an art for mental tourists nor an art of formalistic snob speculation, but essentially Mexican," a public form of art for a democratic state.

In the biographical section of the book, Siqueiros divided his career into five stages: His artistic and political apprenticeship, 1911 to 1921; his search for national roots and development of a political militancy, 1922 to 1931; the search for a publicly functional and modern style of art for the contemporary social function of art, 1932 to 1938; the advance from an experimental technique to a new and modern realism, 1939 to 1950, and a current phase of reflection and self-criticism.

In 1951 David and Angélica began to publish a new review, *Arte Publico*, "Forum of Mural Painters, Sculptors, Engravers and Architects." Besides promoting "public art," it would provide a forum for the exchange of ideas on art between artists. In one of the first issues David addressed the mural decoration of the buildings rising on the new campus of the National University. Since he had called for the integration of art and architecture, he drafted and published a open letter to Carlos Lazo, the architect in charge, urging him to develop plans for integrating murals and sculpture in the university buildings.

After pointing out that it was difficult to imagine the construction of a university city in Mexico without mural paintings or sculpture, he pleaded for immediate action since construction was underway. If the art was added as an afterthought, it would not be integral, or there would not be any mural painting, and a commission should be formed of the most experienced muralists, younger painters with experience and the architects and engineers in charge of the project. He also offered to contribute his point of view to this commission which would supervise the "exterior and interior polychroming of the University City."

Meanwhile he wrote several articles for *Arte Publico* in which he pursued the idea of external murals. In "Premises on the Passage from Interior to Exterior Muralism in Mexico," he explained that just as the Mexican movement had to have been figurative, realistic and modern, our exterior murals should also be figurative, realistic and modern. But since there were no formal or technical antecedents in history for external murals, they had to look to commercial art. Since billboards and posters are figurative and super-realistic, are designed for the out-of-doors and can be seen from great distances. we should adopt the latest materials and tools developed for commercial art.

In a second article, he returned to the idea of commercial art as the only valid antecedent for exterior murals, since billboards and posters are designed to be seen by masses of people in transit. Because of the distances and different perspectives from which they are seen, they employ optical illusions and are painted to last in the sun and the rain. With neon lights they can also be seen at night. Though it is the product of an outdated economic structure (capitalism), this commercial art is a technically advanced art, an "integral art," using painting, sculpture, illumination, etc. in order to match bourgeois architecture.

In the magazine *Hoy*, Siqueiros explained his longstanding differences with Rufino Tamayo. Although he recognized Tamayo as a "good painter, perhaps even a magnificent one," he accused him of having "deserted the Mexican art movement" and joined a trend that was diametrically opposed to that movement. He denied that he had ever said that Tamayo was not a Mexican, but he insisted that though his work contained elements of Mexican popular art, he "deludes himself that his art is really Mexican." To say that he is part of the Mexican school, he continued, would be like saying that Picasso, because he is Spanish, is a product of the Spanish school of painting. Similarly, he argued, "El Greco was a Greek, but his painting was unquestionably Spanish."

Although he had denounced the Mexican government as reactionary, repressive and capitulating to the United States, Siqueiros continued to receive government commissions and was soon working in another government building. The site was less than ideal, a narrow and cramped vestibule at the National Polytechnic Institute, but it was the home of the Institute for the Chemical Investigation of Plastic Materials and he would develop the theme "Man the Master and Not the Slave of Technology," using new materials and techniques.

Instead of painting directly on the building, he created a long horizontal and concave surface just inside the glass doors by attaching aluminum panels to the concrete pillars in the entrance. Working directly on the aluminum, he painted a worker with bare chest and blue trousers in the center. One of his hands points towards a bright red sun, representing the future, while another hand holds a symbol of the atomic age.

Using more somber colors, he painted a deformed hand on the opposite side, mutilated by electrical or mechanical forces, its wrist grasped by a powerful arm coming from the other side, while the foot, leg and arm are imprisoned by turbines and pistons. Over this section he painted a moon, which contrasts with the sun and bright colors of the other side, where man has become the master of the machine.

At the unveiling, David stood in front of the mural and explained his philosophy and interpretation. Atomic energy, which "is now used only for destructive purposes, will be used tomorrow for industrial ends in a world of progress and peace," a world in which the machine will no longer oppress man, but will be in the total control of man.

Man, the Master and Not the Slave of Technology, 1952, Acrylic on Aluminum, National Polytechnic Institute, Mexico, D.F.

The reactions to the mural were mixed. While some visitors were struck by the double effect which the concave surface and polyangular composition created and were convinced that it was one of his major successes, others thought that the forms clashed and that it was one of his least effective murals. Antonio Rodríguez wrote that "the execution is extremely schematic, and the mural does not succeed in either stirring or impressing the observer." Others noted that instead of integrating art and architecture, the large aluminum panels constricted the space of the vestibule and did not complement the architecture. But another reviewer praised his successful manipulation of the forms and described the mural as a "rhythmic architectural machine" which is activated by the spectator and can be viewed from any angle.

Despite his original enthusiasm for painting on aluminum, David had discovered that his plastic-based paints did not adhere readily to the aluminum panels. Undeterred by this technical problem, as well as the negative reactions to the mural, he considered the project a learning experience and continued to search for technical solutions. He was also anxious to apply his new understanding of the "dynamic spectator" and polyangular perspective on a new project.

In the fall of 1951 Siqueiros traveled to Europe and gave a number of talks on the nature and significance of modern Mexican painting. To a group of Latin American and Spanish artists in Paris, he talked about the real significance of the "Modern School of Paris," the historic expression of the bourgeois. In November he visited Warsaw, where he gave a talk to the Union of Polish Painters in which he cited Mexican painting as an example of the contrast between the art of the capitalist world and the art of the democratic socialist world. After a banquet in his honor given by veterans of the war in Spain, he traveled to Prague and Amsterdam, where he made more presentations before returning to Mexico.

At home Siqueiros again was engaged on several fronts, writing articles on "exterior muralism" for *Arte Publico*, giving several talks on socialist realism and initiating a new mural project. In early 1952 he participated with other artists in a panel on "Art Outside and Inside the Iron Curtain." When Lombardo Toledano ran for president, he donated several recent paintings to support the candidate of the Popular Socialist Party.

Despite their well-publicized differences, Rivera, Orozco and Siqueiros were united in their fundamental purpose and frequently cooperated with or defended each other. When President Alemán invited them to suggest ways to promote muralism in Mexico, the three of them met at Orozco's home to discuss a proposal. Arriving late, Diego immediately proceeded to outline a plan for "a City of Art." When Orozco told Diego that the only language that would be spoken in his center would be English, and like everything he did, it would be for the tourists, they almost came to blows. Since they had an appointment with the President the next morning, they agreed that Siqueiros would draw up a proposal that night.

When they met in front of the Presidential Office the next day, they agreed that Siqueiros would make the presentation. After President Alemán greeted them enthusiastically, David proposed the creation of a National Commission of Mural Painting to promote muralism. Members would be appointed for life and should include three younger artists who had demonstrated their ability and understood the social content of the mural movement. Although Alemán agreed with the proposal and promised to act on it, the commission remained an empty promise.

In 1948 Rivera was working on a mural in the Hotel del Prado, a luxurious hotel in downtown Mexico City. When he included the statement *Dios no existen* ("God does not exist") in the mural, the Archbishop of Mexico refused to bless the new hotel unless the statement, made a century earlier by the Mexican liberal Ignacio Ramírez, was removed. During the impasse, some students broke into the building and attacked the mural, scratching out the offensive words and vandalizing Rivera's self-portrait in the mural.

Since Rivera, Siqueiros, and Orozco were on the Board of the Fine Arts Department, whose responsibilities included the protection of painters and their art, Rivera and Siqueiros went to Orozco's studio in Mexico City. When Orozco saw the two Marxists at his door, he asked, "To what do I owe the signal honor that Trotsky and Stalin should call on me—and together? Am I to assume a united front?"

After agreeing to organize a protest against this most recent act of censorship, they marched into the hotel lobby, accompanied by other artists and writers, and while Rivera restored the quotation, Orozco, Siqueiros and the writer Revueltas harangued the startled guests. Nevertheless, the management had a screen placed in front of the mural, thereby hiding its message from the guests, most of whom were North American tourists who could not read Spanish. Several years later Rivera returned to the hotel and over *Dios no existen*, he painted "Conference of Letran, 1836," the place and date of the offending statement. Stepping down from the ladder, he surprised onlookers by declaring that he believed in God.

The protest of the three artists was to be one of the their last public acts together. In September of 1949 José Clemente Orozco died. When his son informed Rivera and Siqueiros of his father's fatal heart attack, they rushed to his home, stunned and grief stricken. From the student strike to his death, Orozco had contributed as much as anyone to modern Mexican art and the mural movement and its international reputation. Frequently compared to El Greece or Goya, he had left an impressive record of prints, canvases and murals.

An iconoclast who attacked current ideologies, Orozco frequently disagreed with Rivera and Siqueiros. Siqueiros once said, "If ten people were in a room and argued for something, Orozco would take the opposite view. His tolerance for fascism only stemmed from our adherence to communism." Orozco had also responded to Siqueiros's enthusiasm for duco paint with "painting with duco is like having a banquet out of tin cans. I can show you fresco that has lasted ten thousand years. That's long enough for me." Commenting on his colleague's portraits, Orozco declared, "The trouble with Siqueiros is that he never has room for the feet."

Although Orozco did not share Siqueiros's politics and they frequently disagreed, he had a great impact on the younger artist and his death was a personal loss for David. After the student strike at San Carlos, they had gone off to fight in the Revolution together, shared poverty in New York, worked together on *El Machete* and had been discharged from their first murals for their antigovernment activities. They had also supported each other on a number of occasions and David had paid tribute to him as the "formal precursor of our painting" in *No hay mas ruta que la nuestra* and painted his portrait. Following his death, Siqueiros joined Rivera and other artists in a final act of homage to their friend and fellow artist.

Siqueiros, Angélica and Diego Rivera in Mexico City, 1950s

Several years later Diego Rivera was working on a mural commissioned by the Mexican government. It was to be part of a comprehensive exhibit of Mexican art through the ages to travel to Paris and other European cities and Diego, whom President Alemán had recently called "a national treasure," had been commissioned to paint a portable mural for the show. Working on panels erected in the Institute of Fine Arts, Rivera was painting *The Nightmare of War and the Dream of Peace* for the exhibit.

In the upper right hand corner, Diego, who had applied for readmission to the Mexican Communist Party, painted a benevolent Joseph Stalin next to Mao Tse-Tung, one hand resting on the Stockholm Peace Petition while the other holds out a pen to the rest of the world. Directly opposite he painted caricatures of Uncle Sam, John Bull and La Belle Marianne. Other sections featured a firing squad, white men whipping slaves, a black man nailed to a cross and Frida Kahlo in a wheelchair, handing out copies of the peace petition.

When the unfinished mural was secretly stripped from its supports one night, a group of artists met immediately and held a press conference to protest this "blatant act of censorship" by the government and demanded the restitution of the mural. As a flood of protest mounted, Carlos Chávez, the Director of the Institute, explained that the mural had been seized to prevent harming relations with friendly nations. Arranging a press conference, Siqueiros proclaimed that the National Front of Revolutionary Painters was united in boycotting the exhibit and they would withdraw their paintings in protest against the seizure of Rivera's mural.

He also announced that the controversial mural was now in their hands and would be exhibited along with another by himself entitled *The Good Neighbor or How Truman Tries to Help Mexico*. The Mexican government was a "lackey," as well as "inquisitorial," he charged, pointing out that other murals with political content remain unharmed, including the one by Rivera in which Trotsky appears in the very same building. Although the exhibit is important to Mexico and its art movement, it will be incomplete because of the political discrimination against the mural of Diego Rivera, he protested.

Two days later Siqueiros explained his position on the mural in *Excelsior*. In spite of his differences with Rivera in the past, he supported him now and condemned the mutilation and hiding of the mural by the government as an act of political censorship. In an article in the communist party organ, he declared that Mexican officials were not the real authors of this brutal attack; the United States Embassy had manipulated them. Since the artist had not been paid and it was not finished or signed by the artist when it was seized, the mural did not belong to the government. He also pointed out that Rivera's mural in Bellas Artes in which Trotsky appears had lasted for seventeen years, whereas the one with Stalin did not last twenty-four hours.

As he had promised, Siqueiros painted a portable mural of Truman as a smiling American soldier, one hand holding the chains that bind a naked Mexican guerrilla fighter, while his other hand grasps a handful of dollars. Entitled *The Good Neighbor or How Truman Tries to Help Mexico*, it was displayed along with Xavier Guerrero's *The Self-Defense of Latin America* in a protest meeting for the "Liberty of Expression and Against Artistic Censorship."

In May the exhibit of Mexican art opened in Paris, but minus the paintings withheld by the protesting artists, a fact which was well publicized. Since many of the paintings belonged to the government, they were shown, including 23 paintings by Siqueiros. On the day of the opening, L'Humanite distributed reproductions of Rivera's *Nightmare of War and Dream of Peace* in front of the Museum of Modern Art.

Not all Parisians were sympathetic, however, and some rightists and unforgiving Trotskyites launched a counter attack. The latter accused Siqueiros of being "an assassin ... whose hands were stained with blood" and called Rivera "a painter who's Stalinism has caused him to degenerate." In its coverage of the Paris exhibit, *Art Digest* accused Siqueiros of aiming "a pistol at one's head, demanding surrender in terms of force" and described Rivera's paintings as "more inflated than ever." Its praise, albeit faint, was reserved for several prints by Orozco.

The controversy surrounding the exhibit also provoked another polemic between Siqueiros and Manuel Rodríguez Lozano. It started when Rodríguez Lozano compared Siqueiros's method of expressing his views on Mexican art as that of an "assassin" who does everything he can to "stifle our art." Instead of defending Mexican art, Siqueiros is trying to demexicanize it and convert it into "the servile art of Russia." His propaganda on behalf of "socialist realism" was an attempt to submit it to the standards of Russia. By propagating socialist realism in Mexico, Rodríguez Lozano charged, Siqueiros had contributed to the suppression of the Mexican people and the stifling of their artists.

Moreover, Rodríguez Lozano argued, for years the "realists" had tried to have themselves considered the only Mexican artists and had hidden behind the mask of Mexican national art. It is lamentable, he added, that Siqueiros and Rivera provoke scandals which have nothing to do with art, affairs which neither help them or art. Therefore, he concluded, the attacks on Siqueiros should not be considered as attacks on the work of other artists.

This feud erupted again several years later when Siqueiros returned from a trip to Moscow and made comments on the negative influence of American imperialism and the school of Paris on Mexican and Soviet art. This time Rodríguez Lozano protested that the art that serves American imperialism or is influenced by Paris is no worse than that which serves Soviet imperialism.

After Paris, the controversial exhibit of Mexican art traveled to Stockholm and London, where it received more favorable reactions. When the show returned to Mexico early in 1954 so that the Mexican people could see the work of their own artists, most of the works belonging to North American museums or private collections were missing. The show which took place in Mexico, therefore, did not have all the works seen in Europe and it received much less attention than the original show had received in the capitals of Europe.

Siqueiros denounced this "debacle" in a speech in Bellas Artes, criticizing the lack of adequate publicity for the show and a catalog that was unworthy of the exhibit. He also protested the inclusion of some younger artists, which combined with the absence of paintings belonging to North Americans, substantially changed the nature of the exhibit which had toured Europe. Next he criticized the lack of any commentary in Mexico on the positive reception of its art in Europe. Certainly the people of Mexico have a right to know how their culture is received in Europe and then he proceeded to read an article by Philippe Soupault on "The Salutary Presence of Mexican Art in Paris."

When he had finished reading this positive review of modern Mexican art, he severely criticized the lack of any substantial analysis of modern Mexican art. At least Soupault understands and says that our movement is more important than any in Europe and has a great future. He writes that in Europe "art is mean and private, while our art is public and monumental." As for Mexican artists, Siqueiros continued, "we do not say that we cannot learn from Europe ... [but] we want to produce a more realistic realism." The Europeans also advise us that in order to be less provincial, in order to universalize ourselves, in order to receive the latest developments, we must imitate the school of Paris. To accept their advice would be tantamount to returning to the cultural situation of the 19th Century under Díaz.

Soupault, he continued, also understands the importance of our participation in the Revolution and enlistment in the Communist Party. Should we abandon painting with a social purpose? he asked. If we do not paint for the people of Mexico with the support of a progressive state or in opposition to a capitulating government, then we will not paint for anyone. We do not need more galleries. The art market destroys artists who paint for it and even in the United States, most painters live on teaching, a method that destroys the master and does not allow the pupil to develop his skills.

Today, he said, that country which used to invite us to paint murals will not even permit us to visit and its galleries and museums exclude the work of any artists with social tendencies. The museums of modern art in Europe, the United States and Latin America are all in the hands of the enemies of figurative or social art. In Los Angeles the Municipal Art Commission removed the work of the "Bolshevik" Orozco from its gallery, not because of his politics, but because of his social criticism and association with our monumental and figurative art movement. "They [the United States] have become intellectually colonial, as we in the countries which suffer from capitalistic exploitation are economically and politically colonial." Now their Inquisition, the State Department, invades Mexico and uses Mexican artists to attack their compatriots.

Tamayo is the worst example, he continued. In New York Tamayo is called "the Mexican counterrevolutionary" and his wife writes letters that attack other artists and the government which supports them. Even Carlos Chávez, a great Mexican composer and conductor, is touched by this imperialist corruption and joins the chorus attacking communist artists as traitors. United States policy corrupts men like Tamayo and Chávez, who recant so that they may work in the United States.

When he was challenged for interjecting politics into a discussion of art, Siqueiros explained that the attack on Mexican art was a political attack on their movement that must be defended on a political-aesthetic basis. Just as the government has an agrarian policy, a labor policy, etc., it should also have a policy and a program for art. While their work is attacked as "official art," in reality the only true official art in the West today is "formalism, the new academic art."

Let us, therefore, call the attention of the Mexican people to those problems of national culture, he declared. Let us tell them that "Mexico can only reap disaster from our friendship with the great American monopolies and the United States government ... it will stifle our culture." We must organize, mobilize and fight! If you admire Mexican painting, you will not be able to prevent its demise unless you are willing to defend it politically, he warned.

Since the movement is entering its second phase, moving from interior mural painting to exterior mural painting, it will be even more dangerous to paint murals on the outside of buildings. Today art exercises as much influence in Mexico as the political program of the Revolution and "we are defending the immediate interests of everyone in Mexico who produces, works and creates; we defend peace and fight against all enemies of peace!" he concluded.

After the uproar provoked by *Nightmare of War and Dream of Peace* had subsided, it was sent to the People's Democratic Republic of China. Although other acts of censorship would follow, mural painting remained respectable and Mexican artists with social messages continued to receive commissions from government agencies, private banks and corporations, including foreign-owned subsidiaries. Even the government's most constant critic continued to receive commissions from its different agencies.

Since his return from exile in 1944, Siqueiros had finished five mural projects, started two others, written innumerable articles and published two books, painted an impressive series of "mural studies" and portraits, and received recognition as a major artist at home and abroad. During the next few years he was busy working on several murals simultaneously, experimenting with new materials and techniques and developing new theories. This relatively peaceful and productive interlude, however, ended abruptly with more acts of censorship, unprecedented in modern history.

XIV. Exterior Murals, Portraits and Polemics

In 1952 the PRI nominated Adolfo Ruiz Cortínes for the Presidency and the government announced that he won the election with three-fourths of the vote. Besides the blatant corruption of the last six years, he faced rampant inflation, an empty treasury, a score of unfinished public works projects and a large trade deficit. Although he purged the bureaucracy and tried to disassociate himself from his predecessor, he pursued the same policies, emphasizing industrialization and productivity over social reform. While foreign capital and tourists flowed into Mexico in record amounts, the real wages of most Mexican workers declined and rural poverty threatened to explode by the end of his six-year term.

The impact of the Yankees and their money was more than economic. Mexico was inundated with American products and the middle class not only acquired a taste for imported goods, but also for American food and culture. Although some writers and artists protested this "cultural imperialism," the deluge continued and the Cold War also spilled over into Mexico and Latin America.

By 1958 there was increasing unrest as workers tried to assert their independence and threatened to strike. Faced with labor disturbances, Ruiz Cortínes chose his Minister of Labor, Adolfo López Mateos, to succeed him in the Presidency. In spite of his liberal reputation and campaign promises, López Mateos adopted a hard-line policy towards work stoppages, arresting labor leaders and using the army to crush the independent unions. One of the targets was Mexico's most outspoken and politically active artist.

In 1952, however, Siqueiros was enjoying official patronage. He had just completed *Man The Master and Not the Slave of Technology* and he was invited to paint a mural in the entrance of the new Social Security Administration Hospital in Mexico City. After analyzing the space, he had the architect transform the narrow lobby into a parabolic and elliptical shell by placing treated canvas and celotex panels over the corners where the walls and the ceiling came together, creating a rounded vault.

Aided by Felipe Estaño, Armando Carmona, Guillermo Rodríguez, Francisco Luna and Epitacio Mendoza, he began to develop "Song of Life and Health: Homage to Science." Using a palette of bright colors, he applied the paint, a mixture of vinylite pigment and pyroxylin, with an airbrush. Though the airbrush permitted a rapid and spontaneous application of the paint, the paint mixture dried fast and hard. When he used an electric sander to erase the hardened material, he liked the textural effects it produced and incorporated them into his painting.

Although he had painted a positive scene of medical progress on a scale model for the Director of Social Security, he changed the original theme to *For the Complete Social Security for All Mexicans*. On the wall to the left of the entrance to the lobby, he painted the inert body of a worker being disgorged from a monstrous machine on a conveyor belt, while his fellow workers look on helplessly. Above this industrial tragedy he placed the dehumanized landscape of a modern capitalistic society, its skyscrapers rising into a stormy sky on the ceiling. Where this wall joins the larger frontal surface, he recreated a humanized sun from *Allegory of Racial Equality and Fraternity in Cuba*. Although he painted its legs and lower back on the concave ceiling overhead, several feet in front of its head, they seem to retreat upward, while the powerfully modeled and foreshortened body thrusts down towards the spectator, its outstretched fist projecting from a red ball of fire. Meanwhile, its receding torso and the pointed skyscrapers draw the eye upward to the ceiling, in the center of which he painted a rainbow and bright red star.

To the right of the Promethean figure, he painted a group of women bearing children and sheaves of wheat. As they march forward, they look upward towards another group of men and women led by a muscular miner, the vanguard of the Mexican working class, his hand pressing the lever of a machine. Behind the miner, he painted a white–robed doctor, a woman in red carrying a Mexican flag and a group of students and workers.

In the background he painted modernistic structures representing modern science in front of the towers of the Kremlin and a Chinese pagoda. In between these symbols of the socialist societies, he placed a Mexican and an Egyptian pyramid, symbols of the Third World. Like the skyscrapers of the capitalist and industrialized world, these pyramid shapes lead the eye upward to the rainbow and red star, representing peace and fraternity and suggesting the merging of both worlds in the future. On the third or sidewall, a large mirror heightens the dynamism of the mural, reflecting and multiplying the vibrant colors and images on the walls and ceiling.

For the Complete Social Security for All Mexicans, 1952–54.
Vinylite on Plywood, Hospital de la Raza, Mexico, D.F.

On March 18, 1954, the anniversary of the 1938 expropriation of the foreign oil companies, Siqueiros unveiled his latest mural.

Translating his painting into words, he declared, "There still exists a world in which machines are the instruments of oppression and homes are prisons," but the people, led by the industrial worker, must provide the solution. Complete social security is only possible in a more advanced society, when there are no limits to the rights and welfare of men and women and atomic energy is an instrument of peace instead of death. The Promethean figure, he explained, is not a God. "It is the light, the sun, a humanized sun, not some mystical thing."

Although linked thematically to *Man The Master and Not the Slave of Technology*, his latest mural was a much more effective and advanced application of his mural technique and constituted a total synthesis of his ideas and experiments to date. Thanks to the concave and elliptical vault on which it is painted, the viewer is immediately enveloped by the bright colors and vibrant forms that surround him. As one moves about, the images of the mural are activated. The figures seem to move and some of them advance and recede simultaneously.

Because of the polyangular perspective and composition, however, the viewer sees these images from different angles without distortion. No matter where one stands in the lobby, the sun-man lunges at the spectator and when one looks at the skyscrapers of the modern capitalist society, they appear to terminate in the rainbow and red star. The same effect occurs when one faces the buildings of the socialist and third worlds on the opposite wall. Siqueiros called this effect or technique an "operating spherical rectilinear perspective," one in which the eye does not receive distorted images or refractions from the wall, but images which are "rectified" and therefore "conform to the distinctive foci of vision." It was an effect, he insisted, which could only be achieved on a concave surface.

At first glance the mural visually assaults the viewer and looks like a political poster. A more careful study, however, reveals its sober and harmonious composition, as well as the recognizable images that are symbolic and real, as well as modern. Impressed by the sense of movement and vibrant colors of the mural, one observer described the tone as "grandiloquent and baroque," while another compared the concave shell to the baroque chapels of the eighteenth century.

Located in the well-lit lobby of a government hospital, *For the Complete Social Security of all Mexicans* is an appeal for brotherhood, solidarity and the peaceful use of technology. Although the modern capitalist world has failed, in the future technology will solve the problems of mankind under a new social regime. The largest and most dynamic of Siqueiros's murals to date, it was the realization of his repeated appeals for an integral, dynamic, neo-realist and modern form of "public art." In the same hospital, Diego Rivera had just completed his encyclopedic, but essentially flat and static fresco on the "History of Medicine in Mexico."

Meanwhile, Siqueiros had undertaken another assignment. Along with José Chávez Morado, Juan O'Gorman and Diego Rivera, he was invited to paint a mural on one of the new buildings of the University City. Although construction was underway before the muralists became involved, the new campus of the national university offered them an opportunity to paint murals, construct sculpture or apply mosaic decorations on the exteriors of modern buildings. Now, Siqueiros declared, the Mexican Mural Movement could advance to its "second stage," the painting of exterior murals.

While Rivera worked on the stadium, O'Gorman on the library, which he also designed, and Chávez Morado on the walls of the Faculty of Sciences, Siqueiros undertook the exterior decoration of the Rectory or main administration building. But the project was fraught with problems from the start, and while the others had finished their murals by the end of 1952, he was still working on his murals in 1954 and it was not unveiled until 1956. Even then, he had only finished one of the several mural surfaces he had agreed to paint.

Determined not to use "archaic" materials or art forms on a modern building, Siqueiros searched for a technical solution. Realizing that purely flat painted surfaces could not compete with the forms and colors of the surrounding landscape, he concluded that exterior mural painting required the integration of sculpture and painting or "sculpted-painting." Therefore he would create an optically dynamic sculpture of four dimensions by combining sculpture and mural painting.

On a small section of the north wall he painted a pair of hands reaching towards an open book on which were inscribed important dates in Mexican history: 1520, 1810, 1857, and 1910 for the Spanish conquest, the independence struggle, the liberal constitution of 1857 and the outbreak of the Revolution, respectively. There is also an undetermined date, "19??," implying a future upheaval in which the "right of the people to culture" will be realized. On the east wall, where a section of the building projects out from a facade of windows, he began tracing a design for the University which was part bald eagle and part condor, a symbol of the two Americas.

For the largest surface, the facade of a two-story section of the Rectory that faces an approaching freeway, Siqueiros designed a "sculpted painting" on the theme of the university at the service of the people. After studying the long rectangular surface from every angle and distance, he began to trace the composition lines on the second story facade. Working without sketches, he painted directly on the surface, creating lines of composition and perspective and some central figures or shapes. After analyzing the optical effects these lines, forms, and colors produced from different angles and distances, he shouted instructions to Luis Arenal and Federico Canessi to make corrections.

Once the composition was outlined, Arenal and Canessi constructed several large sculptural forms on the surface, using steel and reinforced concrete. Although he had planned to cover these forms with electrically colored pieces of aluminum, he discovered that current technology was inadequate and the cost was prohibitive. When he saw that the pigments which he had applied to the wall of the Rectory were fading, he decided to cover the forms with Italian glass tile or mosaic, a material and process which he had described earlier as "archaic" or "Byzantine" and an "anachronism" when used on modern buildings. To avoid the fragmentary effect of mosaic decorations, he ordered larger pieces of the tile.

By the end of 1952 the other artists had completed their projects. While Siqueiros was still experimenting, writing articles and completing his mural in the Social Security hospital, Chávez Morado had completed several large panels using glass mosaic on the Faculty of Sciences, Rivera had finished a bas-relief of reinforced concrete covered with natural colored stone on the stadium, and Juan O'Gorman had decorated four sides of the multistoried library with an elaborate mosaic of natural stone.

When the completed projects of his colleagues received a generally favorable reception and critics attacked his unfinished mural, Siqueiros reacted in a published interview. Those who did not like his murals in the University were "children of a color-blind world" and Rivera's and O'Gorman's use of natural stone was "archaic," "barbarian" and "primitive." New problems require new solutions and there are as profound differences between interior and exterior mural painting as between easel and interior mural painting. The "great spectacle" of the exterior painting presupposes radically different solutions and we are a long way from discovering appropriate materials and techniques.

O'Gorman's reply was equally acerbic. First, he categorized Siqueiros's murals as a defeat for Mexican painting, subjectively and objectively. The workers at the University cannot understand them, he said, and call his symbol of the University "a struggle of roosters or parakeets," while the hands reaching towards the open book is "a series of worms without any foundation." The worst, however, is the south wall, where his figures of men are interpreted as the managers of a factory and it is rumored that it is an advertisement for General Motors.

As for the integration of painting and architecture, O'Gorman accused Siqueiros of doing exactly what he had criticized in others. He had stated that mural paintings should not be like stamps stuck on an envelope, but that was exactly what Siqueiros created, "a stamp glued to an envelope." While he maintains that exterior mural painting must harmonize with the landscape, he has done just the opposite. Neither in color nor in scale is there any harmony between his mural and its surroundings. His work is designed for the colorblind who will see it as the bright red which covers the world in the paint advertisements of Sherwin Williams.

Responding to Siqueiros's accusations of using "archaic" techniques, O'Gorman pointed out that the word itself was archaic since procedure is only archaic for those who are unable to say new things with it. Besides, stone mosaic is cheap and lasts a long time. Meanwhile Siqueiros uses materials developed for the painting of sardine cans or automobiles in order to cover up garbage. Orozco, O'Gorman recalled, had advised Siqueiros to forget about new materials since there was no substitute for talent.

While he was still working on the walls of the University, David was interviewed for *Arte Vivo de Mexico*, a series of recorded interviews of prominent cultural figures. When he was asked about the importance of painting on convex, concave or composite surfaces, he pointed out that his critics were snobs who viewed a painting as a two-dimensional phenomenon produced on a neutral surface. In response to other questions, he declared that the extension of mural painting to exterior surfaces is of major transcendence and constitutes a new profession which involves tremendous problems requiring totally new solutions. A new plastic language is needed, he affirmed, not the Latin that O'Gorman used on the library, nor the frenchified nahuatl (Aztec language) that Rivera applied to the stadium, nor the incorrect and poorly pronounced French of Tamayo and the other artists who are addicted to the Museum of Modern Art in New York.

These polemics involved more than artists or the murals painted at the University. When the University City was dedicated, Siqueiros's unfinished project was covered over. Incensed by this treatment and the failure to mention the contributions of the artists to the project, he retaliated in *Arte Publico*. How, he asked, could the artists be ignored in the celebrations, since it was they who had called for the integration of architecture and painting in the University City? The covering of his own mural and the neglect of the other muralists was another example of the government's appeasement of North American "enemies of Mexican communist art."

When Lombardo Toledano accused the artists of being timid in their most recent murals, charging that they were brave when they painted canvases, but either contradicted themselves or did not live up to their tradition when they worked on walls seen by thousands,

Siqueiros responded immediately. First, he contrasted the conditions when they painted murals under Vasconcelos in the early 1920s with current conditions.

Today the Revolution has been abandoned, the government has capitulated to Yankee imperialists and it seized a work of art that it had commissioned for an exhibit of Mexican art in Europe. Lombardo Toledano and I know the reality of our country today, he continued. "The government of Mexico on the backs of the people, the government of the United States on the back of the Mexican government, and over all of them, Wall Street." But if we painted this on the buildings of the University, he continued, we would be in the same situation we were in when we were expelled from the walls in the 1920s and forced to take up making prints for *El Machete*. Perhaps, he concluded, this would be better than dressing up in counterrevolutionary clothing and is the only viable form of public art during this "reign of terror."

In December David wrote another article on exterior muralism, "a technical problem without precedent in the history of art." After repeating his pronouncement that the painting of murals on the outside of buildings constitutes the beginning of the second phase of the Mexican Mural Movement, he pointed out the lack of any antecedent in the history of art for exterior muralism except commercial billboard art. Since exterior murals presented unique technical problems, they could not be resolved with traditional solutions.

If we were able to achieve an internationally recognized form of art in old and inadequate buildings, then why can't we produce the same under more advantageous conditions? he asked. His experience in Los Angeles on *Tropical America* demonstrated the mistake of assuming that an exterior mural was merely the repetition of the process of painting an interior mural. The difference between exterior and interior mural painting is ten times the difference between painting a canvas and an interior mural.

Referring again to *Tropical America*, he pointed out that a new technical problem required a new material solution, a fact that he had not fully appreciated in his earlier work. Exterior murals could not have the same composition since the angular problems were multiplied many times. Whereas an interior mural is seen from one plane and by a walking spectator, an exterior mural can be seen from many angles and levels and by people walking or passing in cars. However, the murals of Chávez Morado and O'Gorman are "absolutely static, absolutely uniangular... composed in the same academic manner characteristic of the easel canvas, not even common to that of interior mural painting."

Turning to the use of color in exterior murals, Siqueiros charged that neither O'Gorman or Rivera appreciated the problems of color in the sunlight and O'Gorman's natural stone mosaic on a wall around a garden looked like "ancient ruins, naked and without color because of the sun." In their murals at the University, O'Gorman and Chávez Morado had repeated this mistake, producing the effect of a flat stamp stuck on the side of a building.

After repeating his contention that the materials, tools, methods of composition, textures and colors were the causes and not the effects of style, Siqueiros declared that it was a serious mistake to approach a work of art with a preconceived style. Rivera's style on the stadium was not only primitivist, like most of his frescos, but more archaic than much of his earlier work. O'Gorman's "Giotto-like" realism, influenced by Rivera, was used centuries ago by the Florentines while Chávez Morado employed the same style in his murals that he uses in his wood block prints or drawings.

Leaving the analysis of his unfinished mural for the last, Siqueiros pointed out that even though it was not finished, he had not used interior methods and styles and had conducted a thorough search for the most modern means and materials available. The composition was poly-angular, the drawing was accentuated, the color was appropriate to the environment and its textures corresponded to the exterior visual conditions. Its style was not the cause, but the effect, the result of "the coordinated elements in a creative impulse." Although its message was more realist and obvious than those of his colleagues, any judgment would have to wait until it was finished, he concluded.

David's disagreements with the government, University administrators and other artists did not end with this exchange in 1952. When he heard that the architect wanted to remove his scaffolding on the Rectory building, he protested that his scaffolding would not hamper the completion of the building.

Besides, he argued, my exterior work does not interfere with the completion of the interior and how can you speak of the completion of the building when the murals, which are a part of the building, are not yet finished? Even if they removed the scaffolding from the murals, this would create the very impression they are trying to avoid, since the murals are obviously unfinished. They also considered it more important to complete some minor decorations, like gardens or fountains of water, when the proposed integration of painting and architecture is incomplete.

He reminded the architect that he had taken longer because his work was very different from the "primitivist" and "decorative tendency" of his colleagues. Even though they had resorted to pre-hispanic hieroglyphs and colonial symbols in contradiction of the modern and progressive Mexican movement, they have been given another opportunity to continue this style on the new Ministry of Communications and Public Works building. All I am asking, he concluded, is the same opportunity to finish my attempt at plastic integration, a right that my fellow artists have already enjoyed.

When David addressed the Society of Architects two months later, he pointed out that none of the artists had anything to do with the design of the University buildings and since we were commissioned separately, we do not have any responsibility for the architecture which is clearly influenced by European formalism and is full of useless, expensive detail. "In architecture authentic beauty can only be derived from authentic functionality," he continued, and they should study the monumentality, functional logic and constructive realism from the great pre-hispanic tradition.

Turning to the subject of style, he declared,

Style comes as a final consequence of the process of art, not as the beginning ... When style is anticipated, art falls into an academic, decadent routine. Stylism marks the beginning of the end of an artistic period!

When it came to the use of artistic materials, he explained how the neglect of their importance had contributed to a repetition of the mistakes of the past. When an artist needs a new material to solve a new problem, he searches for and discovers it or he invents it. In spite of his disagreements with other artists, we are all fighting for social realism and should argue our views passionately, he concluded.

Meanwhile he had renewed his criticism of abstract art or "the School of Paris" and had exchanged polemics with its Mexican partisans. Tamayo, he said, was a good painter but had deserted the Mexican movement. While he was definitely Mexican and his art contained Mexican elements, he was part of an international current, directly antithetical to that of the Mexican muralist movement. Tamayo responded by attacking the "gangsterism" in Mexican art, but added that he welcomed the chance to engage in a dialogue and prove that Mexican painting was distinguished by its variety and quality.

Several years later Tamayo returned to the attack, declaring that Rivera painted as if he lived in the 15th Century, while Siqueiros imitated David of the Napoleonic Wars, with figures and gestures that crush the spectator instead of convincing him. Rivera, he claimed, had reverted to Fra Angelico with his static figures and Siqueiros was a "megalomaniac" who screams and shouts at the viewer and threatens him if he does not accept his religion, while proclaiming that the essence of his own painting is in "our pre-Columbian tradition." While Siqueiros uses new materials, like "Duco," he creates the same, only harsher effects.

When Tamayo was asked why Siqueiros attacked him, he replied that it was probably because of what he had said about Siqueiros and his work:

> That his symbols are religious rather than social ... and
> dripping with sentimentality ... What is the difference
> between Siqueiros's mothers, bowed tearfully over their

martyred proletarian sons, and the Christian pieta? Or between his tortured Cuauhtémocs and the tortured Christs and saints?

What is most objectionable, continued Tamayo, is their [Siqueiros and Rivera] dictatorship over public taste, government patronage and the souls of the young artists.... Anyone showing a spark of originality is immediately denounced and ostracized. Abstract painting sells well in the United States; the United States dropped the atomic bomb; therefore the abstract painter hates humanity!

Besides, Diego's "anecdotal compositions, portraits and self-portraits" are Italian in style and method while

Siqueiros ... falls back on the baroque perspective of Mantegna and Tintoretto—or on the pretentious official painting of J.L. David! What is the difference between Napoleon in his coronation ermines and Cuauhtémoc in his armor and feathers? And these are the men who call themselves one hundred percent Mexican?

In another statement, Tamayo challenged the claim that they painted for the people, saying that the masses did not understand their work and called their figures "monkeys." He also criticized the talent of the other muralists who painted only a superficial nationalism, a picture of Mexican history and culture, especially the Revolution. He wanted to go deeper in his art, to Mexican roots and from there, to develop something that would be universal and could be understood by everyone, everywhere.

Throughout 1953 David was working on four different murals. Besides the projects at the Social Security Hospital and the University City, he received commissions to paint a mural on the facade of the automobile factory of Fabricas Automex, a Chrysler subsidiary, and to paint a mural for the State University of Michoacan in Morelia.

On the flat facade of the car factory, his assistants constructed a raised elliptical platform, upon which they modeled a man in motion, his raised and greatly foreshortened body appearing to emerge from the flat elliptical surface. While one arm is thrust forward, conforming to the circumference of the ellipse, the other is flung back, like an athlete running or swimming, and intersecting the curve of the ellipse. Its raised chest thrusts forward while the head is flung back and only the upraised chin, nose, and a flock of wavy hair are distinguishable. After the concrete had set, they covered these forms with bright glass tile and filled in the background with more tile and colored cement.

Velocity suggests speed and movement and the juxtaposed forms and brightly colored tile created a sense of movement when viewed by a moving spectator. While it incorporated sculpture, mosaic and painting in what Siqueiros called "sculpture-painting," it was not integrated with the architecture and appeared to be "glued on the building." The "archaic" mosaic tile, which produced a "Byzantine" effect in the hands of his colleagues, has also lost much of its original luster in the polluted air of Mexico City.

For the University of Michoacan, formerly the University of Valladolid where the leader of Mexican independence, Father Hidalgo, had been a student, teacher and rector, Siqueiros decided on a didactic portrait of the national hero. Using pyroxylin, he painted the *Excommunication and Death Sentence of Miguel Hidalgo* on masonite panels.

In the center he placed Father Hidalgo in his priestly robes at the moment of execution, his right hand crossed over his chest and penetrated by two bullet holes, while his left hand remains at his side, its fist clenched. Instead of painting Hidalgo's face at the moment of death, however, he painted a physical likeness that conveyed the strength and nobility of his character. The wall of execution shows the scars of other executions, while the ground is crisscrossed and broken up with broken branches and straw.

To the left of Hidalgo, Siqueiros painted the figure of Bishop Abad y Quiepo, the spiritual assassin of the revolutionary priest, his greater size and rich robes contrasting with the figure of Hidalgo.

The bishop holds a cross with lettering which is also a lance piercing a liberty cap and the earth beneath. This vertical shaft also divides the picture into two parts, so that the figure of Hidalgo balances that of the bishop within the plane formed by the ground and the wall of execution.

The words on the plaque explain that this is the excommunication and penalty of death of Miguel Hidalgo for professing and divulging the exotic ideas of liberty, equality and fraternity, committing the crime of "social dissolution" and therefore, for subversion and betrayal of the *patria*. In an article that he wrote on *Excommunication and Death Sentence of Miguel Hidalgo*, Siqueiros questioned whether history would repeat itself and the Church would ally itself again with the enemies of liberty, peace and social progress.

Excommunication and Death Sentence of Miguel Hidalgo, 1953, Pyroxylin on masonite, University of Michoacan, Morelia, Mexico

Siqueiros was also in demand as a portrait painter. After his successful exhibit of "70 Recent Works" in 1947, he had been besieged with portrait commissions from members of the new Mexican bourgeoisie and during the ensuing years he had the opportunity to paint many portraits. Sandwiching sittings between his mural projects, he painted the portraits of Mexican artists, intellectuals, society women and important political and business figures. He had also completed a government commissioned portrait of Carranza, Chief of the Constitutionalist Forces in the Revolution.

In 1953 many of these portraits were displayed in the Gallery of Mexican Art in Mexico City. In the catalog for the exhibit, David explained that these portraits, less than half of the ones he had completed in the last five years, belonged to his second category of painting, that which was anti-primitivist and had a modern realist objective. He admitted that before 1934 his style was characterized by the "archaism and intellectual archaeologism which still prevails in our contemporary Mexican painting" and which reflected current world tastes. To the press, he explained "the portrait is one of the best and most complete opportunities which the painter-artist has to practice objectivity in reality."

The exhibit was an unquestioned success and the critics noted the originality, strength, vigor, monumentality and sensibility, even the delicacy of the portraits. More than just accurate physical likenesses, the portraits captured the character or psychology of the subject and occasionally contained a hint of social critique. Several writers also noted that Siqueiros himself comes through in all of these portraits and one wrote that he "has always been prone to the monumental ... is impulsive to an extreme" and possesses "an overbearing vitality," the same qualities which predominate in these portraits.

Another wrote that Gide's statement that "Art is an exaggeration" applies to Siqueiros more than any other artist and compared him to Modigliani, in whose work there is a "confession of the psychology of the painter as much as of the subject." He (Siqueiros) uses another person to delineate his own and consistent idiosyncrasy, "portraying himself, finally ... in the portraits of others." In an essay on "Contemporary Mexican Painting," Luis Cardoza y Aragon noted that "the work of David Alfaro Siqueiros is an unlimited projection of himself," in his portraits as well as in his mural or easel paintings.

Several years later Siqueiros elaborated on his views on portraiture and realism. "The direct portraiture places us in the situation of imitating—let us not fear the word—the physical and psychological essence of the subject." It is a sophistry to suggest that a portrait does not have to be a portrait but is only the capricious whim or interpretation of the artist, he continued. Painting a portrait, however, is more than painting just what we can see. For instance, landscapes contain what is known as well as what can be seen and the mental understanding of the problem modifies the concept of objectivity. Therefore the realist imagines because he requires a greater objectivity, a constructive objectivity, and it is important to know whether a painter who has chosen realism can or does not use direct objectivity as a solution to the problem in specific cases.

The painting of a historical or dead figure is a very different problem, however, and requires a very different technique and the realist painter of a social inclination must also understand the problem of objectification. Practicing what he preached, David painted a relatively small but powerful and monumental portrait of the Mexican liberal Benito Juárez. Using photographs, he recreated a physical likeness of the Indian President that appears to be carved out of stone. Combined with Juárez' stern expression, it conveys a sense of the subject's strength, integrity and determination.

When someone accused him of painting portraits for the new rich, he admitted that he had resorted to painting for the homes of the rich, but explained that he had sold the portraits, not his ideology. Even though "I painted a portrait of the architect Carlos Lazo, that does not mean in any sense that I retracted my ideas on the neoporfirism of his architecture." He also admitted to painting beautiful women and "ugly public officials." Naturally, he explained, the most ugly were those who capitulated in the social struggles or were enemies of the people.

In July of 1954 Siqueiros returned to the subject of realism and integral art in a lengthy address sponsored by the Institute of Fine Arts. Speaking ex cathedra, he began his talk on realism in the plastic arts by praising the idea of a discussion on the relationship of art and architecture. After defining "realism" as the objective reflection of the existing social, political and geographical reality without any preconceived impressions or capricious inventions, he addressed nineteen points on the theme.

Starting with "integral" or "unitary art," he explained that it is the simultaneous creation of architecture, sculpture, painting, illumination, etc. During the pre-Hispanic centuries, and to a lesser degree in the colonial period, Mexican architecture was realistic and integral, and was great architecture. The architecture of the early 19th Century, however, reflected the taste of an elite and did not contribute anything to international architecture.

Under Díaz it was even worse, lacking realism or integration, and clearly reflected the tastes of the imperialistic oligarchy. Mexican architecture was still anti-realistic and nothing more than the expression of the new bourgeoisie, their embezzled riches and their surrender to the imperialists who supported them. It would be ridiculous, he continued, to claim that the recently completed buildings at the National University were a reflection of indigenous creativity or had made any contribution to world architecture. The style is a borrowed one. "It is antirealist and theatrical and more than anything else it is like the commercial architecture of the United States, the worst cultural source in the whole world."

Nevertheless, he argued, our movement towards realism and the integration of the arts is the most important in the world. The greatest obstacle, however, was the imbalance between mural painting and architecture and our experiments were thwarted constantly by the antirealism of the architecture. The work of realistic painters did not belong with this architecture. But architecture could only be integrated with art under a realistic political regime and a government that capitulates to the imperialists cannot produce realistic architecture, nor integrate the arts "in the service of the people."

Anti-popular regimes foster spectacular, demagogic
public art, which is impractical and expensive....
architecture born of business speculation is governed by
the economic interests of its exploiters, rather than the
needs of the people.

But, he warned, if our country abandons its responsibility as a leader of Latin America against Yankee imperialism, the immediate enemy of our cultural and economic development, our movement will disintegrate into a parade of professional artists without conscience. "Our cities will continue to be transformed into little Dallases or Houstons," and the cultural roots rediscovered by the Revolution will be buried again. After stating that a popular government would foster an art of Mexico for Mexico, realistic and with universal merit, he concluded his discourse with a challenge. "What conscious intellectual can remain neutral in this inevitable political-aesthetic battle?"

Several years later David returned to the theme of realism in architecture and called Mexico City "the ugliest city in the world" since its architecture has nothing to do with the soil, culture and tradition of Mexico. Skyscrapers, he pointed out, should be prohibited since their only justification is profit, that is to take advantage of the value of the land. The appearance of tall buildings next to small or medium size buildings is unfortunate and the formalism which has been forced on the architects by commercial interests makes the city ugly.

Siqueiros was also critical of the lack of realism in Mexican films and participated in the discussions of a group of artists who were trying to improve the quality of the national cinema. While they all agreed that Mexican films were superficial and had nothing to do with the reality of Mexico, their efforts to improve the quality of Mexican cinema were not very successful.

In 1954 Bellas Artes became the scene of another scandal when Frida Kahlo died. Twice married to Diego Rivera, she had lived a very tragic life, including a childhood accident that left her crippled for life, several miscarriages and a series of painful operations. Although she managed to overcome these hardships, much of her life was spent in bed and in pain. Using a mirror placed over her bed, she had painted herself in some very personal and moving paintings reflecting these tragedies, her pain and her relationship with Diego. While her politics were not as publicized as those of her husband, she shared his Marxism and painted herself discarding her crutches while Marx is strangling Uncle Sam.

After he had recovered from the shock of her death, Diego asked Andrés Iduarte, Director of the National Institute of Fine Arts, to arrange for her body to rest in state in Bellas Artes. While Iduarte made the arrangements, he warned Diego against any political demonstrations, speeches or banners. But just as the first honor guard formed, a young artist stepped forward and placed a shiny red flag with a hammer and sickle on her coffin and the eulogy said more about communism than Frida or her status as a Mexican artist. Afterwards, Rivera, Siqueiros, Iduarte and others shouldered her coffin and carried it out into the rain. At the crematorium Siqueiros exclaimed that he had seen her smiling in the center of a large sunflower, just as she had painted herself.

When Iduarte was dismissed as Director after the incident, Siqueiros immediately denounced it as another example of the interference of the United States in Mexico. If Iduarte had refused Frida the right to an honor guard because she was a communist, he would have violated the constitution. Catholics, he pointed out, have been permitted to have crucifixes placed on their coffins and enjoy religious funeral orations. Therefore Frida Kahlo had every legal and moral right to have the flag of her party, a legal party, on her bier and "no honorable Mexican could have ordered the firing of Iduarte."

His reaction was not shared by everyone, however, as there were many who felt that the incident had dishonored the memory of Frida. Others were sure that Diego had arranged it in order to be readmitted to the Party, a suspicion that gained credence when he was reinstated two months later.

In 1955 David and Angelica left for Europe. In Paris they met old friends, including Fernand Léger. They reminisced about old times and experiences and told stories, often pointed jabs at the foibles or characteristics of their respective nationalities. According to Siqueiros, the subject which most fascinated French intellectuals was the "*pistolerismo*" of the Mexicans, a situation that he had exploited on his first trip to Europe years ago. When Pierre Courtade recalled that he could not turn around in Mexico without seeing a pistol, Siqueiros told them of an Argentine saying, "One Mexican, one pistol; two Mexicans, a fight; three Mexicans, a Revolution."

Not all was in jest, however, and Siqueiros reminded his friends that their views of Mexico were distorted by Hollywood and when they made fun of Mexico, they were making fun of the Mexican Revolution which had a great effect on Mexico and the rest of Latin America. It is not right, he told them, for you to ignore its true nature or its significance. However, his own conduct and the stories he told of firing squads and Pancho Villa did little to disabuse Europeans of their impressions.

After Paris, David and Angelica traveled to Warsaw, where he was offered a commission to paint a mural on the Stadium of the Tenth Anniversary of the Revolution. In his statement to the press, he expressed his gratitude for this opportunity and announced his plans to execute the project with a team of painters and sculptors from Mexico and Poland.

After they attended a show of artists from the Warsaw area, he commented on the pervasive influence of the School of Paris and a return to abstractionism on the part of many Polish artists. In fact, he noted, the exhibit was not significantly different from what he had just seen in Paris. But Polish artists did not have any idea of what it was like to be an artist in a capitalist country since the state bought the greater part of their artistic production. As long as they ignored murals or prints, however, they were destined to imitate Paris and ignore art of a social nature. Before they departed for Moscow, David read an "open letter" to a group of Polish artists in which he critiqued art in the Soviet Union.

When they arrived in Russia, David and Angélica were taken to one of the most luxurious hotels in Moscow. Since Rivera was in

Russia to receive cobalt treatments for cancer, they visited him every morning in a sanitarium. Diego's imagination was more vivid than ever and when he told stories about the past, he described events and personalities that Siqueiros could not recall.

Siqueiros also observed that the Moscow that he and Diego returned to in 1955 was very different from the one they had first visited in 1927. Although Khrushchev had not yet revealed the sins of Stalinism, the personality cult of Stalin was being dismantled. The artists had also changed and Diego, recently reinstated in the Mexican Communist Party, praised the socialist realism of current Soviet artists, whereas Siqueiros criticized their art as "formalistic," "academic" and "mechanical" and not worthy of the popular democracies.

Invited to speak to the Soviet Academy of Art, Siqueiros read an "Open Letter to the Soviet Artists." First he noted the influence of Paris formalism on Polish art, a development that did not coincide with the social transformation of the country. Since Soviet art was state art with the unlimited support of the first proletarian state in the world, Siqueiros said, it is our duty as communists to examine every aspect of our work and criticize each other. While Soviet art did not suffer from the formalist contamination of the capitalist societies, it "suffers from another form of cosmopolitanism: formalistic academicism and mechanical realism."

In Mexico, he read on, our art has forgotten this principle and Soviet painting has perpetuated "old realistic styles" and "you have not learned to create something new from your own national teaching ... you are victims of the dead laws of an international academy." Your formal language has not improved in the last 38 years and you are not interested in finding new material techniques even though you have a state, which would support them, he read. Unfortunately, "Soviet painters ... have remained dominated by the methods of composition and perspective used by academics everywhere." When the President of the Academy, artist Alexander Gerasimov, walked out in the middle of his discourse, Siqueiros continued, accusing Soviet artists of perpetuating the dead tradition of international academicism and not realizing their full potential.

Finishing his address on a more positive note, Siqueiros declared that there were only two important artistic expressions in the world, the Mexican movement, which operated under increasingly difficult conditions, and the Soviet experience, which enjoyed more favorable circumstances. Therefore, Mexican and Soviet artists should help each other to eliminate the negative tendencies and reinforce the positive ones. Soviet artists are professional and are unequaled in expressing psychological phenomena and they are creating monumental art which is integrated with the architecture, but they they must abandon the old routines which tie them down.

Siqueiros addressed Soviet artists on several other occasions in Moscow and Leningrad, each time reminding them of the pernicious influence of the School of Paris and the mechanical realism which he had observed in their art. He always reminded them that he was speaking as a friend and comrade and suggested an exchange of criticisms between the two great movements in modern art with a human focus, those of Russia and Mexico.

During these sessions, David sensed restlessness among the younger artists with the academic formalism of the established painters and sculptors. While he observed that they were working in the latest materials, like acrylics, he felt that they did not appreciate that technique, composition and perspective must correspond to the size and nature of the project. Since content was determined by the state, their "problem is not what to do but how to do it." Nevertheless, they had not advanced very far in the development of a new artistic technology. In the same spirit of cooperation, he invited Russian artists to come and work with him in Mexico or on the mural that he would paint in Warsaw.

Although he did not return to Warsaw and no Russian artist accepted his invitation to work with him in Mexico, his address to the Soviet Academy provoked a discussion among the Russian artists on the points which he had raised regarding the application of a simplistic definition of realism and the use of the old and archaic methods of the old masters. However, his letter was never published in Russia and two years later, when the first Congress of the Syndicate of Plastic Artists of the USSR met, Siqueiros was disappointed when the opening address ignored his criticism and reinforced the retrograde tendencies which he had noted.

In a response to this address by the Secretary General of the Central Committee of the Communist Party, he pointed out that the very artistic production which Shepilov praised did not contain any new formulas and did not correspond to the first phase of political development in the Soviet Union. It did not compare to Soviet achievements in science, technology, industry or even sports, and while it often had a great creative force, it was rooted in obsolete formulas of realism.

Shepilov did not offer the younger artists any new solutions, Siqueiros charged, and his analysis of western art was weak and lyrical and therefore did not help them. While he rejected the idea of novelty for the sake of novelty, Siqueiros agreed that there were positive novelties, realistic and superior, and that is what was lacking in current Soviet art. While Shepilov speaks of a visible progress, Siqueiros continued, the most recent works lack spontaneity and freshness, reflect a stereotyped conformity and display very little talent. When Shepilov said that a painter is not a photographer, he contradicted himself by praising the very paintings which are cold, mechanical and the most photograph-like.

Shepilov also contends that the Communist Party has always helped the union of artists, but I have noted just the opposite, Siqueiros charged. Art pedagogy has always been in the hands of academic teachers who have had the most important positions in the union of artists, leading to mediocrity in artistic production, a situation that requires a change in pedagogy.

Upon his return to Mexico, Siqueiros was interviewed frequently by the Mexican press. While he was critical of Russian and Polish art, he contended that the state protected the artists in those countries while there were sixty thousand painters dying of hunger in France. In Italy, Siqueiros added, the government was not interested in public art and the condition of the artists and painting in that country was a disaster. Picasso, he continued, has not advanced either in the abstract or figuratively, and the pornographic elements in his recent works reflect the decadence of his character. On the subject of teaching art, Siqueiros criticized art schools in Mexico as carbon copies of those of the *porfiriato* or poor imitations of those "pseudo-modern" schools of Paris at the beginning of the century.

He also informed reporters that he had seen Rivera in Russia and though he was receiving cobalt treatments, there was little hope for a complete recovery. After dispelling rumors that Rivera was being held captive in the USSR, he described their conversations in Russia and denied that there was any disagreement between them. It was the enemies of their movement, he charged, that distorted their disagreements on form in order to divide them for political reasons.

Despite their disagreements on art, Rivera and Siqueiros were finally in agreement on the politics of international communism. Their visit and return from Russia coincided with the Twentieth Congress of the Communist Party of the Soviet Union, during which Stalin was attacked, the cult of the personality was declared incompatible with communism and a policy of peaceful coexistence was adopted. While Diego immediately endorsed the new line, Siqueiros qualified his admission that Stalin had made some mistakes in the past by pointing out that they were made under extenuating circumstances. Although neither was actively involved in party activities, both of them continued to make generous contributions to the Party and frequently expressed their opinions on current issues without its approval.

After his return from Russia, David resumed work on his "sculpture-painting" at the University and on March 22, 1956, *The People to the University, the University to the People. For a Neo-Humanistic National Culture of Universal Meaning* was inaugurated. On the overhang of the south face of the Rectory Building, he had constructed five large figures which projected several feet off the surface and dominated the side of the building. These figures are painted or covered with glass tile. One, representing a student, raises his arms in a fraternal gesture, looking towards the other four figures representing the arts and sciences of the University. Behind the student leader a group of students march with banners and a Mexican flag. From one angle it appears that the academicians are offering their knowledge to the students or the people, but from another perspective, they appear to be indifferent to the people's demands for culture and learning.

The People to the University, the University to the People.
1952–56. Bas-relief and Mosaic, Rectory, National Autonomous University of Mexico. Mexico City

The reactions to his latest mural were mixed and Siqueiros himself was disappointed by the results. For some, the sculpted figures were monstrous and seemed to be glued on the building, dominating instead of blending with the structure and making it top-heavy. Some critics complained that it was nothing more than a large poster or commercial billboard. Moreover, while Siqueiros had designed the mural to be seen and comprehended at a glance from a rapidly moving car, the figures are difficult to distinguish and comprehend from a distance and are overpowering when seen close up.

As he had foreseen, the technique was faulty. Over the years the under structure of reinforced cement has rusted, the rust seeping through and discoloring the mosaic tile, and several restorations have been required to preserve the original color. Although the theme is general and direct, the message is unclear and requires more than a passing glance to be understood. Lombardo Toledano also pointed out that even when the message is understood, it does not live up to the revolutionary credo of the artist. Perhaps, he added, this was the result of the artist working for a government whose policies he opposes.

After the inauguration, Siqueiros admitted some of his own disappointment. In an article entitled "My Experience in Exterior Muralism," he reiterated his premise that exterior muralism involves new and unforeseen problems of all types and therefore requires new solutions, and he admitted that he had not completely appreciated the problems of constructing an outdoor mural with all its competing forms and shapes. This failure, he was sure, was due to the newness of the profession or technique, and would require many years of experimentation before these problems would be solved. Nevertheless, he was convinced that flat smooth surfaces could not compete with the other forms and that even pale unpainted sculptural forms were useless, since without any color, they appear shapeless in the outdoors.

He also stated that his recent experience proved his contention that plastic materials determine the form of art and that primitive materials produce primitive solutions. Thus, while he had tried to utilize modern methods, his mural suffered from the defect of archaic materials, namely the mosaic glass tile. "In using mosaic, you call up the ghost of Byzantine art." he wrote. But he was sure that this would be resolved in the future with the perfection of a process of pre-coloring aluminum electrolytically. He also acquired an appreciation of the infinitely greater radius of the spectator in external murals, requiring an even greater polyangular perspective and the development of non-static sculptural forms that can be seen from many different angles.

The use of color, he realized, must also be different then on an interior mural or canvas. Under the direct sun, varying in intensity and elevation at different times of the day or year, the colors also change. For example, white changes completely when used out of doors, either receding or appearing as holes in the surface. Because of his use of mosaics, it was also virtually impossible to make corrections in these color defects after they were discovered. Since this is a very different type of art, Siqueiros concluded, the public would also have to change its viewing habits.

He reserved some of his analysis for a rebuttal of his critics, especially the "antirealists." While they flounder in the metaphysics of that which they call "the objectification of the subjective," and have not improved on the materials and tools invented thousands of years ago, he declared, we are developing the latest techniques and materials available in science and industry. While they are still inured to the canvases they paint for the private market, we are committed to making public art. To their academicism we offer a functional art with a human and social perspective.

When the artist González Camarena described sculpture painting as just another decoration similar to the formal games of the abstractionists, Siqueiros again defended his efforts. Since he had not been afraid to attempt something new and had achieved a successful transformation of the figures when seen from different angles, he was in total agreement with what he had achieved. "All this is the beginning of a better solution," he exulted, and pointed out that the "formalism" of his mural was the result of the technical difficulties he had encountered and not because sculpture painting and realism were incompatible.

In spite of his pronouncements on the coming of the second stage of the Mexican pictorial movement and the importance and nature of exterior mural painting, Siqueiros never finished his two other panels on the Rectory. All that remains are the geometric designs which he had traced on the flat surfaces and over which he had planned to construct sculpted-painting.

Despite its shortcomings, *The People to the University, the University to the People* is the only mural at the University that contains an implicit social message and incorporated new solutions. Although the forms were criticized as too large and overwhelmed the architecture, they were designed to be seen from a distance and smaller figures or excessive detail would have defeated that objective. While he had used mosaic tile instead of colored aluminum for technical and economic reasons, other artists and sculptors have since used anodized aluminum successfully.

Juan O'Gorman later wrote that it was a tragedy that Siqueiros experimented in forms of painting which the Mexican people were not ready to accept, a tragedy which is due to "his artistic power and his political weaknesses." Apparently, his fellow artists were unwilling to take these risks. After completing their murals at the University, O'Gorman and Chávez Morado used mosaic tile on the outside of the new Ministry of Communications and Public Works and Diego Rivera applied mosaic tile to the facade of the Insurgents Theater in Mexico City. The "second phase" of the Mexican Mural Movement, the painting or construction of outdoor murals, was underway, albeit "primitive" or "archaic."

XV. A More Expressive Realism

Between trips abroad, speaking engagements and mural assignments, Siqueiros was busy painting canvases. In the summer of 1956 he exhibited 12 of these recent studies in his own home, including his portrait of Benito Juárez, two portraits of contemporary figures, several landscapes and some semiabstract studies. They illustrated, he explained, the five basic problems of realism: the objectivity of the direct portrait; objectivity in an indirect portrait; non-imitative objectivity in landscape painting; objectivity in the fantasy of predicted technology and pictorial objectivity in political caricature.

In an interview following the exhibit, David elaborated on these concepts. Landscape painting, he explained, poses entirely new problems since there are things that we know about nature that cannot be seen. In the age of the airplane, man cannot have the same lyrical and romantic view of the natural landscape. Objective mentality, therefore, is not the only solution for such panoramas and many problems of volume are better understood from a mental perception than from a strictly visual one.

This mental understanding, then, must modify the simplistic and mechanical concept of objectivity which has prevailed in art. While the cubists confronted this problem, they "concentrated on bowls of fruit, bottles, guitars and coffee mills." In depicting these objects, he explained, they used "objective logic, as well as visual perception," but in landscapes, "they limit themselves to including only that which can be seen from a real or imagined window."

While his portraits of living and dead Mexicans demonstrated the first two types of realism, a painting of a living political figure provided an example of "objectivity in political caricature." His recent landscapes were cosmic panoramas, as if seen from an airplane. Painted in pyroxylin on masonite, *Dikes Against Erosion*, *Industrialization in the Altiplano*, *Forest on Fire* and *Landscape* were heavily modeled and their encrusted forms appeared to emerge from their surroundings. Two semiabstract studies, *Atomic Airship* and *Atomic Foundry*, were futuristic and demonstrated a type of realism based on an objective impression of future technology.

In the fall of 1956 Siqueiros left on a trip to Europe, Egypt, India and China. In Cairo he and Angélica met with Gamal Abdel Nasser. When the French bombed the Suez Canal, Siqueiros volunteered his military services but Nasser politely declined the offer, telling him to carry on the struggle in Mexico.

From Egypt, David and Angélica traveled to Europe and Russia before flying to India. When they arrived in Calcutta, he and Angélica were greeted warmly by Prime Minister Nehru, his daughter Indira and President Sukarno of Indonesia. Following a reception in their honor, David and Angélica flew to New Delhi in the Prime Minster's plane with Nehru and Indira. Their visit to India coincided with a meeting of UNESCO and they were invited to a large reception and banquet for the delegates, at which his lithograph *Child Mother*, a gift to Nehru, was displayed.

From New Delhi, David and Angélica flew to Hong Kong, where they spent several days waiting for visas to travel in the People's Democratic Republic. In China they met with Chou En-lai and discussed the idea of a united front or alliance between the nations of Asia and Latin America. After they visited the Buddhist cave paintings of Tung Hueng and Yuan Kuang, David told his hosts, "If communism doesn't soon achieve a dynamic art comparable to this, then I am afraid I'll have to become a Buddhist." Although they had received an invitation to visit Japan, they returned to Mexico from China, after two months of travel.

Immediately after landing in Mexico, David held a press conference in which he described the highlights of their trip, emphasizing his conversations with world leaders. He also predicted the nationalization of oil in the Middle East and announced the creation of an alliance of Latin Americans against colonialism and imperialism. In response to questions on East-West issues, he agreed that there was some similarity between American and Russian policies, but insisted that it was in the means and not the goals. Why, he asked, is the use of tanks by the Soviet Union to put down a rebellion in a neighboring country wrong, while the overthrow of a democratic government in Guatemala by the United Fruit Company with guns and tanks is considered "good?"

That same year Siqueiros received a commission to paint a mural in the Museum of National History in Chapultepec Castle, the former palace of Maximilian and Carlota in Mexico City. The site was a long narrow rectangular room with a low ceiling and windows along one of the long sides. Since he could not raise the walls or the ceiling, he obtained permission to break through into an adjoining room. By leaving the ends of the common wall in place and using both sides of it, he created a continuous surface of 4500 square feet that wrapped around the walls of the two rooms. Then he announced that he would paint a history of the struggle of the masses and their heroes against Díaz, which he viewed as inconclusive.

When the walls had been cut and the remaining surfaces covered with celotex panels, he had his assistants draw the lines of composition. Using an airbrush and acrylic paint, he began to paint over and around these lines. After he had already painted several sections of the mural, he had strips of fiberglass placed over the vinylite and repainted the finished scenes on the new surface. Unlike fresco, he explained, this would permit the removal of the mural and its reconstruction in another building.

On the end wall he painted Díaz in top hat, his foot resting on the Constitution of 1857 and surrounded by the "usurper" Huerta, Vice President Corral and Limantour, the leader of the Díaz intelligentsia. Behind them he placed rows of government officials and plutocrats in the formal dress of the *porfiriato*. In front of the seated dictator he painted several elegantly dressed society ladies, including a notorious courtesan of the period, dancing and entertaining him.

On the adjoining wall, Siqueiros painted the 1906 strike of the copper miners of Cananea against the mine owner, a Colonel Greene. In the center Fernando Palomares, one of the strike leaders, wrestles with Colonel Greene over the Mexican flag. The Colonel is backed by the dreaded rural police of Díaz and the Texas Rangers, the scourge of Mexicans along the border. Huddling behind them are the reactionary leaders from Sonora, terrified by the striking miners.

Palomares is backed by a group of women and children and three men carrying the body of a miner on their shoulders. One of them is Manuel Diéguez, a leader of the Cananea strike and Siqueiros's commander during the Revolution. On the next section he began to paint the ideological precursors of the Mexican Revolution, with the Europeans Marx, Bakunin and Proudhon in the forefront.

The Revolution Against Díaz, Strike at Cananea. 1957–67. Acrylic on Plywood, Museum of National History, Mexico, D.F.

When he was visited in Chapultepec by the North American writer Selden Rodman, Siqueiros told him that although he could make more money painting canvases, he preferred mural painting. When Rodman asked him why artists exercised so much influence in Mexico, Siqueiros explained that they were never "just artists." We addressed meetings and organized ourselves and others.

> When I led the strike at the Academy in my teens, our
> syndicate made two demands: 'Out with the
> academicians' and 'nationalize the railroads!'...
> Some of us became generals. I am still a reserve
> captain in the Mexican Army and a Lieutenant Colonel
> in the army of Republican Spain. In the old days we went
> to paint with pistols in our belts. They couldn't have
> stopped us if they'd wanted to!

When Rodman asked him about other artists, Siqueiros's response was characteristically critical. "Rembrandt," he said, "painted for the bourgeoisie. That was his limitation." Then he told Rodman that he had imagined a conversation between Rembrandt and Picasso in which Rembrandt asked Picasso when he was going to finish *Guernica*, since it seemed like an unfinished sketch in different shades of gray. "Like all the French," he continued, "Picasso is doing no more than presenting the bourgeoisie with tidy trifles, bits of his complete psyche." While Calder is "a truly great innovator, he makes toys."

Meanwhile, Siqueiros was expressing his views on recent political developments. Upon his return from Europe in 1955 he had given two lectures in which he accused members of his party of being asleep or opportunistic for not opposing the system of "*tapadismo*," whereby the President imposes his successor on the country. Six months later he had called on the party's Central Committee to mobilize all the democratic forces in the country into a National Electoral Front to prevent the continuation of the antidemocratic and counterrevolutionary trend which has prevailed in Mexico since Cárdenas.

In March of 1957 he wrote an article entitled "If I were President," in which he promised to guarantee "effective suffrage," condemn the profiteering of the plutocracy, denounce the bureaucrats and kingmakers from Cárdenas to Alemán and destroy the system whereby the presidents handpicked their successors. As President, he would make Congress truly representative of the people, attack the maneuvering of the new oligarchy and pro-Yankee imperialists and make the next presidential election a truly democratic contest between real political parties.

When the Communist Party did not take a stand on presidential imposition, and announced that any statements by him were personal and did not represent the Party, he attacked the Party for its inaction in a lengthy discourse at a meeting celebrating the 38th anniversary of the Mexican Communist Party. "How can the Communist Party not act in terms of the electoral problem," he asked, "given the urgency and the fact that all other parties, from the right to the left, have taken a position on this issue?" By not participating in the development of new electoral procedures or discussing these issues within the Party, we appear to be supporting the PRI.

He also accused the Party of engaging in a personality cult when it automatically endorsed Cárdenas's proposals for reorganizing the PRI and creating independent political parties. Even if the system chooses a revolutionary candidate who supports our progressive programs, he said, it is still "*tapadismo.*" By participating in the charade whereby the PRI and the government pretend to attack the right in order to protect the Revolution, the Party has aided the bourgeoisie and elected them to the Presidency and the Congress.

Siqueiros then accused different members of the presidential cabinet of protecting foreign capital and oppressing the peasants, while the Minister of Labor has maintained labor peace by controlling the union leaders. The rest of the cabinet has become very wealthy through their positions or as "*tapados*" following the pro-imperialist line of the President. Our country has a new oligarchy of the porfirian type, Siqueiros said, while the people are more miserable and our basic industry is linked to foreign capital from the United States.

After accusing members of the cabinet of selling out the country, controlling labor and enriching themselves, he proposed that the Party organize a Democratic Electoral Front in alliance with all other patriotic and progressive groups or personalities. Besides denouncing the "*tapado*" system, the Party should organize all those who oppose imposition and lead the struggle for national independence and economic and political self-determination.

Although the text of his speech was printed in the press, Siqueiros arranged for its publication in a special pamphlet, in which he also described his unsuccessful efforts to urge Party leaders and progressives outside the Party to oppose the practice of presidential imposition.

In 1957 David's increasing sense of isolation was compounded by a personal loss. Since his return from Russia, Diego Rivera had been convalescing. Although he talked of new mural projects, he spent most of his time arranging his collection of pre-Columbian art in Anacualli, the studio-museum he had designed as a pyramid. In July he called on other artists to support a movement to suspend the testing of nuclear bombs, but his health continued to decline and he died on November 24, 1957.

After a death mask had been cast, Diego's body was taken to the Bellas Artes where former President Cárdenas, Dr. Atl and a sad and stone-faced Siqueiros stood guard. For two days thousands of Mexicans of all classes filed by and paid their last respects to this giant artist and personality.

Thus ended the brilliant and controversial career of Diego Rivera, a life which one writer likened to a giant and colorful fresco, as full of vitality and invention as one of his own murals. In art Rivera was one of the great talents of this century, both in the variety of styles as well as in the quality and quantity of his production. He had progressed from impressionism to cubism to Mexican realism and within the Mexican movement, he had been the most prolific artist. His murals and canvases provide a visual documentation of the history and culture of Mexico, contemporary society, modern technology and his vision of a utopian society.

At the funeral ceremonies government officials, fellow artists and members of the communist party paid their last respects to Diego. Siqueiros, his long time friend, as well as constant critic, honored him as "a man of the Mexican and international working class," whose life and work were an expression of the revolutionary proletariat. After acknowledging Diego's handling of space, volume and color, he praised his pursuit of a new humanism and the social content of his art, which gives him the enormous stature that we revere today.

Siqueiros paid tribute to his fellow artist on many other occasions, not only praising Diego's artistic talents but also emphasizing his role in making Mexican art known to the rest of the world. He also revealed that he had always wanted to paint a portrait of Diego but their pressing schedules had interfered. Now he would paint an objective portrait of Diego, just as he was, with all his contradictions.

For several days after the internment of Rivera, Siqueiros appeared in a state of shock. But when he was interviewed and asked what his responsibility was as the only surviving member of "los tres grandes," he responded immediately that as one of the pioneers of the mural movement, he had to make sure that it was not destroyed or detained.

A month after Diego's death, Siqueiros accepted an invitation to attend the 200th anniversary of the founding of the School of Fine Arts in Moscow. Although he did not participate in the discussions, he was pleased to observe the heated debate that his "Open Letter" provoked when it was read before members of the Union of Soviet Painters and party officials. Before leaving Moscow, he gave a talk on "The Technical Experiences of the Mexican Muralist Movement" at the Pushkin Museum.

Back in Mexico, Siqueiros participated in a series of lectures and round table discussions sponsored by the National Front of the Plastic Arts. Organized in 1952 as "the permanent organ of social and cultural action" to promote the plastic arts and defend the cultural heritage of Mexico, the Front endorsed complete freedom of expression and the production of art forms linked to and at the service of the people. After protesting the seizure of *Nightmare of War and Dream of Peace*, it had sponsored a series of traveling exhibits of Mexican art, especially in Soviet bloc countries.

In 1958 the Front sponsored a series of lectures and debates in which Siqueiros and many other artists participated. When it was his turn to speak, Siqueiros contrasted European art with that of Mexico, where muralism with an ideological content focusing on human problems was emphasized. While the Europeans were ignoring art with an ideological content, rejecting muralism and removing the image of man from their art, he declared, we were emphasizing those elements and moving towards an "integral art." The people of other countries will realize that the different European currents were unilateral and only attacked one problem at a time: "the impressionists, the vibration of light; the futurists, movement; the surrealists, the subconscious; the expressionists, emotion; the cubists, the structure of form, etc." But we asked, "Why take the partial aspects of the problem and not the problem in its totality?"

In Europe, he continued, the print has become a private collector's item, while in Mexico we have converted it into a public art form with an ideological and political function. Our discoveries will have great repercussions. We will show that it is not necessary to expel the image of man from art and in order to achieve a greater realism, we must advance in the dynamic and psychological content of our art. Still young, our movement is like "the stammering of a child before an old man who has lost his memory and creative capacity."

While he recognized the influence of Europe on Mexican art, David explained that the emphasis in European art is on an economy of means and is "bidimensional," whereas "we want to enrich the means because we wish to enrich the expression." If we do not enrich our realism, or if those who follow us, merely repeat us and do not eliminate the negative elements in our work, then realism will be at a serious disadvantage vis-à-vis abstractionism. Our figures must be "more alive, more vibrant, more expressive, more psychological."

In terms of a course of action, we should demand that the government support democratic and public art, just as it must promote agrarian reform, labor laws and economic independence. We must tell the state that it has betrayed the Revolution in the cultural aspect and that we are going to join the people in the struggle to correct this progress. We must explain to the young artists who argue that they must eat from their painting and attempt to justify their art as more advanced and intellectual, that they are the victims and not the perpetrators of these developments. We must demand that the state increase the opportunities for murals without any restrictions on their ideological content or freedom of expression.

In subsequent sessions Siqueiros expressed his view that the history of the art of painting is the history of the search for realism in which the Mexican movement was a participant. Our incomplete search continues, he said, as much in technique as in the scientific elements that intervene in artistic creation, and that explains our preoccupation to develop a better knowledge of space and movement and our search for new materials and equipment. We can enrich realism and "the duty of the young artists is to add more words, to advance!"

When the Mexican paper *Novedades* published an article by artist José Luis Cuevas in its Sunday supplement *México en la Cultura*, entitled "Cuevas Attacks the Superficial and Pampered Realism of the Mexican School," Siqueiros replied immediately in a letter to the editor. Instead of addressing the points raised by Cuevas, however, he concentrated on a campaign against the Mexican movement launched and carried out by the Hearst chain of newspapers, the United States ambassadors in Mexico, *Time* and *Life* magazines and commercial publications throughout the world.

This polemic was fueled by the announcement of the first Interamerican Biennial of Painting and Engraving, scheduled for the Palace of Fine Arts in June, July and August. The National Front of the Plastic Arts and the Taller de Gráfica Popular immediately protested the inclusion of the favorite artists of the dictator Trujillo and the exclusion of exiled artists from the Dominican Republic, the appointment of Juan O'Gorman to the selection jury and the holding of the exhibit during a teachers' strike against the Ministry of Public Education. Nevertheless, the exhibit took place as planned and included artists from all over the hemisphere.

Although he participated as an exhibitor and member of the jury, Siqueiros condemned much of the art as "innocuous copies" of Picasso, Braque or Matisse, or bastard "cocktails of several of them" which emphasized "novelty only for the sake of novelty." Even worse, their copyism is second hand, he declared, since the Latin American artists are copying those of the United States, who copy the Europeans. Dependent on the colonial political-aesthetic of the United States market, they are repeating, "like tropical monkeys," the conventionalisms and mannerisms of the great "bluff" vanguard. Their prestige is not determined by their own people, but by those who are involved in the international business of art with its theoretical base in Paris and its financial seat in New York.

Either naive or opportunistic, Siqueiros continued, these artists practice an "epicurean art" for the enjoyment of a selected "chic" elite which does not exist in their own countries. They are the victims of the scholarships, prizes and purchases from the United States and their critics have acquired their tastes in New York or Washington. It is an art for exportation, for external consumption only. Many of them are ignorant of the traditions of their own people or the problems of their countries and are unaware of this cultural imperialism. They work like angels, above the earth, and have nothing to do with the country of their origin.

Nevertheless, Siqueiros viewed the competition as an opportunity to contrast the work of the Mexican realists with European vanguardism. It would, he said, serve to remind us of the contagion of European vanguardism in America, a "leprosy" which penetrates our movement. When Francisco Goitia, a "pioneer" and "founder of our "anti-abstractionist movement" received the grand prize, Siqueiros proclaimed that social realism had triumphed over abstractionism.

From Caracas came more harsh words for the Biennial as well as for Siqueiros. In a letter to *México en la Cultura*, José Luis Cuevas satirized the exposition and declared that young artists of Latin America are tired of the same old song "there is no other way but ours," which Siqueiros uses to attack the other artists, not in self-defense, as he claims. We are tired of his "grandstanding" and I refuse to "participate in this new comedy staged by this great mummy of our billboard painting," Cuevas continued.

After he described Siqueiros as a dictator in decline, Cuevas likened him to a clown who tries to force out a last laugh while the circus goes on and the public ignores his desperate antics. Although Cuevas conceded that Siqueiros played an important role in a movement that was said to be democratic, he refuses to allow others to express themselves freely. While he attacks bourgeois art, it is he who lives by it with his flattering and sweet portraits and he fears losing the market which he has acquired with the publicity he has received in books printed by North American companies with North American capital.

In the autumn of 1958 Siqueiros participated in a debate with Antonio Rodríguez, Joel Marroquin and Federico Silva at the Workers University on "social painting as art" and "the current status of Mexican painting, realism and abstractionism." After complementing Rodríguez for his efforts on behalf of Mexican art, Siqueiros accused the art historian of ignoring the fundamental cause of the crisis in contemporary Mexican art, which is essentially political. It is the result of the consolidation of the national bourgeoisie and the new Mexican oligarchy, the penetration of Yankee imperialism and the alliance between them and the abandonment, in theory and practice, of the essential postulates of our "pro-realist and national social movement." Since the problem is political, political solutions are required, including the reorganization of labor, the formation of popular democratic parties and the organization of artists.

In 1958 Siqueiros started two new mural projects. The first site was the entrance hall of the cancer unit of the Medical Center in Mexico City, a room with a low ceiling and a flat wall which was broken by a double door and which made several 90 degree turns. Although the surface posed a number of problems, the choice of an appropriate theme was more challenging. What, he pondered, would be fitting for a lobby where cancer patients or their families enter the building to be admitted, receive treatment or visit dying relatives? For many the diagnosis was dreaded and the prognosis hopeless. One might paint a pretty landscape, a history of medicine in Mexico or a strictly ornamental decoration.

Instead he decided to confront the problem directly, painting the illness realistically, but at the same time offering hope for relief through modern science. He would also develop the theme of social problems and man's efforts to overcome them through revolutionary struggle. In effect, human society, through modern science and social change, would cure its physical ills and solve its social problems.

Working with an airbrush, David began to spray bright acrylic colors over a surface of plywood covered with a plastic cloth, sketching the outlines and lines of composition, then filling in with more detail and adding color. On the first wall he painted a barren landscape upon which he grouped several naked and suffering women, their arms outstretched and pleading towards the sky. All is chaotic and the figures are in despair, looking to heaven for relief from devastating epidemics. Next he painted a man leaping across a canyon, fleeing the chaos and misery of the prehistoric cave-dwelling society and searching for solutions.

Moving forward in history, he painted a more orderly human society, in which the classical cultures of Asia, Africa, Europe and America have developed science and medicine and are less dependent upon magic and prayer. For the contemporary world, he painted a woman thanking a group of male and female doctors and scientists of different nationalities behind a bright red and yellow apparatus in which a dark-skinned woman is receiving radiation. Extending this machine onto the adjoining wall, he destroyed the right angle between the two surfaces and created the effect of a continuous plane.

Behind and above this modern machine, he painted a group of men and women, marching in solidarity and raising their arms in celebration. They represent not only the victory of science over cancer, but also the triumph of social revolution over the ills of contemporary society.

Holding his airbrush in one hand, he allowed it to spray freely over the adjoining wall, creating unforeseen shapes that stirred his imagination. Combining these "accidents" with mental images, he formed two hideous monsters, reminiscent of the demons in *Patricians and Patricides* and *The Devil in the Church*. Part human, part animal and part vegetable, they represent the ills of the body and modern society. Although grotesque and terrifying, they are being routed by the advances of modern science and the solidarity of the masses.

The Apology for the Future Victory of Medicine over Cancer, 1958.
Acrylic on Plywood, Medical Center, Mexico, D.F.

The Apology for the Future Victory of Medicine over Cancer is more than just a history of medicine from prehistory to the present and the future, and its subtitle, "Historical Parallel of the Scientific and Social Revolutions," conveys its dual meaning. Rather than avoid the subject of cancer, Siqueiros painted grotesque human forms and monsters representing illnesses and social problems and created a very expressive and human art form.

In the beginning humanity is living in a sort of hell. Placed in a barren landscape and surrounded by prehistoric monsters, man is desperate and imploring. At the same time, however, man is searching for solutions and striving for progress. Eventually, more confident men and women emerge out of this chaos, culminating in the future when man has developed atomic energy for peaceful uses. The scientific revolution is propelled by a social revolution. Together they will solve the problems facing society and modern medicine and science will serve mankind and eradicate cancer.

When the mural was unveiled in November of 1958, Siqueiros explained: "The people, led by the working class, advance towards science in order to offer their solidarity." Pointing to the multitudes surrounding the cobalt apparatus, he expressed his confidence in the future. Man celebrates the victory of medical science over cancer in the advanced society of the atomic era in which current problems are also fleeing.

While he was still putting the finishing touches on this project, Siqueiros had started working at another site. After Diego Rivera had completed his mosaic decoration of scenes from the Mexican theater on the marquee of the Teatro Insurgentes, he had been invited to paint a mural on the same theme in the lobby of the Teatro Jorge Negrete, the headquarters of the national actors' union. But his declining health prevented him from starting the project and when he died, the actors' union turned to Siqueiros. Accepting their offer to paint a mural on "the evolution of the theater in Mexico and the painter's concept of the direction that the theater would take in the future," he began to paint on the panels prepared for Diego.

Working in a frenzy and without a sketch, David traced a series of spontaneous curving lines, ellipses and spheres with an airbrush, creating a rhythmic skeleton of lines on the blank white panels. Gradually he began to fill in this framework. Allowing his airbrush to spray freely, he created a series of accidental forms, the fruits of his imagination and the effects of his tools. When he spotted a mistake, he exchanged the airbrush for an electric sander and erased the fast-drying acrylic paints or shouted directions to his assistants. Working in a mist of paint, he gradually spread his version of the history of the Mexican theater from pre-Columbian times to the present around the walls of the lobby.

His approach, as well as his interpretation, would be very different from Diego's. After stating that he would divide the history of the Mexican theater into three parts corresponding to the three dramatic forms, he explained that tragedy would be represented by the aggression of the government against the workers; comedy by the political bosses, gangsters, union bosses and the violations of the constitution and farce by the follies of the nouveau riche and the corruption of our government. As the mural took shape, therefore, it had nothing in common with Rivera's literal interpretation of the

Mexican theater in mosaic tile. It also differed from that envisioned by the union's Executive Committee.

One morning, only six months after he had signed the contract with the National Association of Actors, Siqueiros arrived at the theater and found the doors padlocked and his mural covered with sheets of plywood. When he demanded an explanation, he was told that the Executive Committee of the union had voted to suspend work on the mural and was going to sue him for breach of contract.

Meeting with a group of reporters, Siqueiros called Landa, the head of the union, "servile," "a grand inquisitor" and "an armed bandit." He defended his right to paint the political and aesthetic ideas which his conscience dictated and compared the imprisonment of his mural to the confiscation of a novel and the prevention of its publication because of its content. He explained that he had been painting everyday and nothing had happened until he began to paint scenes from the living reality of Mexico, since the theater of the future should be based on the real human and social problems of the time. The real issue, therefore, is not artistic but ideological, since Landa and the other directors of the union think that the union movement should be controlled by the government, whereas he had insisted that the workers movement must be independent of the state.

He also reminded the reporters that he was part of a well-known movement and that no one could have expected him to paint any other way. They cannot accuse me of deceit, he said, as they know my political-aesthetic biography. What is even worse is that "the inquisition" has penetrated the field of art and is being exercised by one group of artists against another artist. The members of the union, therefore, should demand that the Executive Committee retract its resolution and attack on my art. After threatening to take the mural out of the theater and into the streets, he warned, "These actors must learn that they live in a real world and that the history of the theater is the history of the real world."

Several days later David protested to the General Assembly of the National Association of Actors that what he had painted in the theater was what they had contracted for since they knew him and his work and they could not assume that he would paint a mural devoid of ideological content. "I have deep political convictions and I cannot change them, and everyone in Mexico and probably in the world knows what they are." he explained. "When they cover up my mural, they are violating my freedom of expression." The conflict, therefore, is over my interpretation of the history of Mexico, a right that is entirely mine. Do they want me to represent tragedy as a drug addict who kills himself and his children? Should I have painted a Greek tragedy? "My mural is not communistic," he protested, "it is a mural painted by a communist, but it is a union mural. There is no red flag, no hammer or sickle."

When the Executive Committee replied that "we asked for pears and he wanted to give us plums," Siqueiros restated his view that the real issue was that members of the committee had political differences with him because he advocated the complete independence of the labor unions from the government since their lack of independence has castrated and corrupted the labor movement for the last twenty years. He also compared the painting of a mural to the writing of a book in which the editor has no right to impose on the author that the contents correspond to his views. What Landa and other members of the Executive Committee have done is to establish an inquisition by one group of artists towards another, he charged.

Siqueiros also took his case to other audiences. Before a meeting of journalists, he defended his mural and summarized the numerous attacks on murals in Mexico since his first experiences in the National Preparatory School to the closure and lawsuit filed against him by the actors' union. As artists, he pointed out, we never accepted themes or interpretations that would limit our freedom of expression. I have not violated any contract and it is only that Landa and some members of the Executive Committee have political differences with me. The government should be censured when it violates the law and attacks the unions, which must be completely independent from the state. In other meetings he explained that his mural in the Jorge Negrete Theater was the fourth mural of his that had been attacked. The difference, he said, was that the other three murals were in Cuba and the United States.

Despite their recent differences, the Communist Party supported Siqueiros and accused the union directors of censorship and the government of violating the constitution. The Popular Socialist Party condemned the closure of the mural as a suppression of freedom of expression and thought and stated that it violated the tradition of this movement in which artistic creation has always been the right of the artist. Since it was in mural painting that Mexican culture had asserted itself at home and abroad, this censorship was a particularly dangerous precedent and was the result of an internal and external conspiracy against the traditional values of our culture. Therefore, the workers and intellectuals should organize against this attack on an eminent painter as well as on the cultural patrimony and independence of Mexico.

As the legal case dragged on, probably unique in the history of art, lawyers argued and judges heard testimony as to whether the mural fulfilled the terms of the contract. When he appeared before the court, Antonio Rodríguez testified that no respectable artist could be expected to conform to a contract which called for history and not art. Moreover, a subject as complex as the history of the theater requires a synthesis, a summary, which instead of being a detailed history, would have to represent its essence. How, he continued, could you expect a man who has known prison, revolutions and wars to paint a didactic mural for school children? That would slander him and his art. Instead of a history of the theater, therefore, Siqueiros has painted its essence and its spirit.

On October 9, 1959, the civil judge in charge of the case visited the site of the mural. As he entered the lobby of the theater, he was confronted by a wall covered with swirling figures of masked actors from the ancient theater and famous actors or singers. When he turned around, he faced the protesting hordes on the opposite wall. Where two walls met at right angles, Siqueiros had painted a large television screen that overlapped the corner, destroying it visually and creating the impression of a continuous plane.

Next to this symbol of the modern theater, Siqueiros had painted a group of poor Indian mothers holding their starving children, their pleading figures similar to the multitudes he had painted in the cancer clinic or the miners and revolutionaries he was working on in Chapultepec. Taking a scene from the current reality of Mexico, he had painted the Indian women of Mezquital, a poor and dry area not far from Mexico City, holding their emaciated children.

In the center he had placed the body of Luis Morales, a young worker who had been shot by the police agents during a demonstration in front of Bellas Artes on the First of May 1952, in which Siqueiros had participated. Based on a photograph of the event, Morales is wrapped in a Mexican flag while his mother, her face torn by grief, holds his head in her hands, a Mexican pietá. Nearby a group of protesting workers look on while blue-eyed soldiers break up a demonstration of workers carrying red banners and trample a book representing the Mexican Constitution of 1917. Meanwhile, history was repeating itself when the army murdered a young railroad worker in 1958 and refused to return his body to his mother, despite protests.

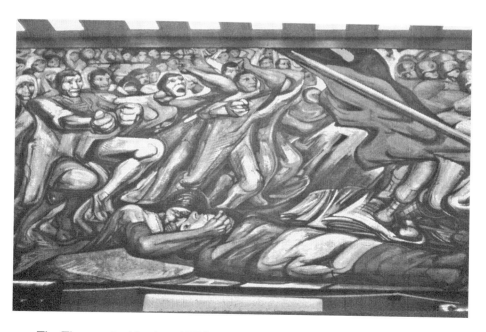

The Theater in Mexico, 1958–1967, Acrylic on Plywood, National Association of Actors, Mexico, D.F.

At the judicial investigation, Siqueiros explained, "In Mexico, in the various stages of the theater, there has been socialist and anarcho-socialist theater. That is why it surprises me that they consider my mural to be dangerous." Although the judicial inspection was inconclusive and the suit was never settled, the mural remained covered for the next eight years.

During a trip to Venezuela in 1960, Siqueiros explained that he wanted to tell the actors to link their art form to the reality of the country and the struggle of the people and therefore, he had tried to paint the theater of the past and how it should be in the future. When he studied the history of the theater, however, he had discovered that there had always been a type of political theater and it was this political theater which he had painted, he explained. But while he was painting, the Mexican government was attacking the workers, arresting thousands of them and torturing and killing some of their leaders. Meanwhile the national and foreign press remained silent and no one knew what was happening in the country. "What could I do under those circumstances?" he asked. I painted "a concrete example of tragedy," the attack by the police and the army on the workers' movement, "blindly obeying the orders of the American State Department, which received its orders from the great monopolies which oppress the whole world, including Mexico and Latin America." Therefore the Executive Committee decided that my mural was an attack on the government and would provoke demonstrations of workers and students, he explained.

If the purpose of the lockout had been to prevent the contents of the mural from being exposed, it had the opposite effect. Both the mural and the artist received more attention than if Siqueiros had been allowed to finish it. Thanks to the lawsuit and the controversy that ensued, many more Mexicans became aware of the mural and the reality which he had tried to depict and the judicial hearings gave him a forum in which he could attack the actors' union and the government, as well as explain and defend the mural. The action taken by the Executive Committee also provided an example of the repressive policies of the government and its control of the trade unions.

Despite this interruption, his mural in the actors' union constituted another advance in the development of his mural technique. After many years of practice, he had perfected his technique with the airbrush, a mastery which not only permitted more spontaneity and freedom but which also greatly enhanced his repertoire of special effects. As he developed an understanding of the inherent properties of the airbrush and the "tricks" which it created, he was able to apply them more effectively and in the process, produce a more direct and expressive form of art.

In his own words, he was trying to make his art more human and more effective psychologically. This mural and those in the cancer clinic and Chapultepec Castle were more direct, more human and more expressive. The figures in his last three murals were very human and their gestures or features reflected the full gamut of human emotions: fear, despair, pain, anguish, grief, hate, fury, love, hope, solidarity, confidence and joy. They were not mere symbols, but real people living out their daily tragedy and struggle. The faces of the women of Mezquital and the mother of Luis Morales expressed their anguish and suffering. Even the distorted and surreal forms of the monsters conveyed the pain as well as the terror which they aroused. Like *Proletarian Mother* and *Echo of A Scream*, they were direct, expressive depictions of the human condition.

These people, however, are not merely surviving. They are advancing, always seeking a better future and the workers are organizing and resisting the government and its agents. They are full of love, solidarity, self-sacrifice and courage and their leaders inspire them to raise their banners and carry on the struggle. The death of Morales, a poor worker, assumes the heroic, while his fellow workers continue the struggle against repression. In *The Revolution Against Dîaz* in Chapultepec, the miners and workers bear the body of their dead comrade on their shoulders and seize the national flag from Colonel Greene.

In the lobby of the cancer unit, the masses, united and allied with the scientists, chase away their individual and collective enemies. These crowds, however, are more than masses of faceless people. They are made up of real human beings, either actual historical personalities or definite national, regional or racial types and the artist has absorbed and expressed their essence. While there is suffering and despair in their faces, there is also hope for those who bear the pain and injustice. Seeking to keep this hope alive, his last three murals were manifestos calling for strength and solidarity.

These murals also demonstrate the difference between the styles and interpretations of common themes by two very different artists and personalities. While Rivera had romanticized the Revolution and depicted the workers and peasants as triumphant in his Ministry of Education murals, Siqueiros described the Revolution as incomplete. In the Institute of Cardiology Rivera had painted a history of the heart and for the Social Security Hospital, he had used a combination of fresco and mosaic to portray the history of medicine from the pre-Columbian era to the present.

In the same hospital, Siqueiros had called for a social revolution and the application of modern science to cure the physical ills, using acrylic paints applied on celotex panels with an airbrush and modeled by an electric sander. In the Medical Center he had treated cancer directly and called for the solution of the dreaded illness as well as the problems of modern society. Both artists, however, shared a faith in the solution of human problems through modern technology and the ultimate triumph of the working class through socialism.

This contrast in styles and interpretation of subject matter is most apparent in their respective treatments of "the history of the theater in Mexico." In his bright mosaic on the facade over the marquee of the Teatro Insurgentes, Diego had depicted highlights of the Mexican theater from the early native cultures to the present, but without any overt social commentary or depiction of current conditions. On the other hand, Siqueiros had painted an incident of police repression and called on the actors to link their art to the lives and struggles of the people.

In technique the two artists were also poles apart. Whereas Rivera worked carefully from predesigned sketches in the classical method and worked in either fresco or mosaic, Siqueiros painted directly, often without any sketches or outlines, and rejected fresco and mosaic tile for the latest in industrial tools and materials. In lieu of sketches he frequently used posed photographs of himself, Angelica or his assistants. More and more he relied on the airbrush, working from his latest inspiration, often derived from the accidents which he observed as he worked, inventing new forms, then correcting them before re-creating new shapes.

The results were as different as their personalities and the techniques which they used. Whereas Rivera's murals tend to tell a story and are stylistically static, those of Siqueiros are less didactic, are more openly critical of existing conditions and make a plea for concerted action. They are also fresher, more spontaneous, more alive and dynamic, and more expressive of human emotions. In both cases, the materials and equipment exerted their influence, fresco and mosaic tile requiring careful planning and execution, while the airbrush and acrylic paints permitted more flexibility, encouraged spontaneity and contributed to a greater sense of movement.

Since 1952 Siqueiros had started seven major mural projects and completed five of them. In the process, he had demonstrated his effective use of new materials and surfaces, contributed to the self-proclaimed "second stage of Mexican mural painting" on the outside of modern buildings and developed a more direct, human and expressive style. He had also painted many canvases or studies, including an impressive series of contemporary and historical portraits. Although he concentrated on his mural in Chapultepec Castle after his lockout from the actors' union, work was suddenly interrupted. This time it was not the mural that was locked up.

XVI. The New Inquisition

In spite of Mexico's recent economic development, the real income of Mexican workers had declined, the gap between the rich and poor had widened and the rate of growth had slowed down, barely keeping up with the population. Fed up with their leaders, many of them government stooges, workers demanded independence and threatened to strike for higher wages, better working conditions and labor reform.

Because of this labor unrest, Ruiz Cortines had chosen his Minister of Labor to succeed him. During his campaign, López Mateos declared that the right of the workers to strike was sacred and his government would be "extreme left within the Constitution." Faced with worsening economic conditions and encouraged by López Mateos's promises, a number of unions took their cause to the streets. In July of 1958 the railroad workers union called for a strike and the telegraph, electrical and petroleum workers promised their support. Although the government agreed to higher wages, the unrest and agitation continued.

A second rail strike was scheduled for August, but the army intervened and took over the railroad facilities before they could be closed down. However, when the workers elected a communist, Demetrio Vallejo, Secretary General of the union, and he brought Valentín Campa back into the union, the communists were accused of taking over the union. Despite concessions by the government, another strike was announced for February. Although the government declared the strike illegal, it granted more benefits in order to avert a work stoppage.

Nevertheless, the railroad workers voted to strike during the Easter holiday, when thousands of vacationers leave Mexico City by rail for coastal resorts. This time the government reacted swiftly. Just hours before the strike was to begin, the army seized installations and telegraph stations throughout the country, while police and soldiers broke into the strikers' homes and forced them back to work at gunpoint. Vallejo and other leaders were arrested and thousands of striking railroad workers were rounded up throughout the country. The dragnet included leaders and members of unions sympathetic to the railroad workers.

Because the prisons were already overflowing, military camps were pressed into service as detention centers. Although some workers were released after a few days, many were kept in prison or military camps without formal charges or any notification of their whereabouts to relatives. The government also charged that two Soviet diplomats had directed the strike and ordered their immediate expulsion from the country.

In May Valentín Campa was arrested. After a long and drawn out legal process, 25 of the labor leaders received long prison sentences. Campa spent the next 10 years in prison while Vallejo was not released until 1972. They were charged with the crime of "social dissolution" under Article 145 of the Penal Code. Instituted in 1941 to prevent sabotage of the war effort by fascist or pro-German elements, this amorphous charge of sedition was applied increasingly to the Left after the war.

Throughout 1958, Section IX of the National Teachers Union was also making demands and had called for a slowdown to publicize its grievances and pressure the government. When a group of teachers occupied the offices of the Department of Education for more than a month, the government granted the teachers a ten percent pay increase. During the summer, there were more demonstrations which the police broke up with tear gas and water cannons. Although some leaders of the teachers union were arrested, they were released by the end of the year by the incoming President as a goodwill gesture. But for the next year and a half, the teachers continued to press their demands for higher wages and better working conditions.

Meanwhile, the leaders of the railroad workers and five thousand workers or supporters remained in prison or military camps. In August of 1959 the government created a martyr for the strikers.

After returning from a meeting of the Communist Party in the capital, Román Guerra Montemayor, a railroad mechanic, was arrested by the military police in Monterey. Taken from his cell at night, he was beaten severely by his captors and then left to die in his cell. Even though a reporter identified a badly mutilated and dismembered body found along a highway as Guerra's, the body disappeared and the army refused to turn it over to the victim's mother.

This was the reality that Siqueiros had tried to paint in the Jorge Negrete Theater. When he was locked out of the building, he protested the censorship of his mural and issued statements criticizing the government. Unable to express his views in paint, he joined other writers and artists in the formation of the National Committee for the Freedom of Political Prisoners and in Defense of Constitutional Guarantees, and was elected President.

At first the small group met weekly at Siqueiros's home, trying to obtain information on relatives held by the police, raising support for their families and arranging a legal defense for the arrested workers. They later moved to the editorial offices of Filomeno Mata, who directed the committee's bulletin, *Liberación*. It contained notices of detained workers and editorials censuring the authorities for violations of the Constitution and urged readers to write petitions to the President, the Congress and the Supreme Court. The editors, however, carefully avoided statements which could be construed as agitation or provoking public disturbances.

Although their primary objective was the release of the arrested workers and their leaders, the committee also focused on the unconstitutionality of the crime of "social dissolution" in Article 145 of the Penal Code, the charge under which the strikers had been detained. A year and a half after their arrest, however, the majority of the workers were still in prison and the few who had been released had to promise not to participate in any strike activities.

As President of the National Committee for the Release of Political Prisoners, Siqueiros made several speeches condemning the government's repression of the strikes. He was also invited to Cuba and in January, 1960, he left for Havana with Angélica and Adriana.

In Cuba he was greeted by old friends, whom he told that the Francisco Javier Mina association of ex-combatants from Spain had chosen Che Guevara as their symbol, because he, like Javier Mina, symbolized the unity of the people of Latin America in their struggle against imperialism. However, he continued, our revolution has begun to capitulate under the increasing pressure of Yankee imperialism and all the governments since Ávila Camacho (1940-1946) have betrayed the Revolution and sold out to North American imperialism. Today there is no worker freedom in Mexico and the prisons are full of workers in order to satisfy the government of the United States. He was hopeful, however, that the Cuban Revolution would inspire a new movement in Mexico.

At the Museum of Modern Art in Havana, he gave a talk on the art of the Cuban and Mexican revolutions. After describing the origins of the Mexican movement, he explained how the Mexican bourgeoisie had sold out the Revolution and served the interests of imperialism. This corruption of the Revolution was reflected in the art of painting and the foreign interests have stepped up their attacks, he charged, using the money of the Organization of American States (OAS) to promote abstractionism and combat our figurative art of a social content. In conclusion, he proclaimed that art without political content was totally compromised and all the truly bold experiments in art belonged to an art of social content.

After several days in Havana, Siqueiros flew to Caracas, arriving in the Venezuelan capital a few days before the scheduled arrival of the Mexican President. While he was there to consider a mural project for the new building of the National Agrarian Institute, he spent most of his time presenting lectures on Mexican muralism and discussing recent political developments in Mexico. At the Central University of Caracas, he traced the history of Mexican painting from Dr. Atl's manifesto of 1906 to his recent experience in the actors union. Now, he said, the Mexican government no longer wants the people to be reminded of their revolution and has not supported the painting of murals or the cultivation of popular culture.

Turning to politics, he pointed out that when revolutions are incomplete, they slide backward, as in Mexico. "The imperialists have achieved this, but they have found many Mexican lackeys to help their cause." Mexico is not what the "pseudo-revolutionary propaganda" wants you to believe, he declared, but since a new revolution is already on the way, we must keep our art public and linked to the problems of the people.

After describing his problems in the actors' union, Siqueiros explained that he had painted the struggles in the street because the Mexican government was committing horrible aggressions against the workers. While thousands of workers were in prison for striking for higher wages, the rest of the world was ignorant of this repression. Therefore, he continued, when I painted that struggle as an example of tragedy, the Executive Committee viewed my mural as an attack on the government. Now "my country, which was in the forefront of the revolution in Latin America, has become a counterrevolutionary hypocrite and the accomplice of imperialism."

At the Museum of Fine Arts, he explained how they had learned to do fresco and then discovered that mural painting was more than just painting larger canvases. Later they learned that exterior mural painting was as different from interior mural painting as the latter was from easel painting. While admitting that he had declared, "Ours is the only way," he explained that any artist who is convinced about what he is creating, thinks the same, that his course is the only way. If not, he is in trouble. While he conceded that beauty could be created by "accidents" and modern art has made important contributions, he had always supported the idea of a collective laboratory for the arts.

Unfortunately, he continued, the Department of State, which serves the interests of the monopolies, has pressured for abstract art and uses the OAS to combat the Mexican pictorial movement. "How can the OAS determine our aesthetic values? It has no right to interfere in our aesthetic affairs, or in our national politics." For many years no figurative painter of a revolutionary social tendency has been invited to exhibit their works in the United States and the

Museum of Modern Art has removed this type of artist from its publications.

The next day David held a press conference before the Venezuelan Association of Journalists. After characterizing the Mexican Revolution as a "frustrated revolution, the Neo-Porfirian and pro-Yankee work of the juniors," he explained how the Left had high expectations of López Mateos and viewed him as another Cárdenas. But when the railroad workers launched a series of strikes, he said, we learned immediately that López Mateos was "the champion of all the other counterrevolutionary demagogues, Ávila Camacho, Alemán and Ruiz Cortines." No other government in this century has conducted such a Nazi and anti-communist policy against the workers.

But, he continued, this aggression against the union movement could not be realized without an explicit arrangement with the government of the United States, the representative of the imperialist Yankee monopolies. In Mexico the legislature, the Supreme Court and the press are controlled by the President and the cynicism of the current administration in talking about "freedom of expression" is greater than under the last three presidents. "The President has so much power that he could be called the Emperor of the Mexican Republic."

The anti-communism of the government, he charged, is obviously dictated by Washington and is much worse than in the time of Calles. The arrest of communists or striking workers in the middle of the night continues unabated. Not only is the government of Mexico cooperating with foreign or North American capital, but it has received in one year more investments of Yankee capital than any other government. Even the artistic program of the government conforms to that of the United States and the functionaries of the OAS who determine the artistic orientations of the whole continent. "Now they don't imprison me, now they imprison my murals!" he exclaimed.

Returning to the subject of Mexican politics, he described the government of López Mateos as the lowest in a period of decline that began with Ávila Camacho, when the uninterrupted process of the counterrevolution was launched. This government is only the most recent work of "the liquidators of the Mexican Revolution." Its authors are the bourgeois sons of the embezzlers who have enriched themselves from the Revolution. However, he warned, there is a powerful movement in my country which seeks solutions and which looks to the Cuban Revolution as a model. The people of Mexico will not wait another fifty years to resolve their pressing problems and those who lead their struggle "will have to make short term plans."

On their return trip to Mexico, David and Angélica stopped off in Havana where he repeated his charges against the government of López Mateos on national television. The policy of repression, he stated, is intended to break the workers' movement for an increase in salaries and is the product of an arrangement with Yankee imperialism. The Mexican government has adopted a McCarthyist policy of repression that must be eliminated by whatever means.

When he arrived in Mexico, he discovered that the press had attacked him and branded him a "foreign agent" and "traitor" for his attacks on López Mateos just before the President's goodwill trip to South America. Holding a press conference to explain his conduct, he started with a question, asking if the proximity of the trip of the President to various countries should have compelled him to hide the truth about the current conditions in his own country? That would amount to an intellectual and ideological abnegation of which I am not capable, he replied. Therefore, I expressed my truth democratically. In Cuba I was very impressed by the unity of the people and since they have accomplished in one year more than Mexico has accomplished in 50 years, the only thing that can explain the President's failure to include Cuba in his trip is his capitulation to the State Department.

Next he summarized his experiences in Havana and Caracas and repeated his charges of the fiction of democracy and a free press in Mexico. The government has expelled two members of the Soviet embassy without charges, has arrested more than five thousand railroad workers and there are frequent assassinations of union and political leaders, including the cover-up of the murder of Roman Guerra Montemayor by the army.

Although Fidel Castro has visited the United States and other Latin American countries, he has not been invited to Mexico and López Mateos did not include Cuba in his itinerary because of the pressure of the United States. When ex-President Cárdenas returned from the 26th of July celebrations in Cuba, he was prevented from holding a public meeting to share his impressions with the people. If the governments of Mexico and Venezuela do not issue a joint declaration in favor of the Cuban Revolution during the President's visit, it will be further evidence of the influence of the State Department in both countries.

Following his press conference, Siqueiros wrote an "Open Letter to My Attackers," listing each of them by name. Published in several Mexico City dailies, it began with a statement made by López Mateos to the effect that one of the greatest virtues of democracy is the possibility that the people may discuss their problems, and then asked when there would be a debate on the President's trip or his policies.

Next he accused his detractors of taking his words out of context or arriving at false conclusions. While they call me a "traitor" and "renegade," he wrote, or described me as "unbalanced," "paranoid," and an "exhibitionist," they also called us traitors when we joined the Revolution. Therefore I am used to being called a "traitor" and I do not know what I have done to deserve such eulogies from this rabble. I did not say anything outside the country that I have not said in Mexico. I did not insult Mexico or the Revolution. I answered the same questions they asked López Mateos, only my answers were not the same.

After proposing a discussion of these issues, so that the people may decide who the traitors are, he stated his political premises for this debate. Mexico, he wrote, does not enjoy full national sovereignty and its position has deteriorated during the last three administrations. Whereas the Mexican Revolution has not lived up to its origins and has declined during the last three presidencies, the Cuban Revolution is destroying the myths of the invincibility of a feudalism sustained by imperialism. Therefore the defense of the Cuban Revolution was important to all of Latin America so that the United States, the enemy of all popular struggles on this continent, does not aid the enemies of the Cuban Revolution.

The problems they faced, however, cannot be solved by the Mexican Revolution of the past. That would be the task of a new movement, more advanced in its program and in its tactics. The policies of the current ruling oligarchy were those of classic capitalism, similar to those of the *científicos* under Díaz, when the people suffered and the country was sold out to foreigners. The program of the President, therefore, does not correspond to the struggle of the people for the national sovereignty and constitutional rights which they aspire to in a more advanced historical period.

When he was summoned to testify as a witness on behalf of a teacher who had been arrested after attending an "illegal" meeting of the Communist Party in Monterey, Siqueiros turned the hearing into a forum to espouse his own ideas, defend the Party and attack the government. To the question of whether the accused had an honest means of living, he answered that he did, since he would not remain in the Party very long if he did not, because no member could acquire any wealth without a thorough investigation by the Party. The only party which can pay its members well is the Institutional Revolutionary Party, the official party that is supported by the government. When he had been paid as an officer of his Party, he had nearly died of hunger. Since the Mexican Communist Party is a legal party of Mexicans, it does not serve other governments, but acts only on decisions made by its members, who are Mexicans.

When he was asked if the Party had anything to do with the student disturbances of 1956, he replied that they were not disturbances but the just demands of the students. Moreover, the current strikes were provoked by the need for a collective contract given the economic conditions of the country. The government knew that if the railroad workers won, other workers would press their demands. That is why it repressed the unions and arrested their leaders.

Next he denied that the accused or the Communist Party had caused any damage to the railroad system, since the Party supports the protection of national properties and contends that higher fares should be charged Yankee companies that have been robbing the country and the government for years. Since the Communist Party is a legal party, the defendant's arrest was illegal since it was based on his political views and his membership in the Party and he had nothing to do with the railroad strike.

Although he continued to work on his mural on the Revolution in Chapultepec, Siqueiros was committed to exposing government repression and expressed his views on many occasions. Between January and March of 1960 he made seventeen presentations, not to mention numerous interviews in which he attacked the policy of the current administration. In May these speeches, press conferences, courtroom testimony and his "Open Letter" were published in a special edition of *Arte Público*. "The History of a Plot: Who Are the Traitors of the Country? My Reply" was addressed to all the patriots and enemies of the antidemocratic policies of the government and the partisans of the Mexican Revolution, as well as to the "liberal" supporters of the *neo-porfirista* and pro-imperialist policies of the last three presidencies. In its conclusion he denied that he had betrayed Mexico or the Revolution. "It is my accusers who have betrayed the Revolution and they hide behind the masks of patriots and revolutionaries."

When the Committee for the Freedom of Political Prisoners held its national congress in July, it drew up a series of demands: The punishment of the murderers of Román Guerra Montemayor; respect for democracy; the independence of the unions; the elimination of unconstitutional police forces; the immediate replacement of the Attorney General of the Republic; the end of government censorship and the repression of art and culture; the nonintervention of the police and the army in the educational institutions and respect for Article 129 of the Constitution, which prohibits the use of the army as a police force. The congress also made plans for a campaign of letters, petitions and appeals, including a day of activities focusing on the prisoners and the unconstitutionality of the crime of "social dissolution."

After the congress, Siqueiros and relatives of imprisoned workers met with the President of the Supreme Court and explained that the prisoners had already been in prison for 15 months without any trial and protested the unconstitutionality of Article 145 of the Penal Code. Although he replied that the Court could not abrogate laws or declare them unconstitutional, he promised to look into delays in the administration of justice. They left, therefore, with only a vague promise of a meeting with the President.

On another front, members of the National Teachers Union continued to press their demands for higher salaries and the independence of their union. During May they had suspended their classes and held a large outdoor meeting without government interference. When a second meeting was held in June, the leaders decided to stage a public demonstration by marching through the streets of the capital to the Zócalo.

On August 4, 1960, a large group of students, teachers and parents left the Teachers College and headed for the central plaza. Before they had advanced very far, they were stopped by the police and told to disperse because they did not have a permit for a demonstration. Meanwhile, more police, some mounted, surrounded and pressed down on the marchers, using clubs and sabers to break up the demonstration. When the protesters tried to regroup, the police used clubs, tear gas, riot guns and a water cannon to break their ranks. Those who tried to escape were pursued and dragged out of nearby homes and stores and beaten. Twenty-eight people were hospitalized and two hundred demonstrators were arrested.

Four days later Siqueiros held a press conference on behalf of the Committee for the Freedom of Political Prisoners. Although it had been arranged long before the teachers' demonstration, and was intended to publicize the activities of the committee, Siqueiros used the opportunity to charge that the students and teachers were the "victims of a premeditated aggression" and demanded that public authorities respect the right of assembly.

After informing reporters of the resolutions adopted by the National Congress in July, he charged that the government had not respected the constitutional rights of the working class and their political parties. Meanwhile, the National Congress will improve its efforts to free the prisoners and mobilize the masses, not only to free them, but also to obtain respect for the Constitution and to eliminate the crime of "social dissolution." Part of this effort, he announced, would be a day of activities focusing on the issue of the political prisoners, including a memorial watch throughout the country in honor of the murdered railroad worker, Ramon Guerra Montemayor, on the anniversary of his death. He then read the resolve of The National Congress to demand the return of the body to his widow, the punishment of the perpetrators, the abolition of the crime of social dissolution and the removal of the Attorney General. Henceforth, the committee must dedicate itself to publicizing the barbarous attack on the teachers and students by the government.

The next day Angélica drove David to Chapultepec, where he was working 12 to 14 hours a day on his mural on the Revolution in order to finish it in time for the November anniversary of the Revolution. When Angélica came to pick him up to drive him home for dinner, he was so preoccupied painting the faces of the socialist precursors of the Revolution that he did not see her waiting at the base of the scaffolding. Though she finally caught his attention and they were soon heading home in their Mercedes, he was still thinking about the mural.

As they neared their home on Tres Picos, Angélica noticed a government jeep and pointed it out to David. When she slowed down in front of the house, several men in peasant dress and straw hats leaped out and ran towards the car with pistols in their hands. Reacting quickly, Angélica accelerated the car, throwing several men to the side, and sped down the street. When another car drove into the center of the street, trying to block their escape, the driver killed his motor and Angélica steered around it.

Suddenly several shots rang out and looking back, Siqueiros saw several men running down the street firing pistols. Reaching into the glove compartment, he took out a .45 pistol and tried to return their fire. But Angélica made a sharp turn down a side street, destroying his aim but managing to evade their pursuers. Once they had put a safe distance between themselves and their attackers, they abandoned the car and took a taxi to the home of Dr. Carrillo Gil.

On the way, Siqueiros pondered what had happened. Was the attack an attempt on his life? Were they political enemies or government agents? If he was to be arrested, why did they not present themselves at Chapultepec where everyone knew he worked every day? With these thoughts running through his head, he decided to surrender to the police.

After they let the authorities know where they were, the police arrived later than night. Although they had no warrant for his arrest, they explained that the order came from "the top" and forced their way into the doctor's home. Recalling the events of the afternoon, David began to have second thoughts about his safety and considered the idea of flight. But when he checked out the exits, he found them blocked by high walls or saw what he thought were police agents stationed around the house. Resigned, he surrendered to the police, who explained apologetically, "What do you want us to do, Señor Siqueiros? This order comes from the top."

Fearing foul play, Dr. Carrillo Gil accompanied Siqueiros to the Inspection General of the Federal District Police. There Siqueiros was placed in a solitary cell while his friend went home. For the rest of the night, all of the next day, and part of the following night, Siqueiros was left alone in his small cell. Sometime early in the morning of the second day, while it was still dark, he was taken from his cell and paraded around through vacant corridors and rooms to what he thought was a room high in the building. Perhaps, he thought, they might throw him off the building and then report that he had tried to escape or commit suicide.

After they sat him down in the room, some other men arrived to question him. Since someone was taking notes as he talked, he jumped to the conclusion that they were going to have him sign a declaration before killing him and he refused to answer any more questions unless it took place in an appropriate time and place and demanded that they inform the Attorney General. When officials from the Attorney General's office did arrive, the interrogation process of the previous night was repeated and after several hours of questions and testimony, he was returned to his cell.

The day after he was apprehended, the government announced that Siqueiros had not been arrested but was being held for questioning and the outcome would depend on his answers regarding his responsibility for certain events. The delay, they explained, was because Siqueiros had not finished his declaration or answered all the questions put to him.

The next morning he was told that many people wanted to see him. Taken to another room, he found himself in front of a crowd of reporters and photographers who immediately began to ask questions and snap pictures. In his statement to the press, he admitted that he had used many methods to change the socioeconomic structure of Mexico but that the Mexican Communist Party prohibited the use of violence.

In response to questions, he admitted that he was a member of the Communist Party and had served on its politburo during the last two months. He denied any involvement with the Worker and Peasant Party whose members were traitors to the Party. As for the stoppage of work by the railroad workers and teachers, he supported them, even though it caused disorders, because it was the only way to achieve union democracy and independence. When he was asked about his association with Othón Salazar, the leader of the striking teachers, he admitted that he had dealt with Salazar as a member of the Committee for the Defense of Political Prisoners. He also admitted that he had never rejected completely the idea of an armed struggle and had praised the Cuban Revolution, even though communists had not made it.

Taking advantage of the presence of the fourth estate, he charged the government with using the communists, or the democratic elements, as bait to fish for loans from the United States. Later, while reflecting in prison, he realized that the Mexican government had been negotiating for loans and had demonstrated its anti-communist policy to the United States by arresting a prominent communist painter, and by repressing the workers' demands for increased wages.

Siqueiros was not the only one arrested in the latest roundup. During a police raid to seize issues of *La voz de Mexico*, the organ of the Communist Party, an old man working in the printing shop protested the illegal entry. When the police asked his name, they were incredulous when he replied, "Filomeno Mata." After checking with headquarters, the police not only seized the last edition of the paper but also arrested Mata, the 72-year-old son of the famous journalist who had defied Diaz and the editor of *Liberación*, the paper of the Committee for the Freedom of Political Prisoners. Like Siqueiros, he was placed in an isolated cell and kept incommunicado until their arraignment several days later.

The disorders they were accused of fomenting, however, did not end with their arrest. While some police were tracking down the whereabouts of Siqueiros, others had been busy breaking up a demonstration by eight hundred student teachers near the Zócalo in which two students were shot and five policemen were injured. Later the police accused Siqueiros of speaking at the college just before this demonstration, which had been banned by the police. A few days after this demonstration, someone tried to blow up the statue of former President Aleman on the campus of the National University. It was not the first attack on the statue and the suspects ranged from anti-alemanistas to anti-communists, who said that it looked like Joseph Stalin, to aesthetes who just found it "ugly."

Mata and Siqueiros were kept in their separate cells until August 13 when they were transferred to the Preventive Prison of the Federal District, formerly the "black palace" of Lecumberri, already familiar to Siqueiros. There the accused exchanged their street clothes, which they had worn since their arrest, for the blue pants and shirt of the prisoners. After being fingerprinted and photographed from the front and side, the 72-year-old journalist and 64-year old artist were conducted to cells in different sections of the prison.

Three days later, in the presence of their families and police officials, they were formally charged with nine violations of the Penal Code. The charges included the crime of social dissolution, dangerous assault, possession of an illegal weapon without a permit, damage to property and resistance to public authorities. Although three of the charges were dismissed, they were accused of having contributed to the commission of other criminal acts since the all-encompassing provisions of Article 145 of the Penal Code not only applied to specific acts, but also to anyone who incited others to commit acts of sabotage, subvert the national life or to cause disorders which affected national order and public peace. Thus, even though they had not participated directly in any of the events which threatened "national order," they could be found guilty as "the intellectual authors" of such acts.

They were also accused of having conducted political propaganda against the government at home and abroad and with espousing the ideas of a foreign power that disturbed the public order and the sovereignty of the Mexican state. Despite their appeal, the judge ruled that they were to remain in prison while the case was being prosecuted.

When it came time for his statement, David attributed his arrest to his espousal of communism, which was political, and he denied that he had participated in the preparation for or the carrying out of any of the demonstrations. "I did not participate," he stated flatly, "because I am not a member" and each of these organizations has their own leaders who are capable of organizing their own protests. Moreover, he continued, there is no evidence that I was present or a speaker at any of the meetings or was present when the demonstration occurred. For a year I have been working 10 hours a day on my mural in Chapultepec and I have not thrown a rock or any other object.

After explaining that the rules of the Communist Party prohibited the use of violence, he attacked the government for following Yankee advice and violating the constitution by attacking the printers and publishing houses and by preventing the circulation of the Communist Party paper. When he was shown some pamphlets, he denied that he had written any of them, but he did share their convictions and would accept them as his own. He also asked the judge to prevent the violations of his own rights since he had been kept incommunicado and without any food except a cup of coffee since his arrest.

After the arraignment, David turned to Angélica and Adriana and asked about "Davidcito," his grandson. When he asked if they could bring him to visit him in prison, they promised to bring him the next day. Just before they led him away, he told them not to worry and disappeared down the long dark corridors of Lecumberri.

On the outside Angélica was busy organizing her husband's defense, protesting his detention and rallying support for his release. The morning after his arrest, she called the press and described the events of the preceding day and night, pointing to the punctured rear tire of their car as evidence of the shots fired at them. Her husband's arrest, she charged, was illegal and had been politically motivated. Some reporters were skeptical, however, and wrote that none of the neighbors had heard any shots and no spent cartridges or bullet holes had been found.

In order to publicize the plight of her husband, as well as to counter the generally unsympathetic and pro-government accounts in the major papers, Angélica mounted and directed a campaign of letters, petitions and articles. Through the Cuban news service she sent an appeal to Pablo Picasso, which was reprinted in papers throughout Europe. She also wrote and published a letter to the President in which she emphasized the valuable services which Siqueiros had performed for his country and the hardships which he had endured in the past.

Despite a silent rebuff from the government, the response from other sectors was immediate and was not limited by social class or national boundaries. In the United States Ben Shahn and Alexander Calder headed a committee which issued a press release supporting Siqueiros signed by 90 important artists, architects and cultural figures and sent a delegation to Mexico to investigate and defend Siqueiros. In Japan a million and a half people signed a petition for his release and in France, Picasso headed a committee of artists working for his freedom. Newspapers and magazines in the United States and England carried signed letters or articles criticizing the government of Mexico and demanding that it drop the charges against the painter.

After visiting Siqueiros in prison, Pablo Neruda wrote a poem to him that compared his imprisoned painting to imprisoning a flash of lightening and ended with, "Mexico is also a prisoner with you." In

Cuba, poet Nicolás Guillén paid tribute to Siqueiros in a poem that instructed the people not to forget the artist whose painting, like him, is "violent, enormous and pure." From Argentina came a poem by Rafael Alberti, "To the Mexican Painter David Alfaro Siqueiros, In Prison." He also received thousands of cards and drawings from elementary school children in the People's Democratic Republic of Germany.

In Mexico there was an immediate reaction to the arrest of Mata and Siqueiros. The day after their detention, the Communist Party issued a bulletin attacking the government. Members of the National Front for the Plastic Arts protested the arrest of one of their members and petitioned the President for his release. A Committee of Artists and Intellectuals for the Liberation of David Alfaro Siqueiros was organized and Angélica coordinated its efforts to free her husband. In an unprecedented display of solidarity, seventy-nine Mexican artists of different aesthetic and political persuasions also joined in a boycott of the Second Pan-American Biennial in Mexico to protest his arrest and the censorship of his mural in the actors' union.

Not all artists were supportive, however. At first Juan O'Gorman refused to cooperate, pointing out that "Siqueiros asked for it," but he later joined other artists in a gesture of support for him. In France and the United States, some artists and writers refused to sign a petition which compared Siqueiros to Van Gogh, Michelangelo and Goya, either because they resented the comparison, or remembered that Siqueiros had resorted to violence in the past and had never been convicted for his attack on Trotsky and the death of Robert Sheldon Harte. They also pointed out that he was able to paint in prison and was receiving excellent prices for his prison paintings.

Besides conducting a political campaign for David's release, Angélica was also active in his legal defense. Although originally represented by a fellow Marxist, Siqueiros appointed a prominent lawyer, José Rojo Coronado, as his attorney and named Angélica, Adriana and her husband to his defense team so that he could see them during the trial. They were also aided in the judicial process by Enrique Ortega Arenas, an attorney who provided free legal assistance throughout the judicial process and printed pamphlets on the government's violation of the constitution at his own expense.

Although they hoped that the charges would be dropped or he would receive a presidential pardon, they decided to apply for *amparo*, a type of writ or injunction which protects citizens from illegal arrest or violations of their constitutional rights by the government. But the magistrates postponed hearings for the flimsiest excuses and imposed bureaucratic regulations to prevent a speedy resolution of the case. As months passed by, they remained in prison.

When he and Mata were brought before the judge handling the case, they flatly denied any complicity in the events, either as inciters or instigators of the "illegal" demonstrations. As the case dragged on, the accused became increasingly fearful that the government would be able to justify their imprisonment by pointing out that one judge had arraigned them and that three other judicial officials had confirmed his decision.

In spite of the delays and the isolation and deprivations of prison, Siqueiros managed to keep his hopes up and immersed himself in prison activities. When other prisoners asked him to design sets for the prison theater, he welcomed the opportunity and painted a folding screen of three sections for a play by a fellow prisoner. It was a satire on a cheating lawyer who took everything his client owned, including his wife, and Siqueiros painted scenes of him going to prison, his dream of liberty, his suffering family, his wife kissing the attorney and the lawyer's transformation into a thief.

Although he offered his opinions on the political content of the plays written and performed by the prisoners, Siqueiros realized that his suggestions were always subject to the approval of the Prison Director. But he also felt that they had more freedom to express their opinions on the President and his policies than was permitted outside of prison. It was the judge of their case who was their real master, he concluded, not the Director of the prison or the guards.

After attending a play performed by other prisoners, he decided to write his own play, a farce called "Troglodita" (Cave Dwellers). Directed at López Mateos, it featured a demagogue who makes speeches about the greatness of Mexico and repeats the phrase, "extreme left within the Constitution, center, not left, but the sensible left." In the legislature, the members' eyes are closed, their ears plugged and their mouths gagged, while they worship the leader who rambles on about the greatness of Mexico in the future while he repeats the phrase "extreme left within the Constitution." When another leader emerges, a few of the legislators dance around him as their choice for supreme leader. In spite of their greater freedom in prison, "Troglodita" was never staged.

When Mexican Independence Day approached, he painted a large cartoon of a locomotive on which "Liberty" was printed in large letters and the tracks were strewn with obstacles that read, "Violations of the constitutional rights of Mexicans by orders from Washington." Placed at the end of the prison corridor on September 16, the next morning it had disappeared.

In November, just as an exhibition of his paintings was opening at the University of Veracruz, David joined Mata, Valentín Campa, Demetrio Vallejo, Encarnación Pérez and other political prisoners in a hunger strike to protest the delays in their cases, the denial of "amparo" and the false charges against them. After six days, they called off the strike, claiming victory when a judge granted the appeal of ten prisoners. While it was a partial victory, most of them remained in prison and their cases continued to drag on without resolution.

Meanwhile, the Siqueiros's cell became an office to help other prisoners. With the assistance of a young lawyer in prison, David helped them prepare their cases or petitions to the Director of the Prison. He also protested the exploitation of the younger inmates by the older and wealthier prisoners.

Not along after his transfer to Lecumberri, Siqueiros had asked to be treated by his physician for a gall bladder problem for which he had been suffering for many years. The judge, however, denied his request, insisting that the prison doctors and facilities were adequate. He was also having some problems with his teeth and he requested to see his dentist as well as his doctor. Several months later, his requests were granted, but when they discovered that the x-ray machine and forceps needed to remove his teeth were not available, Siqueiros had to make special arrangements at his own expense. Using his own case as an example, he pleaded with the prison officials, challenging their professional honor and insisting on the purchase of adequate medical equipment and treatment for all prisoners.

Since the prisoners had to arrange for their own food, Angélica brought him food every day, often accompanied by her grandson "Davidcito." When he and Mata were assigned to the same corridor, she also brought food for him and another inmate. On Sundays the Mata family supplied the food for a "picnic" of the combined families, while the other prisoner provided fresh eggs every morning from the hens he kept in prison.

Although he was also allowed to receive visits from close friends, foreign artists visiting Mexico and reporters, the walls and the daily routine of prison life were suffocating for someone of his temperament. Every day started the same, with the prisoners rising early and preparing their own breakfasts and then cleaning up their cells before they started their jobs or other activities. Even though he worked out an arrangement with other prisoners for some of these chores, the process was time-consuming and left him little time for other activities, especially art, and all activity ceased when the lights were turned off at ten o'clock. On the outside, all of his basic needs were taken care of by Angélica, their servants or his assistants and he could devote himself entirely to his art or political activities.

Despite these inconveniences, David devised ways of overcoming the boredom and frustrations of prison life. After washing in the morning, he would imagine that he was free and walking the streets of Mexico, only to be rudely awakened by the realization that he was still in prison. With another inmate, who had killed his young lover because she had mocked his age and impotence, he would pretend to be walking down the Reforma from Chapultepec towards the Zócalo, flirting with pretty women, insulting the President or shouting obscenities at the driver of a speeding car. Sometimes their strolls took them into the mountains or to a faraway beach, at least in their imaginations. More than just a momentary escape, it was a way of demonstrating that he was stronger than the walls that surrounded him.

Escape was not always so easy, however. In prison, the routine is resented, but when it is broken, it creates a terrible anxiety among the prisoners. Any change is dreaded and exaggerated into a major disaster. Siqueiros was no exception and when Angélica did not arrive at her customary time one day, he paced back and forth and kept looking at his watch. Where is she, he worried, what could have happened to her, why hasn't she arrived yet?

He also used his time in prison to take up his favorite pastime, baseball, buying the uniforms and equipment for the prison team and occasionally playing second base. In the evenings he frequently attended the "Lepe Theater" in the cell of a prisoner with a large television set, bringing an old stool of Angélica's as his seat. On other nights he returned to his cell and read or painted until ten o'clock when the lights were turned off. As the silence of the night closed in, interrupted only by muffled sounds from other cells, David stared into the dark and wondered how many more days and nights he would be imprisoned behind these walls.

XVII. Prison

Locked up in Lecumberri, Siqueiros once again turned to easel painting. During the day and until the lights went out at ten, he painted in his cell, a small room whose walls he could touch with his arms extended. The only light was provided by a single barred window and a light bulb hanging from a cord. When he requested the use of another cell for painting, he was told that every prisoner was entitled to his own cell and there were no exceptions.

He also had to live, eat and sleep amid the toxic vapors of synthetic paints and thinners, and he complained that the fumes affected his liver and kept him in a foul mood. One day, after spilling paint on a blanket, he dashed his furniture against the wall and hurled insults at his unsuspecting neighbors. When one of them retaliated with a personal insult, he stormed out of his cell and fiercely chastised his attacker. Shocked by the fury of his attack, other inmates tried to calm him down. Fortunately for everyone, he was given permission to paint in a vacant cell.

The walls were not his only prison, however. While he dreamed of murals, he was restricted to small canvases or sheets of wood and working from memory. Drawing upon previous subjects or experiences, he painted maternity, a mother and child against a barren landscape, a revolutionary soldier or a self-portrait. Using his imagination and memory to break down the prison walls and recreate the world beyond, he painted landscapes, flowering trees and bunches of flowers. Although many of them were monumental or epic, they were not murals, his first love.

One night, while he was lying awake, he imagined the walls of his cell transformed into a huge mural filled with masses of humanity. In the morning he transformed his fantasy into a small painting in which he is sitting on the floor of the cell, contemplating the swirling figures painted on the walls and ceiling. Besides describing his imprisonment, *Solitary Confinement* expressed his frustration with easel painting and his escape from that reality by designing an imaginary mural. It was the genesis of his most ambitious mural.

Although he was in prison, charged with "subversion," he received a commission from the National Academy to paint a portrait of Alfonso Reyes, noted Mexican scholar, writer and diplomat and a founder of the Academy. Working from photographs, he painted a cheerful portrait of the late Reyes, his arms folded in front of him and his beaming face filling the painting. While it depicted the positive qualities of Reyes, it also suggested Siqueiros's resiliency and determination to overcome his current predicament.

However, when he painted a portrait of himself, it lacked the defiant confidence of earlier self-portraits. Though painted spontaneously and freely, it is brooding and conveys the inner turmoil and changing moods of the prisoner, as well as his advancing age.

Increasingly sensitive to the misery and suffering around him, and more convinced than ever of the failures of the Revolution and the hypocrisy of a government which called itself "revolutionary," he expressed this anguish, poverty and social injustice in his art. In *Enough* he painted a grief stricken mother grasping the lifeless body of her child to her, while in *Fleeing from Terror*, he painted a terrorized mother and child in flight. In *Mother, Father, the Government and Their Little Scorpions* he painted a mother carrying her baby while other naked children implore her for food. But there is no father or government in sight.

On the first day of the hunger strike, he painted several pictures of the innocent victims of the penal system. In one, a pregnant mother stands by the prison gates, holding one child while another pulls at her skirt. From the surface of another emerges the face of a girl, her mouth contorted in pain, her hair standing up in spikes and her eyes full of terror. In *The Executioner* he created a shrouded head grasped by the hands of the executioner. Though faceless, the gripping hands vividly express the anguish and despair.

In *The Black Race Moving Upward* he painted three strong black women carrying their children up the side of a mountain. Although they are fleeing from some disaster or persecution, there is a sense of hope or liberation. When he painted a grandmother holding and comforting a child, he captured the tenderness of the moment and a sense of sorrow in their granite-like faces.

Turning futuristic, he developed an imaginary *Post Atomic Era Landscape* in which the earth is burnt, as if fused by fire, but there is no one left to appreciate its beauty. In a more positive view of atomic energy, he painted an archaeological dig in which nuclear technology has uncovered civilizations of the distant past whose architectural forms are unknown to contemporary man. He was also creating other landscapes, either from memory or as seen from an airplane or imaginary spaceship.

In March of 1961 there was a conference in Mexico on "National Sovereignty, Economic Emancipation and Peace in Latin America." Along with 26 other political prisoners, David drafted and signed a statement to be read at the conference. He also contributed a painting, *The Struggle for the Emancipation of Latin America*, in which the masses threaten to overwhelm a group of soldiers in helmets painted in sinister grays and blacks. Although less than one square meter, the surface is filled with human figures, united in their final struggle against imperialism.

Later that year Nehru visited Mexico. Since he was unable to paint the Prime Minister's portrait, David painted a group of women carrying children across a flat and barren landscape on a sheet of plywood. When it was finished, he signed it at the bottom, "Siqueiros, Preventive Prison, November 15, 1961" and on the back he printed, "To Nehru on his visit to Mexico" and below his own name he wrote in quotations, "But does anyone know–themselves–where we go? Path without Direction."

The paint was barely dry when a committee of artists and writers presented the painting to Nehru. Several days later a paid announcement appeared in several Mexico City newspapers with a reproduction of the painting and a brief statement signed by

Angélica and his brother Jesús. It could only happen in Mexico. A political prisoner paints a picture for a visiting head of state and its presentation is used to publicize the plight of political prisoners in Mexico. Meanwhile, the government also gave its honored guests a book with reproductions of Siqueiros's murals.

In 1961 the National University published the first major study devoted exclusively to Siqueiros and his art. Although *Siqueiros: Introductor de los realidades* (Siqueiros: Introducer of Realities) had been finished by Raquel Tibol before his imprisonment, it was not published until 1961. Through the University, therefore, the government had published a monograph on his achievements as an artist. Later that year, the National Museum of Modern Art sponsored an exhibit of contemporary Mexican portraiture which featured seven portraits by Siqueiros, including his most recent self-portrait, painted, signed and dated in the federal prison.

David continued to sign and date his paintings from the Preventive Prison, alternating between the full "Carcel Preventiva," the initials "C.P.," "Celda 26" for the cell in which he painted, or just "Lecumberri." While reminding the public of his whereabouts, it did not hurt sales and his arrest and the protests for his release increased the market for his prison paintings. The fact that they were painted in prison, or might be his last, undoubtedly increased their value and Angelica was able to peddle them for two to three thousand dollars each as fast as he could paint them. Ironically, the buyers were members of the new bourgeoisie, the social class which he had accused of betraying the Revolution, repressing Mexican workers and selling out to North American interests.

Although he yearned to paint murals, he was earning more money in prison than he had ever received for any of his murals, some of which had cost him dearly, and this was the most lucrative period of his career to date. While he had nowhere to go or anywhere to spend his money, he was able to cover his legal expenses and support Angélica and her family while he was in prison. He was also supporting Jésus and his family, giving his brother paintings to sell when Angélica was not looking.

In December, 1961 David celebrated his sixty-fifth birthday in prison. To commemorate the occasion, Mexican writers, scholars and fellow artists wrote poems and notes to or about him which were printed in an issue of *Nueva Presencia*, a magazine-poster published by a new generation of Mexican artists. Arturo García Bustos declared that "Siqueiros is truly a modern artist" while Francisco Icaza noted that no prison could deprive Siqueiros of his stature as "one of the most important figures of this century." Arnold Belkin, a Canadian artist living in Mexico, wrote that no other painter had been as original or contributed as much in technical materials and composition. José Luis Cuevas pointed out that while he had questioned Siqueiros's antics, he admired and defended him with the same passion. Chávez Morado described him as "a caged eagle," while novelist Carlos Fuentes wrote that it was "Miguel Angel, Rembrandt, Goya and Van Gogh they had imprisoned, the other names of Siqueiros."

Meanwhile, in New York, an "Artists Committee to Free Siqueiros" sponsored a show of his prints and paintings on loan from collectors and the Museum of Modern Art. At the opening more than 500 guests signed a petition to President López Mateos that was given to the Mexican Ambassador in Washington.

In spite of the protests, the case against Mata and Siqueiros dragged on and the accused remained in prison. In May of 1961, a petition for *amparo* was submitted, but it was not until August, one year after their arrest, that they were granted an *amparo* against the objective crimes of "dangerous attack," "carrying prohibited weapons" and "injury to property." However, the charges of "social dissolution" and "resistance to authorities" were not dismissed. When they asked to be told in what way or form they had committed these acts, the judge refused to respond and referred the case to another hearing, to be held in September.

After more postponements, the Fifth Penal Court set the date for the formal hearing and the pronouncing of sentence. On January 18, 1962 the accused were taken from their cells to a small room which could barely accommodate the defendants, their attorneys, their families, a few police agents and the magistrates. Police surrounded it and there was no room for the press or the public. After reading the indictment against the prisoners, the judges explained that the crime of social dissolution applied to anyone who contradicts or disagrees with the programs or standards of the constituted government.

After attacking these charges point by point, the defense argued that the government had not made a single legal case, even within the elastic provisions of Article 145 of the Penal Code. In his statement to the court, Filomeno Mata pointed out that he had been arrested arbitrarily and held for 18 months for crimes that no one had proven that he had committed. Therefore the government should not only pardon him, but also release him without any restrictions on his profession of journalism.

When Mata had finished, Siqueiros began to speak. Standing erect and speaking in a firm voice, he gave a detailed summary of his life, beginning with his enlistment in the army of the Revolution and emphasizing the periods when the government had contradicted its promises or violated the goals of the Revolution. Stunned by his attack on the government and them as its accomplices, the judges, who had almost fallen asleep during the readings of the charges against the accused, now sat up and listened.

After describing the events in which he had participated to carry out the goals of the Revolution and the provisions of the Constitution of 1917, Siqueiros described his arrest, the illegal entry into the home of Dr. Carrillo Gil, the lack of a judicial order and the officers' explanation that the orders had come "from the top."

"We are political prisoners," he declared, and we are here for acts that we did not commit or for acts which are legal and justified. The "education workers" are only fighting for the autonomy of their organizations and we have not participated in their discussions or their preparations for demonstrations because we have not had the time, not because we disagreed. After four hours, he concluded, warning the court that its decision would determine the course of the people's struggle against the antidemocratic and Nazi procedures in our country.

Although the reading of the charges and the hearing of the testimony by the accused had consumed thirteen hours, neither the trial itself nor the statements by the accused received much publicity. Angélica, therefore, published a pamphlet that included his statement before the court as proof of his fifty-year struggle to defend and carry out the Constitution and compared the current regime to that of Porfirio Diaz. His application for *amparo* was also published, preceded by a quotation by a Mexican liberal that the worst injustices are those committed in the name of justice by those sworn to uphold it.

On March 10, 1962, twenty months after their arrest, Siqueiros and Mata were taken to the courtroom to hear the decision of the court. Standing before the rail, they listened while the Secretary of the Court read the resolution of the Fifth Penal Court. After recognizing their advanced age, as well as their defiant attitude, the court sentenced them to eight years in prison, including the time they had already served, and a fine of two thousand pesos each for the crimes of social dissolution, individual resistance, influencing others to resist and causing injuries to police agents.

Although they declared that they would not appeal their sentence because they had no faith in Mexican justice, an appeal was initiated by the court. This process, however, dragged on and despite appeals by the accused and protests for their release or pardon at home and abroad, they remained in prison. When he was asked about the possibility of a presidential pardon, Siqueiros replied, "I suppose that the President will have to consult with the United States before acting."

While their arrests had sparked a protest, there was an even greater outcry when their sentences were announced. Again Angélica directed the campaign to have the sentence appealed or to obtain a presidential pardon, while art critic Raquel Tibol traveled to Europe to enlist the support of artists and writers for the release of Siqueiros. In May Angélica published a letter she had written to López Mateos, reminding him of the contributions that Siqueiros had made to the country and the hardships that he had endured in performing these services.

In another letter she described Siqueiros and Mata as the victims of a political inquisition, an anti-communist policy adopted by the government following the recent Inter-American Conference at Punta del Este. Since they were not involved in the events for which they are accused and because of their stature, she warned, it would be counterproductive for the government. It is an insult that the judges have been commended for being magnanimous for only sentencing them to eight years because of their age. What can the other political prisoners hope for since some of them are only 50 years old? she asked.

Angélica then promised that she would continue to fight for the freedom of her companion and other political prisoners, just as her father had fought the despotic forces of yesterday, which today control the government of Mexico, the union movement and the press. "I will fight, but not alone, for the constitutional guarantees for which millions of Mexicans have fought," she vowed.

While Angélica was busy organizing the campaign to free him, Siqueiros continued to paint, participate in prison activities, issue statements and write letters. In spite of the conditions, life in prison had some advantages, especially for his work. There were no phone calls, no one trying to sell something, no interviews and he could paint without fear of interruption, not even by Angélica.

When the General Assembly of the International Association of Art Critics met in Mexico in 1962, he sent a letter to the delegates, reminding them of the Mexican mural movement, "the only important muralist experience of our time." While there are individual mural painters in other countries, he continued, no other country has had a collective movement. Our art is public and speaks a different social language in a unique style and form and you should use the opportunity to appreciate and judge this art form. Do not take "refuge in a study of archaeology or the art of the commercial galleries."

The following year he wrote an open letter to the meetings of the International Congress of Philosophy in Mexico City, in which he suggested that it would be an opportune time to discuss the controversy between art of a social and political content and art for the sake of art. He reminded the delegates that human content, philosophical discourse and social function had provided the point of departure for our art, whereas Europe had removed philosophical content from art after the Renaissance. After encouraging them to visit the murals in Mexico, he reminded the delegates that he was writing from Corridor "I" of the Preventive Prison, where he has been a prisoner three years and a month, accused of "The Crime of Opinion (Social Dissolution in Mexico)."

Prison also gave him time for other activities. Although the journalist Julio Scherer García had tried to arrange interviews with him, he had always been too busy. After his imprisonment, however, he agreed to a series of interviews and while Scherer García took notes on his typewriter, Siqueiros told stories about his childhood, family members, the Revolution, travels in Europe and South America, political activities in Mexico, his views of other artists and his experiences in prison.

He was fond of telling these stories, spicing them with jokes and double-entendres and recalling details or dates without hesitation. While he told many of them over and over again, each time he added a detail, comment or expression that enriched the story. He was also an actor who needed only one other person to perform, immersing himself totally in the role and using dramatic gestures to convince his audience. After observing him in his cell, Scherer García wrote that he told these stories with a theatrical flair and in a grandiloquent manner, as if he were speaking to a full auditorium rather than a lone journalist.

When Siqueiros read Scherer García's description of his performances, however, he objected strongly, telling the journalist to tell the truth and explain why he shouted or protested the arrest of the railroad workers, who have been held without trial for four and a half years. He also told Scherer García that describing him without mentioning his political activities was like describing a tree by concentrating on its little flowers. "Strip the bark, open it, see the sap trickle, look at that which is truly a tree, at its trunk, its roots and do not concern yourself so much with the flowers."

These stories, published in *Siqueiros: la piel and la entraña* (Skin and Entrails), not only provide information on persons and events in his life, but also offer insight into his personality and character. They reveal the image that he wanted to create or reinforce and suggest some obvious conclusions regarding his personality. His frequent descriptions of executions and carousing during the Revolution, while not exaggerating his role in these events, nevertheless suggest an attempt to demonstrate bravura, or to appear "macho" in the Mexican style. They also reflect his obvious pride in being Mexican and having fought in the Revolution.

Likewise, his descriptions of his childhood, especially under the tutorship of *Siete Filhos*, reinforce the image of a rebellious youth who was nurtured to endure hardship without flinching, to defend himself and to strike back twofold. The accounts that he told of his rebellions at home and in school leave the impression of a maverick, contemptuous of routine or tradition, but also someone who enjoyed the notoriety of being defiant or different.

Although many of his paintings and murals depict the pain and anguish of the victims of modern war, few of the stories he told reveal the misery and suffering of civilians or combatants. Many of his descriptions of tragic events or victims appear hard, cold or matter-of-fact, though there are some moments of tenderness and expressions of empathy.

When he described his experiences in prison, he frequently commented on the human tragedies he observed. On Sundays, it was not uncommon to see a barefoot mother with seven children come to prison to eat better food, shared by the other families, than they had eaten all week. A substantial number of inmates, he knew, returned to prison in order to feed themselves and enjoy the better clothing, food and shelter.

When Scherer y García wrote that he appeared to be disheartened, Siqueiros protested vehemently that he had never been disheartened, that prison for a political prisoner was a field of battle. "If they give me one blow, I will answer with five." Although he admitted that he was frustrated because he could not paint murals, he would not admit defeat and appeared to be content and proud of what he had done with his life.

Besides the theatrical manner in which he told these stories, they are full of incredible detail and vivid descriptions of people, places and events gleaned from a prodigious memory. They also reveal his delight in creating double-entendres as he talked and his appreciation of the ironies of life that he observed around him. There are humorous digressions or expressions and even in the worst of conditions, he could appreciate the humor and irony of his own predicament or the human condition. Aware of the paradoxes or contradictions of his own life, he commented frequently on being revered by the very people and the system he was attacking or on the other hand, were harassing him. Only in Mexico could he be reviled and respected at the same time. Even when he was in jail, he bragged of the unique provisions of Mexican prisons.

He was intrigued by national characteristics and regional differences within Mexico and he imitated the dialect or accent of his characters. When he spoke about Argentines, therefore, he spoke in the Spanish dialect of the *porteños*, the residents of the Buenos Aires. He remembered fondly the nicknames which the prisoners gave to each other, usually very descriptive and emphasizing an unflattering characteristic or physical feature.

When the subject turned to art or politics, he resorted to analogies in order to clarify his basic thesis, drawing his examples or comparisons from history. Or he would use examples from his own experiences to illustrate a point. Frequently there was a statement about the Mexican Revolution, the significance of Mexican Mural Movement, the uniqueness of Mexico or the peculiarities of human behavior.

Although he was proud of his participation in the Revolution, he also expressed doubts about it. After weighing its achievements against the loss of more than a million lives, he concluded that it could not have been more catastrophic. Although the slogans of Madero had been "effective suffrage" and "no reelection," every President since Madero had violated them and one party perpetuates itself and the campaigns were a farce. It started with Cárdenas when he chose Ávila Camacho as his successor instead of General Múgica, whom the revolutionary left supported. Even now, he charged, the *cardenistas* remain in the government, a government which calls itself "extreme left within the Constitution" while it represses the railroad workers.

Just when I had dedicated myself to muralism and developed "my definitive style, a freer, more developed and more integral modern realism," the government's attacks on the railroad workers compelled me to return to politics, he said. I had discovered my more advanced style in the Jorge Negrete Theater and the Medical Center and then I realized that all my previous efforts, at times "excessively cold," now provided the solution.

But he also worried that he might leave prison without any interest in painting or having lost what he had achieved? Even if he returned to painting, how could he paint murals for a government which is a dictatorship of the center, the worst type of government because it distracts the people from finding solutions to their problems, he pondered. How could he continue his interpretation of the reality of Mexico in the actors' union or carry on the ideological development of the Revolution in Chapultepec under this government, especially when they try to ignore all the truly revolutionary and proletarian precursors of the Revolution in favor of the representatives of the bourgeoisie, like Madero and Carranza?

Rejecting such negative thoughts, he reminded himself that he was either a "muralist painter or I am not a painter" and that he must give battle to those who have repressed the railroad workers and kept their leaders in prison for two and a half years. What better way to demonstrate that the government is allied with Washington, he thought, then to break the railroad workers' strike and accuse the Soviet Embassy of giving a million pesos to Demetrio Vallejo. All they can think of is to ingratiate themselves with the North American monopolies in order to receive a few small loans or the rewards of tourism. My first duty as a man, citizen or artist, he vowed, is to contribute to the political transformation of Mexico.

Some of his worst fears were confirmed by news on the fate of his mural *Cuauhtémoc Against the Myth*. Painted in the vestibule of his mother-in-law's home, it was now threatened with destruction. After trying to sell the house to the government, the Arenals sold it to Villasenor, a banker and collector of art who assured them that he would protect the mural. But the new tenants converted it into a place for men to meet their mistresses and the mural became the target of numerous jokes when photographs of couples embracing on a sofa beneath it appeared in the tabloids.

Villasenor, therefore, decided to sell the building, but before putting it on the market, he notified Angélica and they tried to arrange the purchase of the mural by the Ministry of Public Education. Realizing that its removal and restoration would be expensive, they offered to give it to the government if the appropriate institutions would send their technicians to arrange for its removal. The government, however, was not interested and the mural was almost destroyed by the carpenters who dismantled it, while the two sculptures were sold to a private gallery.

The National Front of Public Artists immediately protested that they have not only imprisoned Siqueiros, they also destroy his murals. From prison David wrote a letter to the Director of the Institute of Fine Arts, protesting its failure to protect his mural. Citing past experiences, he asked how could a government which claims that muralism was a major achievement of the Revolution and has classified paintings by Orozco and Rivera as national treasures which cannot be taken out of the country, refuse to prevent the destruction of my mural which has been offered free to the government.

Although the government later arranged for the reconstruction and restoration of *Cuauhtémoc Against the Myth* in the chapel of a former monastery in Mexico City under the direction of Luis Arenal, the incident was another source of aggravation for the penned-up artist and confirmed his charges that the government had abandoned the Revolution and its artists.

Despite these distractions, David continued to paint and these years were the most prolific in terms of easel paintings. Although he told Scherer García that his real prison was not the walls of his cell, but the small dimensions of the panels on which he painted, he was creating mural-like paintings with a monumental effect. By recreating his dreams and memories and filling up the picture plane with crowds of people, blossoming trees, bunches of flowers, vast panoramas of nature and figures of Christ, he not only transcended the picture plane, but also his surroundings.

Freed from the objective constraints of reality, he developed a freer, more spontaneous and more expressive style. Prison was a place for dreaming, he said, and even after the lights were turned out, he would lie awake on his cot and imagine the walls of his cell covered with murals. Lacking models or scenery to paint, therefore, he worked from memory or recreated the images from his nighttime fantasies, uninhibited by realistic detail. The result was a series of paintings or mural studies, drawn freely, like sketches and bordering on the abstract.

While he had developed a lighter and more spontaneous style in recent murals and pre-prison paintings, he had never painted so much over a long period of time and he experimented with his technique and style. With practice, came confidence and his control of the medium and brush strokes were more assured, more definite and less labored. His depictions of maternity became lighter, less sculptural and less encrusted with paint. The rich textures and heavy impasto began to yield to more economical brush strokes and a lighter style that created a more dramatic sense of movement. At the same time, some of the landscapes and the figures in them are barely distinguishable and only hint at reality.

His new style also demonstrated his belabored thesis that the tools and the form of art determine the style. Since he was now painting with delicate brushes on small pieces of wood instead of working on large walls or ceilings with an airbrush, his style necessarily changed. The subject matter and the tone also changed, he explained, since an easel painting is for a home, a place of peaceful contemplation, whereas a mural is a "discourse, a proclamation or a sermon" to be viewed by the masses in a public place. Many of his canvases, however, were anything but peaceful and could preach as well as disturb.

In the spring of 1963, David pondered what to give Angélica on her saint's day. He thought of painting a picture of her grandson Davidcito, of whom he had already made a number of sketches. Instead, he decided to paint some "living flowers," that is, uncut and living where they had been planted. When Angélica came to prison, he presented her with a painting of red and white flowers and apologized for not being able to give her the real thing. On it he had written, "Angelica, on your day, for our cause."

A month later he gave her another painting of a "Window of Flowers" on which he wrote, "For you Angélica, with all my love, on this anniversary of your life. Siqueiros, *Carcel Preventiva*." On the back he explained that only an artist could give flowers without killing them. Several months later he painted "a structural portrait" of himself holding his grandson and gave it to Adriana on her saint's day.

He also painted a number of bright and colorful pictures of flowers and flowering trees, bushes and cacti, unique to specific regions of Mexico and painted from memory. While the plants and their flowers dominated, he painted large groups of human figures at the base of the trees, dwarfed by the much larger forms of nature. In *The Tree of the Sad Night*, the legendary tree at the foot of which Cortés and his men recovered after their rout by the Aztecs, he painted a burned out tree surrounded by small white figures carrying lances, ghosts of the past. *The Blue Fig Tree* depicts a white tree trunk topped with bright red flowers, at the foot of which a crowd is suggested by streaks and dots of color.

From an uncharacteristic source came another inspiration. After a wealthy collector contacted Angélica and asked her to have him paint a picture of Christ, he accepted the commission. In a few days, using a small burnished statue of Christ and drawing upon his memory of the crucifixes and religious paintings he had seen as a child, he painted the head of a Mexican Christ. Angélica liked it, however, and convinced him to let her keep it.

As a replacement, therefore, he painted a *Mutilated Christ*, a figure without legs and suspended from above, on which he wrote that first his enemies crucified him, then his friends mutilated him at the end of the Middle Ages and today, after the Ecumenical Councils, his new friends were trying to restore him under the pressure of communism and it is to them that this small work is dedicated.

In another painting of Christ, *The Defeated Redeemer*, he painted a dejected and mutilated Christ, his hands cut off at the wrist, head bowed in defeat. Later he explained that He bears the weight of the crisis in which his doctrine of "peace on earth" has been buried by two thousand years of war, each one more devastating than the previous one. He also painted a *Black Christ* with bowed head and blood pouring from his wounds. It is a Mexican or mestizo Christ, dark skinned, bleeding and mutilated, like those in churches all over Mexico.

On another painting of Christ, based on his memory of those "terrible Mexican Christs of the people which I believed in as a child," he wrote, "He who paints Christ, believes in Christ." He later clarified that the statement had been made by Fra Angelico and did not imply that he had converted to Christianity. While he might paint Coatlicue, a goddess of ancient Mexico, it would not mean that he worshipped her. Besides, he explained, Christ was a major symbol of humanity, a revolutionary who was arrested and crucified for his ideas, a victim of the crime of "social dissolution," and his mutilation shows what his friends and enemies have done to his teachings since his death.

In contrast with these vivid paintings of a suffering Christ, he painted the figure of a little Jesús in a red smock entitled *Jesús will be a Saint*. Using the same quick and economical brush strokes, he painted a dark purple sun on a reddish sky over a black and chaotic landscape barely suggested by several flowing strokes of black paint. Despite the economy of means, the painting expresses the ominous mood of its title, *The Death of the Sun*. With the same technique, he painted a reclining female figure, relaxed and serene, her eyes closed and her head resting on a pillow. While one picture is turbulent and foreboding, the other effectively conveys a sense of serenity and intimacy.

Some of his other paintings, including one of a grandmother embracing a child, a bunch of flowers, *The Two Davids*, *Little Jesus* and *Woman Resting* also suggest a new sensitivity and tranquility and reveal his ability to capture tenderness or paint scenes of pure natural beauty. But, in a different mood, he could paint with a fury, expressing his outrage against injustice and human suffering by painting a series of terrorized women and children in flight. *The Storm* features a group of women and children in greens, browns, yellows and white, their shawls blown violently by the wind, while in *Women of Mezquital,* he painted a group of emaciated mothers holding their starving babies. In *Flight* a mother grasps her child as she flees in terror while *Women in a World of Hunger and Terror* featured a woman with her arms raised in protest.

Like many of his prison paintings, these pictures are characterized by a lack of detail, spontaneous and free brushstrokes and a sense of agitation or movement. He also created a number of abstract studies for murals or as experiments in technique. When circumstances permitted, he announced, he would incorporate them into new murals. Meanwhile Angélica sold them to galleries and private collectors at lucrative prices.

In February of 1964, half way through his fourth year in prison, the convention of the Electoral Front of the People (FEP) nominated Siqueiros, Mata, Campa and Encarnación Pérez as candidates for the Senate in the July elections. In his campaign statement, Siqueiros called for an end to the president's control of the Congress, respect for the principles of "effective suffrage" and "no reelection" and eliminating the repression of the working class, the peasants and the intellectuals.

Although his campaign for the Senate, conducted from his cell in Lecumberri, was unsuccessful, not long after the July elections, Siqueiros was released. In the waning days of his administration,

López Mateos had decided to issue a pardon and on July 13, 1964, just 27 days before he would have completed four years in prison, Siqueiros left prison for good. While the official version stated that his pardon was in recognition of his services to the nation through his art, it is more likely that López Mateos wanted to spare the incoming President the embarrassment of having a famous artist in prison.

Since prison regulations required that he turn over all his tools and materials before leaving the prison, David had to surrender his brushes and paint the day before his discharge. Unwilling to cease painting, however, he continued working, using shoe polish and a crude brush to paint on pieces of paper.

On the day of his release, Siqueiros was greeted by several hundred people of all social classes. After they presented him with bouquets of flowers, they lifted him onto their shoulders and carried him, shouting "*vivas*" and singing the *Internationale*, to his waiting car. Although overwhelmed by the reception and the outpouring of emotion, not to mention his freedom, he maintained his composure and expressed his gratitude for those who had worked for his release. When someone inquired about his health, he joked, "I feel fine. You know you can't kill an old baseball player!"

At his home the 67-year-old artist, his thick hair almost completely gray and his forehead creased by furrows, was surrounded by old friends in a grand fiesta. While the rum flowed and a mariachi band played in the background, he roared out greetings and exchanged toasts with his friends and members of the press. When he was asked about his plans for the future, he said, "To work and get back to my party activities. My art is my life but my party is my duty." He also added that he had developed a new concept of color which would enrich his mural painting technique. Now I will return to the greater art of murals armed with superior technical weapons.

Then he announced that he would meet with artists and students in front of his mural in Chapultepec in a few days and would explain why he had painted small canvases and urge them to support the continued development of the muralist movement. After reading the official statement of his pardon, he expressed gratitude for the campaign for his freedom, which he felt, was the greatest recognition he could receive, since it was without national or social boundaries and demonstrated to the world the importance of the Mexican pictorial movement.

Therefore, he explained, he was proud to have been a fundamental part of that movement and would continue to be "an enthusiastic promoter," since it was as a member of that movement that I won my freedom and I will continue fighting for the popular leaders still in prison.

A few days later he met with young artists and students in Chapultepec and exhorted them to continue their support of muralism and to defend freedom of expression since "a muralist must lay out his theme, the mural is his pulpit." Within a few days, he was back working on the mural, resuming the feverish pace which had been interrupted so abruptly four years ago.

XVIII. A Modern, Humanist Realism

Before he resumed work on *The Revolution Against Díaz*, Siqueiros realized that the style he had developed in prison was more fluid and if placed next to the sections painted four years ago, would create the impression of a mural painted by two different artists. Since he did not want to abandon his new style or repaint the already finished sections, he decided to blend the two styles as much as possible, while avoiding the direct juxtaposition of one style against the other.

With a team of assistants, which included Luis Arenal and his niece Electa Arenal, an accomplished artist, he began to outline the remainder of the *Revolution Against Díaz*. While his assistant of many years, Epitacio Mendoza, prepared the paints, Siqueiros either directed their application or wielded a long brush or spray gun himself. Driven by his stored up energy and ideas, he worked day and night, sometimes without eating, declining interviews and refusing to allow himself or the mural to be photographed.

Where a pair of French doors interrupted the flow of the already painted surface, he had the doors covered and then painted more rural police and several cowering supporters of the *porfiriato* on the new surface. In the corner where the walls depicting the court of Díaz and the strike of Cananea come together, he painted another courtesan, her figure overlapping the juncture of the walls and visually destroying the right angle. Then, by connecting the mass of sombreros of the rural police with the top hats of the Díaz court and the reactionary officials with the dancing courtesans, he not only created the impression of a continuous surface, but also linked

Díaz and his supporters to the forces of repression and the strike of Cananea.

One day, perhaps exhausted by his feverish pace, he lost his balance and fell off the scaffold, seriously injuring his spine. Again work had to be suspended while he convalesced, frustrated by one more interruption in the project.

Several months later, still feeling the effects of the fall, he started on "the precursors" of the Mexican Revolution. Using photographs collected by Epitacio, he painted Ricardo and Enrique Flores Magón, members of the Mexican Liberal Party, the artist Posada, Andrés Molina Enríquez, a writer who criticized the policies of Díaz, and John Kenneth Turner, a North American reporter whose articles undermined Díaz's image in the United States. Before he finished, he had painted the portraits of more than two dozen men and women, marching together under the red and black banners of the workers' movement and led by Marx, Bakunin and Proudhon.

In the spring of 1965 David and Angélica went to Europe. In Rome he was given a reception at the House of Culture, during which Mario de Micheli cited his innovations and contributions to modern realism and his influence on other artists in Latin America. During his visit, Siqueiros expressed his frustration in having to paint small pictures in prison and commented on the dependency of Latin American art on the market of the United States.

Upon his return to Mexico, Siqueiros immediately resumed work on the mural in Chapultepec. On the wall facing the Díaz court, he painted three soldiers representing the three major types or factions of the Revolution: the Yaqui Indian, the northern cowboy troops of Villa and a southern peasant guerrilla type. On one side of them, he placed Francisco Madero, the first President of the Revolution, and on the other side, Adelita, the most famous *soldadera*.

Behind the soldiers he painted the leaders of the major factions and their lieutenants: Carranza and Obregón, Pancho Villa and Felipe Ángeles, Zapata and Otilio Montaño, along with other major participants in the struggle against Díaz. He had placed the common soldiers in the foreground, he explained, to emphasize their pivotal role in the conflict and the revolutionary potential of the masses.

Their solidarity also depicts that phase when the *carrancistas, villistas,* and *zapatistas* were united in the struggle against Díaz and Huerta.

The Revolution Against Díaz, Revolutionaries, 1957-1967, Acrylic on Plywood, Museum of National History, Mexico, D.F.

Working in his new and freer style, he painted a procession of faceless and semi-abstract figures on the next section, the least visible of any of the surfaces. On the reverse side of this wall that divides the two rooms, he painted a mounted soldier. Painted freely, this anonymous revolutionary is reigning in his horse and coming to an abrupt stop, creating a sense of suspended movement.

Where this wall meets the adjoining wall, he painted a red pyramid that overlaps the corner formed by the walls and creates the impression of a continuous surface. On this surface he paid tribute to the victims of the revolt against Díaz. From a photograph taken after a battle in Zacatecas, he painted the bodies of revolutionaries, stretched out on a mountainous terrain, their feet stripped of their shoes. The first corpse is that of Leopoldo Arenal, Angélica's father, killed during the attack on the plaza of Nochistlán in 1913.

Although this wall of the martyrs concluded his depiction of the revolution against Díaz, there was one more surface to paint. In the corner next to the only exit from the room, Siqueiros painted a frozen or petrified Díaz in somber grey, sitting alone in a frozen and barren landscape. The implication was twofold: The dictatorship was barren and the forces of reaction were dormant, not dead.

Though he was hampered by his recent injury and was working simultaneously on two other projects, Siqueiros was nearly finished by the end of 1966. In a brief ceremony before its official inauguration, he explained how the museum function of the room had determined the theme as well as the documentary approach of the mural. When he had first seen the space in 1957, he had decided to paint a large documentary mural with portraits of the revolutionaries which could be taken in by the moving spectator.

The Revolution Against Díaz, The Martyrs, 1957-1967. Acrylic on Plywood, Museum of National History, Mexico, D.F.

A few days later and two weeks short of his 70th birthday, Siqueiros was awarded the National Prize for Art and was honored, along with diplomat and writer Jaime Torres Bodet, in a ceremony in the National Palace. After receiving the award, which included 100,000 pesos ($8000), and words of congratulations from President Díaz Ordaz, Siqueiros explained that they were also honoring the Mexican pictorial movement which had emerged from the Revolution and whose intellectual precursor was Dr. Atl. He also recognized the contributions of Vasconcelos, Lombardo Toledano and President Obregón, without whom the movement would not have occurred. In honoring me, "Señor Presidente," he concluded, you have honored the painters of our transcendent movement, the most important of our time, which emerged in a country that because of colonialism, had lost the power of creation that it possessed before the conquest and in spite of the colonial oppression of Spain.

Despite his disagreements with the government, he cherished the prize and always considered it to be his greatest honor. He was proud to be Mexican and while he had received commissions from the government, neither his art nor his contributions to Mexican muralism had been recognized officially in Mexico. Now, in spite of his disagreements with the government, he had been recognized as a national treasure and had joined the select company of Mexico's most celebrated writers, thinkers and artists.

When he was asked during an interview if he had changed since he was in prison, David replied, laughing, "as a man in the sexual sense? I continue to be a man!" After the question was rephrased, he responded that he did not know whether he had changed, but perhaps others could judge more objectively. He also announced that his mural in Chapultepec was a point of departure for a new phase in Mexican muralism and he would finish it on the anniversary of the 1907 strike of the textile workers in Rio Blanco.

During the next month and a half, David and his assistants worked night and day to finish *The Revolution Against Díaz* in time for the scheduled inauguration. After applying the final touches the night before, he arrived early the next morning in suit and tie to help President Díaz Ordaz cut the ribbon and inaugurate the mural. In response to questions from the press, he noted that the final recognition and acceptance of the Mexican movement was more than a nationalist one, it was a "transcendental one." He also revealed that he did not plan to rest but would continue to work on his next project, the largest mural ever painted, which he would complete in time for the 1968 Olympic games in Mexico City.

In spite of the confining space of the room and the flat vertical walls on which he had to paint, Siqueiros had painted one of his most effective murals. What he could not do vertically, he had done horizontally by expanding the original surface and painting a mural that wrapped around the adjoining walls. Where the walls met at right angles, he had used overlapping images and strong horizontal lines to create an illusion of a continuous surface while linking the scenes thematically.

Like *Portrait of the Bourgeoisie*, this mural is a documentary film which spectators activate by their movement. From the only entrance to the room, one sees the central scene of the struggle at Cananea, with the striking miners backed by the European socialists and the Mexican precursors of the Revolution. As one walks around the room, the story of the Revolution unfolds, proceeding from the decadent dictatorship through the scenes of struggle, full of recognizable portraits, to the martyrs of the Revolution. As one turns to leave the room, one is confronted by the frozen forces of reaction.

The surging masses, striking miners, armed revolutionaries and the mounted horseman create a sense of movement, not only appearing to lunge towards the viewer, but also against the dictator and his armed forces. The figure of Colonel Greene is bending backwards, suggesting the inevitable triumph of the workers and the revolutionaries. These crowds are not faceless, however. They are real Mexicans, humble folk, their misery and pain, as well as their courage and determination, written on their faces. In fact, the mural conveys several moods, from the comic and burlesque portrayal of Díaz and his court to the heroic struggle of the masses and the tragic deaths of the martyrs of the Revolution.

When he was asked about the predominance of the color red in his mural, David explained, "Color is a voice, an expressive term, and therefore must be linked intimately with the theme of the painting."

Therefore, he continued, a painting of a revolutionary theme must have the color of blood, pain and victory, or red.

By painting recognizable portraits and the faces of real Mexicans, he had painted a description of that conflict which could be understood by the peasant, worker, housewife or student. It is not, however, a glorification of the struggle and does not point to any achievements of the Revolution. Instead, it implies that the Revolution is incomplete, that the goals for which the martyrs fought and died have not been realized and that the forces of reaction have not disappeared. It also stresses the revolutionary potential of the masses and solidarity, without which the overthrow of Díaz would not have been possible.

The reaction to *The Revolution Against Díaz* was overwhelmingly positive. After visiting Chapultepec when Siqueiros was in prison, John Canaday had written in the *New York Times* that the partially finished mural was a "powerful work of art and propaganda" and praised the abstract geometry of the lines of composition traced on the walls. When he read Canaday's article, Siqueiros commented that it was like being damned with faint praise and by lumping him together with Orozco and Rivera, he had failed to make any distinction between their art.

When the French scholar and statesman Andre Malraux visited Chapultepec, he remarked that "there is nothing like it in the world" and it is truly "one of the culminating works of western art in the Twentieth Century." *Time* magazine described it as "architectural art, active painting for the active spectator." Antonio Rodríguez wrote that Siqueiros "has absorbed the pain, bitterness, suffering, and despair of the people and kindled the spirit of revolt in the hearts of those who have to bear the misery and injustice." Others praised the mural as his most effective yet and commented that at the age of 70, he was stronger and more creative than ever.

The more than 60 historical portraits in the mural clearly demonstrated his mastery of the art of "indirect" or historical portraiture. While some of these portraits were of well-known revolutionary leaders like Villa, Zapata, Madero, Obregón and Carranza, they also included several foreign writers and thinkers, as well as miners, union leaders, peasants and soldiers who contributed to the revolt against Díaz.

While these portraits provided a historical explanation of the Revolution, it was not without controversy. Some conservatives and nationalists objected to the inclusion of Marx, Bakunin and Proudhon in a mural on the Mexican Revolution, since the roots of the movement were indigenous and certainly not marxist, socialist or anarchist, and demanded that the room be closed to the public. Siqueiros, however, explained that the European thinkers had influenced some of the more advanced Mexican liberals and had pointed to the need for a fundamental social change in Mexico.

Following on the heels of his seventieth birthday, the National Prize for Art and the positive reaction to his latest mural, Siqueiros received another honor. In April of 1967 it was announced that David Alfaro Siqueiros, along with three others, would be awarded the Lenin Peace Prize for his opposition to the United States' invasion of Vietnam and intervention in Latin America. Although he had scaled down his political activities since his pardon in order to concentrate on art, he had contributed to the Mexican Committee of Solidarity with Vietnam.

With this award, Siqueiros joined the only two other Mexicans to receive this honor, President Cárdenas and Heriberto Jara, a general of the Revolution, and the likes of Fidel Castro and Pablo Picasso. After receiving messages of congratulations from all over the world, Siqueiros declared his support for the Soviet Union's struggle for peace and his opposition to the Vietnam War. He then announced that he would donate the prize money of 28,000 rubles ($30,000) to the "heroic people of Vietnam," which, he estimated, would be enough to purchase two artillery pieces.

The Lenin Prize was followed by another honor. In spite of the fact that he had directed much of his criticism at official academies and academicians, he was made the first President of the Mexican Academy of Art. Although his selection was well deserved in terms of his contributions to Mexican art and his stature as an artist, the Presidential decree which established the Academy had stipulated that the presidency should be rotated among its members, proceeding alphabetically. Alfaro Siqueiros, therefore, became its first President and at its first meeting, he declared that he would do everything possible to make sure that the Academy did not become just another useless bureaucracy.

In 1967 David was also honored with a retrospective show at the National University, commemorating sixty years of art from 1907 to 1967. The exhibit, which ran through August and September, included 200 paintings, from his childhood copy of Raphael's "Virgin of the Chair" to a recently completed "Study of Zapata" for another mural.

During the opening ceremony, a young student approached Siqueiros and shouted "Viva MURO!" in reference to a conservative student organization whose acronym means "wall." While he and other students handed out leaflets accusing Siqueiros of the assassination of Trotsky and the surrender of Mexico to the Russians, other students rallied to his defense, shouting "Viva Siqueiros!"

José Luis Cuevas contributed to the controversy by writing in an article that Siqueiros had been dead artistically for some years but prison had rescued him. Sounding like Siqueiros chastising Rivera, Cuevas characterized the bouquets, landscapes and volcanos as superficial and decadent paintings "to charm the tourists." While he promised to defend Siqueiros's fine work, Cuevas explained that when Siqueiros says, "ours is the only way", he really means "my way" rather than "ours."

Despite these inauspicious rumblings, the show was very successful, attracting around two thousand viewers daily for two months. In her review of the University exhibit, Margarita Nelken wrote that it was a revelation of his easel work and constituted a culminating event in the history of Mexican art. His self-portraits, she wrote, revealed the inner psychology as well as an intentional simplicity in their depiction of the physical features. After praising his "grandiloquent baroque concept," another review proclaimed that he "is a master of easel painting."

Antonio Rodríguez wrote that his self-portraits amount to a "psychic and plastic biography of the artist," revealing not only his age but also the artistic periods through which he has passed. To illustrate his point, he compared the confident and combative *El Coronelazo* with the more pensive self-portraits done in prison. Moreover, Rodríguez added, his abstract paintings were plastically rich and show that he could have been a fine abstract painter. Even these abstract forms, however, reveal the artist and his landscapes are only a "pretext for projecting his personality and vision of the world over them."

In a televised interview on the exhibit Siqueiros responded to his critics and when he was asked if it was not true that he sold his paintings, he replied, "Sure, I sell my paintings! A painter of society does not paint for free." When he was asked about his fall from the scaffold while working on his mural in Chapultepec, he made a play on the Spanish verb to fall (*caer*), saying, "That's how I am, if I do not fall prisoner," referring to his arrest while working on the same mural, "I fall from a height of four meters."

When Raquel Tibol interviewed him for the catalog, Siqueiros told her that "to paint in a rectangle, no matter how large, would be so painful and so difficult for me that I suppose that I simply could not dominate the emotion which is lacking in order to create." He had always preferred grand compositions and had been inclined towards muralism from the start. That was why the Mexican muralists were not interested in exhibitions and why he had never painted easel paintings in the strict sense of the term. If he painted a figure or a tree, he was thinking in terms of a mural he was going to paint.

He also revealed many of his ideas on art, including his often-repeated remarks on the differences between easel and mural painting. Easel painting developed, he explained, when the private art market emerged along with the bourgeoisie. It is less difficult, offering fewer problems than painting murals in fresco and therefore is a lesser art. It has nothing to say and is determined by the market place, since it can be purchased by a buyer, whereas a mural conveys a message and can transform the viewer.

On the subject of art museums, Siqueiros was equally adamant. He declared that the art of museums was not public art since it cost money to see them and an artist must be successful, which means he is selling in the market place, or is dead, before his paintings will be purchased by the museums. Therefore, during the time when the artist is most productive and needs to communicate with his public, his paintings are in private homes where only the owners and their friends can see them.

In response to Raquel Tibol's questions on realism and what he had learned since his first attempt at muralism, he replied that realism also meant a reality that does not exist without movement. Everything else is statuary and is completely dead. I want sculpture to move, it is necessary to move everything. "In painting it is necessary to move the clouds because the clouds, in reality, move."

When asked whether the public appreciated his work, Siqueiros was sure that they did because it always included the representation of man. In fact, he declared, the majority of the public understands my realism, it is the intellectuals and young artists who do not understand me. Easel painting has closed off the brain of most artists and I will paint an artist in a gold frame, which is also a guillotine.

On the relationship of art and politics, Siqueiros stated that there was nothing more barren than those who wanted to separate the ideology of an artist from his work. Anyone who thinks in terms of this duality lacked two things, creative capacity and political conscience, and was living in "a state of semi-consciousness." It was, he said, "intellectual parasitism and those painters who paint for themselves and not for man, lock themselves up egotistically in the intimacy of their studios."

How is it possible, he asked, that those artists who opposed fascism, have now turned away from an art form that does not express any love for mankind? One of the virtues of the Mexican government is its support of realistic art, a support that we earned by our participation in the armed struggle and politics and by the strength and insistence of our demands. Only in Mexico have revolutionary artists been able to develop an art form which serves the masses and because of our success, young artists will be able to continue muralism.

At the close of the exhibit, David exhorted the younger artists to continue the Mexican movement, warning them to reject "the useless pastry shop" in which European artists are engaged. The school of Paris, he added, did not influence our movement, it was its antithesis. Serving man is fundamental to all artistic endeavors, he concluded, and the Mexican pictorial movement is as international and universal as any other movement. What started in Mexico will spread to the United States and the Soviet Union.

David repeated many of these views in another book. Entitled *A un joven pintor Mexicano* (To a Young Mexican Artist), it was part of a series of publications to a young novelist, architect, artist, etc. Written in the tone of a manifesto, it was really addressed to a young muralist or neo-realist painter. After establishing his premise that the history of the art of painting was the history of the search for realism, he cited several examples beginning with the development of the *claroscuro* by Massacio and his disciples. Later the baroque artists sought an active space and were the investigators of dynamism in the form of space. The impressionists' search for the vibration of light was a scientific investigation of reality. At a time when art was losing its objectivity, Cezanne searched for a geometric structure of form in order to place art in its realistic framework. Even the non-figurative painters have contributed to the enrichment of realism through their development of new materials, texture or optical tricks.

But, he continued, realism involves more than just a recreation of a social reality. A painting may be realistic in its idealistic position, its theme and content, but not in its science or style. Modern realism requires a universal reality encompassing human reality, the reality of its social-historical function, the reality of its theme and content, the reality of its scientific knowledge, the reality of its technical and professional material and the reality of its form.

This realism must be neo-humanist or be derived from its service to man and must speak with a language of its time, not in Latin or an archaic tongue. Since we do not speak in Latin, but in the language of our people, why in art do we continue speaking in Latin or the language of the academy? he asked. He also warned young artists to be aware of decorative trends and to avoid "archaeological and museum nationalism ... The realism today must be modern if it does not want to lose the support of the man of our time."

Turning to the Mexican movement, Siqueiros wrote that the Mexican experience followed the path of realism in the real sense of the word and marked a return to professionalism in international art, that is, an attack on the problems and not as a flight from them. Just as there is enrichment in language, the duty of the younger artists is to add more words in order to move forward. We also showed that it is not necessary to remove the image of man from art in order to create the art of the future, he wrote. However, he continued, our movement was only the stammering of a young child before an old man who has lost his memory and has arteriosclerosis of his creative capacity.

Siqueiros saved some of his strongest language for the so-called "avant-garde." If we look closely at their work, he wrote, it is the most reactionary movement in the history of culture. It has not developed anything new in composition or perspective and has lost much of that which has been accumulated over twenty centuries. It is based on the hysteria of novelty for the sake of novelty, in order to satisfy a parasitic plutocracy. The artist who changes his style every 24 hours is the best-known artist. When he has exhausted all the solutions, the others become his followers and sink into repetitious imitation. That is why most artists in the United States support themselves by teaching in the academies or doing commercial art if they are lucky.

Avant-gardism, therefore, not only wants to escape from human problems but also from professional difficulties. They reject composition, space, volume, movement, the relation between form and color and all discipline. This is a bohemian attitude in culture and as a result, their art consists of decorations for the bankers, industrialists, oligarchies, upper bourgeoisie and the more prominent intellectuals. We all know of the great fraud perpetrated by the great art dealers.

Although he admitted that he had painted for the market, as well as for the state, the difference was that while many of the younger artists painted just for the rich, we sold to the rich that which we painted. In my case, he explained, I painted some nudes, flowers and intimate things, but they were always studies for murals that I was painting or wanted to paint and they did not betray the epoch of muralism.

There are some who think that if the world goes bad, they must be bad also. But man has an obligation to be social and charitable with the rest of man, to receive from them but also to give. That is why our social sense was opposed to nihilistic individualism, masturbation and solitary and infertile love. Pornography "is immoral because there is nothing more anti-social."

In terms of recommendations or solutions, Siqueiros was adamant about the need for discussion and criticism. To those who say that painters must paint and not discuss, he countered that there had never been an important artistic movement that did not have a corresponding theoretical discussion or controversy based on the common principles of the participants. For us, public controversy was the most practical way of moving forward, and our boldness, in spite of its faults, explained the vitality of our movement.

But, he continued, I do not believe that our movement has entered a mortal crisis and its transcendence is too great to be liquidated. While "conscious or unconscious agents of imperialism will try to bury it, there is a rebirth of humanism in many other countries ... The young ones must put it on the right track." In art the process is always upward and forward, with ups and downs, but always forward, he argued, and the younger ones must overcome or surpass that which we have done now, doing all we could not do and completing that which we left unfinished. Just as the Vatican had been the director of Catholic art, they must oblige the state to take action. The duty of the young ones, therefore, was not to defend the positions which the older artists have already abandoned in their technical and artistic development, but to fight from more advanced positions.

In his challenge to the new generation of artists, he advised them to abandon all the stagnation that was alienating the masses for they advanced rapidly. If the younger artists break away from the already established tradition, they will be opposing us from behind and not from more advanced positions, he declared. Therefore, "do not be in the rearguard, assume all the historical responsibility which responds in culture to an authentic vanguard!"

Despite his age, Siqueiros was not ready to relinquish his position to anyone. He was full of energy and enthusiasm and the recent honors and respectability reinforced his beliefs and spurred him to even greater exertions. In prison he had dreamt that he had painted a gigantic mural and Picasso, Braque, Orozoco, Rivera, Matisse, and Degas were all astonished when they saw it. But the mural disappeared and each time he went to find it, there was only a small easel painting in its place.

Afterwards he lamented, "I must work in easel while I dream of frescos," and compared himself to a novelist who is told that he can only write a page a day. But Siqueiros's dream was more than a subconscious expression of his frustration in painting small pictures. It was an expression of his ambition to paint a monumental mural that would surpass all others and impress his fellow artists, living and dead.

After his release from prison, he had rushed to Chapultepec to finish his mural and renewed his efforts to complete *Patricians and Patricides* in the old customs house. But neither of these projects permitted the application of the ideas, images and style that he had developed in prison. He longed for a site where he could realize his vision of a totally integrated mural and while he was applying the last touches in Chapultepec, he signed a contract for another mural, the most ambitious ever attempted. Conceived in a small prison cell, it would be his magnum opus, the culmination of all his theories and aspirations and the realization of his prison dreams and mural studies. It would be the largest mural ever painted and would occupy him and an international team of artists for the next six years.

XIX. The Polyforum

Not long after his release from prison, Siqueiros accepted a commission from Manuel Suárez y Suárez, a wealthy industrialist and owner of the hotel Casino de la Selva in Cuernavaca, to paint two large panels for the hotel at 60,000 pesos each. Although they had attended the Academy of San Carlos and fought in the Revolution together, Suárez had become a rich businessman and had openly supported Hitler and Mussolini. He had also purchased some of Siqueiros's prison paintings, including some for López Mateos, and it was rumored that he had persuaded the President to pardon Siqueiros in 1964.

Since the government had not sponsored any new mural projects for several years, Siqueiros welcomed the opportunity, and when he learned that Suárez planned to expand the hotel into a convention center, he proposed that he paint a larger mural for the addition. Suárez agreed and promised to cover the costs of the project, including a fully equipped workshop and a team of artists and technical workers, while Siqueiros would paint a mural of 2,000 square meters.

Siqueiros immediately hailed the project as "the fourth stage of Mexican Muralism." Instead of painting a mural on the walls of an existing building, he would be able to plan his mural and integrate it with the architecture while the building was under construction. Furthermore, it would not be painted in place, but in a special studio-workshop where the large panels could be prepared and painted before being mounted in the building. In the future, he predicted, artists would work with the architects and mural decoration would not just be painted on the walls, it would constitute the walls themselves.

Anxious to get started, Siqueiros directed the construction of the studio-workshop next to his home in Cuernavaca, the first of its kind devoted exclusively to muralism. Designed to handle large and heavy panels, the main working area was a hanger 13 meters high, 42 meters long and 20 meters wide, with large doors so that the large panels could be moved in and out of the work area. Strung across the ceiling were iron rails for mechanical cranes to raise and lower the large and heavy panels. Because Siqueiros had suffered from vertigo after his fall in Chapultepec, he had trenches constructed directly beneath these rails so that he could paint on the panels as they were raised or lowered in these trenches without mounting a scaffold.

Equipped with an air compressor, electric sanders and grinders, metal pounding and shaping machines, welding equipment and scaffolding, the workshop resembled a small factory. There was also a laboratory where paints and materials could be tested and a photography studio. Later, a large metal framework was erected outside on which the finished panels could be assembled and checked for compatibility and continuity. When the workshop was completed, David and Angélica broke a bottle of champagne and baptized it "*La Tallera,*" converting *el taller* (workshop or studio) to the feminine.

Next, Siqueiros set out to realize another lifelong goal, that of directing an international team of artists working on a collective project. This was not only necessary because of the size of the project, but it would also allow him to apply his contention that the only way to teach muralism is to have students work under a master artist on a mural project. Hence the workshop was officially known as the "*Escuela Taller Siqueiros*" (Siqueiros School Workshop).

After he issued an invitation to join him, artists came from Argentina, Guatemala, Japan, Italy, Israel, Belgium, France and the United States to work on the project in Cuernavaca. Although the number of assistants fluctuated, more than 50 different artists and technical workers eventually participated. Since he sought to create an integral work of art, he tried to eliminate preconceived tastes or mannerisms by weeding out those who could not subordinate their personal styles. After observing how well they assimilated his own style, he divided them into teams headed by a master painter or sculptor.

In spite of its international flavor, the *Escuela Taller Siqueiros* was a family operation. His brother-in-law Luis Arenal was a key member of the team and worked on several pieces of sculpture for the mural. After assisting Siqueiros in Chapultepec, Electa Arenal also joined the team of artists in Cuernavaca while her father, Leopoldo Arenal, was responsible for the acquisition and "technical control of materials." Angélica was the "Administrator" and handled the bookkeeping and business arrangements.

Rounding out this nucleus were Epitacio Mendoza, Mario Orozco Rivera and José Gutíerrez. Mendoza was a longtime assistant while Orozco Rivera, a muralist and teacher from Veracruz, became the artist-director of the school workshop. The Director of the National Institute for the Testing of Plastic Materials, Gutíerrez was in charge of the laboratory where pigments and surfaces were tested before they were used by *el maestro*.

The theme for the mural had come to David in prison and was as ambitious as the project itself. It would be the history of humanity, a procession of all the oppressed people of the world, struggling against all the evils, suffering and misery of the past, but marching towards a positive and victorious future. Since he realized that the history of mankind was too extensive, however, he decided that "the march of humanity in Latin America" was more appropriate and manageable. Though rooted in Mexico, it would be "the history of man seen through the filter of our own history; it is his evolution and his destiny."

After conducting experiments with different materials and consulting with Gutíerrez, they decided to construct the large panels out of reinforced asbestos-cement, to be supplied by one of Suárez's factories. Although each panel would weigh between 350 and 1000 kilograms, they would resist saltpeter, humidity, settlement and fungus, "the great enemies of murals."

Now that the *Revolution Against Díaz* was finished, David was able to devote himself almost exclusively to planning and executing the mural for the Casino de la Selva. Since his home was next door to the workshop, he was able to spend more time on "*La Capilla Siqueiros*" (The Siqueiros chapel), its latest name. Some days he worked 15 to 17 hours, without pausing for lunch, and then returned in the evening to inspect the day's work and paint after everyone else had gone home.

After a scale model of the rectangular building was constructed, David sketched the outline of the *March of Humanity* on its walls. When the huge asbestos-cement panels were moved into place, he began to paint the outline on them, creating a series of zigzag patterns using an airbrush or spray gun. Working from the general to the specific, and pausing only to change nozzles or paints, he recreated many of his prison paintings on the panels, albeit greatly enlarged and simplified. There were mothers with babies, women in flight, crowds surging forward, men struggling, a volcanic landscape and a flowering tree, as well as prehistoric monsters, reminiscent of those on the walls of the cancer center and the unfinished *Patricians and Patricides*.

During the day, the studio was full of noise and activity and looked and sounded more like a machine shop in a factory than an artist's studio. Shouting over the din, Siqueiros directed his assistants or guided the younger artists as they mounted scaffolds and worked on the upper sections. While his aides prepared the panels, moved them into place, and mixed paints, he wielded a long-handled brush or spray gun, frequently interrupting his work to explain the project to a steady stream of visitors.

Like a major construction project, everything was carefully planned. When the panels were finished, they were moved to the outside patio where they were assembled together on a special framework. After checking for compatibility and the effect from different perspectives, they were photographed from different angles. Photographs of the finished panels were then placed on the model in order to check for any compositional problems or optical distortions. From time to time, photography was also used to enlarge and transfer paintings or sketches to the blank surfaces of the panels, after which they were painted by his assistants.

In 1966 the nature and location of the project were suddenly changed. Instead of expanding the Casino de la Selva, Suárez was persuaded by President Díaz Ordaz to move his project to Mexico City. In a large open space on Avenida Insurgentes, one of the major arteries of the capital, Suárez would build a brand new hotel and convention center, the largest in Mexico City. On the same site he would erect another building for cultural events and Siqueiros would paint a mural on its interior and exterior.

This change in plans called for much more than the enlargement of the original project or a mere change in location. Instead of decorations painted on or attached to standing walls, the mural panels would form the very walls of a building. By working with the architects in the design of the building, Siqueiros would be able to integrate mural painting and architecture in "the fourth stage of the Mexican movement." Since it would also serve as a cultural center for concerts, dance performances, art exhibits and public meetings, it would be known as "The Siqueiros Cultural Polyforum" and would be finished in two years, in time for the Olympic Games scheduled for October 1968.

Working closely with Siqueiros, the architects Guillermo Rosell and Ramón Miguelajauregui designed an octagonal building with inclined walls that would eliminate any angles between walls and the ceiling. This would permit the painting of a continuous or "active surface" with no interruptions between adjoining walls or the walls and the ceiling, the perfect "plastic box." The exterior was designed as a dodecagon, its twelve sides to be painted by Siqueiros. The total surface was 4,331 square meters, more than twice that of the mural for the Casino de la Selva, and there were tentative plans for a separate exterior sculpture painting honoring the masters of modern Mexican painting.

Despite these changes, Siqueiros would continue to work in Cuernavaca, preparing and painting the panels before they were transported to Mexico City and mounted on the framework of the building. Only the ceiling, therefore, would be painted in place, using acrylics on a plastic acoustical material. Since the theme had not changed, he would be able to use most of the panels which he had already painted.

Nevertheless, there were frequent changes throughout the project and if he did not like the effect of the panels when they were assembled on the framework next door, he would make changes on the model before repainting or making the necessary corrections. He had always contended that murals posed more problems than easel paintings because the total space was active, and given the magnitude of this project, the compositional problems were even greater and required more corrections.

He also decided to add another dimension by including polychromed sculpture and creating a sculpture painting. He would create an "integral art" of mural painting, sculpture and architecture by attaching painted sculpture directly to the interior walls and covering the twelve exterior panels and the wall surrounding the site with a sculpture painting. Declaring that he had always been a sculpture-painter, he explained, "Painting helps me move sculpture and sculpture serves to move the painting." By combining sculpture and painting, I can speak with two voices, he said. I can be more eloquent, more understandable.

The responsibility for the sculptures was assigned to Luis Arenal, Armando Ortega and Adir Ascalón. After experimenting with different materials, they decided to create the sculptures from cold rolled steel. Once they had been cut out, shaped, and welded together, these metal sculptures were sandblasted to specific requirements, treated with a coat of inorganic zinc and covered by an anticorrosive resin used on boats. Then they were spray-painted with acrylic paint and attached to the asbestos-cement panels.

Although he worked incessantly on the mural, David frequently interrupted his work to show visitors around the workshop. With a fedora or straw hat in place and a cigarette dangling from his mouth, he explained his latest project and reiterated many of his ideas on art. It should be taught in active workshops, in the process of creation and not as "mere pedagogical expression," he pointed out, while he reminded his visitors that he had first called for an integral art of painting, architecture and engineering in his 1921 Barcelona manifesto. He also emphasized the unique demands of mural painting. Unlike an easel painter, a muralist must know about everything that affects his work, including chemistry, optical problems, even acoustics.

Contrasting his approach to that of other artists, he declared, "My art is related to my life; technically, politically, everything is in relation to my art." Great art, he contended, is that which provokes thought, which teaches and takes its subject matter from life.

When former President López Mateos visited the workshop and approached a paint spattered Siqueiros with open arms, they embraced like old friends. Later he explained that he had no choice since the man whom he had attacked as a counterrevolutionary and who had him arrested and imprisoned, had approached him with open arms, in the Mexican fashion, as if to apologize and forget the past. What was he to do, he asked, call him a bastard and refuse to accept his gesture of friendship? One also has to distinguish between the man and the act, he added. It was not the individual but the pervasive influence of imperialism which was responsible for his conduct.

In spite of their public name-calling, José Luis Cuevas was a close friend and frequent guest. After inspecting the mural, he would join David and Angélica and other friends in their home next to the studio. While they sipped cognac or ate dinner, David exchanged stories with his guests, reveling them with stories of the Revolution, his travels or experiences in prison, and expounding on his latest views on art or politics. Although she had heard the stories many times, Angélica listened patiently, diligently covering up the food to keep it warm or sending it back to the kitchen to be reheated. When the Russian poet Yetushenko came to Cuernavaca, David showed him around the studio and painted his portrait while they chatted.

Like a modern Medici or Pope, Señor Suárez also visited the workshop frequently, observing the process and talking to the artists.

He not only referred to the project as "the Siqueiros Chapel," but he also saw himself as "Julius II" and Siqueiros as "Michelangelo," and had a lookout tower constructed in the workshop so that he could observe the process without interfering. Relations between patron and artist were not always harmonious, however. A shrewd businessman and art collector, Suárez had acquired rights to any works of art produced in the workshop and insisted that the mural not contain any political statements. While Siqueiros apparently accepted these conditions, he insisted that he had total artistic control and balked at Suárez's suggestions about any changes.

Much to Angélica's consternation, Siqueiros was so enthralled by this unprecedented opportunity that he did not worry about the added expenses and neglected to negotiate a new contract. Not only was the space to be more than doubled but sculpture painting was much more expensive. Although a cabinet minister arranged to have a government steel factory supply the steel for the sculptures and the framework of the building, the additional costs soon surpassed the funds provided by Suárez.

When they needed a machine to shape the metal for the sculptures, therefore, Angélica arranged some portrait commissions to pay for the machine. When some workers were discharged without pay, David paid them out of his own pocket. Suárez, however, continued to insist that the studio-workshop and all of the models and sketches for the mural belonged to him. Meanwhile, the skeleton of a building was rising in Mexico City while a team of artists constructed, sculpted and painted its walls in Cuernavaca. Although he directed their work, Siqueiros was engaged on several projects or activities simultaneously.

After he finished the mural in Chapultepec, Siqueiros worked sporadically on his problem-plagued mural in the old customs house. When the actors' union withdrew its lawsuit and invited him to finish his mural in the lobby of the Jorge Negrete Theater, he proceeded to complete his depiction of The Theater in Mexico. He left the scenes of the flag-draped body of Morales and the soldiers breaking up the workers' demonstrations and trampling the Constitution just as he had painted them. As events unfolded, conditions had not changed since the 1958-1960 disturbances and the scenes of repression were as timely in 1968 as they had been ten years earlier.

On the wall opposite these scenes of contemporary Mexico, he created a sculpture-painting portrait of singer and actor Jorge Negrete, the founder of the actors' union. Working in his more spontaneous and fluid style, and adding strips of metal and several bas-relief mask-like sculptures to the two-dimensional surface, he painted his version of tragedy, comedy and farce in the theater of the past.

In the fall of 1967 David and Angélica left for Europe and the Soviet Union. As a recipient of the Lenin Peace Prize, David had been invited to the celebrations of the Fiftieth Anniversary of the October Revolution in Moscow. During the meeting of the Congress of the Communist Parties, he saw many old friends, including veterans from Spain, and they reminisced about old times. When he visited the Moscow Academy of Fine Arts, of which he had been made an honorary member, he sensed that some Soviet artists had assimilated his "Open Letter" and were looking for new forms in their monumental art.

After Moscow, they traveled to Belgrade where they visited with Marshall Tito before heading home. When they landed in Mexico, David commented on the tremendous progress he had seen in Russia since his last visit and the lack of humanism in European art. Although the Europeans attack us as government employees, they are employed by members of a social class that made art a commodity and are increasingly dependent on the galleries that dominate the art market. He also defended his National Prize for Art. Whereas in Europe, government awards are given only to academics, our art has served the state and therefore it has been recognized and rewarded by the state. This prize also demonstrates that even a communist can be honored by the government and any award for a revolutionary is a victory for the progressive forces. In my case, he explained, it is also a victory for art with a human content.

While he conceded that Picasso was "the most powerful painter of his generation and tendency, the greatest innovator in that period of inventive hysteria," he described his art as a collection of sketches, "an informal art made at high speed" in which there is the "greatest repetition, monotony and formal poverty of all times." The recent Picasso exhibit demonstrates the depressed state of European artists. In Mexico, however, we have created a more sincere and humbler art, not as an end in itself but as a point of departure. Picasso, he charged, was only "a dilettante of the revolution." Although he was a member of the Communist Party, he was not a militant or active member. If he had been more active in the party of the working class, he would have been more critical, like us, Siqueiros added.

Although he had concentrated on his art since leaving prison, government repression of the Mexican student movement prompted him to speak out. In 1968 the students were not only demanding more liberal admission policies to the University, but also the release of Demetrio Vallejo, in prison since 1959. They also opposed the Olympic games scheduled for October and protested U.S. involvement in Vietnam. Since other sectors also opposed the Olympic games because of the tremendous cost, and because the eyes of the world would be focused on Mexico during the games, the student leaders decided to press their case during the summer of 1968. When the government reacted with unprecedented force and violence, the original conflict escalated into a national crisis and tragedy.

It started when a schoolboy rivalry erupted into a riot between the students of two schools and the Chief of Police of the Federal District dispatched the *Granaderos*, or riot police, to separate the students. This use of paramilitary forces violated the tradition of campus autonomy, further polarizing the students and generating more support for a national strike.

In the following days there were more encounters between students and the riot police, leading to more arrests and repression. Students reacted to the use of force by marching on the Zócalo, commandeering buses and erecting barricades behind which they pelted the police with stones. When students barricaded themselves in an old school building in the heart of Mexico City, the *Granaderos* used a bazooka to break down its massive doors. More united, the students held mass meetings on the campuses and issued new demands for the settlement of the strike. These demands included the release of all students in prison, the freedom of all political prisoners, the disbanding of the *Granaderos*, the firing of the Chief of Police and the repeal of the crime of social dissolution.

When talks with the government broke down, tension mounted and on August 27, the National Student Strike Committee organized the largest antigovernment rally in Mexican history as one million students and supporters paraded and chanted antigovernment slogans in front of the Presidential Palace. After dark, tanks and armored cars moved in, and this plaza, the scene of many bloody confrontations in the past, became a battlefield in which one student was killed.

As the date of the opening of the Olympics approached, army troops invaded the campus of the National University, where some of the athletic events were scheduled to take place. There were reports of snipers firing on the troops from campus buildings and hundreds of students were arrested. Realizing that time was running out and hoping to capitalize on the sympathy for their cause, the strike leaders called for another outdoor rally on October 2 in the Plaza of Three Cultures in Tlateloco, only a few days before the opening of the Olympic games.

Siqueiros was naturally sympathetic towards the striking students, especially since their demands included the freedom of all political prisoners and the repeal of the crime of social dissolution. After the first incident, he issued a series of statements condemning the use of excessive force by the government against the students and endorsing their cause. Following the bloody confrontation in the Zócalo, Siqueiros published an announcement entitled *"Basta Ya"* (Enough Now), in which he reminded readers of his participation in the student strike of San Carlos and condemned the last eight years of "ignominy" in which the Supreme Court, the Congress and the Army had become oppressors of the people. He called for the release of political prisoners and an end to the policy of sending provocateurs among the workers and the students.

In another statement, he commended the students for having brought about the discussion of the crime of social dissolution by a congressional commission and asked to participate in that process. When the House of Deputies met to discuss the crime of social dissolution, he testified at length, citing his own case as well as that of other victims of the law, and called for its suppression as a monstrosity. In an interview after his appearance in the House of Deputies, he told a reporter that he should oppose a law that arrests people for their opinions. He also announced that he would suspend work on two exhibits scheduled for the Olympics.

On the evening of October 2, 1968, David was sitting in the office of the Minister of the Interior, Luis Echeverría, who was in charge of internal security. Around eight the phone rang and David watched as a distraught Echeverría received obviously distressing news. When he hung up, he turned to Siqueiros and explained that the army had attacked the student demonstrators in Tlateloco and there were reports of many casualties. As Echeverría expressed his concern for his own children, Siqueiros was convinced of his sincerity, as well as his ignorance of what was taking place in the Plaza of Three Cultures.

The rally had started off peacefully and was smaller than earlier gatherings, but when the police and the army surrounded the plaza with tanks and armored cars, the crowd refused to disband. Using billy clubs and tear gas, the *Granaderos* began to disperse the protesters when firing broke out. While the army claimed that it had been fired on, other witnesses later testified that the army had shot first and then snipers began to shoot back from surrounding apartment buildings. Photographs later showed plainclothes police with rifles, purportedly provocateurs, on the outskirts of the crowd.

After the first shots, the army opened up with rifles and machine guns from short range, catching hundreds of innocent people in a crossfire while helicopters flew overhead and dropped flares and tear gas on them. When it was over, there were more than 300 dead and thousands injured, although the government denied that more than 40 had been killed. Thousands of protesters were arrested and the following day the jails of the capital were filled with several thousand more students. Several hundred of these prisoners, including faculty members, remained in custody for several years without trial.

The bloodbath of October 2, 1968 ended the student movement of that year, but it did not resolve any of the outstanding issues and the intransigence of the government radicalized some sectors of the population and provoked more violent tactics in the future. Although President Díaz Ordaz assumed full responsibility for the actions of the government, many blamed Luis Echeverría for unleashing the troops on the students. The Olympic games, which was never a central issue of the student strike, took place as scheduled and in spite of the bloody prelude and cloud of repression in which the games took place, Mexico was the first Latin American or developing country to host the games.

Although David had threatened to suspend work for the coming exhibits, he attended the openings of two exhibits of his work in the tourist area of Mexico City between September and November. One of them was entitled *Against War* and featured a "retrospective self-portrait" of him brandishing a machete and some paintings of war victims, their ghostly figures wrapped in acrylic flames of napalm. Other recent works included *The Storm*, in which an offshore drilling platform is enveloped by a storm, and a scowling Olmec-like cat whose greenish-yellow coat reflects sulfur and the envy and greed that it inspires. The most striking piece, however, was *The Mastiff*, a large dog symbolizing war, whose insatiable appetite consumes everything while it remains a skeleton. The exhibit also included 10 lithographs which he had recently finished for Pablo Neruda's epic poem, *El Canto General*, and a series of lithographs condemning the war in Vietnam. They were dedicated, he said, to all those people who fight for the independence of their countries.

Following the events of October, Siqueiros concentrated on completing his mural in the Jorge Negrete Theater and in December, he applied the last strokes of paint to the walls of the lobby. Except for some bas-relief sculptures and some minor stylistic changes, *The Theater in Mexico* was the same interpretation of comedy, tragedy and farce that had provoked its censorship nine years earlier. Like his recent murals, it expressed the full range of human emotions, the fear, terror, despair, hate and anger as well as the love, idealism, confidence and solidarity of the masses. This time the directors of the actors' union gave their stamp of approval and the official inauguration was scheduled for January.

Before the official ceremony, Siqueiros made a brief statement in front of the mural. After talking about his experiences in the Revolution and praising the contributions of Orozco and Rivera to Mexican muralism, he explained that he had not made any changes in the mural since the conditions that he had painted earlier had not changed.

When he was asked what his images of struggle had to do with the theater, he pointed out that the essence or spirit of the theater, especially revolutionary theater, is based on the drama and reality of everyday life, the conflicts, feelings and interests of the different classes, groups or individuals. Actors, like artists, he proclaimed, must take their message to the streets and express the living reality of the people.

Early in the morning, two days after he had finished the mural, twenty men broke into the building. After knocking the watchman unconscious and tying him up, they ripped off the curtains covering the mural and began to attack the painted figures. Using sharp instruments, they gouged the figures of the soldiers, the workers and the Indian mothers and then poured paint thinner on the surface of the mural.

When Siqueiros learned of the attack, he rushed to the theater to inspect the damage. After blaming the ultraconservative student organization MURO (University Movement of Renovating Orientation) for the attack, he minimized the destruction and promised to restore the damage without cost. He also pointed out that the mural did not specify in which country the repression of the workers is taking place since he had removed the number "17" from the trampled book, thereby removing the specific reference to the Mexican Constitution.

However, some viewed this deletion as a betrayal of the student movement and the railroad workers' strike, since it removed any direct connection between the soldiers and workers in the mural and recent events in Mexico. By making the statement against the use of military force more general, it was argued, he had weakened the message and destroyed the effectiveness of the mural. Although the body of Luis Morales, wrapped in the Mexican Flag, was still there, the charges of betrayal did not go away.

After he had restored the damage to his latest mural, David concentrated on the *March of Humanity*, dividing his time between a new studio-home in Mexico City and "*La Tallera*" in Cuernavaca. At 72 he was full of energy and ideas and thrilled by the magnitude and challenge of the project before him. Even though the original deadline had long since passed and the mural was far from being finished, he continued to test new ideas and techniques. He was also planning new projects, more ambitious and experimental than this one.

Attracted by news and rumors about the artist and the project, visitors poured in from all over the world and besieged him with requests for interviews. While he freely granted interviews, he also canceled them just as abruptly when the mural required his undivided attention. Never one to shun publicity, however, he enjoyed talking to his guests, especially friends and allies from past struggles, and showing them around and explaining his project. When he was asked to do a portrait of Abraham Lincoln for Arthur Landis' book on the Abraham Lincoln Brigade, the American volunteers in Spain, he obliged and completed the commission without charge.

In the spring of 1969 he suffered a great personal loss. While she was working on one of the scaffolds, his niece Electa fell when the scaffold began to move and then stopped abruptly when one of the wheels caught in a crevice. Crashing to the floor, she died instantly when her head hit the pavement as her father and David watched. Electa was just 40 years old, an accomplished painter and sculptor and had a promising career ahead of her. David felt her loss deeply and though he returned to work with his usual energy and enthusiasm, close friends noticed a decline in his spirit and a more pronounced aging process thereafter.

He was also saddened by the loss of two friends. Although he had only met the mysterious writer B. Traven recently, he had sensed an affinity with the writer and his novels on the struggles of the oppressed in southern Mexico. The following year, when he and Angélica were in Paris, they heard that Cárdenas had died. While they had disagreed in the past, they were close friends and the loss he felt was personal as well as political.

Although he refrained from any direct participation in domestic politics, Siqueiros continued to issue statements on national and international issues and to endorse different causes. Several times he expressed his view that the governing party of Mexico was becoming radicalized and the Mexican Revolution was about to enter a new and more advanced stage. The PRI, he felt, was ready to adopt a more positive and advanced attitude and even the clergy had dropped its reactionary stand on important issues. He suggested that the PRI discard "*tapadismo,*" permit more democracy and stop being a blind instrument of the government. While land reform has not gone far enough, the nationalization of oil, the railroads, the utilities and sulfur had been important.

In September David was made an honorary member of the Academy of Fine Arts of the Soviet Union. In bestowing this honor on him, the academy not only recognized his art and service to humanity, but also the positive developments that his criticism of Soviet art had stimulated. Meanwhile, he was serving as the President of the Mexican Committee of Solidarity with Vietnam. Later in the year, when students and other prisoners launched a hunger strike, David and Angélica expressed their solidarity and called on the government to release them.

In 1970, their efforts were finally rewarded when Congress voted to abolish the crime of social dissolution under articles 145 and 145 B of the Penal Code. A few days later, President Díaz Ordaz signed the act which eliminated the crime of social dissolution and released Demetrio Vallejo and Valentín Campa, in prison since the 1959-1960 disturbances. A victim of these articles and an active participant in their repeal, Siqueiros had cause to celebrate and praised the President for convening a special session of the Congress and calling for the study and nullification of Article 145. Although he applauded the repeal of Article 145, he also warned that the vague sections of the reforms regarding national security might cause problems in the future.

Meanwhile he was involved in another imbroglio with his own party. When the Mexican Communist Party condemned the Soviet invasion of Czechoslovakia and called for an immediate withdrawal, he defended the use of force as a necessary defensive effort under the Warsaw Pact. It was not the first time that he had disagreed with the direction of the Communist Party and he joked that his unruly head of hair was caused by the agitation of party politics. However, he had not only publicly opposed the decision of the Central Committee but he also accused the party of precipitate and antidemocratic action in reaching its decision.

If his violation of party discipline and public criticism of the Party were not enough, the Party had other concerns. While David had cooperated with the Party during the student strike, he had made statements endorsing the Olympics, and the deletion of the number "17" from his mural and his reassurances to the army were viewed as unacceptable compromises with the enemy. He had also made a number of positive statements about trends within the governing party and had been photographed embracing López Mateos. Others questioned his comfortable life style, including the two Mercedes cars and new house he had purchased in Mexico City, and his relationship with Suárez.

The real crunch came, however, when he publicly endorsed Luis Echeverría for the Presidency in 1970. Not only was Echeverría blamed for the bloody events of October 1968, but his nomination by the PRI perpetuated the *"tapadismo"* which he himself had consistently opposed. According to Siqueiros, his reversal was motivated by his realization that the past strategy of automatically opposing any official candidate had failed. He was also encouraged by the candidate's statements about "unlimited freedom" of expression in art, the threat of imperialism, the need to protect the rights of Mexico, the achievements of Fidel Castro and his respect for the independence of unions. He was also convinced of Echeverría's innocence in the massacre of Tlateloco.

When the Central Committee, of which he was a member, voted to protest "the electoral farce" by boycotting the Presidential elections, Siqueiros disobeyed party policy and went to the polls to cast his vote for Echeverría and candidates of the Socialist Party that had endorsed him. The Central Committee reprimanded him, declaring that his participation in the election not only supported the demagogy of the government, but also violated party discipline and contradicted its policy.

After Echeverría's inauguration, Siqueiros issued an "Appeal to Communists," in which he reminded party members of past mistakes, including his own, and pointed out that by not supporting Echeverría, the Party was repeating the mistake when it did not support Cárdenas. The Party ignores the positive developments of Echeverría, he wrote, especially his attack on corruption and promises to respect the independence of the unions. To judge a priori is not a marxist method, he counseled, and we must wait to see if his deeds and words coincide.

Our tendency to label dissenters from party decisions as traitors, Trotskyites, agents of imperialism, revisionists, reformists, government supporters or anarchists has also been unfortunate, he continued. The disagreement over Czechoslovakia, he said, was not a party matter since the abstention of the other members of the Warsaw Pact was a betrayal of a sister country threatened by North American imperialism and the decision of the Mexican party to oppose the invasion was "antidemocratic." However, he denied that he was anti-party and hoped that they could overcome sectarianism and become an effective marxist-leninist party.

In its response, the Central Committee accused him of not raising these issues within the Party before making them public. His call for support of Echeverría, they said, is based on some public phrases of the candidate. By his participation in the farce of no reelection, he disguises the fact that the same class remains in power. Because he is no longer actively involved in the Party, he conceives his criticism of the Party superficially and by publishing these criticisms, he causes serious damage to the Party. Why didn't he express his views on the invasion of Czechoslovakia before the Central Committee before publicly opposing its decision? they asked.

Following this reprimand, Siqueiros withdrew his "Appeal to Communists" and decided to seek cooperation and unity. Meanwhile he declared that he would maintain his position as stated in the press, and while he had always disciplined himself within the Party, he reserved the right to express his own opinions. The movement towards open democracy in Mexico deserved support, he continued, since the opposite, the domination of the country by ultra-reactionary pro-imperialists, would constitute a disaster for the people.

Several days later Siqueiros was expelled from the Central Committee of the Mexican Communist Party. While there was a motion to expel him from the Party, it was postponed indefinitely because of his declining health. Although he continued to compare Echeverría to Cárdenas and complimented him on his adherence to the program of the Revolution, his record as a party militant and renown artist, as well his generous contributions, outweighed lapses in party discipline and he remained in the Party for the rest of his life. He also continued to protest the tendency of the Party to expel any dissenters and pointed out that the inquisitors of today were themselves the victims of other inquisitions. If the party faithful were troubled by these statements or his continued support of Echeverría, his next commission was probably not very reassuring.

XX. The March of Humanity

Although he had painted several portraits of Christ in prison, Siqueiros had denied that he believed in Christ and had condemned what the friends and enemies of Christ had done to his teachings. More recently he had admitted that he believed in God, "a universal, infinite and cosmogonic God" and was a Christian by inheritance. In his view God included everything. "God is the mystery of the universe, God is everything ... He cannot have the small image of man because he is much greater than our own world."

When representatives of the papacy invited him to paint a portrait of Christ for the new Vatican museum, Siqueiros accepted immediately and began work on a figure of Christ. Eight days later he presented his *Christ of Peace* and explained. "Christ was the first revolutionary of history, who rebelled against oppression, against the status quo...for the benefit of all humanity." Everyone on the left recognizes "Christ as a combatant in the struggle for the transformation of human life!" Attached to the painting was a plaque on which he had inscribed, "Christians, what have you done to Christ in more than two thousand years of his teachings?"

The *Christ of Peace* is sculptural, characterized by strong modeling, an exaggerated foreshortening which breaks the plane of the picture and a bold contrast between the strong features of Christ and a solid white background. Working from a photograph of himself, he had painted Christ in profile with strong Semitic features, his foreshortened arms extending forward and his interlaced hands pleading for peace. It is also a Mexican Christ, with a crown of piercing thorns, bloodied features and knuckles dripping with blood.

Siqueiros explained that he did not want to paint a conventional Christ, an Italian, French, or Spanish savior, but "*a la Mexicana*, though just as he was, a Jew. I painted a gory Christ, more like a modern martyr than a conventional Christ."

In other statements he confessed that he admired Christ, not as a religious leader, but as a political leader of his time. "Christ was the first anti-imperialist leader of history since he had the courage to confront the powerful Roman oppressors without any support ... The same ones we now have north of the Rio Bravo."

He also compared Christ to Lenin since they were both founders of a new doctrine opposed to war and oppression. One was a revolutionary of the past and the other, a revolutionary of the present, and they killed him "as today they kill communists throughout the world." He was "a political prisoner, crucified more for his revolutionary political ideas than for his religious ideas ... like a Bolshevik of his time." He suffered the same repressive violence as "Vallejo and Campa, the same that I suffered over the years ... Christ was a man, a caudillo, a leader."

Although some Mexicans considered these comparisons blasphemous and objected to his unconventional portrait, the *Christ of Peace* joined paintings by other modern artists in the Vatican museum, but without the plaque. Siqueiros continued to be fascinated with the image of Christ and he designed a greatly enlarged *Christ the Leader* for one of the twelve exterior panels of the Polyforum.

As work progressed in Cuernavaca, workmen were busy erecting the framework on which the sculpture painting was to be mounted in Mexico City. When it was ready, the finished panels were trucked from Cuernavaca to the site and mounted in place using large construction cranes. There were 72 of these panels, weighing between 350 and 1000 kilograms each, and they were to be assembled in four sections of 18 each. The spaces between the panels were filled in with an epoxy paste mixed with asbestos powder, after which a fiberglass cloth was laid over the paste. When the materials had set, they were painted over so as to create an uninterrupted flow of painting from one section to another.

Polyforum Siqueiros and Hotel de Mexico, Mexico, D.F.

While the panels were being set in place, Siqueiros and a team of artists were already working on the ceiling, creating a series of generalized human figures rising from the sidewalls and culminating in the center of the ceiling. Meanwhile, other crews were mounting the 12 panels on the exterior of the building and a large sculpture-painting wall was being assembled along the perimeter of the site.

Nearing the end of his most ambitious project, David worked harder and longer and talked enthusiastically about the activities that would take place in the Polyforum. To visitors he proudly pointed out the different features of the project and the international "symphony" of artists and technicians working on it. He also talked about future projects and the chemical breakthroughs he would use in them. When he heard a visitor comment that the lynching of a black and the monsters attacking women in the mural were pessimistic, David replied. "Society is always moving forward. It never stops in its progress. Sometimes it moves slower because of the repressions of imperialism, but the people never stop in their democratic progress!"

On December 15, 1971, six years after he had started the project and only two weeks before his 75th birthday, David participated in the inauguration of the Polyforum Cultural Siqueiros. While President Echeverría presided, Siqueiros was joined on the platform by his patron, Manuel Suárez, former President Miguel Alemán, Rufino Tamayo, the writers Carlos Fuentes and Salvador Novo, the architect Guillermo Rossel de la Lama, and other government officials and cultural figures.

When it was his turn to speak, Siqueiros talked at length on art and the Revolution and explained his sculpture painting. After stating that art speaks to the masses and expresses their most profound feelings realistically, he attacked paintings which were painted as an object of exchange and speculation in a capitalistic society. Muralism, on the other hand, is an art form that belongs to the people who view it. When Siqueiros was finished, Echeverría spoke about the cultural achievements of the Revolution and lashed out at "capitalistic imperialism."

At the press conference that followed, Siqueiros was pressed by reporters on the contradictions between this project and his former murals or political views. While he insisted that the Polyforum was "a collective experience," available to the masses, he refused to comment on the absence of any political statement in the mural and declared that they should leave him alone to paint what he wished.

When the speeches and ribbon cutting were over, the Polyforum Siqueiros was opened to the public. Besides displaying a mural, the largest ever painted, its several levels provided space for the display and sale of handicrafts, exhibits of contemporary art and performances of theater or dance. The main forum, on the third level, is reached by elevators in glass tubes, like space capsules, or by a circular stairway. Here *The March of Humanity on Earth and Towards the Cosmos* is presented in a large auditorium, the walls and the ceiling covered with more than two thousand square meters of sculpture painting. The floor is a rotating platform on which spectators can sit and listen to a recorded explanation of the mural in Spanish, English and French as the floor rotates and lights illuminate the scenes on the walls.

Upon entering the room, one sees a great procession of figures and is overwhelmed by the visual assault of the dense array of forms, bold colors and protruding metal sculptures. Instead of viewing passive images, one senses that the figures in the mural are looking back. It is the march of the oppressed people of the world from prehistoric times to the present, a victorious march leading to an inevitable and universal revolution.

On the south wall, Siqueiros had painted the march towards the democratic bourgeois revolution. The violence of slavery and racism is depicted by a large metal sculpture of a lynched black man, his mutilated and scorched body hanging from a rope. A sculpture of the mythological animal, the *nahual*, represents evil and ancestral prejudice. Despite their suffering, the masses surge forward towards liberation, led by mothers shielding their children. A clown, representing demagoguery, prematurely celebrates the revolution before the masses dressed in rags, while the forces of militarism loom below. Where the end wall interrupts this flow of humanity, Siqueiros had inserted an enlarged and simplified version of **Our Current Image**. The outstretched hands of this large and faceless male figure, part sculpture and part painting, offer science and technology to humanity.

The north wall represents the march of humanity towards the revolution of the future. This march is also characterized by violence and struggle, beginning with an erupting volcano, a metallic sculpture of a *nahual* attacking a woman and a landscape of dead trees and barren soil. But good triumphs over evil as a man chops down a poisonous tree of evil, flowers spring forth from the *amate*, a tree which never blooms, and a woman raises her arm in the quest for social justice and revolutionary progress. The blossoming flowers represent the new leaders, while another volcano provides energy. On the end wall, directly opposite the man of science and connected to it by converging lines on the ceiling, a faceless female figure symbolizing culture extends her open hands for peace and harmony in a new society.

The March of Humanity on Earth and Towards the Cosmos,
1967–1971, Sculpture-Painting on Asbestos Cement,
Siqueiros Cultural Poyforum, Mexico, D.F.

Overhead three figures are trying to put man on the moon, while the two nations engaged in the space race are represented by an eagle and a red star. In the center of the ceiling, waves of energy, like rays of the sun, burst forth from a cosmic energy source and cascade down the walls to the marching throngs. Rising up from these same throngs, energy flows back towards the center of the ceiling, uniting the multitudes of man's past on earth with his future in the cosmos. Thus, the two end walls, with their symbols of science and culture, along with the ceiling, form a plastic unity of man and woman united in peace and love, the beginning of a new and positive future.

For the exterior of the Polyforum, whose twelve sides radiate out from the center like the faces of a diamond, Siqueiros had designed a sculpted mural of twelve separate panels of 2,750 square feet each. On these panels, representing "The March of Humanity in Latin America," he painted 12 themes: Leadership; Dry Leafless Tree and Reborn Tree; Circus, a Transition from Spectacle to Culture; the End of Aggression; Moses Breaks the Tablets; Christ the Leader; The Dance of the Indian

People before the New Divinity; Flight: A Sacrifice for Liberation; Winter and Summer; The Mingled Races, the Drama Unleashed by the Conquest; Music; and The Atom for Peace, Not War.

Christ the Leader, Exterior Panel, Cultural Polyforum Siqueiros, Mexico, D.F.

Around the perimeter of the site a two-sided mural-wall was erected. The side facing the street consists of a procession of generalized or sketched human figures. On the inside he had constructed sculpture-paintings of five major figures in modern Mexican art: Diego Rivera, José Clemente Orozco, José Guadalupe Posada, Leopoldo Méndez and Dr. Atl. Between the portraits of Orozco and Posada there is an abstract metal sculpture entitled *Crepúsculo* ("Twilight"). Made of welded bands of steel, it looks like a mummified body, its mouth open, placed against the outline of a head. Was this a self-portrait, the last of "los tres grandes?"

The Polyforum was Siqueiros's magnum opus. It was the largest mural ever painted, more than three times the size of the Sistine Chapel, and it was the first building designed to house a mural and the mural and the structure formed a single entity. It was also a synthesis of his ideas of designing a modern building with architects, of creating "unitary art" by integrating mural painting, sculpture and architecture, and of conducting a large team of artists and technical workers in a fully equipped workshop, using the latest in materials and equipment.

"Here we have been able to create an integral work," he explained. "Architects, engineers, artisans, sculptors, painters and even acoustics engineers have worked together to create the Polyforum. It is true collective art." It is a symbiosis of architecture, sculpture and painting, a "plastic cube" in which the audience sees the whole from any point of view as well as individual details. "People will become part of the walls and the floor, which in turn, will become part of the people." He also pointed out that there was no sequence to the mural, since "in art, one should be able to start and end anywhere."

Conceived in prison, the Polyforum was a dream which he had converted into a massive reality. It incorporated many of the images from his prison paintings, the vivid portrayals of motherhood, terror and flight, flowering trees, large multitudes, volcanoes, figures of Christ and hideous monsters which afflict mankind. It was also painted in the freer and more fluid style that he had developed in recent years.

Characteristically, it was not designed to please or to placate. It is a polemic and the language is brutal and direct. Like a baroque church, the interior is a total and overwhelming experience and there is no denying the emotive force of the sculpture painting. It attacks the senses, seeking to convince the viewer of the inexorable progress of humanity from misery and suffering to an inevitable explosion and liberation. Man is central and will triumph after centuries of suffering and struggle, Siqueiros explained. "It is the history of man seen through the filter of our own history; it is his evolution and his destiny."

Founders of Modern Mexican Art, Metal Sculpture-Painting Wall, Siqueiros Cultural Polyforum, Mexico, D.F.

Not everyone, however, was impressed. While some of the criticism focused on the art, much of it focused on the inherent contradictions of the project. It was pointed out that the site of the mural was a hotel-convention center for wealthy businessmen or tourists and that "polyforum" was English, not Spanish. Not only was it located in an affluent section of Mexico City, but the entrance fee of 50 pesos (more than two dollars) would prevent working-class Mexicans from viewing his masterpiece. It was also a form of speculation for Siqueiros's patron and owner of the hotel, Manuel Suárez, just as paintings were objects of speculation in the art market. Since the project had been viewed as a tourist attraction from the start, it was referred to as "Suárezlandia" and Siqueiros's charges that Rivera only painted for the tourists came back to haunt him.

Questions were also raised about whether the mural was comprehensible to the masses. Since his latest style bordered on the abstract, it is difficult to understand the profusion of forms, shapes and colors without a printed guide or recorded narration. There are no familiar portraits or flags and many of the symbols are obscure and require explanation. Despite his admonition that "a mural is a permanent discourse, destined to be read," neither the language nor the message is easily deciphered. While one can recognize and appreciate individual sections, the tendency to focus on those sections destroys the plastic unity and obscures its unifying theme. After the opening ceremony, one reporter commented that the entrance fee, the time required to interpret the mural and its dedication to one man made the Polyforum elitist and private, as opposed to collective, and was, therefore, "the coffin of Mexican muralism."

The most severe criticisms were leveled at the lack of coordination between the geometric structure of the building and the sculpture painting. Even though the building was designed for the mural and the sculpture painting forms the very walls of the building, it did not form a harmonious whole and the murals dominated or obscured the structure. While critics agreed that the interior had a plastic unity, they were also unanimous in pointing out that there was no continuity in the exterior panels and they looked like large easel paintings stuck on the side of the building. Only two of the twelve Polyforum panels contained recognizable figures and there was no apparent theme or coherent message in the exterior mural. This fragmented appearance, however, may be attributed to the Polyforum's diamond-like structure, designed to support *The March of Humanity* on the interior, as well as the process of preparing the panels in a workshop in Cuernavaca instead of painting directly on the walls of a finished building.

Still others lamented that the use of the rotating platform reduced the spectators to passive viewers and violated Siqueiros's idea of the dynamic spectator. There were criticisms that the illumination was unimaginative and distorted the three dimensional sculptures, as well as suggestions that the lights could have been integrated more effectively in the panorama. Although there were no objections to the portraits of the masters of modern Mexican art, it was pointed out that the wall on which they were placed obscured the view of the Polyforum from the street, isolating it from its environment and making it less accessible or private.

While Siqueiros had opposed Suárez's idea of installing a revolving platform, as well as the construction of a sculpture-fence around the site, their existence contradicted his claims of complete artistic control. Combined with the commercial nature of the project, Suárez's changes and insistence on an apolitical mural also reaffirmed Siquieiros's frequent statements about the relationship between the social function and the content or form of art.

Some of the strongest reactions, however, were provoked by the size and elaborate style of the Polyforum. Reacting to the profusion of forms and the violent clash of shapes and colors, critics used terms like "gigantism," "unnecessary bigness," "spectacular," "rhetorical," "grandiloquent," or "pseudo revolutionary emphasis" and one called it "The Polyforum of Frustration." One commentator wrote that the figures did not sing, but shouted in loud voices that could deafen.

However, these comments were subjective and perhaps reflected the fact that the Polyforum was an entirely different art form and neither the public nor the critics had acquired the necessary tastes or standards of judgment. The absence of any systematic analysis of the style and composition of the mural also suggests that the magnitude of the project had overwhelmed the critics and even enthusiasts limited themselves to commenting on its heroic, monumental or universal qualities.

Also missing was a discussion of the incongruities between the content of *The March of Humanity* and Siqueiros's previous work and the original premises of the mural movement. Besides the lack of recognizable portraits and national symbols, there is no mention of the present, positive or negative. There is struggle and revolution, but they are in the past or the future, and there is no mention of the current reality of Mexico, only a vague suggestion of future liberation through technology. Since the artist and the mural movement had always been linked to national issues and social conditions, the absence of either in *The March of Humanity* served the interests of the ruling party.

Seeking international acceptance, recent presidents had made extensive trips abroad, Mexico had hosted the Olympics and World Cup soccer matches and the PRI now wanted to attract foreign capital as well as tourists. Internationalism, moderation and stability, therefore, were to replace nationalism, revolutionary politics and social conflict, even in works of art, especially one commissioned as a tourist attraction by a member of the new oligarchy. At the same time, the regime could maintain the fiction that the Revolution was still alive, and like the mural, assure the world that the problems of the present would be resolved in a "safe" future. By ignoring the present and not making any political statement, therefore, the Polyforum not only betrayed the struggle in Mexico, but ironically confirmed Siqueiros's earlier statements that "anti-popular regimes foster spectacular demagogic public art" and that murals painted for demagogic reasons or tourism were inferior.

Criticisms and contradictions notwithstanding, the Polyforum stands as a monument to a tremendous imagination and creative impulse. For Siqueiros it represented the opportunity and the challenge to realize many of his lifelong dreams and he had applied all of his energy, skill and experience to make it a reality. It was another experiment in his constant drive to develop a more effective plastic language, to create a new realism for a modern age. Consistent with his purpose, it assaults and overwhelms and like much of his art, it depicts all aspects of the human experience, from terror and suffering to love and solidarity. It is brutal but it also shows tenderness and love.

As Antonio Rodríguez wrote,

> No one in Mexico ever showed such an integral image of the drama of man as he [Siqueiros]. Rodríguez Lozano saw desolation; Orozco, cruelty and tragedy; Cuevas, the unhinging of man. Siqueiros embraces the whole scale of suffering. Dead workers, martyred heroes, sobbing women, beings dominated by anguish, crowds whipped by hunger were the leitmotifs of his work... He mixes the sobs and

cries to convert them into cries of protest ... The people of Siqueiros suffer and die, but they are not resigned, in order to encourage the rebellion of those who, in terrorized march, move onward towards the star. The Polyforum therefore, appears as the last and polished image of the dream which nurtured his life.

Any evaluation of the Polyforum should include the contributions of the many artists, architects and workers who contributed to the project. Despite his differences with Manuel Suárez, Siqueiros recognized that no one had ever provided the economic and moral support for a project of this magnitude in the history of art and he was grateful that Suárez had provided him with this unique opportunity. He insisted that he did not have to compromise his ideas or interpretation to suit his patron, or to please the public, and he saw no contradiction in working for a millionaire who had the vision and financial resources to invest in a project that would cost several million pesos and which could only be left to posterity.

Before he had finished the Polyforum, Siqueiros was planning new projects. When the State of Mexico invited him to decorate a large new building at the university in Toluca, he immediately began working on it in Cuernavaca, despite his declining health. After constructing a monumental pyramid based on those of pre-Hispanic Mexico, he created an imaginary landscape of pyramids on some leftover asbestos cement panels, like an ancient city, behind which lines of composition and perspectives disappeared into infinity. While he was working on this project, he received an invitation to paint a mural in Geneva, Switzerland for the new headquarters of the International Organization of Labor.

When a retrospective exhibit of his work, including some of his latest paintings and lithographs, was scheduled to open in Tokyo in 1972, he and Angélica applied for transit visas for their trip to Japan at the American Embassy. Despite his age and declining health, not to mention his international reputation as an artist, the U.S. Embassy only gave them permission to spend two days in California. After resting in Los Angeles, he and Angélica flew to Japan and the opening of his show.

Upon their return, Siqueiros resumed work on the mural for the university in Toluca, alternating between his workshop in Cuernavaca and his home and studio in the capital. But he lacked his habitual energy and found himself tiring easily. When he could no longer bear the strain of mural painting, he sat down and directed the drawing of compositional lines and the painting of figures from a chair. Like a film director, he used a megaphone to shout directions to the artists working on the scaffolds, telling them to add some color or to extend a line.

When visitors arrived, he would rise and dramatically apply some strokes with a long handled brush to the unfinished panels. But it was a painful and frustrating process, especially for an artist who put all his energy and feelings into his work and enjoyed the physical process of mural painting. How could he rest now that there were so many projects to be done, so many possibilities now that he had broached the fourth stage of Mexican mural painting?

After he complained of a pain in the lower part of the spinal column and began to lose his appetite, Angélica insisted that he enter a hospital for a checkup. But he was impatient to return to his work and refused to stay in the hospital more than two days for the prescribed treatments. While he agreed to undergo some therapy in Cuernavaca, he abandoned the treatment after several visits.

Although he had rejected an invitation to do some lithographs for a "Mexican Masters" suite, he agreed to participate when Angélica insisted that they needed the money and he realized that Tamayo, Cuevas and the artist-sculptor Zúñiga would also each submit two lithographs. His first attempts, however, were disappointing and after the plates were destroyed, he recreated two of his paintings, *Maternity* and *Repose*, in two of his finest lithographs.

Late in 1972, David and Angélica made arrangements to convert his studio in Mexico City into a museum of mural composition where his models, tools, "mural studies" and compositional drawings could be studied. The "Sala de Arte Publico" (Museum of Public Art) is not only a museum of his work, but also a center for exhibits, lectures, panels and film presentations on art and national or international issues.

In the spring of 1973 David and Angélica took a trip to Europe and Russia. In Paris, they visited the lithography studio of Mourlot where he signed the lithographs for two series based on some of his earlier paintings. From France they went to Geneva so that he could see the site for the projected "March of Humanity" which he was to paint in the offices of the International Organization of Labor.

Next they flew to Moscow to attend the celebrations for the First of May. As if they were on a pilgrimage, he and Angélica visited the museums, exhibits and sacred sites for comrades. When a speaker noted that Siqueiros was present at a meeting and described his 50-year struggle as a communist, the audience rose and gave him a standing ovation. Sensing that he was getting tired and experiencing more pain, Angélica canceled their trip to the south of Russia and they spent the rest of the time visiting museums or artists in their studios and meeting with old comrades.

When they returned to Mexico, David tried to keep up his usual pace, but he lacked the strength and energy. Following Echeverría's "State of the Nation" address, he wrote an open letter to the President, in which he endorsed his continuation of the Revolution, but warned against allowing the progressive measures to be undone by his successors, as happened after Cárdenas. He also urged Echeverría to allow the workers, peasants, students and intellectuals to create their own organizations for the purpose of transforming society.

Meanwhile, he continued to paint as time and energy permitted. But he was experiencing severe pain and was admitted to the hospital a week later. On September 11, 1973, Angélica met with the doctors and learned that he had an advanced case of cancer of the prostate and had only a few months to live.

When she returned to his room, he was watching television in horror as the armed forces attacked the presidential palace in Santiago, Chile, killing thousands of civilians and Salvador Allende, the popularly elected socialist President of Chile. As the blood bath in Chile continued, they received news that the military junta had ordered the destruction of his mural in Chillan. Fortunately, those rumors turned out to be false and *Death to the Invader* still condemns imperialism, past and present.

A few days after the coup, they received news of the death of Pablo Neruda from cancer. In a letter to Pablo in care of his countrymen, Siqueiros described him as "the greatest muralist poet, singer of the hopes of all the oppressed people of our Latin America and the whole world" and he assured Pablo that the struggle would be won in spite of the humiliation of the Chilean people by Yankee imperialists and their criminal native allies.

David's health continued to decline and during the last few months of 1973, he experienced increasing pain. Although confined to his bed, he never gave up hope that he would recover and return to his tools and the projects waiting him in the studio next door. Refusing to accept any negative prognosis and not wanting to dampen his hopes, Angélica never told him of the doctor's prediction. When David asked her if he was going to die, she reassured him, "No, what do you mean? You will live for many years." A week before his seventy-seventh birthday, he stumbled weakly into the street to look at his workshop and unfinished panels, talking enthusiastically about his plans for the future.

On January 5, he told his brother Jesús that he doubted that he would ever see him again. The next day, he died without uttering a word while Angélica, Adriana, Leopoldo and two nurses stood by his bed. For the first time since birth, he was serene and quiet, his restless energy finally spent. After embracing her lover and comrade of more than 40 years, Angélica tried to suppress her grief and prepared to meet the public. Immediately messages of condolence came from all over the world, as friends and admirers expressed their sorrow and paid tribute to Siqueiros's life and his work.

One of the first to visit and convey his condolences was President Echeverría. After paying his respects to Angélica, he decreed that David's body would lay in state in Bellas Artes and there would be 24 hours of public mourning and homage. The next day he joined members of the cabinet, Angélica, Jesús, members of the Arenal family and many old friends and comrades in an honor guard at the side of David's flag-draped casket. Burying past differences, Carlos Chávez and Rufino Tamayo also stood guard over their fellow artist.

During the day, several thousand Mexicans of all ages and social classes filed by, some stopping to kiss the flag and honor their friend and ally for the last time. To commemorate his death, Roberto López Moreno and Mario Orozco Rivera composed a folk ballad or *corrido*, "The Death of Siqueiros." Even in death, however, his differences with his Party continued to haunt him. Some members wanted him expelled posthumously because of his support of Echeverría and resented that the President had handled the ceremony and the national flag had been placed over his coffin instead of the communist banner.

The next day his body was taken to the Rotunda of Illustrious Men with an escort of cadets from the Military Academy. While thousands listened or watched on radio and television, the pallbearers carried the coffin to the gravesite and Angélica and Echeverría placed a large wreath at the foot of the coffin. After the Mexican flag was removed, folded and given to Angélica, the coffin was lowered slowly into the ground while hushed mourners sung the *Internationale.*

XXI. Epilogue: Only in Mexico

The day after his death the front page of the *New York Times* announced "Siqueiros Dies in Mexico at 77." Besides a photograph of him, there was a news photo of a father carrying his son, wounded by an artillery barrage in Cambodia, and a picture of President and Mrs. Nixon leaving church services in San Clemente. The father and son could have stepped out of one of Siqueiros's paintings and the juxtaposition of their pathos with the Sunday ritual of the Nixons suggested an updated *Portrait of the Bourgeoisie*.

The *Times* also featured two articles on Siqueiros. Although John Canaday called him "a mountain" and emphasized his talents as a "pure artist or artist-propagandist," he concluded that the Mexican Renaissance had not survived the 1940s and Siqueiros had "outlived his movement." In his obituary, called "A Tumultuous Life," Alden Whitman wrote that Siqueiros was "a showman with an invincible ego" who had become a national institution in Mexico in his last years, "a status the old revolutionary obviously enjoyed." In spite of their praise for Siqueiros as an artist, the tone of both articles was patronizing and reflected a bias against social realism. They not only described him as a propagandist or strutting clown, but also dismissed the Mexican Renaissance as "nationalistic," "anti-esthetic" and "visual propaganda."

Although Canaday's verdict that the mural movement had not survived the 1940s reflected recent trends in Mexico, it overlooked the murals painted by Siqueiros and other artists since 1940. While the Revolution may have ended with the reforms of Cárdenas and a new generation of artists was breaking away from social realism, the poverty, repression, and imperialism had not disappeared and many artists continued to describe these conditions and express their views in their art.

There was also no mention of the factors that brought about a shift in official patronage or acts of censorship. Increasingly dependent on American tourism and hoping to attract foreign capital, the government sought to portray a modern and stable society. Although it still glorified the leaders of the Revolution, the new elite was not interested in social reform or artists who contradicted the image of stability and prosperity. When one of the founders of the mural renaissance tried to paint current conditions and protested government repression, he was not only locked out of his mural site, but was arrested and sentenced to eight years in prison.

Not just government priorities had changed. New galleries had opened, catering to wealthy Mexicans or foreigners who preferred picturesque scenes or abstract paintings by younger artists. These artists had not participated in the struggles of the past and their art reflected a different Mexico. Lacking a revolutionary government to back them, they painted for a market that was greatly influenced by international cultural currents. With some exceptions, nonfigurative easel painting supplanted social realism and mural painting became a form of decoration to attract foreign visitors.

Despite these trends, the Mexican Mural Movement, which began in 1921, was an important and distinctive countercurrent in modern art. Since it expressed contemporary issues using modern materials, equipment and techniques, it was more than a revival of the art of the European Renaissance, of large frescos painted by a master artist and a team of assistants. It gave mural painting a new and modern vitality, developing new techniques and materials, adapting to modern architecture and building materials, and painting exterior murals.

Although there were attempts to revive mural painting before 1910, it was not until young artists, lacking a market for their art and inspired by their participation in the Revolution, turned to a sympathetic government to sponsor mural painting. While their first murals were tentative, they developed new techniques and painted themes that were less traditional, more Mexican and militant. Like their counterparts in literature, music and dance, they sought to develop themes and forms of expression which reflected the traditions and conditions of their country and which would serve the Revolution.

In contrast with the prevailing artistic currents in Paris and New York, their art was realistic and figurative and made a social or political statement. Instead of removing man from their art, they made the human condition the central focus of their artistic expression. While they drew from the Mexican experience, their depictions of maternity, the family, suffering, anguish, greed, fascism, imperialism, war, modern technology, solidarity and revolutionary struggle were universal.

The Mexican muralists also viewed themselves as "cultural workers," not elite artists working in the isolation of their studios, and they participated directly in the political struggles of Mexico and other countries. They committed themselves to "public art," not for the enjoyment or speculation of wealthy collectors, but to enlighten, inspire and mobilize the masses. Often, however, their "proletarian art" was appreciated more by the bourgeoisie they were attacking than the masses they hoped to inspire.

It was "public art" in every sense of the term and the artists and their work provoked heated discussions. When they disagreed with each other, public debates ensued in which workers, as well as artists and intellectuals, took sides. Nowhere, at any time, had the subject of art or artists generated such excitement and controversy or were artists treated as national celebrities. When they died, they were mourned as national heroes and they willed their studios and collections of art to the people of Mexico.

Despite its fitful origins, the mural movement not only survived, but also received international recognition and several muralists were invited to paint in the United States. While most of the excitement focused on their murals, the drawings, prints and paintings of Orozco, Rivera and Siqueiros also received critical acclaim and were purchased by the major museums or private collectors in Latin America, the United States and Europe. Today Mexicans of all social classes visit their murals while retrospective exhibits of their work draw crowds in the United States, Asia and Europe.

When unemployed American artists petitioned their government for support, the Roosevelt Administration responded by hiring artists to decorate public buildings with murals as well as to draw, paint and photograph the American scene. Since they had no experience in mural or fresco painting, they either studied the work of the Mexicans in the United States or went to Mexico to view their murals. In the 30s and 40s African-American artists were also influenced by the revolutionary forms, techniques and content of the Mexicans, especially "Los tres grandes." More recently, minority artists have followed the example of the Mexican muralists, protesting injustice or expressing their pride in their culture and community on the walls of their neighborhoods.

David Alfaro Siqueiros was not only a founder and participant in the Mexican Mural Movement. Insisting that an art movement must have a theoretical base and can only progress by constantly reassessing its production, he drafted a series of manifestos, engaged in public debates and wrote articles and books on art in which he hammered away at certain basic theses, reminding himself and others of the founding premises of their original movement, the uniqueness of mural painting and the need to develop a new and modern realism for a modern age. In spite of their polemical and dogmatic tone, these statements constitute the major theoretical formulation of the Mexican Mural Movement and Siqueiros was its self-appointed ideologue.

When he was accused of imposing his views on other artists and trying to monopolize artistic expression in Mexico, he responded that given the conditions and needs of our country, the mural movement was "the only way." It was unique, he argued, the cultural expression of the Mexican Revolution in the arts, and no other country has developed a comparable movement, even those with similar histories or cultures, or produced as many outstanding muralists. Since their murals were intended to serve the Revolution and it was incomplete, they had to continue the struggle and defend muralism against new apolitical trends in art.

Accusing artists who paint in the isolation of their studios of "cerebral masturbation" and developing innovations for the sake of innovation, he stated that the so-called "avant-garde" artists had not contributed anything new to the development of modern plastic materials, equipment or technique. While he recognized their talent and innovations in perception, he protested the monopoly of modern art by "the school of Paris" and contended that they had become stagnant, forming exclusionary schools, copying the work of the recognized "masters" and developing formal stylisms.

Responding to charges that the Mexican muralists were "government lackeys," he declared that an artist who paints for wealthy collectors, chic galleries or influential art critics is no more free than an artist who is hired to paint a mural by a government which respects freedom of expression. To those who criticized modern Mexican art because of its political content, he reminded them that the great art of the Renaissance was ideological and no one would reject it because it was religious or was commissioned by the government or the Catholic Church. Besides, artists who ignore the turmoil and conflict around them are making a political statement by their silence. When their art was criticized for being nationalistic and lacking universal meaning, Siqueiros pointed out that while a national past or culture might be the starting point for an artist, a platform on which to develop a universal message, it should not be an end in itself.

Insisting that truly great art was "integral," he explained that the schools of modern art were concerned with only one dimension of art: impressionism with light; fauvism with color; expressionism with emotion; surrealism with the subconscious; cubism with the structure of form and futurism with movement. Great art, he contended, is "integral" or "unitary," combining all the elements and integrating painting, sculpture and architecture.

Siqueiros also rejected the currents of abstract or nonfigurative art and proposed the development of a "neo-realism," using the latest discoveries of industry and science. It would not only employ new techniques and materials but also the mental and visual understanding of nature derived from modern science and technology. Although he explored the possibilities of "the controlled accident" in his own work, in order to enhance the sense of reality, he ridiculed the idea of a movement based on trivial accidents, created by throwing or dripping paint on a flat surface.

After proclaiming that the great art of the past had been public, Siqueiros participated in one of the major public art movements of the 20th Century and painted twenty-five murals in five countries. Practicing what he preached, several of his projects became schools for other artists and he employed teams of artists on all of his major mural projects. His final mural, the Polyforum Siqueiros, engaged more than 50 artists, technicians and architects in a fully equipped workshop. There he conducted a symphony of artists, creating the master design, directing its execution and maintaining a harmony of style.

It was from these experiences that Siqueiros derived his theories, especially about mural painting. After discovering how the tools and materials affected art, he also concluded that mural painting involved much more than enlarging an easel painting. It was totally different and more difficult than easel painting, requiring more physical strength and very different techniques, materials and composition. Murals must compete with other structures or architectural forms and since they were seen from different angles by moving spectators, they needed a multiangular perspective. Since exterior mural painting was very different from interior mural painting, it also required new materials, techniques and solutions.

Following this discovery, Siqueiros worked constantly to develop new techniques for resolving the special problems of mural painting. Aware that moving spectators saw murals from many different angles, he developed a multilinear perspective for "the dynamic spectator." Employing optical illusions, multiple images and concave surfaces, he created realistic effects and a sense of movement which the spectator activates. At the same time, the figures may be viewed from different angles without distortion.

Siqueiros also insisted that mural painting involved the painting of the total architectonic space, including the ceilings, vaults or arches and even the floors of the mural site. By integrating architecture, mural painting, sculpture and polychroming, the expressive language of the artist was enhanced, while the more active concave surfaces could be used to create a sense of movement. Besides demonstrating his idea of truly integral art, the Polyforum was also a testimony to his restless energy, expansive imagination and constant search for new solutions.

In his drive to develop and enhance his new realism, Siqueiros experimented with and used the latest discoveries of science and industry. When he was accused of using materials developed for painting commercial products, he explained that the materials and tools of art had always come from industry or the laboratory and you could not paint modern art with archaic materials or equipment. Archaic materials or techniques could only produce archaic art. A modern age calls for modern materials, equipment and techniques, appropriate to the intent of the artist and the function of his art. New tools and material enable us to expand our vocabulary, to enhance and make our plastic language more eloquent, more effective. Fascinated with film and cinematography, he envisioned making a film of a mural as the final statement or work of art.

Since Siqueiros always insisted that he was a muralist and that his small paintings were preliminary studies for murals, it is not surprising that many of his easel paintings appear in his murals. By themselves, however, many of them are virtual murals, monumental, heroic or allegorical in nature. In some of them the figures thrust forward, visually assaulting the viewer, or they retreat, drawing the viewer into the recesses of the painting. In others the picture plane is filled with masses of humanity or gigantic forms of nature, while many of them describe the human condition, make a statement or instruct. The effect, therefore, is of a much larger painting or space, more like a mural than a flat two-dimensional space surrounded by a frame.

There is also a sense of movement in these pictures, the human figures or inanimate objects appearing to vibrate, swirl about or interact with each other. His still life *Three Squashes* creates the impression of three living objects interacting with each other, while many of his landscapes are turbulent, the earth and mountains seeming to move like molten lava. This sense of movement gives his art a baroque quality in which the sinuous forms move about and envelope each other or the viewer.

When he was not working on a mural project, Siqueiros was able to support himself by selling his easel paintings or painting portraits. While the portrait assignments helped him to develop his skills for painting historical figures in murals, he also developed a unique style in which he depicted the inner psychology, personal character and emotional state of the subject. Even his numerous self-portraits are autobiographical, describing his state of mind, emotional condition or predicament, as well as his changing features.

Whether painting murals or small canvases, Siqueiros's plastic language is direct, graphic and sometimes brutal. The impact is emotional, evoking a gamut of feelings and provoking a response. In *The Sob, Echo of a Scream* and *Mothers of Mezquital* one cannot avoid feeling the pain and anguish of the victims or condemning the causes of their suffering, while his many depictions of maternity convey the strength and tender love of mothers, as well as their despair. Many of his paintings are also visual allegories in which he made a statement about humanity or society.

Although the emphasis in many of his smaller works is on repression, poverty, fear and suffering, he could also express the tender love of a mother for her children, natural beauty, the confidence, strength, and courage of individuals and the solidarity of the working class. In prison he painted flowers or flowering trees, a grandmother tenderly holding her child and a sleeping woman, serene and peaceful.

Despite his differences with his father, Siqueiros absorbed many of Cipriano's artistic preferences and developed a personal style that belongs to a tradition of baroque art in Mexico. Before his exposure to the Italian futurists and the film techniques of Serge Eisenstein, his preoccupation with movement had already been triggered by the active compositions and flowing forms of the Mexican baroque.

Although he was a modern and revolutionary artist in terms of technique and content, stylistically he was a baroque artist.

Unlike Rivera's relatively static and flat compositions, Siqueiros created three-dimensional compositions in which the figures either thrust forward toward the observer or draw him back into the painting and surround him. His art is agitated, spontaneous and impassioned, as if he were speaking through his images and trying to provoke or challenge his audience. It expresses or evokes strong feelings, often unpleasant, and its sinuous forms are half real, half fantasy. In contrast with Rivera's more classical style, it is fresher, more alive and bursting with emotion.

His theories on "integral art" and the integration of painting, sculpture and architecture also belong to the baroque and many of his murals, from his first mural assignment to his last project, the Polyforum, are modern baroque chapels. While Tamayo called his paintings of maternity "Mexican madonnas," his paintings of Christ also recall the *cristos* that he had observed in baroque chapels with his father.

Art and politics were inseparable for Siqueiros and his preference for social realism and mural painting was motivated by a desire to communicate with and mobilize the masses. While Picasso's marxism had little impact on his art, Siqueiros's art was a vehicle for expressing his opposition to war and fascism, condemning capitalism, denouncing racism and bigotry, combating imperialism and glorifying the struggle of the masses. Although it may be appreciated from a purely aesthetic point of view, such an approach is one-dimensional and ignores the very purpose of his work and the intimate connection between his political views and the form, style and content of his art. Similarly, his search for new materials and equipment for a "neo-realism" was part of a consuming drive to make his statements more visible, enduring, and effective.

An inveterate activist who was involved in many struggles on several continents, Siqueiros boasted that he had been arrested and deported from more countries than anyone else in history. Throughout his life his outbursts of creative energy were interspersed with direct political engagement, as if he needed to regenerate himself, revive his political consciousness or renew his contact with the masses, whose struggle he sought to depict and serve. Since his art was linked to that struggle, however, he was never disengaged from that cause, even in prison.

Not only did he participate directly in the struggle, but he also founded, published, and edited a series of publications from poster-like broadsheets to journals on art, albeit most of them short-lived. These publishing ventures constituted another form of public art in which he expressed his ideas on a wide range of topics, including art, modern architecture, national cinema, imperialism, Mexican politics and international affairs.

Siqueiros's life story is also important in terms of understanding his art. Just as the style, form and content of his art were affected by his politics, his art and his politics were also a reflection of his personal character, shaped by his nationality, family background, his childhood, the political and intellectual climate of his formative years and his young adult experiences. While his life story helps to explain his art, that art reflects and illuminates Siqueiros the man.

Born into an upper class Mexican family at the turn of the century, David Alfaro Siqueiros grew up in a period of intellectual and political ferment and a resurgence of Mexican nationalism. Between 1900 and 1910 Mexico experienced increasing unrest as attempts to organize the workers were repressed and resentment mounted against the perpetuation of the Díaz dictatorship and its surrender to foreign interests. In 1910 these factors came together in an armed revolt against Díaz.

During the next seven years, the country was torn by political intrigue, foreign intervention and a devastating civil war. Politically naive in 1910, the overthrow of Díaz, the student strike at San Carlos and the assassination of Madero radicalized Siqueiros, while his participation in the Revolution accelerated his political indoctrination. By his own account, his revolutionary experience was crucial, exposing him to the real conditions of his country and its rich cultural heritage. It also removed him from the secluded halls of the art academy and destroyed the idea of becoming an elite artist, working in a private studio and painting commissions for the rich.

If there is a major theme or image in the art of Siqueiros, it is that of maternity, repeated many times in his mural and easel paintings. While motherhood has always inspired artists and he had been exposed to hundreds of madonnas and pietas in the churches he visited with his father, his frequent depictions of the strength and love of mothers also suggests the loss of his own mother at a tender age. The subject of motherhood is inescapable in Mexico and the ubiquitous mother surrounded by her offspring is a constant reminder of the poverty and suffering and a natural subject for an artist who sought to describe these conditions. But their love and strength also offer hope for the future, symbolizing solidarity and the struggle for a more just society.

Another pervasive image is that of the victims of an unjust system, war or imperialism, including tortured prisoners, dead miners and martyred revolutionaries. First depicted in *Burial of a Worker*, he created similar images in *Accident in the Mine*, *Proletarian Victim*, *Tropical America*, *Echo of a Scream*, *Death to the Invader*, *Portrait of the Bourgeoisie,"* *New Democracy*, *For the Social Welfare for All Mexicans*, *The Theater in Mexico*, *The Revolution Against Diaz*, and many other paintings or studies. Like the figures of motherhood, these inert cadavers or martyrs are graphic reminders of human tragedy and suffering.

Since his father and grandfather were the most important men in Siqueiros's life during his formative years, they played a very important role in his character development, contributing to or reinforcing his fierce pride, even arrogance, a strong sense of dignity and personal integrity, personal courage and apparent disregard for danger, a combative or aggressive nature, a zest for life and tremendous dynamic energy. He exuded confidence and refused to admit any self-doubt or discouragement.

Siqueiros was also being molded by the social environment and national culture and many of his personal traits conformed to those expected of young Mexican males. Although he received awards from foreign powers and international recognition as an artist, the honor that he cherished the most was the Mexican National Prize for Art. He was extremely proud of having contributed to a modern art movement unique to Mexico and stylistically his art is more akin to the Mexican baroque than any other style or school of art. He also loved to tell stories about the uniqueness of being Mexican and was fond of describing the distinctive regions, cultures and peoples of Mexico.

During the Revolution he proved his mettle in combat, drawing on the skills and fortitude nurtured by his grandfather. He also witnessed the terrible carnage and apparently learned to accept or endure the violence of war, as well as to participate in acts of violence. He was very proud of his participation in the Mexican Revolution and many of the stories he told about that conflict or the war in Spain featured firing squads and the defiant courage with which the victims met their fate. While some of these tales were intended to impress his audience, they also reflected the brutality of these conflicts and the impression that these experiences made on him.

Long after the civil war Mexico remained a violent society in which political differences were settled by assassination or armed revolts against the government. When the artists began to paint their first murals in the Preparatoria, they were attacked by students and had to defend themselves with pistols. As a union organizer in Jalisco, he had to use weapons in order to protect himself against company goons, *cristeros* or government agents. He helped to break up the "Gold Shirts" in the Zocalo by firing into their ranks, he led front-line troops in Spain and he organized an assault on the fortified home of Leon Trotsky in which a young American was killed.

According to his own testimony, he continued to carry a pistol and when police agents surprised him outside his home in 1960, he reached for the pistol in the glove compartment of his car while Angélica sped away. Given the Mexican male's strong sense of honor and the use of violence to settle political or personal differences, it was not unusual, however, for a male of his generation to carry a pistol. In view of his outspoken political views and frequent antigovernment activities, not to mention numerous amorous escapades, he probably had good reason to look out for his personal safety.

Siqueiros's experiments and use of untested materials and equipment as well the initiation of projects which were unprecedented in scale or technique, also suggest a tremendous self-confidence and a powerful ego. His choice of mural painting as a means of expression indicates that he not only had something to say, but was confident that it was important and that he could express it effectively through his art. Mural painting offered him a larger stage and audience than easel painting and he was just as dramatic in his art as he was in his public speaking. The Polyforum is not only a testimony of his fertile imagination, restless energy and artistic talent. Unprecedented in conception, size, materials, techniques, construction, employment of artists and technicians and the integration of architecture, sculpture and mural painting, it is also a monument to an indestructible ego.

Siqueiros had a great imagination and flair for the dramatic, and whether speaking to a large audience or telling a story to an intimate group of friends, he was very theatrical, sitting or standing erect and speaking dramatically. Although he matched Rivera's flair for attracting publicity or generating controversy, his outbursts were not limited to protesting injustice or repression. Throughout his life he also attacked fellow artists and accused them of abandoning the spirit of the original mural movement; painting for tourists, reactionary governments, or modern imperialists; removing man from their art; ignoring social issues; imitating the work of established artists; becoming folkloric or picturesque and using archaic methods and materials in their art.

Although Siqueiros sprinkled his praise for Orozco with critical comments, his favorite target was Rivera. While he recognized Diego's genius and contributions to modern Mexican art, he attacked him for his "counterrevolutionary road," archaic methods and betrayal of the goals of the movement. Diego attributed Siqueiros's attacks on him to their political differences and his need to prove his good faith to the Party, but there also seems to have been a personal rivalry or competition between the two in which the younger Siqueiros, consciously or unconsciously, sought to surpass Rivera.

After Orozco and Rivera died, Siqueiros concentrated on Rufino Tamayo and José Luis Cuevas, defending muralism and the school of realism against their apolitical tendencies and accusing them of betraying modern realism or the mural movement. Although he was accused of trying to monopolize Mexican art or to impose his views on a new generation of artists, his conduct was consistent with his dialectical approach to life, art and politics, always challenging whatever was static, in vogue or official. Conflict and confrontation, thesis and antithesis, whether political or chromatic, were the modus vivendi. Nor did he spare himself, prodding him to develop more advanced techniques and plastic materials for a new and more effective realism.

Notwithstanding his strong ego and dogmatic manner, Siqueiros was a charming man. He enjoyed the company of others and loved to be surrounded by friends and admirers, and in private, he was a good friend with many of his public adversaries. Although he was married three times, he never had any children, but he adopted Angélica's daughter Adriana as his own and was a doting and affectionate grandfather to her children and caring uncle to his niece.

Women were attracted to him and he certainly enjoyed their company, causing each of his wives considerable anxiety. He always needed a woman, not just as a female companion, but also as a coworker or comrade who shared his political views and would sacrifice herself for him. His three wives were dedicated to him and it is clear that he needed and depended upon them and that they sacrificed their lives and careers when they were with him. They also shared the risks and hardships of his political activism and career in art.

His widow, Angélica Arenal de Siqueiros, was a very strong and talented woman who gave up her own career as a journalist to live and work with him and not only participated in his political activities, going into hiding and exile with him, but also helped to write and edit many of his publications and manage his business affairs. Since he never learned to drive, she drove him back and forth to his mural projects and delivered his meals everyday when he was in the national penitentiary. During the Polyforum project, she managed the books, paid the artists and the workers, handled the correspondence and arranged commissions when new equipment or materials were needed.

After his death Angélica announced that he had left his studio in Mexico City and all of his archives and library to the people of Mexico. It is now the Sala de Arte Público, an archive on his life and work, as well as a gallery and forum for discussions on art and politics. Before her death, Angélica worked unceasingly, promoting his art all over the world, editing and publishing his memoirs or writings on art and managing his former studio in Mexico City. She also promoted his hope that the workshop in Cuernavaca, built especially for the Polyforum project, would become an active workshop in which students from all over Mexico would learn mural painting by working on new projects. Through her efforts, the legacy of Siqueiros lives on, while his paintings and murals continue to remind us of the human condition and the constant struggle for liberation and social justice.

NOTES

I. "A Young Chinaco"

p. 5 Most of the information on Siqueiros's childhood, family and personal life comes from his memoirs, published posthumously, *Me llamaban El Coronelazo. Memorias de David Alfaro Siqueiros,* ed. by Angélica Arenal de Siqueiros, (México: Biografias Gandesa, 1977); Angélica Arenal de Siqueiros, *Páginas sueltas con Siqueiros* (México: Editorial Grijalbo, 1979); Julio Scherer Garcia, *Siqueiros: La piel y la entraña*, (México: Ediciones Era, 1974); Raquel Tibol, *Siqueiros: Introductor de realidades*, (México: Universidad Nacional Autónoma de México, 1961); idem, *Siqueiros: Vida y obra*, (México: Colección Metro Politana, 1973); and idem, David Alfaro *Siqueiros: Un mexicano y su obra,* (México: Empresas Editoriales, 1969).

p. 7 Except where the title cited is in English, the translations from Spanish are by the author.

IV. "Renaissance"

p. 59 The sources on the origins of the Mexican Mural Renaissance are: Jean Charlot, *Mexican Mural Renaissance*; Anita Brenner, *Idols Behind Altars: The Story of the Mexican Spirit*, (Boston: Beacon Press, 1970) and Antonio Rodríguez, *A History of Mexican Mural Painting*, trans. by Marina Corby, (New York: G.P. Putnam, 1969). Siqueiros also addresses the factors or individuals which contributed to the revival of mural painting in México in his articles in *No hay mas ruta que la nuestra*.

p. 62 There is some disagreement over who discovered the formula for fresco and painted the first modern fresco in Mexico, though the latter honor probably belongs to Charlot.

V. "Labor Leader"

p. 89-92 Siqueiros's activities as a union organizer and his personal experiences are based mainly on his own accounts in *Me llamaban El Coronelazo*; Tibol, *Siqueiros: Vida y obra*, pp. 63-69 and idem, *Siqueiros: Un mexicano y su obra,* pp. 30-46.

VI. "Prison - Taxco"

p. 109 When Siqueiros later changed the title from *Peasant Mother* to "The Deported Woman" the painting took on another meaning, implying that she and her child are the victims of U.S. immigration policy during the Great Depression, when thousands of Mexicans, including many who were legal residents, were threatened or deported. When the "Deported Woman" reference is used, it not only refers to specific events but also converts a static composition into a dynamic one, adding a sense of movement to this monumental painting. Although he painted it in 1931, the date has been changed several times to suggest an earlier completion. *Portrait of Decade*, p. 121.

p. 111 Moisés Saenz was Undersecretary of Public Education in the Calles administration who promoted rural schools, traveling libraries and cultural missions. A member of the ruling establishment, his home in Taxco was a cultural center and frequent residence of American visitors and he was one of Siqueiros's first patrons. Siqueiros did a lithograph study and an oil portrait of Saenz. *Portrait of a Decade*, p. 142.

p. 111 Siqueiros had apparently visited Taxco previously and may have received favored treatment, since other political prisoners were kept in prison. After the completion of an all weather road in 1931, Taxco became a tourist attraction and cultural center.

p. 115 The woodcut of the hammer and anvil was later used for the cover of *Art Front*, the magazine of New York artists' union in 1936. Because few collectors could afford oil paintings during the Depression, many artists turned to prints and Spratling became their agent in Mexico, arranging for their printing and sale in New York at the Weyhe Gallery. *Portrait of a Decade*, p. 139.

p. 116 In some rural areas it was customary to have the portraits of dead children painted by a local artist or to decorate them with flowers and ribbons before having them displayed for a day or so, propped up in a chair or laid out on a table, as part of a wake.

p. 118 After the defeat of the Spanish Republic in 1939 the Casino Español became a conservative social and cultural center for Spanish residents in México and was the site of a victory party celebrating the triumph of Franco and the Nationalists.

p. 118 Siqueiros referred to his American patron as Alicia Mayer in *Me llamaban El Coronelazo*, while other sources refer to an Alice Myers who was a collector from Santa Fe.

VII. "Exile: Los Angeles - Buenos Aires"

p. 129 For information on Siqueiros's art work in Los Angeles in 1932, see Shifra Goldman, "Siqueiros and Three Early Murals in Los Angeles," *Art Journal* 33, Summer 1974; Laurance Hurlburt, "David Alfaro Siqueiros: The Quest for Revolutionary Mural Form and Content, 1920-1940" (Ph.D. diss., University of Wisconsin-Madison, 1976); idem, *Portrait of Present-Day Mexico, A Mural by David Alfaro Siqueiros*, (New York, Christie's, 1969) and idem, *The Mexican Muralists in the United States*, (Albuquerque: University of New Mexico Press, 1989).

Siqueiros also referred frequently to his experiences in Los Angeles in his many articles and speeches on mural painting and the Mexican Mural Movement. His personal life and experiences in California are based on his memoirs, *Me llamaban El Coronelazo*,

Arenal de Siqueiros, *Páginas sueltas con Siqueiros*, and conversations or interviews with Shifra Goldman, Harold Jones and Millard Sheets.

Portrait of Present-Day Mexico was donated to the Santa Barbara Museum of Art and has been installed intact on its original walls in the entrance to the museum In Santa Barbara, California.

p. 139 The description of the process involved in *Tropical America* is partially based on an interview with Harold Jones, an art teacher at Washington High School in Los Angeles and one of Siqueiros's assistants on the project, July 24, 1983. Following his expereience on "Tropical America," he offered a high school class in fresco, working with a shop teacher whose students prepared and applied the wet plaster.

p. 143 Recent attempts to restore *Tropical America* are discussed in Goldman, Shifra, "Tropical Paradise: Siqueiros' Los Angeles Mural: A Victim of Double Censorship," *Artweek*, July 5 1990, pp. 20-21. Thanks to a persistent effort by Shifra Goldman and others, The Getty Conservation Institute has undertaken the preservation and restoration of "Tropical America."

A few years ago, *Street Meeting* was rediscovered under several coatings of paint by artist Dave Tourje, who is trying to arrange for the purchase of the building and the restoration of the mural in a new Siqueiros study center.

p. 144 Siqueiros's address to the John Reed Club, September 2, 1932 is reprinted in Tibol, *Siqueiros: Un mexicano y su obra*, pp. 101-115.

p. 146 According to *Los Angeles Times* critic Arthur Millier, Siqueiros was also working on another mural in the John Reed Club with a class of students, a project which was either never finished or was subsequently covered over. Hurlburt, "Siqueiros: Quest for Revolutionary Form and Content," p. 76n.

p. 156 While Siqueiros was still working on "Plastic Exercise," Blanca had taken up with Natalio Botana, his patron. She later became a supporter of Juan Perón and moved to Chile when he was overthrown in 1955. She also insisted that she and Siqueiros had never been divorced after their marriage in Los Angeles in 1932. *Portrait of a Decade*, p. 146.

VIII. "A New Realism"

p. 164 Siqueiros's well publicized relationship with María Asunsolo is alluded to in his letters to her from New York and Spain, as well as in *Me llamaban El Coronelzao*. Additional information and insight was obtained in interviews with friends or acquaintances.

Though she was never an art dealer, María's apartment was a meeting place for artists and she arranged sales for many prominent Mexican artists, frequently with Mexican politicians who were laundering their illegal gains by buying art. She also sponsored other cultural activities and visited prisoners in Lecumberri. Throughout her life rumors proliferated about how she preserved her beauty and she later married a wealthy American who owned ranches in Mexico. During their affair, Siqueiros had given her "The Virgin of the Chair," his first oil painting, along with "The Abduction,"and a crucifix which he had stolen from a church in Taxco. Fabienne Bradu, *Damas de corazón*, (México: Fondo de Cultura Económica, 1994).

p. 167 Lola Alvarez Bravo saw Siqueiros and Rivera "rehearsing" their confrontation in front of the restrooms in Bellas Artes before the incident. *Portrait of a Decade*, p. 51n.

p. 176 Although I described *Explosion in the City* in an previous edition of this book as an experimental work done in 1936, which foretold the nuclear explosion at Hiroshima nine years later, it was actually painted in the 1950s and the date was altered to reinforce the image of artistic innovation and personal prescience. Dates, as well as titles, were also changed for other paintings for biographical reasons or to change the meaning as circumstances warranted.

IX. "El Coronelazo"

p. 189 Mexico's reaction to the Spanish Civil War, the government's support of the Republic and the participation of Mexican volunteers in the conflict are chronicled in Patricia Fagen, *Exiles and Citizens: Spanish Republicans in Mexico*, (Austin: University of Texas Press, 1973); Lois E. Smith, *Mexico and the Spanish Republicans*, (Berkeley: University of California Press, 1955); T.G. Powell, *Mexico and the Spanish Civil War* (Albuquerque: University of New México Press, 1981) and D. Anthony White, "Mexico in World Affairs, 1928-1968" (Ph.D.diss., University of California, Los Angeles, 1968).

p. 190 Siqueiros's participation and experiences in the Spanish Civil War are based on accounts in *Me llamaban El Coronelazo*; Arenal de Siqueiros, *Páginas sueltas*; Carlos Contreras, "David Alfaro Siqueiros en la guerra española" in Tibol, *Siqueiros: Un mexicano y su obra*, pp. 249-254; Andres Iduarte, "Un artista en la guerra," in Arenal de Siqueiros, *Vida y obra de Siqueiros*, pp. 45-50; José Renau,"Mi experiencia con Siqueiros," *Siqueiros: Revolución plastica*, Revista de Bellas Artes, No. 25, January-February 1976 and an interview with Andres Garcia Salgado, México City, March 1977.

Some of Siqueiros's war stories have been challenged by others, including the Mexican poet Octavio Paz. In *Mexico and the Spanish Civil War*, Powell writes that Siqueiros had no combat experience or military training, thereby dismissing his participation in the Mexican Revolution, and states that his military rank in Spain was due to his position as a political commissar for the Republic. While Siqueiros's participation in the Spanish Civil War may have been distorted in the frequent retelling of his war experiences, it appears from the testimony of other veterans of the conflict and officers of the Spanish government that he took many risks and engaged in frontline combat. Given his participation in other forms of combat or political violence before and after the war in Spain, and the testimony of witnesses to those events, as well as his committment to the struggle against fascism, it would have been out of character if he had avoided combat in Spain.

p. 200 According to Siqueiros, he had intervened to save Barnabe Barrrios, a Mexican volunteer who had been involved in the Experimental Workshop, from execution for desertion. *Me llamaban Él Coronelazo*, p. 105-106.

X. *"Agent Provocateur, Fugitive and Exile"*

pp. 217-221 Although the attack on the fortified villa of Trotsky in Coyoacan is well documented, there seem to be as many versions as there are accounts. Moreover, even 37 years later the court records on the first attack in May, 1940 have either disappeared or are not available to the probing scholar. The description of the attack, therefore, is based on a combination of contemporary newspaper accounts, the published testimony of several of the participants, the depositions of several of the alleged attackers, a book by the investigating police officer, interviews with associates of Siqueiros, and secondary works on Trotsky, Mexican politics and history during this period.

Thanks to the issues, ideological positions and personalities involved, Trotsky's assassination still evokes strong feelings and many of the accounts of his life or death are subject to distortion and should be read with the ideology of the authors in mind. While the general story is well known, the details of the first attack and the conspiracy or plan leading to the assassination are either shrouded in mystery, some of it deliberately concocted by the participants, or they have become confused in the profusion of versions of the events between May and August, 1940.

The role of Siqueiros is described in his memoirs *Me llamaban El Coronelazo* and Arenal de Siqueiros, *Páginas sueltas*, as well as in many other public statements by him, the alleged leader of the mass assault on Trotsky's refuge. The arrangements for Trotsky's asylum and his activities in México between 1937 and his death in 1940 are described in Joel Carmichael, *Trotsky, An Appreciation of His Life*, (New York: St. Martin's, 1975); Isaac Deutscher, *The Prophet Outcast, Trotsky, 1929-1940*, (New York and London: Oxford University Press, 1963); Herrera, *Frida*, and Leon Trotsky, *Writings of Leon Trotsky, 1939-1940*, (New York: Pathfinder Press, 1973).

One of the participants in the May assault, Nestor H. Sanchez, briefly describes his role in *Memorias de un combatiente*, (Oaxaca: "Carteles del Sur," 1976), while Valentín Campa explains the position of the Mexican Communist Party in *Mi testimonio, memorias de un comunista mexicano*, (México: Ediciones de Cultura Popular, 1978).

Although they concentrate on the assassination of Trotsky and the identity of his actual assassin, Isaac Don Levine, *The Mind of An Assassin*, (London: Weidenfeld & Nicolson, 1959); Nicolas Mosley, *The Assassination of Trotsky*, (London: Michael Joseph, 1972); and Victor Serge and Natalia Sedova Trotsky, *The Life and Death of Leon Trotsky*, trans. by Arnold J. Pomerans, (New York: Basic Books, 1975) also provide information on the first assault on the villa in Coyoacan.

General Leandro A. Sanchez Salazar, the investigating police officer, later published his version, *Murder in México, The Assassination of Leon Trotsky*, trans. Arnold J. Pomerans, (London: Secker & Warburg, 1950), which describes his investigation of the first assault, the assassination and the arrest of Siqueiros. While based on his own experiences, it was written with the collaboration of Julian Gorkin, a Spaniard who joined the POUM, and amounts to a trotskyite attack on Stalin, the NKVD and the GPU. There is also a novel on Trotsky and his assassination by Bernard Wolfe, *The Great Prince Died*, (New York: Charles Scribner's Sons, 1959).

More recently, an autobiography of a former KGB officer states that Siqueiros was the leader of one of three separate teams, unknown to each other, which were assigned by the GPU to assassinate Trotsky. The French "Jew" was actually Iosif Grigulevich, whom Siqueiros met in Spain and a KGB agent who later planned an attempt on Tito and wrote biographies of Simon Bolivar, Pancho Villa, Che Guevara and Siqueiros. This version contends that Robert Sheldon Harte was murdered because he recognized Grigulevich, also known as I. Lavretsky, at the door. Even though the Mexican Communist Party denied that Siqueiros was a member of the Party, there is a party membership card in his name dated 1939. *Portrait of a Decade*, p. 64-65.

In addition to the above, I was also able to obtain the depositions of several of those arrested after the first attack. From several of my contacts in Mexico, I obtained interesting but not always reliable information on the plans for the attack, the identity of the attackers, the killers of Robert Sheldon Harte and the identity and personality of Trotsky's assassin.

p. 233 Siqueiros was the first Mexican artist to paint Cuauhtémoc, the Aztec leader who succeeded Moctezuma and Cuitláhuac and who surrendered to Cortés after leading a fierce resistence against the Spaniards. Today he represents Mexican nationalism or resistence to foreign invasion or influence. Interview with Raquel Tibol, México City, Februrary 2, 1977.

p. 239 After the Trotsky affair, the FBI, and later the CIA, monitored his activities carefully, the former agency accumulating a dossier of 50,000 pages on him. Except for a temporary transit visit to attend an opening of his work in Japan, he was repeatedly denied a visa to enter the United States. During my research, I encountered cases of other Latin American artists, writers and journalists who were denied visas because of their public statements or association with leftist organizations or causes.

pp. 239-242 The murals in Cuba are described in Tibol, *Siqueiros: Vida y obra*, pp. 119-122. Since the promethian or sun-man image and flying female figures appear in his Cuban and later murals, they may have been partly inspired by comic-strip or film characters like Superman and Tarzan, who made their appearance in the 1930s, especially since he was so intrigued by film and commercial art. Irene Herner, "Siqueiros, El artista sujetado or la experimentación," Oliver Debroise, ed.*Otras Rutas Hacia Siqueiros*. (México: Instituto Nacional de Bellas Artes, 1997). On the other hand, Siqueiros's first mural, painted in 1923, featured an angel-like figure and the nude females in "Plastic Exercise" seem to be hurtling through space.

XII. "El Maestro"

p. 270 In *Contemporary Mexican Painting In a Time of Change*, Shifra Goldman describes the transition from muralism to easel painting, the emergence of private galleries, the cultural imperialism of North American cultural organs and corporations, and the confrontation between the old generation of social realists and a new group of younger artists opposed to "official political art" in the postwar period. pp. 27-40.

Although they abandoned the reformism of Cárdenas, the post 1940 governments continued to support realism in art, thereby creating the impression of being revolutionary or progressive. At the same time, they endorsed abstractionism in order to promote Mexico's new international posture. (Goldman, p. 39). While Mexico pursued a seemingly independent course in foreign affairs and cultivated an image of revolutionary nationalism, the government was increasingly repressive and counter-revolutionary at home.

XIV. "Exterior Murals, Portraits and Polemics"

p. 306 The dead worker in *For the Complete Social Security of All Mexicans*, as well as the grey cadaver in *New Democracy*, resemble the dead soldier in Uccello's *Rout of San Romano*, and an illustration of this painting in a book which Adriana gave to Siqueiros is surrounded by notes on foreshortening in his hand. The image of the dead worker was also based on a photograph of Siqueiros lying on the floor of his studio in his paint-covered overalls.

XX. "The March of Humanity"

pp. 448 Leonard Folgarait provides a thorough and provocative analysis of the Polyforum, including the historical, political and social context of the project, its political meanings, Siqueiros's explanations, the reaction of the critics and its inherent contradictions in *So Far From Heaven*.

Rumors were rampant during the project that Suárez was broke and that the hotel might be sold to North Americans. Other versions contended that the government was paying for its completion and that Echeverría, who was accused of profiting from new hotels in Cancun and other resorts which his government had promoted, was the new owner of the hotel and the Polyforum.

BIBLIOGRAPHY

Books and Pamphlets by David Alfaro Siqueiros

Siqueiros, David Alfaro. *A un joven pintor mexicano*. México: Empresas Editorialies, 1967.

_____. *Como se pinta un mural*. México: Secretaria de Educación Pública, 1951.

_____. *Mi repuesta, la historia de una insidia. Quienes son los traidores de la patria?* México: Ediciones de "Arte Público", 1960.

_____. *El muralismo de Mexico*. México: Ediciones Mexicanas. 1950.

_____. *No hay mas ruta que la nuestra. Importancia nacional e internacional de la pintura mexicana moderna*. México: Secretaria de Educación Pública, 1945.

_____. *Siqueiros. Por la via de una pintura neorrealista o realista social moderna en México*. México: Instituto Nacional de Bellas Artes, 1951.

_____. *La trácala. Mi replica a un gobierno fiscal-juez*. México: Ediciones de la Tracala. 1962.

Collections of Articles, Letters, Manifestos and Speeches by Siqueiros

Arenal de Siqueiros, Angélica. *Vida y obra de David Alfaro Siqueiros*. México: Fondo de Cultura Económica, 1975.

Carrillo Azpeitia, Rafael., ed., *Siqueiros*. México: Secretaria de Educación Pública, 1974.

Siqueiros, David Alfaro. *Art and Revolution*. Translated by Sylvia Calles. London: Lawrence and Wishart, 1975.

Tibol, Raquel. *David Alfaro Siqueiros. Un mexicano y su obra*. México: Empresas Editoriales, 1969.

_____. *Documentación sobre el arte mexicano*. México: Fondo de Cultura Económica, 1974.

_____. *Palabras de Siqueiros*. México: Fondo de Cultura Económica, 1996.

_____. *Textos de David Alfaro Siqueiros*. México: Fondo de Cultura Económica, 1974.

_____. *Siqueiros, vida y obra*. México: Colección Metro Politana, 1973.

Books on The Life of Siqueiros

Arenal de Siqueiros, Angélica., ed. *Me llamaban El Coronelazo. Memorias de David Alfaro Siqueiros*. México: Biografias Gandesa, 1977.

_____. *Páginas sueltas con Siqueiros*. México: Editorial Grijalbo, 1979.

Scherer Garcia. Julio. *Siqueiros: La piel y la entraña*. 2d ed. México: Ediciones Era, 1974.

Stein, Philip. *Siqueiros, His Life and Works*. New York: International Publishers, 1994.

Tibol, Raquel. *David Alfaro Siqueiros*. México: Empresas Editoriales, 1969.

_____. *Siqueiros, introductor de realidades*. México: Universidad Nacional Autónoma de México, 1961.

Zabludovsky, Jacobo. *Siqueiros me dijo*. México: Organizacion Editorial Novaro, 1974.

Books, Catalogs, and Pamphlets on the Art of Siqueiros

Crespo de la Serna, Jorge J.. *David A. Siqueiros*. México: Editorial Espartaco, 1959.

Debroise, Olivier, ed. *Otras Rutas hacia Siqueiros.*. México: Instituto Nacional de Bellas Artes, 1996.

Folgarait, Leonard. *So Far From Heaven: David Alfaro Siqueiros'The March of Humanity and Mexican Revolutionary Politics*. Cambridge: Cambridge University Press, 1987.

Gual, Enrique. *Siqueiros*. México: Galeria de Arte Misrachi, 1965

Harten, Jurgen. *Siqueiros/Pollock: Pollock/Siqueiros.*. Dusseldorf: Kunsthalle Dusseldorf, 1995

Instituto Nacional de Bellas Artes. *Exposición de Siqueiros*. México: 1972

_____. *45 autorretratos de pintores mexicanos*. México: 1947.

_____. *Iconografía de David Alfaro Siqueiros*. México: Fondo de Cultura Económica, 1997.

_____. *Portrait of a Decade, David Alfaro Siqueiros, 1930-1940*. Mexico: 1997

_____. *70 obras recientes de David Alfaro Siqueiros*. México: 1947.

_____. *Siqueiros. Exposición de homenaje*. México: 1975.

_____. *Siqueiros: Revolución Plastica*. *Revista de Bellas Artes* no. 25, January-February 1976.

Luna Arroyo. Antonio. *Siqueiros, pintor de Nuestro Tiempo*. México: Editorial Cultura, 1950.

Micheli, Mario de. *Siqueiros*. Translated by Ron Strom. New York: Harry N. Abrams, 1968

_____. *Siqueiros*. México: Secretaria de Educación Pública, 1985.

Rodríguez, Antonio. *Siqueiros*. México: Fondo de Cultura Económica, 1974.

Sala de Arte Publico. *Siqueiros: El lugar de la utopía*. México: 1994

Spratling, William. *David Alfaro Siqueiros:Trece gradados en madera*. Taxco: 1931.

Suárez, Orlando *David Alfaro Siqueiros, A Guide to The Study of His Life and Work*. Special Edition of *Arte Público*. México: Sala de Arte Público, 1969.

Tibol, Raquel. *David Alfaro Siqueiros*. Pinacoteca de los genios. Buenos Aires: Editorial Codex, 1965.

Universidad Nacional Autónoma de México. *Siqueiros, exposición restrospectiva, 1911-1967*. México: 1967.

Index

About the Author

D. Anthony White, Ph.D. is Professor Emeritus from Sonoma State University. A graduate of Phillips Andover Academy, Stanford University, the Universities of California at Berkeley and at Los Angeles, he learned Spanish playing and coaching basketball in Bilbao, Spain. After writing his dissertation on Mexican foreign policy, he received his doctorate from U.C.L.A. and taught Latin American History, United States-Latin American Relations and Global Studies at Sonoma State for 37 years. The recipient of a research grant from the National Endowment for the Humanities, he conducted research for this biography in the artist's archives and interviewed his widow, family members, friends, artists and art historians.

Made in the USA
Lexington, KY
27 November 2010